The Disciples of King Gambrinus

Volume 1

Twenty-Five Unfortunate Lives

Also by Herman Wiley Ronnenberg:

Disciples of Gambrinus VOLUME II: *Capitalists and Town Fathers*

Material Culture of Breweries (Guides to Historical Artifacts)

John Lemp: The Beer Baron of Boise

Beer and Brewing in the Inland Northwest

Jeanette Manuel:
The Life and Legend of the Belle of Fabulous Florence

Pioneer Mother on the River of No Return:
The Life of Isabella Kelly Benedict Robie

The Politics of Assimilation

The Disciples of
KING GAMBRINUS
VOLUME I

Twenty-Five Unfortunate Lives

Herman Wiley Ronnenberg

HWR

Heritage Witness Reflections Publishing
Troy, Idaho

The Disciples of King Gambrinus, Volume 1
Twenty-Five Unfortunate Lives
Copyright © 2013 Herman Wiley Ronnenberg

First edition published 2011
Second edition 2013

Paperback ISBN: 978-0-9818408-7-1
Ebook ISBN: 978-0-9818408-9-5
Hardback: 978-0-9818408-3-3
Hardback LCCN: 2010916862

HWR

Heritage Witness Reflections Publishing
P.O. Box 356
Troy, Idaho 83871

Cover painting of King Gambrinus by Liz Hess

Book design and cover photography by Robert and Erik Jacobson
www.LongfeatherBookDesign.com

Dedication

This volume is dedicated to all the Idaho brewery owners and workers, malt makers, barley, and hop growers, and all the retailers of beer of the Micro era, from 1985 to 2010. For a quarter of a century these dedicated men and women have used the resources of the third largest malting barley-growing state, and third largest hop-growing state, to return Idaho to its historic tradition of slaking its thirst with locally made brew. May your lives be smoother, hoppier, more effervescent, and more full-bodied, and ultimately more satisfying than those covered in volume I. *Cheers!*

Acknowledgments

So many have provided so much to the research and writing of this book, that I fear any list will thoughtlessly omit as many as it includes. Nonetheless, let me thank a few who made mighty contributions: Thanks to Lillian Heytvelt for the many inter-library loans she procured for me. Thanks to Carol Hill for her editorial work. Thanks to Robert and Erik Jacobson for the book's cover and interior design. Thanks to all the hard-working professionals at the Idaho Historical Society Library and the Library of the University of Idaho.

Table of Contents

Illustrations

Adolph

1. Gold Mines historical sign. Rocky Bar had a large initial population, which made a brewery a reasonable business. Adolph, John Krall, and G. W. Hiatt owned the Boise Brewery and Bakery there until August of 1865.
2. Salem Beer Bottle. Adolph brewed in Salem, Oregon, for many years, although this bottle is not from his brewery.
3. Toll Gate Historical Sign. Toll road to Rocky Bar where Adolph invested in the brewery, also owned by John Krall & G. W. Hiatt.
4. Adolph's Salem, Oregon home.
5. The Adolph home viewed from the rear.
6. Sign at the historical Samuel Adolph home in Salem shows its 21st Century usage.
7. *Tri-weekly Statesman* 27 August 1864

Bernhardt

8. Greater Coeur d'Alene Region map.
9. Newspaper ad for the brewing company stock.
10. The magnificent Coeur d'Alene Brewery. Photo North Idaho Museum.
11. Coeur d'Alene Brewery workers, including two children, pose at the loading dock.
12. Newspaper ad offering spent brewery grain.
13. Prince of Pilsen beer label. This Panhandle Brewing Company replaced Bernhardt's.

Weimann

Williams

Turn Verein

The Disciples of
KING GAMBRINUS

Series Introduction

THE HARD-WORKING MEN who made Idaho a part of the American nation worked up a mighty thirst in the process. European-born— mostly Germanic—men saw a need and a business potential and brewed beer for them. Beer to quench their thirst, to feed the inner man, to bind the society, and to save that society from whiskey-induced rages and excesses. Saintly altruism was not the only motive, perhaps not a motive at all; profit motivated the men who pursued brewing. The brotherhood of brewers was not quite a cult, not quite a guild, not quite a profession, but it had elements of all three. European legend and lore said medieval King Gambrinus invented beer. The legend conveniently forgets the first few thousand years of brewing history in the Old World, but it offers a definite starting point for the brewers to begin their own historical epoch. A European brewer considered himself, if not a descendant from the legendary king, at least a disciple. This series of collective biographies tells the lives of the Disciples of Gambrinus as they lived, worked, and died in the Gem State. As with any large group, there were the saints and the sinners, the sane and the insane, the wise and the foolish, the successful and the failures. Some committed murder; some had murder committed on them. Some became enormously wealthy, while some filed for bankruptcy. They were a microcosm of the human condition, but their link to brewing endowed them with a certain essence that was theirs alone.

There is hopefully a place where genealogy, family history, biography, local history, tales of the western frontier, and brewing history all meet and interact. That elusive spot is the one I am aiming for. The lives of these brewers contribute to all of these but cannot be pigeonholed into any one.

Volume I covers the life treks of 25 men who experienced tragedy. From gunfights, to shipwrecks, to falls, to unprovoked attacks, potential tragedies stalked them all and overtook quite a few. This volume also has appended a large history of the Germans in Idaho, and in particular, how this ethnic element fit into the brewing history of the state.

Volume II covers the men who were successful in building businesses and in public service. So much of the local history of the state was built on foundations financed and envisioned by local men who took their brewing profits and capitalized other local ventures.

Volume III tells the lives of other men who deserve to be remembered for their lesser impact on the state's history. Lesser impact, yes, but not less interesting or less steeped in the human condition. This series is my personal, perhaps idiosyncratic, tribute to the men who brewed the beer long ago and in the process built much of the foundation of Idaho: The Disciples of Gambrinus.

Introduction: VOLUME I

Twenty-Five Unfortunate Lives:
Violence and Accidents, Suicide and Insanity

A MAN WHO GETS UP EVERY MORNING, goes to work, and then returns home to his family each evening has a good life, and I would not disparage the interest that one should take in such people. Brewers, in general, were noted for their steadiness, hard work, dependability, and strong family connections. Nineteenth century brewing required about 18 hours of uninterrupted labor per day. Steady attention to these requirements made other, more interesting, activities rare and difficult. Such men, however, make dull subjects for stories. This first volume in this series covers the exceptions, however, not the rule. These 25 men all suffered tragedies or problems that add an exclamation mark to their lives and, frankly, make them more interesting. Lumping these men together does create a biased picture of the profession that later volumes will dispel. Few brewers, in general, died as these men did, from gunfights, shipwrecks, suicides, or murders. Most died from age or illness. Looking at these particular men's lives does reveal the manifold potential disasters waiting just out of view on the western frontier for the teetotaler or the Disciple of Gambrinus alike.

These stories are meant to round out the reader's understanding of the past, the brewing profession, and the dangers from within and without that a businessman on the frontier faced. The large appendix on the history of the ethnic Germans in Idaho puts great emphasis on the role of brewers in German American culture. Compared to eastern states, Idaho had few Germans-but those few cut a wide swath.

The bibliography for the entire series is found in this first volume. Therefore, some items listed there are not referenced in the text in this volume. Any new material uncovered before the subsequent volumes are published will be put in a small supplemental bibliography in each.

ISHS stands for Idaho State Historical Society. End notes are short form; complete references are in the bibliography.

1

SAMUEL ADOLPH

Buggy Accident Victim

ON THE 17TH OF SEPTEMBER 1893, about four in the afternoon, Salem, Oregon brewer Samuel Adolph hitched up a pet yearling colt and started for a drive with his young son, Joseph.[1] He had scarcely gotten away from the house when the inexperienced young animal took fright and overthrew the buggy.[2] Joseph jumped and saved his life, but Samuel was not so lucky. His right leg was broken in two places, his right arm was also broken and badly lacerated, and his head was lacerated. Doctors Smith and Reynolds were called, but all they could do was make him comfortable. He was conscious until midnight, and then took a short nap and the death struggle began. The most successful brewer in the short history of Salem was dead.

His obituary described Adolph as 59, born in Prussia, and he had been in Salem since 1866. His previous business experience in Portland and Boise was noted. The newspaper said he was successful at everything and he left a good fortune for his wife and six children. They described him as a man of genial disposition, openhanded to the needy, who enjoyed an extensive circle of admiring friends.

Catherine Lemp of Boise left immediately to be with her newly widowed sister, Mary. Daughter Eva was visiting in Chicago and hurried home for her father's funeral.[3] Samuel had been a Mason, and the first plan was to take his remains to Portland for burial in the Jewish cemetery. The plan was to postpone the funeral until Sunday, the 24th of September, to allow the relatives to gather. Plans were changed and the funeral was performed by the Masonic order at the graveside and he was buried in City View Cemetery.[4] Friends gathered at the home at 2:00 and cars took them to the cemetery. The funeral was largely attended, with seven horse-drawn cars and 75 buggies going to the cemetery.[5] The Masons observed their rites in a most impressive manner. Catherine Lemp left for Boise the following Tuesday.[6]

Samuel Adolph was an extremely successful brewer in Salem, Oregon, but he had an earlier, little-known career in the Gem State. Credited with building the very first cabin in Boise, Adolph was involved with several pioneer Idaho brewers.[7] Adolph met and joined forces with John Krall, who had sold his brewery in Placerville, Idaho in 1864 and then opened a bakery, saloon, and brewery in Boise City. Early businesses and partnerships came and went rapidly. At first, Krall was partners with Thomas Paulson, and they operated under the name of John Krall & Co. In August 1864, they dissolved partnership and Krall took Adolph as a partner.[8]

Soon Adolph paid William Brockie $225 on 22 August 1864, for lot 4, block 42 of Boise City as he began to acquire real estate.[9] On 28

2. Salem Beer Bottle. Adolph brewed in Salem, Oregon, for many years, although this bottle is not from his brewery.

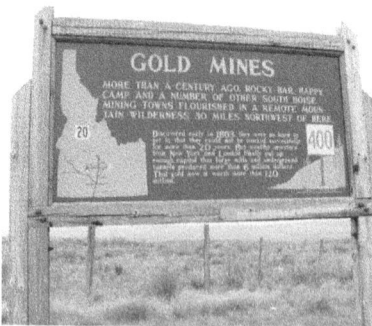

1. Gold Mines historical sign. Rocky Bar had a large initial population, which made a brewery a reasonable business. Adolph, John Krall, and G. W. Hiatt owned the Boise Brewery and Bakery there until August of 1865.

April 1865, John Hoy bought half of the City Brewery and Bakery and the lots they were on-9 and 10 of block 9-, from his partner, George Englehardt, for $900.[10] This was undoubtedly preliminary to the sale a few days later of the whole brewery to John Krall. On 2 May 1865, the John Krall Company, consisting of John Krall, John Lemp and Samuel Adolph, paid $1300 to John Hoy for the lots he had bought four days before.[11] Lemp, the Beer Baron of Boise, would remain in brewing for 50 years and would soon be a brother-in-law to Adolph, but he was allied with Krall only briefly.

3. *Toll Gate Historical Sign. Toll road to Rocky Bar where Adolph invested in the brewery, also owned by John Krall & G. W. Hiatt.*

On 8 July 1865, Albert Held paid Samuel Adolph $750 for lot 4, block 42 in Boise City—the lots he had bought from Brockie. On 13 July 1865, three major sales were transacted regarding the brewery. Samuel Adolph paid John Krall $600 for a one-quarter interest in the Boise Brewery on Main Street, lots 4, 5, 6 of block 34.[12] The same day John Lemp paid Samuel Adolph $1200 for half of the brewery.[13] Also Lemp paid Krall $3000 for lot 3 block 3 and the City Bakery which sat thereon.[14]

Krall dissolved partnership with Adolph in the City Bakery, Boise City in July of 1865.[15] Adolph also dissolved partnership in the Boise Brewery and Bakery in Rocky Bar with John Krall and G. W. Hiatt in August 1865.[16] Adolph retained other partnership interests. On 6 February 1866, Peter Sturzenacker and Fred Vetterlein paid John Krall and Company [the company was Samuel Adolph] and John Lemp $900 for lot 9 and 10 of block 9 of Boise City.[17] On 15 February 1866, Samuel Adolph paid Lemp $1200 for a half interest in the lots 4, 5, 6 of block 34 and the Boise Brewery.[18] On 9 May 1866 Henry Kohlepp, brother-in-law to both Adolph and Lemp, paid them and their wives, $2000 for the lots and the Boise Brewery and lot 10, block 3 and the ice thereon. Mary Adolph signed with a mark.[19] On 8 September, Mary Adolph paid $1,000 to Henry Kohlepp, her brother, for half of the brewery and the lots it sat on and lot 10 of block 3.[20] On 13 September John and Kate Lemp paid Kohlepp $1,000 for his half interest in the

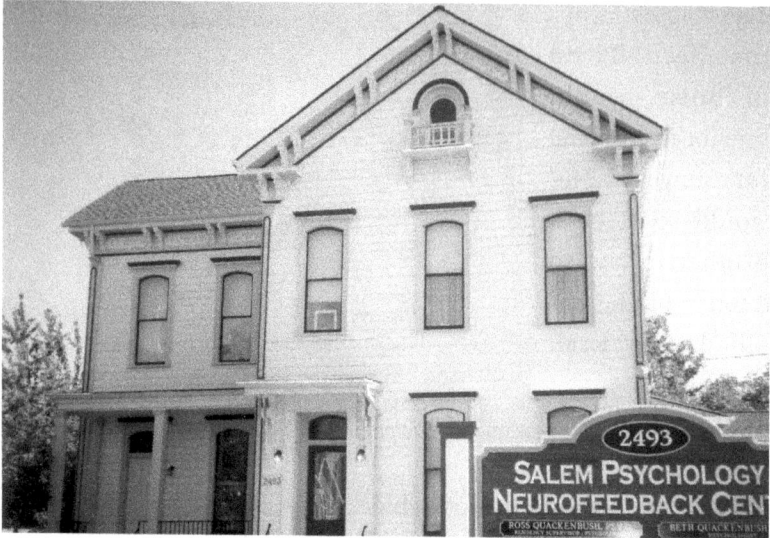

4. Adolph's Salem, Oregon home.

brewery and the lot in block 10.[21] On 24 October 1866, Samuel and Mary Adolph sold their half interest in the same property and business to John Lemp for $1000.[22]

In August of 1866, Ada County paid Krall and Adolph $25 by warrant to satisfy an unnamed bill.[23] Adolph soon married John Lemp's sister-in-law and went into business with Lemp.

On Federal Tax records, Adolph paid tax on his income and his gold watch in May 1865 at Boise City.[24] Adolph was briefly a brewing partner with John Lemp there in 1866. On the Federal Tax Records of May the partners paid for their fermented liquor license, and in

5. The Adolph home viewed from the rear.

June 1866, Lemp and Adolph at Boise paid tax on 12 barrels of beer.[25] In July they paid for brewing 12.5 barrels.[26] In August they paid for brewing 12 barrels—$12—and their brewer reassessment of $16.67. In September they paid for 15 barrels brewed, and on the October 1866 Federal records, Lemp and Adolph paid tax for 16 1/2 barrels of beer brewed.[27] The newspapers of those years failed to even list Adolph's first name. After his marriage, Adolph moved on to Salem, Oregon, in late 1866, and remained a successful brewer there for nearly three decades. Lemp and Adolph announced their dissolution of partnership on 22 October 1866, with Lemp to receive all accounts due.[28]

On 26 March 1867, Samuel and Mary Adolph sold their Warm Springs ranch to her father William Kohlepp for $700.[29] All the Adolph financial ties to Boise were ended.

However, in 1889 when Samuel returned for a visit with his wife and daughter, the wealthy, successful Salem, Oregon, brewer finally got some detailed mention in the Boise press.[30] Despite these over-sights, he had a significant link to Idaho and the brewing hierarchy: he was married to Mary Kohlepp, sister of Mrs. John Lemp (Catherine Kohlepp, wife of the Boise Beer Baron), brewer George Kohlepp, and other Kohlepp siblings with connections to brewing. Thus he occupied a branch on the great, extended Lemp family tree. From Boise, he had gone to and remained in Salem, Oregon.

There is a Samuel Adolph on the 1860 U.S. Census at Fort Laramie, Wyoming, which was in the Nebraska Territory at that moment. I suspect this was our subject and he was on his way west at the time. The surname is very hard to read on the manuscript. This 23-year-old person was working as a blacksmith at this area dominated by the military. If other Census records were right, Adolph would have been 26 then, but perhaps he fibbed a bit on his age.

Records in Salem seem to indicate that Samuel Adolph arrived in 1862, which is possible if he left for a while to go to Boise and then returned.[31] Probably he got there later. In January of 1866, Adolph paid his Federal Tax for fermented liquor in Boise City, Idaho.[32] He opened the Pacific Brewery—the first in Salem—at

6. Sign at the historical Samuel Adolph home in Salem shows its 21st Century usage.

Cottage and Trade streets (on the south side of Trade) with John Brown as a partner. His lager supplied the 13 saloons of the town.[33] In 1869, a fire destroyed the brewery and Samuel moved his location three blocks, to the southeast corner of Trade and Commercial streets, and built a new plant with a bottling works he called the Salem Brewery.[34]

One of Adolph's early rivals in Salem was Louis Walcott's Star Brewery. Walcott wanted the money paid for hops to stay in Oregon and helped teach hop growers to cure their hops more carefully. He could be considered a pioneer in the Oregon hop business.

The U.S. Census for 1870 and 1880 listed Adolph in East Salem of Marion County. In April of 1875, the Samuel Adolph family lost their 5-month-old daughter and her death notice was published throughout the state.[35] Another Samuel Adolph, most assuredly his son, was born in Marion County, Oregon, on 1 October 1880. He registered for the World War I draft with that birth date and location. He was also listed with his wife and son on the 1920 Census. On the 1880 Census, Adolph was 45, wife Mary was 38, son Will was 11, daughter Eva was 9, son Lyen was 7, daughter Meta was two. In 1885, Samuel, Sr. joined with two employees, Maurice Klinger and Seraphin Beck who moved the location to the northeast side of the corner and built the even larger Capital Brewery.[36]

The next week after Adolph's funeral, the assessments for improvement of several streets in Salem was listed in the local newspaper. Adolph had owned a prominent section on Commercial Street.[37]

The brewery continued on until Seraphine Beck died in 1900. His widow bought out Klinger in 1901, and in 1903, Margarite Beck sold to the Kola Neis Hop Company of Albany, Oregon, and to Leopold Schmidt of the Olympia Brewing Company.[38]

The Adolph family continued to live in Salem. In 1901, for instance, Mrs. John (Catherine) Lemp of Boise came to visit, and then took her niece back with her to visit Boise.[39]

In 1903, the Salem Brewery Association bought Adolph's old business and brewed Salem Beer. Salem voted dry in 1913 and the

Association moved to Portland. When Repeal came, the company re-incorporated in Salem. Famous Northwest brewing entrepreneur Emil Sicks bought the Salem plant in 1943 and ran it until the building was razed in 1955. It had a party room on the 2nd floor and a large sign on top for "6 Sick's Select Beer."

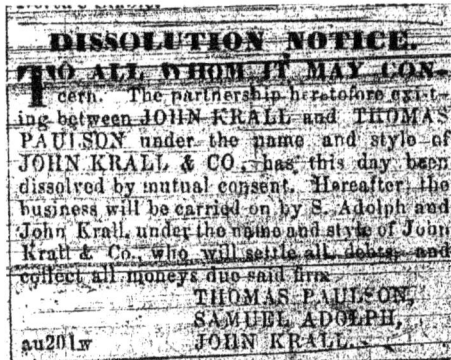

7. Tri-weekly Statesman 27 August 1864

Samuel Adolph had a brief sojourn as an Idaho brewer, but he is definitely a Disciple of Gambrinus, and an associate member of the Idaho branch of the mythical lodge.[40]

SAMUEL ADOLPH FAMILY

Samuel Adolph	(husband)
Birth Date:	1834
Birth Place:	Prussia
Death Date:	17 Sep 1893
Death Place:	Salem, Oregon
Occupation:	Brewer
Religion:	Jewish

Mary Kohlepp	(wife)
Birth Date:	Circa 1842
Birth Place:	Prussia
Spouse Father:	William Kohlepp (1813-1869)
Spouse Mother:	Martha E. ? (1813-1881)

Children:	Eva, Samuel, Joseph, Will, Lyen, Meta

Eva Adolph	
Birth Date:	Circa 1871
Birth Place:	Oregon

Samuel Adolph Jr.

Birth Date:	1 Oct 1880
Birth Place:	Marion County, Oregon
Death Date:	Mar 1981
Death Place:	Salem, Marion County, Oregon
Spouse:	Lottie V. ?
Birth Date:	Circa 1885
Birth Place:	Pennsylvania
Children:	David

David Adolph

Birth Date:	Circa 1905
Birth Place:	Oregon

Joseph Adolph

Birth Date:	1882
Death Date:	1942
Spouse:	Lillie
Children:	Rex, Alden

Will Adolph

Birth Date:	Circa 1869
Birth Place:	Oregon

Lyen Adolph

Birth Date:	Circa 1873
Birth Place:	Oregon

Meta Adolph

Birth Date:	Circa 1878
Birth Place:	Oregon

END NOTES

1   *Evening Capital Journal*, Salem, Oregon, 18 September 1893, p. 4, c. 4.
2   *Idaho Daily Statesman*, Boise, Idaho, 22 September 1893, p. 6, c. 4.
3   *Capital Journal*, Salem, Oregon, 19 September 1893, p. 4, c. 1.
4   *Evening Capital Journal*, Salem, Oregon, 20 September 1893, p. 4, c. 1.
5   *Evening Capital Journal*, Salem, Oregon, 25 September 1893, p. 4, c. 1.

6   *Evening Capital Journal*, Salem, Oregon, 26 September 1893, p. 4, c. 2.

7   *Idaho Daily Statesman*, 22 September 1893, p. 6, c. 4

8   *Tri-Weekly Statesman*, Boise, Idaho, 27 August, 1864, p. 4, c. 1.

9   Ada County Deed Book 1, p. 115.

10 Ada County Deed Book 1, p. 142.

11 Ada County Deed Book 1, p. 152.

12 Ada County Deed Book 1, p. 229-230.

13 Ada County Deed Book 1, p. 232-3.

14 Ada County Deed Book 1, p. 233-4.

15 *Tri-Weekly Statesman*, 20 July 1865, p. 3, c. 2.

16 *Tri-Weekly Statesman*, 3 August, 1865, p. 2, c. 4.

17 Ada County Deed Book 1, p. 431-2.

18 Ada County Deed Book 1, p. 444.

19 Ada County Deed Book1, p. 531-2.

20 Ada County Deed Book 2, p. 32-3.

21 Ada County Deed Book 2, p. 34-35.

22 Ada County Deed Book 2, p. 35-36

23 *Idaho Tri-Weekly Statesman*, 14 August 1866, p. 2, c. 2.

24 Federal Tax Records, 1865-1866, University of Idaho Library Microfilm # 558.

25 Federal Tax Records, 1865-1866, Microfilm # 558.

26 Federal Tax Records, 1865-1866, University of Idaho Library Microfilm # 558.

27 Federal Tax Records, 1865-1866, University of Idaho Library Microfilm # 558.

28 *Idaho Statesman*, 27 October 1866, p. 4, c. 4

29 Ada County Deed Book 2, p. 226-7.

30 *Idaho Daily Statesman*, 27 August 1889, p. 3, c. 2.

31 Meier and Meier, Brewed in the Pacific Northwest, p. 70.

32 Federal Tax Records for Idaho, 1865-1866, University of Idaho Library Microfilm # 558.

33 Gary Flynn, "Salem Brewery Assn," *American Breweriana Journal*, No.149, September-October, 2007, pp. 13-16.

34 Meier and Meier, Brewed in the Pacific Northwest, p. 70.

35 *Morning Oregonian*, Portland, 1 April 1875, p. 2, c. 2.

36 www.salemhistory.net/Agriculture/ Hops/Beer. p. 1.

37 *Evening Capital Journal*, 28 September 1893, p. 3, c. 2.

38 Gary Flynn, "Salem Brewery Assn," *American Breweriana Journal*, No. 149, September-October, 2007, pp. 13-16

39 *Idaho Daily Statesman*, 15 November 1901, p. 5, c. 4.

40 In 2001 the Samuel Adolph house at 2493 State Street was on the agenda of the Historic Landmarks Advisory Commission in Salem, Oregon. Internet site, www.open.org/-sedev/Agenda726.htm

2

CHRISTIAN BERNHARDT
Driving Force Behind the Coeur d'Alene Brewery

BY THE EARLY YEARS OF THE 20TH CENTURY, people who lived within a hundred miles found that excursions on the swank steamers that crisscrossed Lake Coeur d'Alene in northern Idaho were a certain way to beat the summer heat. Many of these people were from Spokane, Washington, due west, the largest city in the region. Up to 2,500 customers swarmed the docks on any given Sunday morning to get aboard one of the Red Collar Line's 50 large boats. If the world-famous natural beauty was not enough, the boats had scrumptious meals, live bands, and interesting docking sites for seeing local attractions.[1] The town of the same name as the lake, based on lumber, agriculture and these tourists, was growing and incorporated as a city in 1907. Yet all the beer for which these workers and merrymakers hankered had to be shipped in, just as far as the tourists were. With a ready-made customer base, could a brewery in Coeur d'alene possibly fail?

Coeur d'Alene village originally grew up around Fort Sherman, and a post office was established in 1878. Twenty soldiers rode their horses inside a saloon called the "Idaho Brewery" on Independence Day 1887.[2] This was a retail branch of Henry Reiniger's brewery in nearby Rathdrum, not an actual manufacturer of beer, and this was the first reference to a local brewery in the lake city.

Christian Bernhardt owned a brewery in Canal Dover, Ohio, from 1902 to 1904, but then he decided northern Idaho was the place to expand his business goals.[3] In June of 1907, he was in Coeur d'Alene

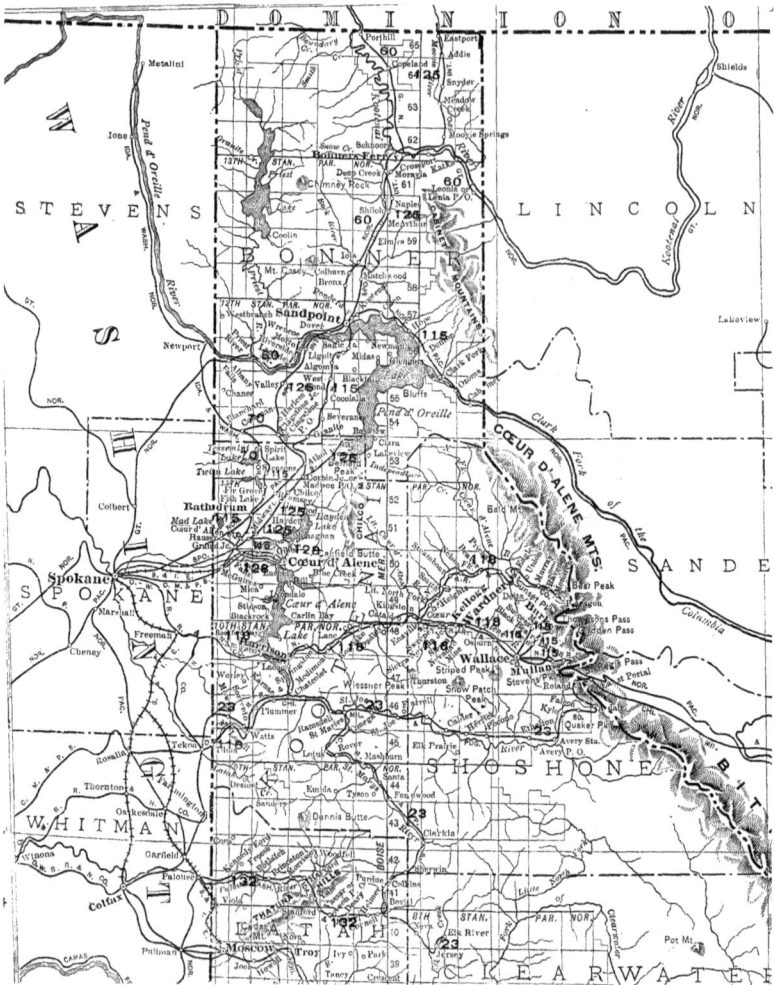

8. Greater Coeur d'Alene Region map.

peddling stock in a proposed brewery there.[4] He envisioned no nickel and dime venture; capital stock was $200,000, and shares were $100 each. An investor could pay 10 percent down and 10 percent a month. This may have been a scam from the beginning, but the brewery's later business troubles seem more a case of mismanagement than questionable intent. The planned brewery was not only announced in the local media, but news of it was carried in nearby Wallace to try to sell more stock there. "As sure to pay dividends as a brewery" was

Coeur d'Alene Brewing Company, Ltd.

Do you want to own stock in a brewery?   An investment which guarantees good returns.   Breweries never fail.

Mr. Chris. Bernhard, an Ohio brewer, representing considerable eastern capital, has selected Coeur d'Alene as a location for a new brewery, after a thorough investigation of local conditions. Associated with him are several influential business men of this city. The capital stock of the brewing company is $200,000, over $75,000 of which has already been subscribed.

The company wishes the co-operation and support of the community in which it is to make its home. In order to secure this support and good will, it offers for a limited time, shares of stock to the citizens of Coeur d'Alene and the tributary country on terms within the reach of all. Operations will be begun at once. A cut of the brewery will appear in a later issue of this paper.

You Have a Chance to Get in on the Ground Floor

Stock may be purchased by payment of 10 per cent down and 10 per cent every thirty days thereafter $100 per share. Stock subscriptions will be received at the office of Sanders & Flynn or at the Exchange National bank, Coeur d'Alene, Idaho.

9. Newspaper ad for the brewing company stock.

one come-on employed in a half-page ad.[5] The ads also said Coeur d'Alene residents had already bought $100,000 worth of stock.

One of the ads gave a bit of biography about Bernhardt.[6] It described him as a German who understands every department of the brewery business and who has already bought $30,000 worth of stock himself. Another selling point was that nine-tenths of the saloon keepers in Coeur d'Alene had made a purchase and many Wallace-area ones had also bought in.[7] They would certainly sell the beer from a brewery in which they owned stock, and saloon sales were vital for success in an era when little beer was consumed at home.

In September of 1907, the owners ordered 400,000 bricks, and they started construction at the site where old Fort Sherman had once stood.[8] William Griesser of Pittsburgh designed the massive six-story structure.[9] Bernhardt again made the short train trip to Wallace to inform the investors there that the 400,000 bricks had arrived.[10] While the construction progressed, some business developments took place. The new incorporation of Bernhardt, William Dollar, and Earl Sanders was listed in *Western Brewer*.[11]

Earl Sanders made a pilgrimage to Wallace in late October to report and to try to sell more stock.[12] Things seemed all right. In April, the Wallace newspaper gave a long, detailed architectural description of the nearly completed plant.[13] Bernhardt went to Wallace in May of 1908 to talk to stockholders and tell them the product would soon be on the market.[14] A contest offered $100 in stock for the best name for the new beer.[15] Prince of Pilsen was the winner. In July, the brewery offered lots in the area for sale on good terms.[16] Beer must have been flowing by October of 1908, because the brewery offered spent grain—a post-brewing byproduct—to stock raisers at 20 cents per bushel.[17] No sooner was the brewery in operation than a hail of lawsuits struck.[18] The brewery owners had not paid any of the creditors. For example, Branson and Max successfully sued for $318.63 plus interest and attorney fees for unpaid goods, wares, and merchandise in April of 1909.[19]

By April of 1909, liabilities were approaching $150,000. The Exchange National Bank, the Idaho Bank and Trust Company, and William Dollar, on behalf of the stockholders, all filed suits.[20] The suits alleged that the liabilities were $150,000 and the business could only be sold for $100,000. The banks said they were owed about $30,000, and Dollar's group was

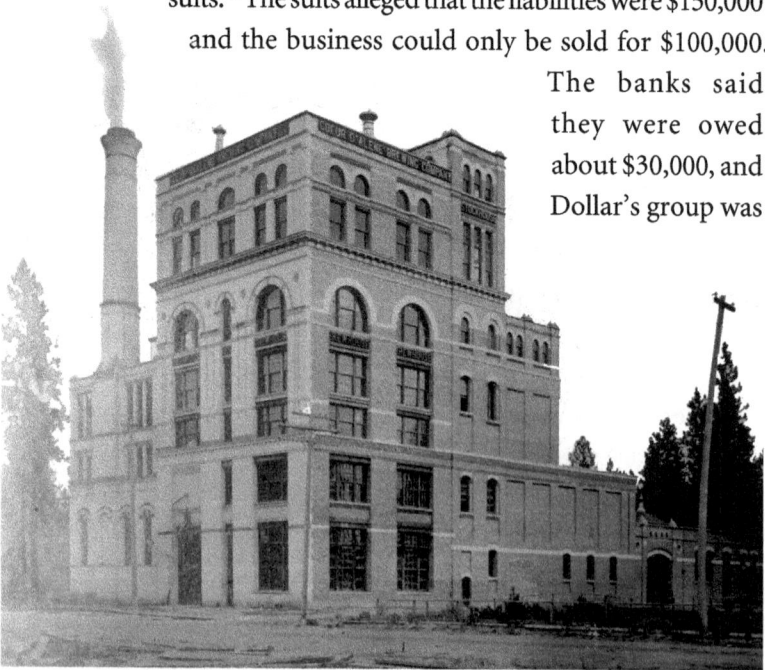

10. *The magnificent Coeur d'Alene Brewery. Photo North Idaho Museum.*

11. *Coeur d'Alene Brewery workers, including two children, pose at the loading dock.*

owed about $15,000. His group also wanted, in addition, 10 percent in attorneys' fees. The Washington Brick and Lime Company, the Brewery Equipment & Supply Company, and the Lake City Hardware Company all filed additional suits.

The next day, another regional newspaper continued the story. [21] By then, assets were $300,000 and liabilities $150,000. The St. Joe Bank was among those filing claims. Bernhardt and secretary Earl Sanders were the ones being accused. Dollar, H.F. Moore, and Leon DeMars alleged that Bernhardt and Sanders issued themselves blocks of stock worth at least $25,000 "without paying for the stock or accounting in any way for it." The stockholders believed Bernhardt and Sanders were running the brewery for their personal gain, rather than for the benefit of the stockholders. The stockholders were also seeking a receiver to protect themselves, and believed that one appointed at the behest of the creditors would injure them.

A month later, many of the

ATTENTION RANCHERS
AND OTHER OWNERS OF CATTLE AND HOGS

Commencing October 27 we will have spent grain from the brewery to dispose of at 20c per bushel measure.

Coeur d'Alene Brewing Company

12. *Newspaper ad offering spent brewery grain.*

13. *Prince of Pilsen beer label. This Panhandle Brewing Company replaced Bernhardt's.*

stockholders held an informal meeting in Coeur d'Alene to work on the situation.[22] O.D. Jones, William A. Simons, Louis Sweet, and John H. Nordquist, all of Wallace, Gus Nelson of Burke, John Carlson of Gem, and Curtis Lightner of Enaville all attended the meeting.

The report from the meeting said that only the small creditors were howling for money, so the stockholders wanted to get them together and settle. Brewing was continuing, and the business in Coeur d'Alene City alone would meet expenses.

An ad in the Coeur d'Alene newspaper listed 10 retail establishments that carried the local brew.[23] Apparently these were not enough.

Early in June, another meeting created a complete business reorganization.[24] A number of Wallace stockholders took an 18-month

14. *The brewery in winter snow with a loaded wagon in front. Photo North Idaho Museum.*

option on $73,400 of the treasury stock and decided to try to collect $19,000 due in subscribed stock. They hoped this much cash would make it possible for the stockholders to negotiate with the creditors of the business. O.D. Jones, president; L.L. Sweet, vice-president; William Gulickson, secretary; and William Dollar, treasurer, were the new officers. Bernhardt was still on the board of directors, along with Sweet, Jones, Gulickson, Dollar, and John H. Nordquist, William Simmons, D.E. Keys, Leon DeMars, E.E. Horst, and George F. Bittner. All these plans did not get a chance to reach fruition.

On June 30, the

15. The brewery makes the background for a posed photo. Photo North Idaho Museum.

business was declared bankrupt.[25] Vice-president Sweet said they thought everything was fixed, but a new claim was filed for $1,900 that refused to wait for payment. Sweet blamed the Spokane Brewery for forcing the issue and thus eliminating competition. Sweet said now the investors would all lose their money. A week later, the report was that things were settling down and the bankruptcy would take its natural course.[26]

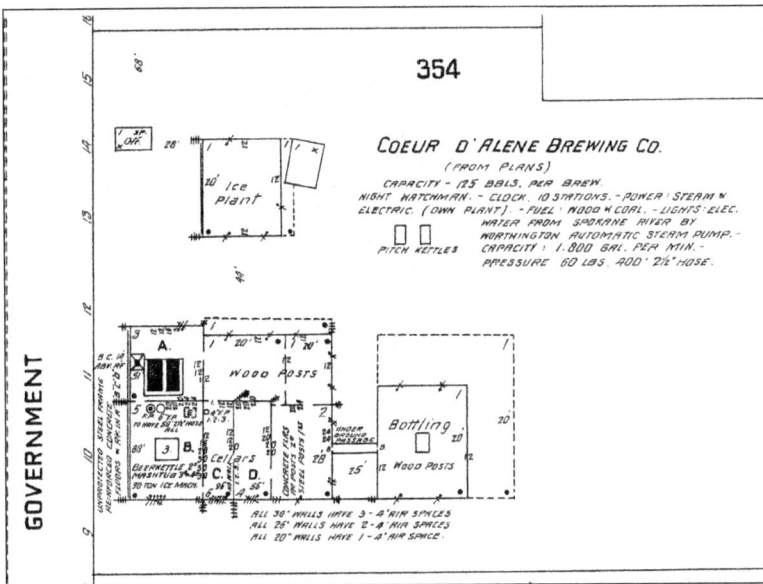

16. Coeur d'Alene Brewing Company from the fire insurance map.

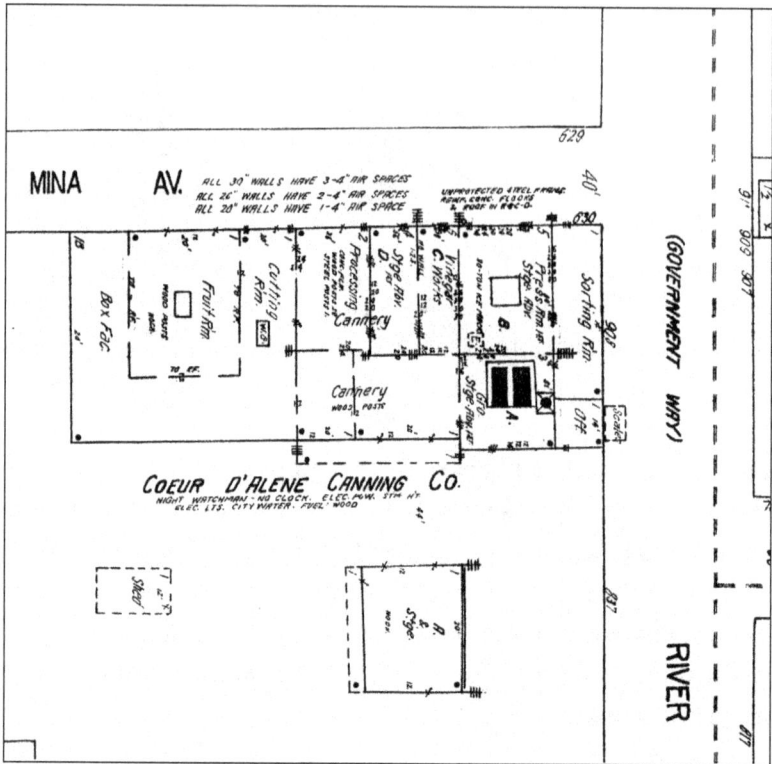

17. *Coeur d'Alene Canning Company has replaced the brewing company in the great brick building.*

In September 1909, the case of *Horace H. Hubbard, Trustee of the Coeur d'Alene Brewing Co. Ltd. vs H. G. Herold* was filed. The case was delayed twice, but on 1 June 1910 Earl Sanders and Christian Bernardt testified in court in Coeur d'Alene in the case, which was ultimately dismissed in a non-jury trial.

The business went on to be closed and then sold and then reopened before statewide prohibition shut it down for good. But what of our subject Christian Bernhardt? The 1910 U. S. Census listed him as 37 years old, born in Ohio, and living in Kootenai County, Idaho. The next thing I learned of him, he was opening a saloon two and a half years later in Coeur d'Alene at an area called Coney Island.[27] [I wonder where they got that name?] The building was partially outside the city limits and he was hoping to avoid paying city saloon taxes.

Towering over the grounds of old Fort Sherman, the brewery was destined to have other incarnations. It became a cannery, then a meat and grain storage site, a boat shop, and in the 1930s the U.S. Forest Service used it for storage on blister rust control projects.[28] In 1965, five stories of the main building

PANHANDLE BREWING CO.

"Prince of Pilsen"
B E E R

18. Newspaper ad for Prince of Pilsen beer.

were torn down by the United Brick Salvage Co. of Spokane. Bricks were shipped to Seattle, Portland, Yakima, Pasco, and Pullman. In September of 1967, Dr. Henry A. Novak sold the site to Victor and Donald Swofford, who operated the Swofford Quality Cut Shop. On 12 September 1968, the business was completely destroyed by fire. Eventually the land was sold to North Idaho College.

In the 1850 to 1951 Idaho marriage index there is a listing for a Christian Bernhardt (sic). He married Alice Targler on 6 July 1921 in Kootenai County, Idaho.[29] Bernhardt would have been 48 at the time.

END NOTES

1   Singletary, *Kootenai Chronicles*, p. 46.

2   Letter from John A. McTraland, Museum of North Idaho, to the author, 2 August 1982.

3   Van Wieren, *American Breweries II*, p. 265. The subject's name is often spelled Bernard also. This may be an Anglicization.

4   *Coeur d'Alene Press*, Coeur d'Alene, Idaho, 13 June 1907, p. 4.

5   *The Times*, Wallace, 10 July 1907, p. 4, c. 1-7.

6   *The Times*, Wallace, 11 July 1907, p. 4, c. 1-7.

7   *The Times*, Wallace, 12 July 1907, p. 4, c. 1-7.

8   The tennis court of North Idaho College are at this site in the 1990s. One source said 5 million bricks were used which I believe is a drastically large error. See Robert Singletary, *Kootenai Chronicles*, p. 46.

9   A brief discussion of the construction is found in Ronnenberg, *Beer and Brewing in the Inland Northwest,* p. 50.

10   *The Daily Times*, Wallace, 6 September 1907, p. 4, c. 6.

11   *Western Brewer*, vol. xxxiii, no. 2, 15 February 1908, p. 115.

12   *The Daily times*, Wallace, 27 October 1907, p. 6, c. 5.

13   *The Daily times*, Wallace, 3 April 1908, p. 3, c. 5.

14 *The Daily times*, Wallace, 12 May 1908, p. 2, c. 4.

15 *Western Brewer*, vol. xxxiii, no. 5, 15 May 1908, p. 233. Randy Carlson, "From the Archives," *American Breweriana Journal*, November-December 1984, p. 13.

16 *Coeur d'Alene Evening Press*, 22 July 1908, p. 3, c. 5 & 6.

17 *Coeur d' Alene Morning Journal*, 28 October 1908, p. 4, c. 2 & 3.

18 *Coeur d'Alene Evening Press*, 23 April 1909. p. 1, c. 1.

19 Kootenai County Records, ISHS, Reel 1, p. 324.

20 *Coeur d'Alene Evening Press*, 23 April 1909, p. 1, c. 1.

21 *The Times*, Wallace, 24 April 1909, p. 1, c. 1.

22 *Daily Idaho Press*, Wallace, 21 May 1909, p. 1, c. 2.

23 *Coeur d'Alene Evening Press*, 24 May 1909, p. 3, c. 5 & 6.

24 *Coeur d'Alene Evening Press*, 9 June 1909, p. 1, c. 1. *Idaho Press*, Wallace, 10 June 1909, p. 1, c. 4.

25 *The Idaho Press*, Wallace, 1 July 1909, p. 1, c. 6.

26 *The Idaho Press*, Wallace, 8 July 1909, p. 1, c. 4.

27 *Coeur d'Alene Evening Press*, 26 December 1911, p. 1, c. 3.

28 Singletary, *Kootenai Chronicles*, p. 46.

29 *Idaho Marriage Index 1850 to 1951*, Family Tree Maker, CD-ROM.

3

JOHN CORAY
Murder Victim

JOHN CORAY ACHIEVED HIS BRIEF NOTORIETY the way anyone with a choice would elect to avoid—he was a murder victim. Idaho City was a boomtown full of shady characters and frequently awash in violence in 1864 when Coray and Adam Pefferlee operated their Idaho Brewery there. Shortly after 11 o'clock on a nondescript Monday night, the 29th of August, seven or eight men were singing German songs and taking one last late-evening social glass of beer behind the closed doors of Coray's brewery saloon.[1] A stranger knocked on the door and demanded admittance. Coray said to go away, they were closed for the night, but Pefferlee went to the door and opened it to see what was wanted.

The stranger, who later proved to be an Irishman named Thomas Fitzgibbons, asked if they knew where he could find a man named Harry or Henry. Pefferlee said he knew several men with that name. Fitzgibbons said he sought the one from Auburn or Mormon Gulch. Pefferlee said he thought there was such a man at Buena Vista Bar, which was about a mile from Idaho City. Pefferlee gave complicated, detailed directions on where to go to cross the bridge on the road to that little settlement. Fitzgibbons ambled off; Pefferlee locked the door and joined the men inside for another drink.

Soon, Fitzgibbons was back rapping on the door. Again, Coray said not to open it, but somebody overruled him, and again Fitzgibbons asked the location of a man named Harry. Coray said to Fitzgibbons, "Go away, we don't want any of your kind, or any drunken bummer here at this late hour."[2] Fitzgibbons flew into a rage and called no one in particular "a son of a bitch." Coray went toward Fitzgibbons and said, "Who do you call a son of a bitch?" "You, you son of a bitch," Fitzgibbons shot back as he backpedaled into the dark street. Coray followed him until he was 12 to 15 feet away from the Irishman and

19. Idaho City Cemetery.

they were about 30 or 40 feet into the street. A single shot rang out. Brewer Coray was hit in the chest a little right of the sternum, in the pit of the stomach, yet the slug pierced the lower part of the heart, according to the *Boise News*, which obviously had no anatomy professor on staff. Coray lived another 10 or 15 minutes and his only words were "I'm killed."

The editor of the local newspaper was returning from the theater at the time and heard the shot fired on Montgomery Street immediately to the rear of the Washoe Saloon, which fronted on Main Street. However, he did not learn until the next morning that Coray had been shot and killed.

At 10 o'clock Tuesday morning Justice Walker, acting as coroner, summoned a jury of six "good and lawful men" who reported to the Idaho Brewery to examine the evidence in the case. Doctors Harris and Hogg examined Coray's body in the presence of the jury and extracted the ball, which was a navy-sized slug. The testimony indicated that Coray never had any idea he was in danger, nor did anyone think he intended to do any injury to Fitzgibbons. "Everything seemed to be going on in a spirit of playfulness and pleasantry at the brewery until the fatal shot was fired."[3] Dr. Hogg, who had been in the brewery laying on a table when all this was occurring, thought nothing of the events at first, but thought it was a "skylark" until he heard the shot and Coray's words "I'm killed."

The jury also determined that Coray was a 29-year-old native of Switzerland, a good citizen, and a peaceable man. Several individuals in the area who had known him for years at Yreka, California, attested to this.[4]

THE LYNCH MOB

Tuesday morning as the coroner's jury met, Deputy Sheriffs Underwood and Whiting became suspicious that a mob would try to take their prisoner, Fitzgibbons, after Coray's funeral.[5] With the help of John Keenan, who had made the arrest the night before, they summoned a large, well-armed posse and stationed them in the yard around the jail. At 4 o'clock that afternoon Paxton's brass band, playing a mournful dirge, led the hundreds of mourners who escorted Coray's earthly shell to the cemetery. On the walk back to town about 100 men stood on the hill overlooking the jail and prepared to assault it. They were game to put instant justice around the neck of Thomas Fitzgibbons and deport his Irish soul to County Purgatory without benefit of court proceedings.

Several men spoke against this hasty action and Judge Parks gave the most influential speech. Parks climbed on a tree stump to be seen and heard above the throng. His audience, which had swollen to several hundred, listened attentively. He asked them to point out a single instance where a criminal had escaped punishment since Sumner Pinkham had been sheriff.[6] Had even one escaped the vigilance of the officers in bringing them to trial, or had a single defendant once found guilty gotten away? No one could cite a single instance. Where then was the necessity of disgracing the land with scenes of mob violence? Wait until Monday next and a grand jury would be impaneled, and if they return an indictment, a

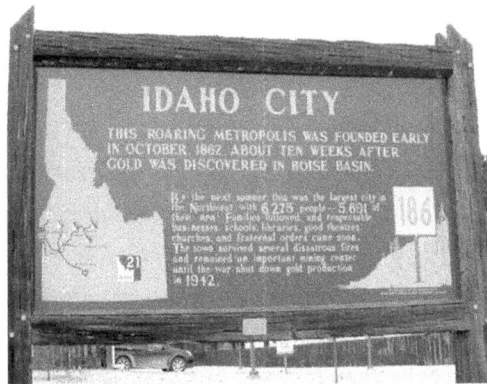

20. Idaho City historical sign.

trial jury of 12 men would pass upon his guilt or innocence. When Parks finished the word was whispered among the crowd, "let's go home." Eventually, everyone wandered away without incident.

Sheriff Sumner Pinkham, to whom the judge referred, was appointed sheriff soon after the organization of the territory in 1863.[7] In the fall of 1865, he was himself shot dead in Idaho City by low-life Ferd Patterson. Patterson was acquitted, but later shot dead while he sat in a barber chair in Walla Walla, Washington.

The local paper philosophized long and deeply about the mob dispersing without a lynching, and managing to praise those on both sides, yet deeply thanking those who gave "sober second thoughts before plunging the whole community into anarchy and confusion." They called the defendant a "poor deluded wretch … with no hope of escape."

THE FITZGIBBON TRIAL

The Grand Jury returned an indictment of murder in the first degree.[8] The first witness at the trial on 12 October 1864 was Adam Pefferlee, who said five men—John Coray, Adam Pefferlee, Mitchell Scholl, and the two barkeeps, Jim Hogg and Charley—were in the saloon that night when a man came to the door. After Coray went out, he was shot and said, "Oh, Adam, I am shot." Pefferlee followed the suspect a bit, but then came back to help the others get Corey inside the saloon.

The next witness was Scholl, a saloonkeeper who had shut his place that night and then went to Coray's. Scholl had little new to add. James Hogg testified next and explained a bit more about how they locked the door and put a bench in front of it.

The judge gave the jury detailed instructions before deliberations. Murder is killing with malice aforethought; express malice is deliberately taking the life of another person. Murder in the second degree is "where the killing is willful and malicious, but without deliberation."

Fitzgibbons was convicted of second degree, not first-degree murder, when the verdict came.[9] In 1865, the Boise District Attorney pointed out that of 60 deaths by violence in the young territory, there

had not been one con-
viction for capital
murder. It seems that
when the bloodlust of
the lynch mob abated,
it left a curiously
weak-willed attitude
that favored judicial
compromise.[10]

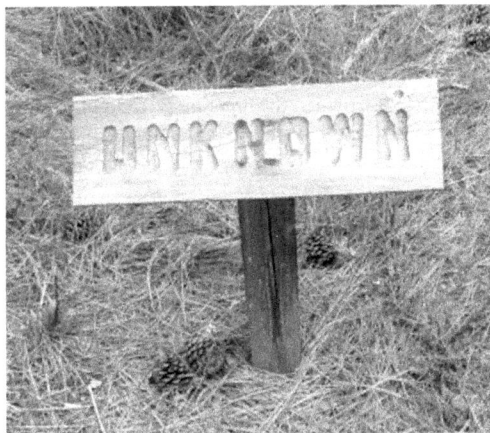

21. *One of many unknown graves in the Idaho City Cemetery. John Coray's grave is not marked.*

John Coray was the first, but not the last, brutally murdered member of the Idaho branch of Gambrinus' fraternity. In May of 1865, the brewery he had owned was a $6,000 loss in the fire that swept Idaho City.[11]

END NOTES

1 *Boise News*, Idaho City, 3 September 1864, p. 2, c. 2. This was a very long detailed article and appeared on the same page as an account of the lynch mob that followed the killing. The story appeared in shorter form in a letter from "Tycoon," a regular contributor to the Boise newspaper from Idaho City. See *Tri-Weekly Statesman*, 1 September 1864, p. 3, c. 1. This reporter said the events happened at "Chronies" Brewery in the rear of the Washoe Saloon.

2 *Boise News*, Idaho City, 3 September 1864, p. 2, c. 2. The speeches were quoted in the newspaper.

3 *Boise News*, 3 September 1864, p. 2, c. 2.

4 If Coray indeed worked at a brewery in Yreka, California it must have been either the one owned by Gottfried Gamble who later went to Lewiston, Idaho (1862 to 1869) and then Steilacoom, Washington from 1879 to 1882, or the one owned by Charles Peters from 1860 to 1888. See Bull, Friedrich and Gottschalk, *American Breweries*, p. 38.

5 *Boise News*, Idaho City, 3 September 1864, p. 2, c. 3.

6 Pinkham was appointed sheriff, along with many other official appointments, by the governor and confirmed by the council on 27 February 1864. He was also U. S. marshal.

7 Hawley, *History of Idaho*, 1920, p. 864-5.

8 Boise County Criminal Records, reel #40 of Boise County Records. All the subsequent material on the trial is from this source. The court reporter could neither write nor spell.

9   Bancroft, *History of Washington, Idaho and Montana,* p. 457-458. Bancroft records this whole incident, making Coray the only Idaho brewer he mentioned.

10 An 1896 article in the *Statesman* could only find seven men who were legally executed in the history of the state to that point. *Idaho Daily Statesman,* Boise, Idaho 23 May 1896, p. 3, c. 1 & 2. [11]*Idaho World,* Idaho City, 20 May 1865, p. 2, c. 1 & 2.

4

OTTO FRIES

Unexplained Insanity

Moscow, Idaho, is the home of the University of Idaho and a prosperous village that has had two brewpubs in the 1990s. Go back over a hundred years, and the town was an infant with an uncertain future. The area had no furs or minerals, and hence little early interest was generated. William Ewing, a cattleman, arrived in the general area in 1869, and A. A. Lieuallen started farming three miles east of the present site in 1871.[1] The abundant growth of camas plants led to the name of Hog Heaven (hogs love to eat camas) for the area. Then, the settlers renamed it Paradise Valley until 26 December 1876, when "Moscow" was chosen in honor of Moscow, Pennsylvania.

In February of 1882, the local press released news that Moscow would soon have a brewery.[2] Property records indicate that the two new brewers, Otto Fries and Joe Neiderstadt, jointly purchased lots 11 and 12 of the block at A and Main streets in 1882.[3] A. J. Frye and Miriam R. Frye sold the two future brewers a lot measuring 125 feet on A Street and 120 feet on Main Street for $200 on February 6, 1882.[4] By March 30, the carpenters were framing the building and the Lewiston newspaper predicted "before the orators have a chance to sling the British Lion by the tail over their heads for the admiration of an applauding audience of free-born American citizens on the next Fourth of July, we will have Moscow beer to drink, and as Sam Woods says in quoting scripture (or is it Shakespeare?), Beer is good for the stomachs ache."[5] They were giving Fries and Neiderstadt a lot of pre-opening publicity. Finally, Mr. Fries actually got his name in the Lewiston paper but he had to settle for their phonetic spelling, "Frees."[6]

The U.S. Census listed Otto as a resident of San Francisco County, California in 1870. He was 43, had $200 in personal property, was from Prussia, and "works in brewery." All his neighbors also "worked in brewery." On the R. G. Dun Mercantile list for 1883 was Fries and Co., brewery, Moscow (p. 111).

The Moscow brewery was opened in June, and in a few years Moscow had its own newspaper, the *Moscow Mirror*, and daily activities were recorded.[7] C. B. Reynolds, a practicing attorney, was moonlighting as editor-publisher during the early years, and despite his often-editorialized claim to being a teetotaler, he became fast friends with Otto. The numerous references to Otto in the newspaper sounded like barroom banter between joking buddies.

In one instance, the news report was that "Otto has left" to locate his "sweetheart who lives in the lower country."[8] Otto had supposedly been receiving mysterious letters for several months and complained of feeling poorly. Reynolds predicted that when Fries' girl brought him back, the band would be out and the boys would be around. Otto did return, because just two weeks later, Reynolds reported that he had been going around with his hand in a sling. By listening through key-holes and down chimneys, the newspaper man learned his girl had gone back on him and Fries "made a determined effort to put an end to himself, but weakened after pulling the trigger and tried to stop the bullet from coming out the muzzle with his hand."[9] This certainly sounds more like an inside joke than a report of a would-be suicide. Considering later events, however, there is room for doubt.

Before long, Reynolds kidded Fries about taking a stroll every evening with the lady with red ribbons in her bonnet, and Otto "tells the boys that he has not enjoyed weekly prayer meeting so much since he had the measles."[10] Her identity never surfaced. The following January, Otto made news again, but of a more substantial nature. There was a new "city" six miles east of town on the Bronte (or Bronta) Cabin Place, which was christened "Otto," "after our townsman Otto

22. Moscow Brewery with the Grand Army of the Republic
posed in front for the 4ᵗʰ of July parade.

Fries."[11] The same issue of the paper announced that there would be a big dance there in the new hall at Otto on January 21st with "good music, fine dancing and a grand supper"—tickets $1.50.[12] Just how or why the place was named after Otto remained unclear. One can speculate that he bought property there or moved to the area. In 1895, the village was officially founded by Mason Cornwall and was generally known as Cornwall throughout its history.

In just two months the press announced that the partnership of Fries and Neiderstadt had dissolved due to the ill health of Fries, and Neiderstadt would continue the brewery alone.[13] According to the dissolution notice, they were marketing beer eight miles away in Pullman, Washington, as well as in Moscow.[14] In early April, Fries' brother (name not listed), came up to visit from California and liked Moscow so much that he announced his intention to stay.[15]

Apparently Fries' illness was mental or a physical illness with mental symptoms. In December, the paper announced that Otto was in a mental asylum in California.[16] In two months, the *Mirror* announced Otto's recent death.[17] That April, Yontis, Coburn, and Boice, attorneys at law, came up from Lewiston to appraise Otto's

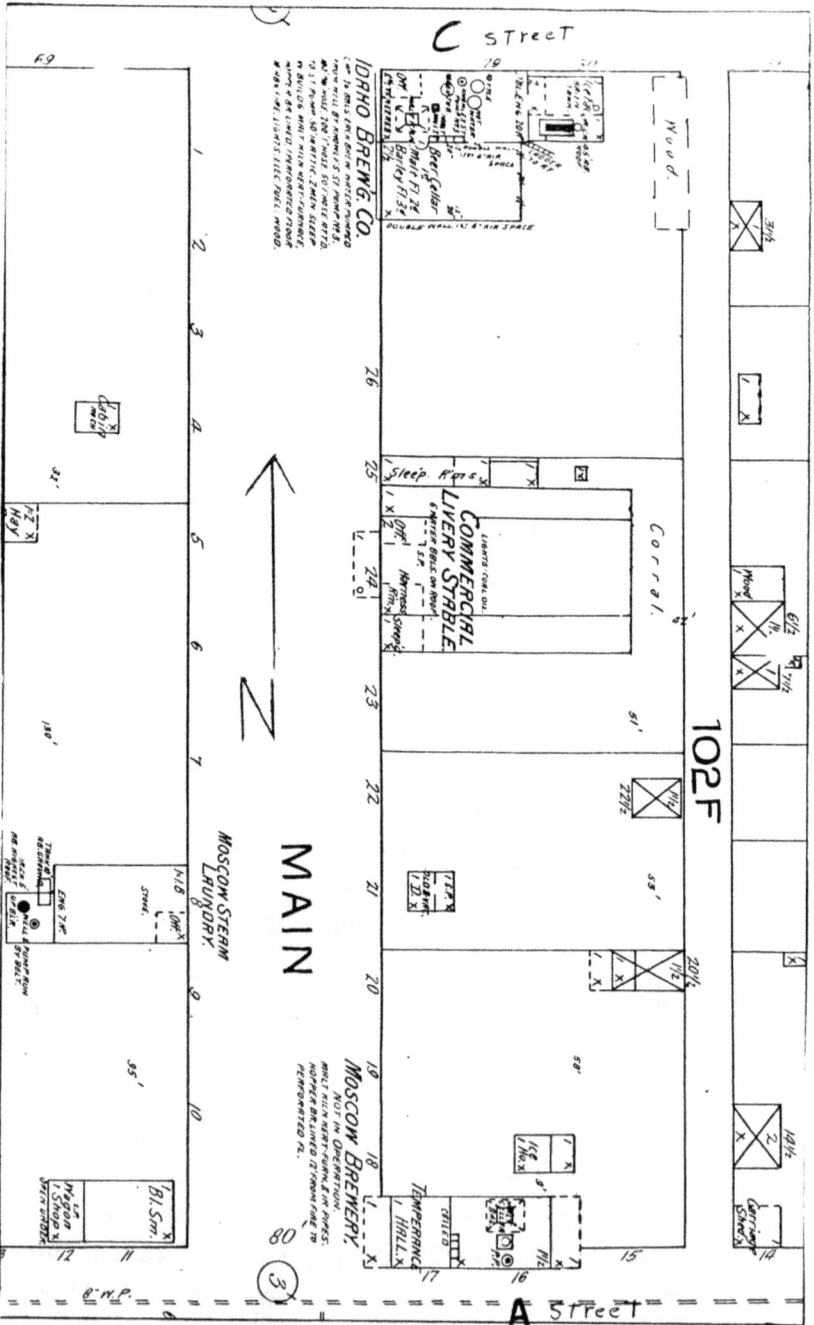

23. *Moscow Brewery and Idaho Brewery on Main Street*
at the corners of A and C in 1893.

estate.[18] Apparently, his move to California before his commitment to the asylum must have been in haste, since all his possessions were still in Moscow. Apparently, he suffered a breakdown.

Fries appeared to be so popular and so ready to grow with a new town, but he ended up making almost no impact. He was one of several Gem State brewers to end their days in mental institutions.

END NOTES

1   Lalia Boone, "Post Offices of Latah County," *Quarterly Bulletin* of the Latah County Historical Society, Moscow, Idaho, Vol. 7, no. 4, October 1978, p. 3.

2   *The Nez Perce News*, Lewiston, Idaho, 16 February 1882, p. 1, c. 6.

3   Records of the Latah County Title Company, Moscow, Idaho.

4   Nez Perce County Deed Record Book, p. 88.

5   *The Nez Perce News*, March 1882, p. 2, c. 1.

6   *The Nez Perce News*, 13 April 1882, p. 1, c. 4.

7   *Lewiston Teller*, Lewiston, Idaho, 22 June 1882, p. 3, c. 2.

8   *Moscow Mirror*, Moscow, Idaho, 6 November 1885, p. 3, c. 3.

9   *Moscow Mirror*, 20 November 1885., p. 3, c. 2.

10 *Moscow Mirror*, 2 December 1885, p. 3, c. 2.

11 *Moscow Mirror*, 15 January 1886, p. 3, c. 2

12 *Moscow Mirror*, 15 January 1886, p. 3, c. 2.

13 *Moscow Mirror*, 26 March 1886, p. 3, c. 2.

14 *Moscow Mirror*, 4 April 1886.

15 *Moscow Mirror*, 9 April 1886, p. 3, c. 1. In 1893 an H. Fries owned a saloon in Lewiston, Idaho, 30 miles from Moscow.

16 *Moscow Mirror*, 24 December 1886, p. 3, c. 1.

17 *Moscow Mirror*, 25 February 1887, p. 3, c. 1.

18 *Moscow Mirror*, 15 April 1887, p. 3, c. 1.

5

GOTTFRIED GAMBLE

Angry, Execrating and Execrated

Gottfried Gamble was one of the first brewers in Idaho, one of the first councilmen in Lewiston, and one of the first men to have a case heard in the Territorial Supreme Court. Gamble was a brewer in Yreka, California, at the Pacific Brewery on Oregon Street from 1858 to 1870, according to some sources.[1] He founded the brewery there in Siskiyou County, and may have had a financial interest for those years, but definitely not a physical presence there after 1862. He sold the brewery to John Miller, who in turn sold it to Charles Frederick, Leopold Lunker, and John Hessenauer in 1865.[2] At a special meeting of the Yreka fire department in April of 1860, they filed a petition for control of the new engine, and G. Gamble was one of the petitioners. Soon, Klamath Engine Company Number 2 was organized.[3] This gives some idea of Gamble's activities while in Yreka. The 1860 U. S. Census listed him as 40 years old, from Bavaria, a brewer with $4,000 in real estate and $2,000 in personal estate. He lived near brewers John Hesseman and Charles Peters.

When gold was discovered in Oro Fino, Elk City, and Florence, Yreka endured a violent case of gold fever, which swept many citizens to northern Idaho. In May of 1862, Gamble wrote to the *Yreka Weekly Journal* that the Salmon River mines—the Florence area—was a greater humbug than the Frazier River gold excitement had been, and that he intended to work in Portland only long enough to get money to pay his way back to Siskiyou County, California.[4] The same issue of that newspaper said speculators at Lewiston were selling lots from $400 to $2,000. They likened this to "buying a stone quarry for a gold-bearing quartz lead."[5] Others believed the deals were sound, and soon Gamble had changed his mind and stayed in Lewiston to use his brewing experience and expertise.

Gamble, making beer in Lewiston by 1862, was one of the first three brewers in the future state of Idaho. Mr. A. Charles Brown and Gamble started the "California Brewery" that year. Back in Yreka, the District court heard the case of John P. Miller v. G. Gamble and issued a judgment on foreclosure.[6] Possibly, there was no reason to return to California for Mr. Gamble. Ernest Weisgerber, who already had a brewery in operation in Lewiston, bought the Brown/Gamble brewery, or part of it, from Brown on 16 October 1863.[7] Gamble then disappeared briefly from the historical record. Ernest advertised himself as the sole proprietor of the brewery by October of 1863.[8] Gamble was buying up real estate these years, and most of it eventually passed into Ernest Weisgerber's hands. In August 1863, Gamble sued Caesar Hoeflein in the district court in Walla Walla County, Washington.[9] Eventually, the case was dismissed with Plaintiff Gamble paying $10.25 in final fees after about $19 had been collected from both men for other fees. This is all I know about this case, but I suspect Hoeflein was brewing for Gamble, because Hoeflein later owned a brewery in Boise Basin when that gold rush was ablaze.

In August of 1865, Gamble paid Federal Tax on 77 barrels of beer brewed in Lewiston; in September he brewed 11 barrels of beer; in October Gamble paid for 9 barrels of beer, and in November of 1865 Gamble paid for a federal brewer's license.[10]

Gamble bought the south half of Lot 1, Block 4 on First Street of Lewiston for $300 from E. R. and Jane Marshall of Boise.[11] From Charles Haas of Bamberg, Germany, on 19 November 1866, he purchased, for $50, the land under "The What Cheer House," and from M.E. Goodwin of Umatilla County, Oregon, he purchased, on 29 April 1867, land adjacent to the brewery called "The Alta House" for $300.

The 1866 business directory listed Gamble as the only brewer in Lewiston.[12] This has to be an oversight. Gamble paid federal tax on fermented liquor in June 1866 on the Federal Tax Records.[13] In July he brewed 25 barrels of beer.[14] In September 1866, he paid for 24 barrels brewed.[15] By 1867, the firm was called Gamble and Weisgerber.[16] Gamble also had a newspaper ad published in 1867 to the effect that he was the "authorized agent for sale of lumber at Lewiston, during our absence. /E. A. Starr & Co."[17]

The first ever meeting of the Common Council of Lewiston was held on 1 April 1867, and Councilman G. Gamble was one of the five elected members present.[18] Soon, he turned his attention to the mining camp of Warren.

Gamble was involved in a court case that eventually reached the Idaho Supreme Court and was decided in January of 1869. Gamble was the respondent versus Dunwell, Ankney, et al., the appellants.[19] The case came from the first Judicial District, which included Lewiston. Gamble owned a way-station known as Twelve-mile House in Nez Perce County on the Nez Perce Reservation. He apparently bought it from a Mr. Nixon, or gave Nixon a mortgage on it. Nixon then sold it again to two men, both surnamed Ankney. The local court returned the title to Gamble and the state Supreme Court upheld that decision. The court wrote that the complaint, the answers, and "other particulars, are almost incomprehensibly drawn." They also ruled that they had no jurisdiction on Nez Perce land, but that did not matter since this was a case in equity and the person involved was in their jurisdiction.

On 1 March 1869, Ernest Weisgerber gave Gamble $600 for "The Alta House."[20] He also purchased another piece of land nearby from Gamble. Gamble's successful court case may have given him some new directions in business. All of this together became the site of the Weisgerber family home and the greatly-enlarged brewery of later years. Shortly after this, Ernest Weisgerber's two brothers, John and Christ moved to Lewiston, and Gamble headed permanently to the booming gold camp of Warren.

In Idaho Supreme Court business on January 5th of 1870, the case of G. Gamble vs. S. Devinish was heard.[21] The appeal was dismissed

California Brewery,
Near Head of First Street,
LEWISTON, I. T.

GAMBLER & WEISGERBER,
IS OUR AUTHORIZED AGENT FOR SALE
of Lumber ... During our absence.
Jan. 17, 1867. — ... E. A. STARR & Co.

FRESH BREWED LAGER BEER ALWAYS
on hand and for sale by the Keg, Gallon, or
Glass. Also, a good BAR, supplied with the
Choicest of LIQUORS and CIGARS.
January 17, 1867.   n1 tf.

and the judgment of the court below affirmed. The record was unclear as to the particulars of the case.

Gamble came to the gold camp of Warren "mounted on a splendid charger, smiling and supercilious," according to his critic, future Idaho governor Willey. He tried mining and had a great deal of capital acquired in Lewiston to finance the venture. Some historians remembered that the first sawmill in Warren was built in 1868 by Shessler (sic) and William Bloomen, and about the same time Godfrey Gamble installed a five-stamp mill that used waterpower.[22] Stamp mills pulverized ore preliminary to extracting the minerals. Gamble's Rescue Mine was going great guns in March of 1872 when a second chimney of good ore had been reached in drifting east about 200 feet from the terminus of the tunnel.[23] On the 9th of March, the day before they intended to make a cleanup of two weeks run, the sheriff served all the owners-Charles Isenbeck, Richard Hurley, Moses Hexter, Levi Hexter and Godfrey Gamble-with an order to "desist and refrain from further prosecuting any work on said mine." The order was made at the insistence of parties who claimed ownership.

In late October, Gamble was involved in a court case of Williams and Maxwell v. Gamble and Root.[24] The court took the case under advisement on October 29 and on the 30th, said they would decide it at a later date.

Also in October, a report on mining in Warren gave a glowing report of Gamble's mine.[25] They described the Rescue load as about one half mile from town and owned by Gamble. Considerable work had been done on 1,200 feet of the mine. One shaft was 182 feet deep, and 60 feet below the surface the first run went 130 feet east and 116 feet west. The second level, at a depth of 120 feet, runs 170 feet east and 80 feet west. The third level down 180 feet had runs east of 320 feet and west 150 feet. Crosscut tunnels were under construction. Their main vein was producing $25 to the ton. Gamble had a ten-stamp mill at the plant, which he kept in constant operation. The last 37 days' run had produced $11,522.38.

In late December, Godfrey Gamble and company were running five stamps and had struck ore in the west level that looked very good.[26] They had good hands at work and everything looked prosperous.

In January of 1873, the Idaho State Supreme Court ruled in the case of Alonzo Leland, Appellant vs. Chas. Isenbeck and Godfrey Gamble, Respondents.[27] The long decision gave a great deal of information. In District Court in Idaho County, Leland had showed that he had title and the premises of the mine had been withheld from him. Isenbeck and Gamble claimed Leland's title had been divested by a sale by the sheriff of Idaho County to Alexander and Co. on an execution of a judgment against E. B. Johnson. Gamble also pled an estoppel. Gamble and Isenbeck had won their case in the lower court.

The court ruled that the judgment that gave title to Alexander and Co. was invalid, and therefore the purchase of the mine by Isenbeck and Gamble was invalid even if done in good faith. Isenbeck further argued that he and Gamble had invested large sums in developing the mine and that Leland never even informed him of his claim to the property. They were unable to show the judgment from Johnson to Alexander and that was declared void. Hence further future sales were all void also.

Isenbeck had sold his share of the mine to Gamble on 23 February 1872. The court said Gamble had full knowledge of the Leland claim then and thus could not assert the same defense that Isenbeck could have asserted. The court called Gamble's pleadings "extraordinary and irregular as they must appear to all, it will be seen from the amended answer that all the matters averred therein are either redundant, irrelevant, or immaterial to his defense, ..." The decision was by Justice M. E. Hollister, with W. C. Whitson concurring. They court forced Leland to pay half the costs because he had brought a record "containing a mass of redundant matter, which greatly increases the costs in the case ..."

After this legal battle, the title to the Rescue mine in the Warren area was given to Alonzo Leland from Charles Isenback and Godfrey Gamble.[28] Twenty-six local men, including Leland, Saux, former brewer Manuel, and news correspondent and future governor Willey, formed the corporation known as the Rescue Mining Company.[29]

The newspaper account that announced the formation of the mining corporation also gave a detailed history of the mine. It was located in 1868, and the next year a 120-foot main shaft was sunk. Over $74,000 in gold was extracted from the quartz ore before the legal troubles shut the mine down. There was a blacksmith shop, large storehouse, boarding house, etc. all in good shape at the mine.

In April of 1873, Gamble left Warren, and future Idaho governor N. B. Willey wrote a scathing denunciation of the man.[30] He said Gamble held "a prominent position in quartz matters hereabouts for the last six years." He sank $20,000 into quartz operations, but left behind debts to enterprises and personal obligations that great again. He left on snowshoes in the dead of night in "sorrow and anger, execrating and execrated, shaking off the dust from his feet as he went..." His few remaining friends supposedly gave him a stake to get to San Francisco. Why was he a failure? Willey answered himself: Because he knew nothing of the business and "luck won't always do to depend upon."

A. Leland and the other new owners sued Gamble—despite his physical absence—and his fellow investors in

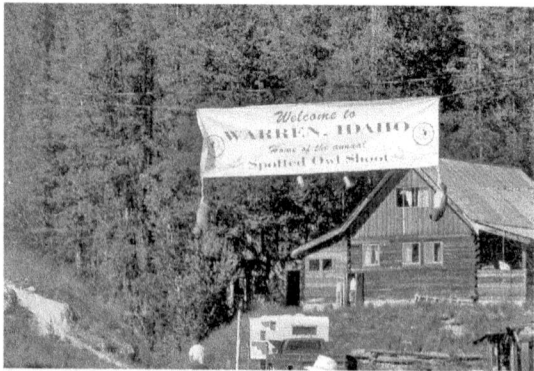

24. *Warren, Idaho in 1991. The spotted owl shoot conveys their attitude toward outsiders making rules for them.*

August 1873 over conversion of gold quartz.[31] The cause was discontinued as to all except Gamble, and judgment was ordered for the sum of $27,900 against Gamble with costs. He could never return to Warren with that debt hanging over his head.

In early October the new Rescue Mine owners purchased "a large quantity of tools which were formerly in the use of Gamble and Co."[32] It is unclear from whom they actually bought them.

It's hard to believe Gamble ever showed his face in civilization again after Willey's denunciation, but he did—and not in San Francisco. He was soon in Steilacoom, Washington, brewing beer in partnership with Mr. Mayer Kaufman.[33] First their enterprise was called the Steilacoom Brewery, but then it became the Puget Sound Brewery and it lasted until 1887.

Gamble's sojourn as a business pioneer of Idaho was long forgotten by then.

END NOTES

1   Dale P. Van Weiren, *American Breweries II*, p. 46. In some sources his first name is spelled Godfrey. This is probably an Anglicization.

2   *History of Siskiyou County, California, Illustrated with Views of Residences, Business Buildings and Natural Scenery, and Containing Portraits and Biographies of Its Leading Citizens and Pioneers*. Oakland, CA: D. J. Stewart & Co., 1881, p. 216C.

3   *History of Siskiyou County, California, Illustrated with Views of Residences, Business Buildings and Natural Scenery, and Containing Portraits and Biographies of Its Leading Citizens and Pioneers*, p. 190.

4   *Yreka Weekly Journal*, Yreka, California, 3 May 1862, p. 1, c. 3.

5   *Yreka Weekly Journal*, 3 May 1862, p. 1, c. 4.

6   *Yreka Weekly Journal*, 14 May 1862, p. 3, c. 2.

7   Taylor, Weisgerber and White, *A Man, His Family and His City*, 1982, p. 7. A month later he bought another lot from Brown but sold it back in June of 1864.

8   *The Golden Age*, Lewiston, Idaho, 24 October 1863, p. 2, c. 5.

9   Superior Court Records, 1859-1909, Walla Walla County, Washington, cage 407, Book of District Court Costs, p. 55. Washington State University. Holland Library, Special Collections.

10 Federal Tax Records, 1865-66, University of Idaho Library, Microfilm # 558.

11 Taylor, Weisgerber and White, *A Man, His Family, and His City*, 1982, p. 9

12 *Langely's Idaho Directory*, 1866, p. 2 of partial copy in University of Idaho Special Collections.

13 Federal Tax Records, 1865-1866, University of Idaho Library Microfilm # 558.

14 Federal Tax Records, 1865-1866, University of Idaho Library Microfilm # 558.

15 Federal Tax Records, 1865-1866, University of Idaho Library Microfilm # 558.

16 *Lewiston Journal*, Lewiston, Idaho 4 February 1867. p. 4, c. 3. 5 April 1867, p. 3, c. 2. 4 July 1867, p. 4, c. 3.

17 *Lewiston Journal*, 15 February 1867, p. 4, c. 5.

18 *Lewiston Journal*, 5 April 1867, p. 2, c. 4.

19 *Idaho Reports*, Vol. I, 1866-1880, case decided January 1869, pp. 268-271. Minutes of the Idaho State Supreme Court, Microfilm #128, University of Idaho Library, original pages, 197-198.

20 Taylor, Weisgerber and White, p. 13.

21 *The Capital Chronicle*, 8 January 1870, p. 4, c. 1. Minutes of the Idaho State Supreme Court, Microfilm #128, University of Idaho Library, original pages, 293-294, 300, 303, 305-306.

22 *History of Idaho*, Volume I, Chapter 11, p. 20. *History of Idaho, The Gem of the Mountains*, 1920, Vol. I, Chap. 33, p. 6.

23 *Idaho Signal*, Lewiston, 16 March 1872, p. 3, c. 1.

24 *Idaho Signal*, Lewiston, 2 November 1872, p. 3, c. 3.

25 *Idaho Signal*, Lewiston, 16 November 1872, p. 1, c. 3 & 4.

26 *Idaho Signal*, Lewiston, 28 December 1872, p. 3, c. 2.

27 *Idaho Signal*, Lewiston, 29 March 1873, p. 1, c. 2-4. Idaho Reports, 1873, pp. 469-476.

28 *Idaho Signal*, Lewiston, 29 March 1873, 29 March 1873, p. 1, c. 2-4.

29 *Idaho Signal*, Lewiston, 12 July 1873, p. 1, c. 2-5.

30 Helmers, *Warren Times*, n. p. Author cites, *Idaho Tri-Weekly Statesman*, 26 April 1873.

31 *Idaho Signal*, Lewiston, 23 August 1873, p. 3, c. 1.

32 *Idaho Signal*, Lewiston, 11 October 1873, p. 2, c. 2.

33 Dale P. Van Weiren, *American Breweries II*, p. 384.

6

GEORGE GOODING

Accidental Fall Victim

ON THE 1870 U.S. CENSUS, George Gooding was living at Placerville, Idaho, in the Boise Basin, a 41-year-old "brewery keeper," born in Bavaria of Bavarian parents, with $800 in real estate. He lived with his partner, George Miller, another Bavarian, and a brewery worker, John Fischer. Gooding and Miller became partners in the brewery in the boomtown of Granite Creek, also in the Boise Basin area, the previous year. Miller had owned a saloon there since at least 1868 and had previously been a deputy sheriff there in 1866.[1]

In May 1869, at Granite Creek "George Miller has lately added to his place a large and finely fitted brewery."[2] Another reporter toured the Boise Basin in August 1869 and found "George Miller is succeeding with his lager beer brewery."[3]

The partnership did not last long. An Idaho City friend who stopped by in October said Gooding had bought out Miller already.[4] Miller stayed in Granite Creek in mining. Miller was more a saloonkeeper and Gooding more of a brewer. The beer had not suffered from the change, and the brewery and one saloon were about the only places in Granite Creek doing any liquor business. There is no record of the brewery continuing into 1871. Gooding moved to Centerville, which is near Placerville, also in Boise Basin, and operated a brewery again. In October of 1873 George fell 12 feet from the landing at the top of the stairs at his brewery and was severely injured.[5] He fell on Tuesday the 23rd and died on Thursday the 25th, two days later.

Gooding is a fairly common name, helping to obscure the faint trail

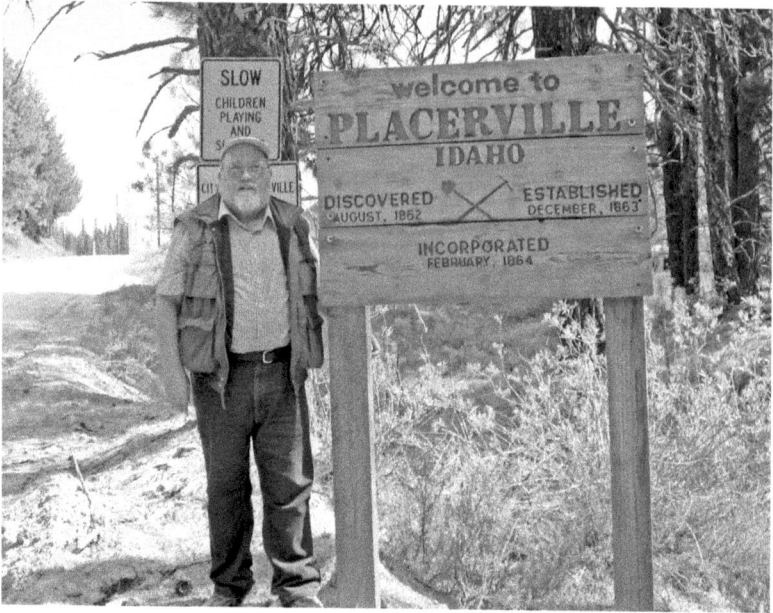

26. *The author poses by the Placerville, Idaho, welcome sign. 2008 C. E.*

left by this Disciple of Gambrinus.[6]
Death at the brewery is service
indeed to King Gambrinus.

END NOTES

25. *Road sign in Placerville shows the general locations of Boise Basin towns.*

1 *Idaho World*, Idaho City, Idaho, 8 September 1866, p. 2, c. 5. *Idaho Semi Weekly World*, Idaho City, 23 November 1867, p. 2, c. 2

2 *Idaho World*, Idaho City, 13 May 1869, p. 3, c. 4.

3 *Idaho World*, Idaho City, 5 August 1869, p. 2, c. 2.

4 *Idaho World*, Idaho City, 29 September 1870, p. 2, c. 1.

5 *The Walla Walla Statesman*, Walla Walla, Washington, 18 October 1873, p. 2, c. 5.

6 There is a George Gooding on the U. S. Census in Nye County, Nevada in 1880, 1900, and 1910. There is also a George N. Gooding there in 1880. Relationship to our brewer, if any, is unknown. A George Gooding opened a real estate company with J. J. Fuller in Weiser, Idaho in 1904. See *Evening Capital News*, 22 June 1904, p. 2, c. 1.

7

PAUL GRAF
Accidental Shooting Victim

IN THE EARLY MORNING OF OCTOBEr 10, 1904, William Murphy, night watchman at the Sunset Brewery in Wallace, Idaho, shot and killed his friend Paul Graf.[1] Was it murder, an accident, a settling of an old grudge, or a defense of the property Murphy was paid to guard? The coroner's jury made their decision, but the facts left plenty of room for doubt.

At one o'clock in the morning, Murphy ran across the street from the brewery to the house of brewery engineer Fred Inman. "Fred get up, there's somebody robbing the office," Murphy shouted. Before Inman could get out of bed, he heard a shot, and a moment later, two more. Inman jumped to the window and Murphy called to him, "Fred, watch the front and I will go around back." Inman heard another shot and Murphy ran back to say, "I got one of them Fred, but I don't know where the other went to." Murphy then ran up the street, where he soon met night officer Quinn running up; together they went back of the brewery. Murphy came running back to Inman with the ghastly report, "My God, Fred, I have killed Paul."

THE CORONER'S INQUEST
The Wallace coroner's jury met later that same day and tried to figure out how such a thing could have happened. The deceased man, Paul Graf, was the brother-in-law of Jacob Lockman, the manager of Sunset Brewery. The local paper said Graf had worked at the brewery on and off for seven or eight years. They seemed to forget that it had

only been in business for three years. Graf had a key to the back door of the brewery and no one had ever asked him to turn it in when he quit working there three weeks before.

Graf's friend, Mark Oppenheimer, testified at the inquest that Graf had spoken earlier that evening about some faro cards at the brewery that had come from a closed saloon, and that he wanted to go up to the brewery to fetch them. Graf had been drinking and he showed Oppenheimer the keys to prove he could get in. Oppenheimer also testified that Graf never carried a gun but relied on his muscles if trouble ever developed.

Others testified that as the fatally wounded man lay dying he was heard to ask, "Billy, why did you shoot me? I was getting the mail." Later, after being taken to the hospital, Paul Graf whispered, "that man who killed me is my best friend, he made a mistake when he killed me."

The story of getting the mail cropped up several times, but no mail, nor the faro cards he had mentioned, were found on Graf. Bill Murphy testified at length before the coroner's jury. He claimed he could see two men crouching behind the desk in the office and had watched them a while before going over to Inman's to report the break in. "Then I ran nearly to the center of the road," Murphy explained, "I fired two shots from there. I did not aim at anything. I saw them run out from the back office. I ran alongside the office and fired through the front window at them. Then I ran back of the office. As I got there, one of them was coming out of the door, coming backward, pulling the door shut. I hollered to him, 'hands up,

27. Sunset Brewery ad from Coeur d'Alene Souvenir.

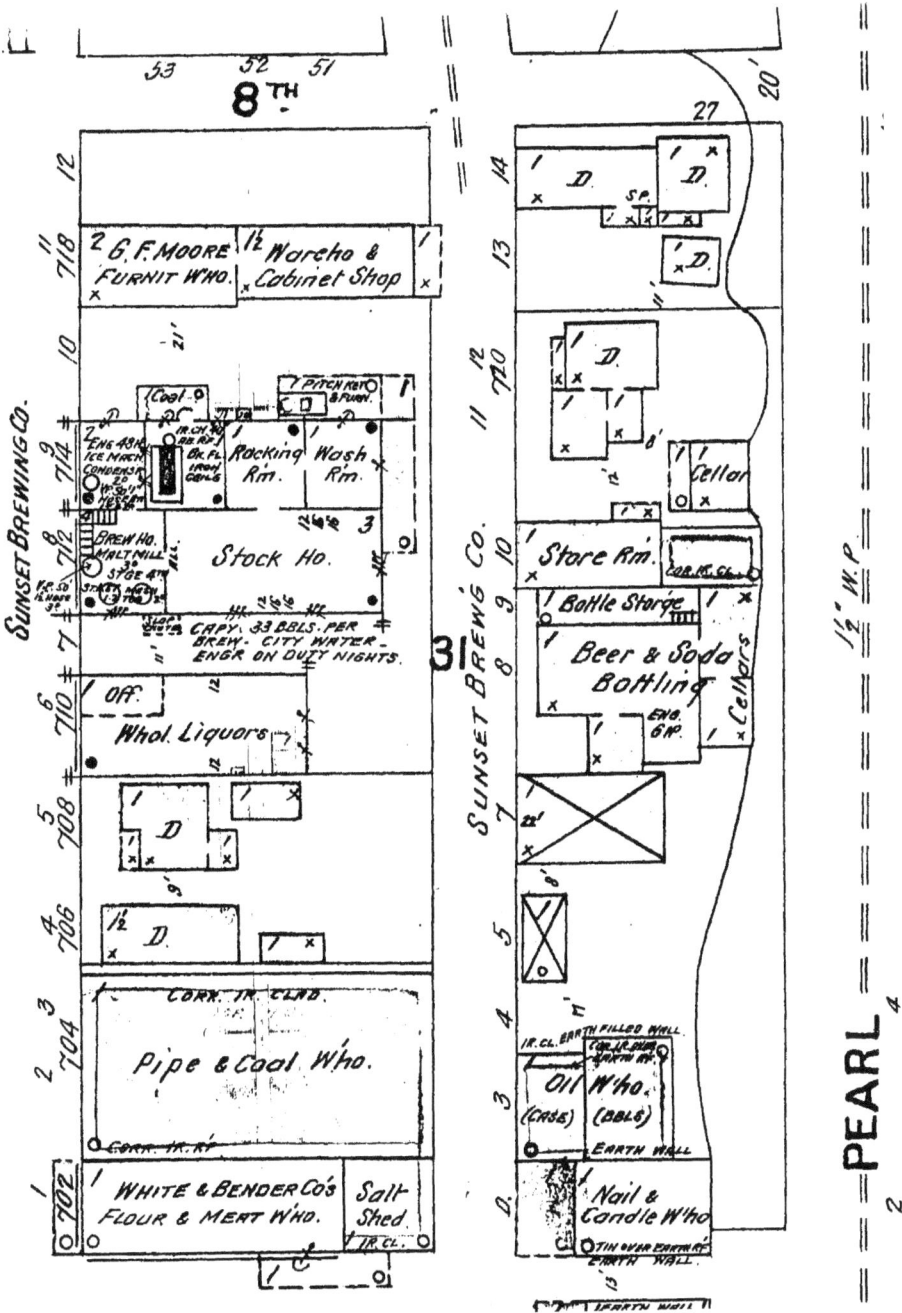

28. Sunset Brewery on the Wallace fire insurance map.

Something Good

米

Sunset Beer...

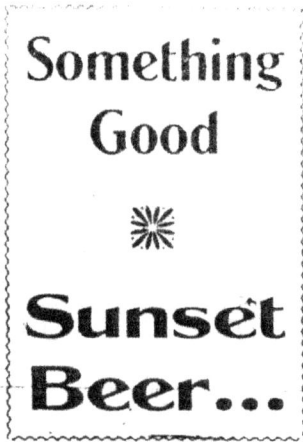

29. Sunset ad from January 1907.

there.' Just as I did he wheeled around toward me and I thought he was going to fire at me and I fired at him. As soon as I fired, it was the last cartridge I had. I heard him holler, and I turned and ran."

No one else saw a second man and no one came forth to admit being there. The coroner's jury deliberated briefly and reached the verdict that Paul Graf had died from a shot fired by William Murphy and "we find the killing to be justifiable homicide."

Was Murphy confused about what he saw? Was he deliberately lying? Perhaps the ultimate question was the one the dead man's father asked at the inquest: "Mr. Murphy, are you instructed by the Sunset Brewery to shoot any man that comes there at night?"

END NOTES

1 The major source for this chapter, and the source of all quotations is *The Idaho Press* Wallace, Idaho, October 15, 1904, p. 6, c. 1-5. An article in the *Idaho Capital News*, Boise, Idaho (13 October 1904, p. 3, c. 7) gives a brief synopsis. They use "James" as Murphy's given name. They also said Graff (sic) was one of the best known young men in the Coeur d'Alenes. See also *Idaho Daily Statesman*, Boise, Idaho, 11 October 1904, p. 3, c. 4. This chapter has been published as an article in several periodicals: "The Shooting at the Sunset Brewery," *High Country*, June 1981, p. 8. Reprinted in *Suds and Spuds*, April 2006, p. 3-4.

8

HENRY GROTEWALD

Murder Victim

GROTEWALD WAS A PARTNER with Frank Gindorff in the brewery in Bayhorse in Custer County, Idaho, in 1885. Several Idaho newspapers briefly mentioned his unexpected death that year: "Word comes to us as we go to press that a German by the name of Groutwell (sic), who owned a brewery and ran a lodging house in Bayhorse, was found dead beside the road about a mile this side of the town last Monday. It is supposed that he was murdered for his money?" *Houston* [Idaho] *Press*" "Henry Grotwald (sic) was found above the Bayhorse Brewery yesterday. Particulars unknown. Coroner Kileup has gone over and will hold an inquest today." *Messenger* Nov. 3"[1]

Gindorff had owned a tin shop in Bonanza, Idaho as early as 1879, and supplied the capital for outfitting a brewery. He employed a succession of brewers and partners in the brewery. He was apparently minimally involved in the actual brewing and spent his days at his hardware and metal shop. One newspaper report accused him of murdering his partner, Grotewold, whose body was found in Bayhorse Creek, Custer County, in November of 1885.[2] Gindorff was put under $1,500 bond to appear before the Grand Jury. He was apparently never formally charged nor convicted. The brewery's business listing continued to be Frank Gindorff, aka Gindorff and Grotewald, until 1887.[3]

On 7 May 1886, Emilie Grotewald gave a power of attorney in regard to land and leases to William J. Teloar. In May of 1886, Emile sold the Sunday Mining Claim in Bay Horse to William Teloar for

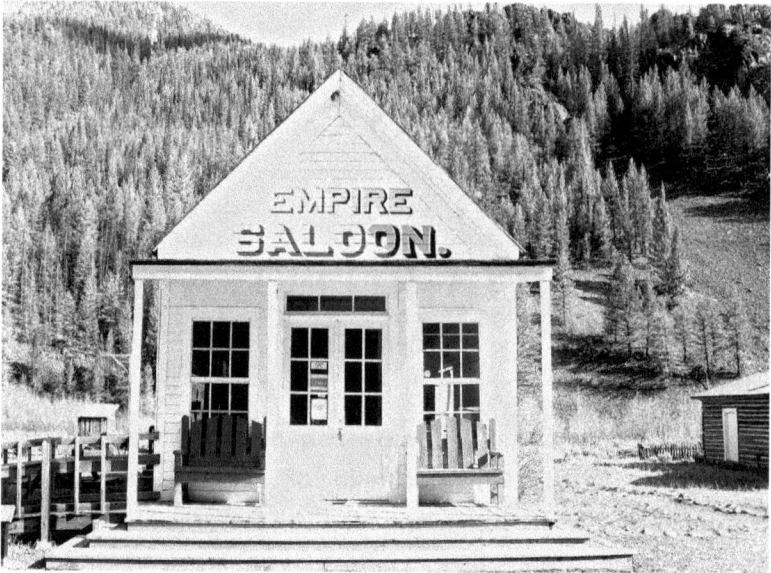

30. *Empire Saloon, Custer, Idaho.*

$150.[4] Was this Henry Grotewald's widow? I presume so.

On 28 May 1886, Amelia Grotewald married Seigle Hopper at nearby Challis, Idaho with the ceremony performed by James Burns.[5]

In July of 1905 a report said Frank Grotewald and Otto Koeninger came into Bayhorse from the Dewey and Minnie Moore mines and said they had struck it rich.[6] I suspect this was a relative of the previously murdered Grotewald.

Grotewald was one more unfortunate follower of King Gambrinus, and one whose trail is difficult to follow.

END NOTES

1   *Boise City Republican,* Boise, Idaho,14 November 1885, p. 1, c. 4 & 5.

2   *Idaho Tri-Weekly Statesman,*Boise, Idaho, 8 December 1885, p. 1, c. 2.

3   MyFamily.com Internet site. Citing the San Francisco California Directories, 1889-91.

4   Custer County Records, ISHS, reel 8, p. 405.

5   Custer County Records, ISHS, reel 1, "Marriage Certificates."

6   *Idaho Daily Statesman*, Boise, Idaho, 1 July 1905, p. 8, c. 2. Koeninger was perhaps a relative to Robert, Conrad, and Herman, all of them were sporadically in the brewing business.

9

JOSEPH HELMUTH
"Lager Beer Joe" Went Down With the Ship

NOT EVERY MAN IN A MINING CAMP earned a nickname, and not every nickname was remembered for any length of time. "Lager Beer Joe" Helmuth's moniker outlasted him. Joseph Helmuth was a pioneer brewer of Walla Walla, Washington, and one of the very early brewers in Idaho, but he was also one of the first brewers to leave the boom camp life of Boise Basin. In 1863, he built the first brewery in Placerville, Boise County, Idaho Territory, and earned a spot in the collective memory of Boise Basin as the legendary figure, "Lager Beer Joe."[1] He invested over $15,000 in his brewery and an adjacent saloon that year but then pulled out and returned to Walla Walla, where he had previously brewed, still owned businesses, and had a wife.

Helmuth began advertising the brews of his previous brewery business, The Walla Walla Brewery, in the local newspaper there in Washington Territory by 20 December 1861, close to the time the *Statesman* of that town began publication.[2] His ad proclaimed him a manufacturer of lager beer, and a wholesale and retail dealer in wines and liquors operating on Main Street in Walla Walla. Herman Francis Reinhart, who worked for rival Walla Walla brewer Emil Myers, remembered "Lager Beer Joe" as running the only other brewery in town, and living in "the second house south."[3] Reinhart also remembered local Walla Walla farmers growing barley to sell to either Emil Meyer or Lager Beer Joe.[4]

In December of 1864, Helmuth's ad reappeared in Walla Walla's newspaper. He was home from Idaho, back at the "old stand" on Main

Street, and brewing beer and ale "warrant(ed) to be equal in quality to any manufactured on the coast."[5] He was also again wholesaling wines and liquors and retailing to everybody who had 12 1/2 cents for a drink.

Helmuth was born in 1830 in the city of Damboeh, Alsace, which was then a part of France.[6] In 1850, he came to America, and in 1858, to Walla Walla. Helmuth had been one of the original Walla Walla, Washington, citizens calling for the establishment of county government there.[7] He was also one of the original petitioners asking that the name of Walla Walla be applied to this new town being laid out near Mill Creek in 1858.[8]

An unsigned letter from Walla Walla to the *Oregon Statesman* of Salem in April of 1859 described the town as adjoining the Nez Perce reservation, with four retail dry goods stores, "six whisky shops," and a 100 pounds of flour or a gallon-and-a-half of whisky could buy an Indian horse.[9]

THE WALLA WALLA FIRE DEPARTMENT

By 1860, Helmuth was pushing for a fire department in Walla Walla. As one of the first and certainly the most dedicated to this goal, he won a lasting place in the municipal history of that city. On the 1860 U. S. Census, Joseph Helmuth was a 31-year-old grocery keeper with $3,000 in real estate and $2,000 in personal estate, and was born in Prussia.[Alsace had changed hands.] The Helmuths lived next to Emil Meyer, the first brewery owner in Walla Walla, and anywhere east of the Cascades. Joseph's wife, "Oudile" Helmuth, was 23, born in France. Odile (often called Odelia), according to her tombstone, was born 15 April 1835 in Saverne, France, and her married named was spelled "Hellmuth."[10]

By February of 1862, Helmuth's efforts had helped create the Union Hook and Ladder Co. No. 1. It had been organized very loosely and was at that time trying to assess each member $6.20 to pay its debts. They had hooks, ladders, and buckets distributed throughout the town, and the local newspaper said, "It is in the interest of every citizen to lend this company substantial aid in relieving them from their present embarrassed condition."[11] The infamous theater performance in April of 1862 at which Cherokee Bob Talbot, the Confederate-loving desperado, shot and stabbed several Union soldiers, had been arranged to benefit the Union Hook and Ladder Company in the first place.[12] Helmuth was not taken aback by this mayhem and continued his efforts to raise money for fire protection.

Helmuth won some fame and respect by actually getting a fire department started after the first of Walla Walla's four big fires on 11 June 1862. He circulated a subscription paper for buying a fire engine and then published a notice of a meeting to organize a fire company.[13] Interest lagged, and the meeting was never held. After two unsuccessful attempts to hold meetings, Helmuth ordered a fire engine from San Francisco on his own volition.[14] He still hoped to receive subscriptions, but was not going to wait. He persevered and rounded up subscriptions totaling $1,600 and then advanced $500 of his own money to buy this Hunneman "tub" fire engine.[15]

31. Walla Walla Fire engine. Helmuth worked long and hard to get fire protection in Walla Walla.

Helmuth received a letter from H. Webster when his fire engine had been shipped on the steamer *Pacific* on December 17. Again Helmuth called for a citizens' meeting to organize a fire company.[16] As we shall see, the *Pacific*'s karma included a future encounter with Helmuth that did not involve fire engines.

The engine arrived in December of 1862 and a company was organized to take charge of it. The Washington Engine Co. No. 2, which must have been a competing group, held a ball on Christmas Eve to raise money.[17] Helmuth was elected the first foreman of the Walla Walla City Fire Department. Since there were three big fires soon to come in Walla Walla, it remains unclear how successful the endeavor was. There is extant an 1863 photo of the fire department with the Hunneman tub engine in front of the Belle-Creole saloon.[18] Tiger 19 Engine Company No. 2 still owned and operated the hand engine in 1875.[19]

In October 1862, A. Kyger sued Helmuth. The fees were $14.90 and the case was settled, but the record said little else.[20] Every small business owner was involved in suits over unpaid bills.

HELMUTH AT PLACERVILLE

Helmuth must have been traveling between Boise Basin and Walla Walla frequently these years of the mid-1860s, which is neither a short nor easy journey. That next spring of 1863, he was temporarily through with Walla Walla's fire troubles and was brewing in Placerville, Idaho Territory. On 12 August 1863, Helmuth paid George McCarty $50 for 25 feet of claim 22 and 25 feet of claim 29 in the Idaho & Ophir Quartz lead in South Boise County.[21] As with everyone else in a gold-rush area, buying mineral claims was also a potential new endeavor.

Walla Walla pioneer Herman Reinhart quit brewery work and began freighting into Boise Basin, where he saw Helmuth's prosperous saloon and brewery.[22] In late December of 1863, Walla Walla City Councilman Kyger presented for consideration at the city council meeting a deed for city lots they were buying from Joseph Helmuth.

The next meeting, 5 January 1864, the deal was closed. Helmuth got $1,000 for 30 feet of ground on the corner of Main and Second streets.

In May of 1864, Picard and Businger purchased the Walla Walla Brewery from Helmuth, apparently with a mortgage, and they continued it as a brewery and saloon.[23] They must not have been able to make their payments to Helmuth, because by December he was again the operator of the brewery.[24] He then apparently returned to Idaho.

At the Democratic Convention for Boise County, Idaho Territory, on July 5th 1865, Joseph Helmuth was a representative from Placerville.[25] In May and June 1865, Helmuth paid federal tax as brewer and retail liquor dealer, and for a billiard room in Idaho; in July 1865 he was again listed; in August 1865, he brewed 16 barrels of beer in Placerville and paid $16 in tax; in May 1866, Helmuth paid for his wholesale liquor license.[26] Some of this must have been done while physically back in Walla Walla. When he prepared to permanently leave Boise Basin, he advertised for sale his brewery, saloon, dwelling house, pool tables, and fixtures at "A bargain," and as "a good speculation."[27] The *Idaho World* said that Helmuth wished to return to Europe in the fall and was doing a fine business.[28] Charles

32. Magnolia Saloon in Placerville not quite as old as Lager Beer Joe Helmuth's time in town.

Kohny bought the brewery and continued the business for many years.[29] Ten years later—a long time in gold camp reckoning—Kohny still described his establishment as "Lager Beer Joe's old stand."

The invitation committee from Placerville for the Grand Fenian Ball to be given by the Emmett Guards to be held in Idaho City on the Fourth of July, 1866, included Helmuth.[30] Also in June 1866, Joseph Helmuth was listed as a delegate from Boise County to the Territorial Democratic Convention at Boise City.[31] Helmuth's Idaho sojourn was over, however.[32]

A suit of O. S. Whiting et al vs. Jacob Haubrick et al [which included Helmuth] over Idaho mining property was filed in 1868.[33] By this time Helmuth was so poorly remembered in mining circles that he was first listed anonymously as John Brown and unpleaded, and then relisted as "John" Helmuth. The plaintiff was successful in having the defendants enjoined from using their mining ditch. The case came again to the courts and Helmuth and Haubrick were ordered to pay $800 in damages to the ditch.[34] The Haubrich brothers were also brewery owners in Boise Basin, which may explain how they became acquainted with Helmuth.

BACK TO WALLA WALLA

There are scant references to Helmuth the next few years. In 1867, the fire department was at last reorganized on an efficient basis. Washington Engine Co. No. 1 of the Walla Walla Fire Department issued cards to their members. An 1868 example that is extant has Helmuth's signature as foreman.[35]

In late October of 1870, a report from Walla Walla said there was a depression in the grain market. The price was down to 50 cents per bushel and the millers were full and were not buying any more. "The principal purchaser now in the market is Mr. Joseph Helmuth, who is paying 50 cents cash."[36]

An advertisement in the *Walla Walla Union* for R. H. Parker's skating rink said it was in Helmuth's Hall, which gives some idea of the property owned by Mr. and Mrs. Helmuth.[37]

Walla Walla held a billiard tournament in the winter of 1874 for the championship of Eastern Washington.[38] A silver mounted cup and a cash purse were the prizes. The contestants played seven games of 300 points each or a total of 57 games for the eight contestants. Joseph Helmuth was one of the eight competitors. His interest in bringing billiard tables into Idaho City at an early date probably related to his own interest in the game.

When Walla Walla was raising subscriptions for bringing a railroad to town in early 1875, Helmuth, or perhaps his wife, pledged $100.[39] In August of that year, Helmuth arrived back in Walla Walla on a stagecoach from the Landing (probably Umatilla, Oregon, on the Columbia River).[40] He had driven a band of horses to Winnemucca, Nevada, the previous autumn. The horses did not sell in the spring, and Helmuth had waited till summer when he sold at a good price. The newspaper said they were "glad to see Joe back again, and trust he will long remain one of us." Long he did remain one of them, but not long among them.

ABOARD THE *PACIFIC*

Helmuth and his wife, Odile, decided to take a trip back to Germany that fall after the relatively long separation due to Joseph's horse-selling venture. They made no general announcement, and few people in Walla Walla knew of their departure. She took $10,000, mostly in coin, in a satchel to pay for the trip.[41] On the first leg of the journey, she deposited $2,500 in the bank of British Columbia in Portland, Oregon, and took the remaining with her on the initial sea portion of the trip. The only jewelry she owned she was wearing on the ship, according to the executor of her estate, Thomas Quinn. From Portland, they traveled north to Vancouver, Canada. The couple then boarded the steamer *Pacific*, bound for San Francisco, for the first sea leg of the journey.

The *Pacific*, which had once hauled the fire engine for Walla Walla, had fresh paint, new bolts, and polished brass fixtures, but it should never have been allowed to sail. The ship began its life in New York in 1850, a part of the gold rush fleet, and soon was sold to the United States Mail Steamship Company. Her 10-foot-stroke walking-beam engine made her one of the fastest steam vessels in the Americas, according to author Robert Belyk.[42] By 1851 she was regularly on the San Francisco to San Juan, Nicaragua, route.

The Pacific Mail Steamship Company bought the aging vessel in 1872, for service between San Diego and Mexico. Soon the ship was put in mothballs, facing a likely future as scrap. The gold rush in the Cassier District of northern British Columbia made ships capable of hauling passengers valuable again, and the ship was re-outfitted and returned to service.

On October 26, 1875, the *Pacific* left San Francisco. She entered Victoria harbor on October 30, where she discharged passengers and cargo, then steamed on to Tacoma, where she loaded 2,000 sacks of oats, 128 bales of hops, 18 casks of tallow, and assorted hides and buckskins. She took on 35 passengers at various Puget Sound ports and returned to Victoria on November 4.

The *Pacific* sailed from Victoria, British Columbia, on 4 November 1875 at 9 o'clock in the morning.[43] She was a wooden side-wheel steamer of about 900 tons, carrying $25,000 worth of oats and —ironically from our perspective—hops, as well as $75,220 in gold, and Mr. and Mrs. Helmuth. The *Pacific* collided with the American square-rigger *Orpheus* off of Cape Flattery, Washington—the northwestern most point in the lower 48 states—that first night out. There were about 238 people on the *Pacific,* but only five lifeboats with a total maximum capacity of 160. The crew was insufficient and too undisciplined to actually lower these boats in the emergency, according to the inquest jury report. Later, the report said the vessel had been rebuilt and repaired several times and was not considered safe for travel, but was somehow still permitted to run.

The fearful incident began about 40 miles south of Cape Flattery, when the *Pacific* approached the *Orpheus.* The *Orpheus* saw the light from the ship off her port bow and should have maneuvered to keep it in that position. Instead the *Orpheus* put the helm hard to starboard and crossed the *Pacific's* path. The captain of the *Pacific* was Jefferson D. Howell, brother-in-law of Jefferson Davis, President of the Confederacy a decade earlier. The *Pacific* had a man at the wheel, one supposed to be at the lookout, and a third mate, a "young man of doubtful experience" on duty. The inquiry jury found this inadequate to keep a proper lookout. When *Orpheus* inexplicably got in front, the *Pacific* struck the ship on the starboard side with her stern. It was a very light blow and should not have caused great damage if the *Pacific* had been a sound ship—but she was not sound! The *Orpheus* captain, Charles A. Sawyer, hailed the side-wheeler but was not answered, and thinking of his own ship's condition, sailed away after the collision and did not remain to ascertain the amount of damage done to the *Pacific*.

Henry F. Jelley was the survivor who gave the most detailed account of the collision and the events afterward.[44] Jelley was a native of Ireland and for nine years a resident of Canada. A railroad surveyor, at age 22, he was vigorous enough to survive a situation that would—and did—kill nearly anyone. He believed the steamer was leaking all the first day at sea as it sailed against a strong southwest wind. The crew was busy pumping water, trying to keep an even keel. They put water in the boats on the high side of the ship and then let it out and pumped water into the other side when the list of the ship changed. Jelley said that when the boat listed, it had trouble coming up again, probably due to having considerable water in the hull. That first evening, as he was preparing to retire, Jelley felt a heavy shock and heard a grating sound as though the ship had struck a rock. He immediately ran to the deck, where captain Howell shouted: "Don't be alarmed, we have merely struck the side of a ship." The passengers seemed reassured and most went below. Jelley circulated among the passengers a while and then went back to his stateroom. There was no confusion or excitement. While undressing, Jelley felt a heavy lurch toward port, and the ship remained in that position.

Jelley again went on deck, where he heard the captain tell a crewman to lower the boat with the ladies in it. Jelley asked the captain if there was a signal gun or lights on board and was told he could find them in the wheelhouse. The crew had abandoned the wheelhouse though the ship was still under a full head of steam. One passenger was there already and he asked Jelley if he knew the direction of the shore, since the man vowed to steer the ship himself if no one else would. Jelley then went to the lifeboat forward of the paddle box. The majority of ladies were put in it, and the first engineer seemed to be in charge of it. Some of the women said there was water in the boat. Finally the ship was so low that this boat floated free and the pilothouse also floated free of the ship and toward them. Jelley and four others clung to the boat as the ship went down. Jelley and another man then got on top of the passing pilothouse.

Jelley said the water was calm when the ship went down, he saw hundreds of people in the water, and was almost sure one of the lifeboats full of passengers went down with the ship. If women were in this boat, Mrs. Helmuth may well have been among them. Jelley cut a rope off a lifeboat that went by and used it to lash himself and his companion to their makeshift pilothouse raft. Through the night, the unnamed companion drank from a flask of whiskey and seemed in a good mood. Jelley declined to drink. The other man finally fell into a deep sleep in the early morning hours. When a wave broke over his face without awakening him, Jelley checked and found him unexpectedly dead. After a whole day without rescue, Jelley cut the rope and rolled the body—now nameless forever—into the sea. All he knew was that the man was a miner from Cassiar and seemed to have a large quantity of gold dust on him. During the day, Jelley saw other rafts with survivors, but none of them could make themselves seen or heard by the ships that passed at a distance.

The next day, Saturday, Jelley was spotted by Captain Gilkey of the *Messenger* who had observed wreckage and was scanning the sea with his spyglass. Jelley was more dead than alive, but he did recover to tell this tale. Another version of the events was told by Nell O. Henley, quartermaster of the ill fated *Pacific*, and the only other survivor. He had been on a boat with the captain and several people, but they had all washed overboard or died on the boat. He was rescued by the *Oliver Wolcott* and taken to Neah Bay, where the Indian agent cared for him.[45]

Charges against the Orpheus' captain soon developed. As one newspaper reported:

"The Lost Pacific/Inhumanity of the Captain of the Ship Orpheus that ran into the Pacific. It is now coming to light that the Captain of the ship *Orpheus* disregarded all maritime rules, and if he did not actually try to run into the steamer *Pacific,* he was reckless in the management of his ship, he did not care for the consequences; and it was next to impossible for the steamer to have dodged him at the rate of speed the two vessels were under. Besides this, after the collision had taken place, the steamer followed his vessel and hailed him three times for help, and when he was informed by his wheel-man that the steamer wanted help his reply was G—d——the steamer, and directed the wheel-man to keep his ship on her course. The evidence on this point is positive from all the men on his own ship, who were on watch at the time. The steward of the ship *Orpheus* said they could see the lights of the steamer twenty minutes after they struck her. The steward's wife said she could hear the people from the steamer calling for help. Charles Thompson, who was at the wheel on the *Orpheus*, made affidavit that he saw the lights of the steamer fifteen minutes before the collision, and had he kept the course he was on the *Orpheus* would have passed two miles to the leeward of the steamer. The mate first told him to head for the lights of the steamer. The Captain afterwards told him to keep the ship on her course, but afterwards changed his order and told him he wanted to speak to the steamer; but when Captain Sawyer gave the order to port the helm hard down it was obeyed, but it was too late to avoid a collision. After ascertaining that the ship had not sprung a leak the Captain ordered her on her course.

The steamer followed the ship and hailed her three separate times but no answer was returned and the ship kept on her course, and the steamer was not able to keep up with her and fell behind, and the steamer was lost sight of in about 15 minutes after the collision. The ship was going eight knots an hour, and the night was clear, but afterwards it blew very hard and rained.

Aug. Hartwig, Cash. J. Brown, and Alfred Buhue swear that they were on the same watch, and corroborate the statement of Chas. Thompson, the wheel-man.

If these statements are true, which we have not much reason to doubt, the Captain's statement itself condemns him to a great extent, he ought to suffer the highest penalty of the law. Why he has not been arrested and held to answer for the collision is a little strange. We are told, however, that there is great feeling of indignation against Captain Sawyer. Indignation is poor satisfaction for so many lost friends, even his life would be no recompense, but his punishment might be a warning to other navigators."[46]

Rescue ships went out, and a few bodies and a few trunks were recovered. No one remembered the Helmuths or mentioned their names in any context. Passenger lists that were published throughout the region gave the first knowledge to the Walla Walla public that the retired brewer and his wife had been on the *Pacific*.

The *Orpheus* became disabled by the collision but cruised on until 5 o'clock that morning when she mistook the light at Cape Beale for the Tatoosh light and ran ashore.[47] The captain and crew were later found sitting on the beach. The ship was a total loss.

The final report of the *Pacific* disaster was that only two on board had survived.[48] The steamship *Gussia Telfair* returned to Victoria, British Columbia, in the evening of 11 November having found only five bodies in its search in the area for survivors.[49] The sinking of the *Pacific* remains the worst sea disaster on the Pacific Coast of the continental United States.[50] Charles A. Sawyer, master of the *Orpheus*, never escaped the memory of his brief encounter with the *Pacific*. Shortly before his death in 1895, he was playing cards with several friends when he said, "There it is again! Didn't you hear it?" What, his friends asked, was he talking about. "The whistle of the *Pacific*," he told them.

Many press reports listed Mr. and Mrs. Helmuth, Walla Walla businessman and wife, among those lost. Helmuth's fellow Walla Walla firefighters offered this evaluation of their fallen comrade: "His love of the institutions of his adopted country; his public spirit and enterprising disposition was known to all. He was unusually affable and courteous, a genial companion and a true friend, … [the firemen] will miss in their future deliberations his frank avowals, his disinterested advice and his safe counsels."[51] "…Joseph Helmuth, was called hence, to answer our roll-call no more…"

The story was not over yet! Later that month, Mrs. Helmuth's body was recovered from the sea and was reported forwarded to friends in Portland.[52] Our brewer, her husband, was never found. Mrs. Helmuth's body was found floating near Cape Flattery, about 12 miles west of Race Rocks, a few days later and the *Walla Walla Union* announced it was being brought back for burial.[53] An inquest was held at Victoria on the four bodies recovered from the wreck.

The *Walla Walla Statesman* in her obituary labeled her "a woman of more than ordinary shrewdness and her judgment contributed largely toward acquiring the fortune of which she and her husband died possessed."[54] She had arrived in Walla Walla in the late 1850s

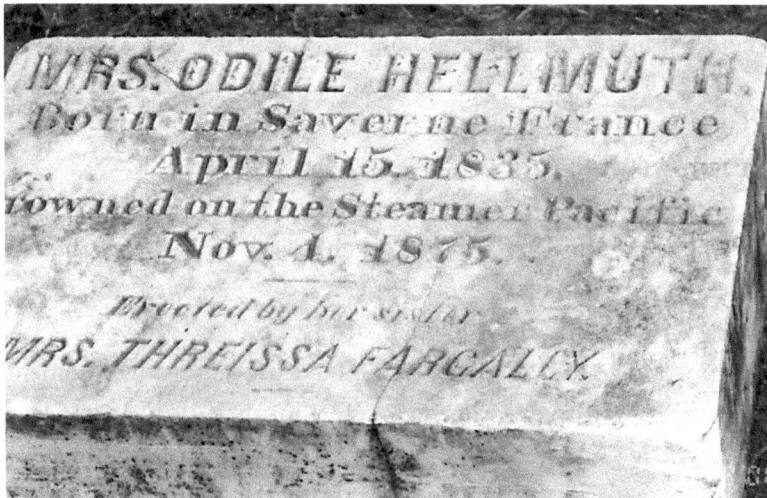

33. *Odile Hellmuth tombstone in Walla Walla.*

with her husband, Joseph, and begun acquiring property. She had rental income of about $2,000 from Main Street alone, and had several thousands invested in bonds and mortgages. She gave to any cause that offered to improve the general welfare. Her liberal subscription to the railroad subsidy was a case in point. She also cheerfully gave to the less fortunate. Her home was an exhibition of grace and refinement. She was less than 40 years old and had everything to live for. "Peace to her ashes."

Odile's remains were shipped to Portland from Port Townsend and then, in obedience to telegraphed instructions from Mrs. Farg-Aly (sic) her sister, prepared for shipment to Walla Walla.[55] The body was first put in a metal casket filled with alcohol. The body arrived in a good state of preservation in Portland and the alcohol was changed preparatory to the final leg of the shipment. At this point, several discoveries were made. The bone of the right leg near its attachment to the body was badly crushed. There was a long, deep cut on the inside of the thigh, which appeared to have been inflicted by a blunt object with ragged edges. She was wearing, at the time of the disaster, a thick flannel underskirt, which was cut and torn as if struck violently by a piece of wood or iron. Some believed that the boiler exploded the moment the steamer sank and a fragment of iron from it struck her. There was also a small abrasion on her nose as if it had been struck by some light object. If the explosion was the case, the newspaper opined incongruously, she was probably killed outright and "spared the horrors of death at the hands of the merciful waves."

Thomas Quinn was made administrator of the Helmuth estate. He was related to the family through marriage.[56] The estate was valued at over $20,000. Most of this was the personal property of Odelia—Joseph was hardly mentioned by the probate court—and was presumed to go to her heirs.[57] Quinn made the usual advertisement for those having claims against the estate to come forth.

An article published in the *Echo*, an Olympia, Washington, newspaper, charged that the Captain of the steamer *Goliath*, who recovered her body, robbed the corpse of Mrs. Helmuth of money and jewelry.[58]

Administrator Quinn published a public letter dated December 20th "in order that no wrong be done to innocent parties." He believed her $7,500 worth of gold coins was still in its original satchel at the bottom of the sea. He had received all the jewelry she wore that fateful night and that was all the jewelry she owned, so she could not have been robbed of it. Quinn said he did not want slander to "be the reward of those kind-hearted men who assisted in saving the living and returned the dead to their relatives."

Mrs. Helmuth was buried in Mountain View Cemetery in Walla Walla in the Catholic section. Her tombstone inscription reads that it was erected by her sister Mrs. Fargally (Fargaly).[59]

Did you know, old Gambrinus, Lager Beer Joe has up and gone away?

END NOTES

1　*Idaho Tri-Weekly Statesman*, 16 November, 1875, p. 3, c. 2. Some sources spell the name with two "l"s.

2　*Walla Walla Statesman*, Walla Walla, Washington, 20 December 1861, p. 3, c. 1.

3　Herman Francis Reinhart, *The Recollections of Herman Francis Reinhart, 1851-1869*. Austin: University of Texas Press, 1962, p. 204.

4　Herman Francis Reinhart, *The Recollections of Herman Francis Reinhart, 1851-1869*. Austin: University of Texas Press, 1962, p. 216.

5　*Walla Walla Statesman* 13 January 1865, p. 4, c. 3.

6　*Walla Walla Union*, Washington Territory, 3 November 1875, p. 3, c. 3. This is his obituary.

7　Frank T. Gilbert, *Historical Sketches of Walla Walla, Whitman, Columbia and Garfield Counties, Washington Territory*. Portland: A. G. Waling, 1882, p. 228.

8　Gilbert, *Historical Sketches of Walla Walla*, p. 298-299.

9　April 12, 1859. as reprinted in Baird, Mallickan and Swagerty, *Nez Perce Nation Divided*, p.17.

10　Her grave is in Mountain View Cemetery in Walla Walla, Washington. It is in the Catholic section Block 1, row 4, grave 30.

11　*The Washington Statesman*, Walla Walla, Washington, 1 February 1862, p. 2, c. 1.

12　*The Washington Statesman*, 12 April 1862, p. 2, c. 3. Talbot got away on a stolen horse as the soldiers searched the town in defiance of their commanding officer, and civilian and military authorities blamed each other for the problem.

13　Gilbert, *Historical Sketches of Walla Walla*, p. 302

14 *The Washington Statesman*, 25 October 1862, p. 2, c. 2. An announcement of a meeting the previous week drew no support. *The Washington Statesman*, 18 October 1862, p. 3, c. 3

15 Lyman, W. D. Lyman's History of Old Walla Walla County Embracing Walla Walla, Columbia, Garfield and Asotin Counties. Chicago: S. J. Clarke Publishing Co., 1918. Vol. I, p. 149

16 *The Washington Statesman*, 29 November 1862, p. 2, c. 1. The previous October (1861) the long time commander of the *Pacific*, G. W. Staples was killed by Ferd Patterson when he tried to mediate a quarrel between Patterson and a Mr. Dodge. *Yreka Weekly Journal*, 24 October 1861, p. 1, c.2. Later Patterson was in the Idaho City area when he shot and killed former lawman Sumner Pinkham and set off a period of vigilante conflict in the Boise Basin.

17 *The Washington Statesman*, 20 December 1862, p. 3, c. 1.

18 Robert Bennett, *Walla Walla, Portrait of a Western Town*, 1804-1899, p. 68.

19 *The Washington Statesman*, 9 January 1864, p. 3, c. 3. Alturas County Records, ISHS, reel 1, p. 85.

20 Superior Court Records, 1859-1909, Walla Walla County, Washington, cage 407, Book of District court Costs, p. 22. Washington State University. Holland Library, Special Collections.

21 Alturas County Records, ISHS, reel 1, deed book, p. 85

22 Herman Francis Reinhart, *The Golden Frontier: The Recollections of Herman Francis Reinhart, 1851-1869*. Austin: University of Texas Press, 1962, p. 221.

23 *The Washington Statesman*, 24 June 1864, p. 3, c. 4..

24 *The Walla Walla Statesman*, 23 December 1864, p. 4, c. 3. In giving the lineage of the United Union Brewery of Walla Walla, which was purchased by W. D. Bryan in 1943, Robert A. Bennett (*Walla Walla: A Nice Place to Raise a Family, 1920-1949*, p. 165.) says the plant was begun by Helmuth in the 1850s and sold to Emil Meier in 1862. I believe this is erroneous.

25 *Idaho World*, Idaho City, Idaho, 8 July 1865, p. 2, c. 2

26 Federal Tax Records, 1865-66, Microfilm # 558.

27 *The Idaho World*, 5 August 1865, p. 3, c. 2..

28 *The Idaho World*, 29 July 1865, p. 3, c. 1.

29 See the biography of Kohny.

30 *The Idaho World*, 16 June 1866, p. 2, c. 5.

31 *The Idaho World*, 23 June 1866, p.3, c. 2.

32 The Pacific Coast Directory of 1867 listed Joseph Helmuth as brewery, liquor and billiards merchant in Placerville, Boise County, Idaho territory. I am unable to properly explain this.

33 Boise County Judicial Records, Idaho State Historical Society, Microfilm reel # 35.

34 Judicial Records of Boise County, Idaho State Historical Society, Microfilm reel #35.

35 Robert Bennett, *Walla Walla, Portrait of a Western Town, 1804-1899*, p. 68.

36 *The Boise Weekly News*, 29 October 1870, p. 3, c. 2.

37   *Walla Walla Union*, Walla Walla, Washington, 8 June 1872, p. 3, c. 6.

38   *Idaho Signal*, Lewiston, Idaho, 7 February 1874, p. c. 5.

39   *Walla Walla Statesman*, 13 February 1875, p. 3, c. 2.

40   *Walla Walla Statesman*, 14 August 1875, p. 3, c. 1.

41   *Walla Walla Statesman*, 25 December 1875, p. 3, c. 4.

42   Robert C. Belyk, *Great Shipwrecks of the Pacific Coast*, p. 37.

43   *The Olympic Transcript*, Olympia, Washington, 4 December 1875, p. 2, c. 4.
     This was a report from the inquest held over the body of passenger Thomas J.
     Farrell. A well researched account of the *Pacific* tragedy is in Robert C. Belyk,
     Great Shipwrecks of the Pacific Coast (New York: John Wiley & Sons, 2001).

44   *Walla Walla Statesman*, 20 November 1875, p. 1, c. 3-6. *Walla Walla Union*,
     13 November 1875, p. 2, c. 2. *The Olympic Transcript*, 20 November 1875, p. 2,
     c. 3.

45   *The Olympic Transcript*, 13 November 1875, p. 2, c. 2.

46   *Tri-Weekly Statesman*, 27 November 1875, p. 2, c. 1.

47   *The Olympic Transcript*, 13 November 1875, p. 3, c. 3.

48   Snowden, Clinton A. *History of Washington: The Record of Progress of An
     American State*. New York: The Century History Co., 1909, vol. IV, p. 270.

49   *Idaho Tri-Weekly Statesman*, Boise, 16 November 1875, p. 2, c. 3.

50   Robert C. Belyk, Great Shipwrecks of the Pacific Coast, p. 37.

51   *Walla Walla Union*, 13 November 1875, p. 3, c. 3.

52   *Idaho Tri-Weekly Statesman*, Boise, 23 November 1875, p. 3, c. 1.

53   *Walla Walla Union*, 20 November 1875, p. 3, c. 1. One body found was
     George Vining of Puyallup who had on his person bills of lading for hops
     shipped from Tacoma. His watch had stopped at 9:30.

54   *Walla Walla Statesman*, 20 November 1875, p.3, c. 2.

55   *Walla Walla Statesman*, 27 November 1875, p. 3, c. 3. The whole article was
     attributed to the *Oregonian* of Portland.

56   *Walla Walla Statesman*, 4 December 1875, p. 3, c. 2.

57   *Walla Walla Statesman*, 11 December 1875, p. 3, c. 3.

58   *Walla Walla Statesman*, 25 December 1875, p. 3, c. 4.

59   A Therese Fargaly, born in 1820 in France, is listed on the Individual Record
     of the LDS genealogical web site. FamilySearch. On the 1880 U. S. Census she
     was 60, living with her daughter's family in Walla Walla, and born in France.
     Her daughter's father was Belgian.

10

JOHN HENDEL

Convicted of Manslaughter

JOHN HENDEL WAS A BREWER and saloonkeeper with an erratic personality bordering on insanity. Leander Hollstrom was a Finnish miner who had wrestled for prizes and brawled in the streets of Hailey, Idaho, on more than one occasion. In the wee hours before dawn one night, they quarreled and fought at Hendel's saloon. Hendel and his hired man, Louis Roder, each fired one revolver shot toward the unarmed Hollstrom. One bullet lodged harmlessly in the ceiling and one ripped fatally through the Finnish miner's heart.[1]

The frontier judicial system of Hailey had many questions to answer before justice could be served. Who fired which bullet? Was there a third shot fired? And above all, what really led to the murder of an unarmed man? Before most of the truth was established and justice dispensed, the mining town of Hailey had to endure inquests, trials, perjurers, sleight-of-hand lawyers, insane defendants, and even an exhumed corpse.

This trial tells us a bit about the place of the brewery in frontier society, and a bit about the justice system in a prescientific age, but mostly it reconfirms the old adage that truth, like beauty, lies in the eye of the beholder. Though lacking the strong sexual overtones of the original, the story became an occidental version of Roshomon. Everyone involved saw reality through his or her own unique lens.

THE SETTING AND HENDEL'S BACKGROUND

Today, Hailey is a town near the famous modern ski resort of Sun Valley, Idaho. It was named for the "Stagecoach King," John Hailey. In March of 1893, though, when the Hollstrom shooting took place, it was a hard-rock mining center. There was a substantial community of Finnish men who worked in the mines and, as most new immigrants do, tended to keep to themselves.

As a single Bavarian immigrant, Hendel was already a brewer in 1880 when he worked for and boarded with Henry Gilbert, proprietor of the Gilbert Brewery in Virginia City, Montana.[2] That old brewery survived into the 21st Century with most of its old equipment intact and remained a popular landmark as that city declined in population and switched to a tourist economy.

Hendel first appeared on the Idaho scene six years later when he was working as a cooper in Boise in John Brodbeck's brewery. At one point, Hendel built a tub on the second floor that held 73 barrels of water.[3] He made it out of two inch planks. It featured automatic shutoff when full, and furnished water to the brewery all day after being filled at night. Shortly after his sojourn in Boise, a newspaper reported in June 1886, that Hendel and Herman Jacobs were looking for a place to start a brewery and had settled on Shoshone, Idaho.[4] This venture was obviously short-lived if it got into operation at all. Six months later, Hendel was in Hailey alone to start a brewery.

In November of 1886, former business partner Herman Jacobs sued Hendel for $3,000.[5] Back in court the next June, the case had been settled and was dismissed at the plaintiff's cost.[6] Apparently some disagreement stemmed from the Shoshone brewing venture.

John Hendel soon built his brewery—the second one in operation in the small town of Hailey (about 2,000 population) at the time.[7] Colonel James Ballentine may have had a financial interest in the venture, because later he owned the brewery building. In April of 1889, Hendel offered his beer for families at $3.50 per keg.[8] In June of 1889, Hendel built a sidewalk in front of his brewery.[9] The Bradstreet's Commercial Report of September 1889 listed John

Hendel as a brewer in Hailey and Hendel and Sonnleitner as saloon owners.[10] The brewery had a bar room or saloon attached to the brewing area, and Hendel and his wife lived on the premises in a back bedroom. There were no closing hours prescribed by law on the frontier, and a group of miners out on the town and coming into the brewery late that fateful night was too common for anyone to suspect it was the start of a long drama.

HAILEY LEARNS OF THE SHOOTING

Just before 4 a.m. on March 17, 1893, a commotion spread through the night owls of Hailey—a murder had just been committed in John Hendel's brewery.[11] Sheriff A. J. Jackson was awakened and he bolted from bed and ran to the scene. The corpse was still warm when he arrived. Hendel and his hired man, Roder, were still on the scene, and each admitted firing a shot from his revolver. Jackson arrested them both and took them to the county jail. Hendel seemed unable to comprehend that he was in real trouble. He said he would only be held two or three hours and wanted to stay in the

34. Gilbert Brewery, Virginia City, Montana

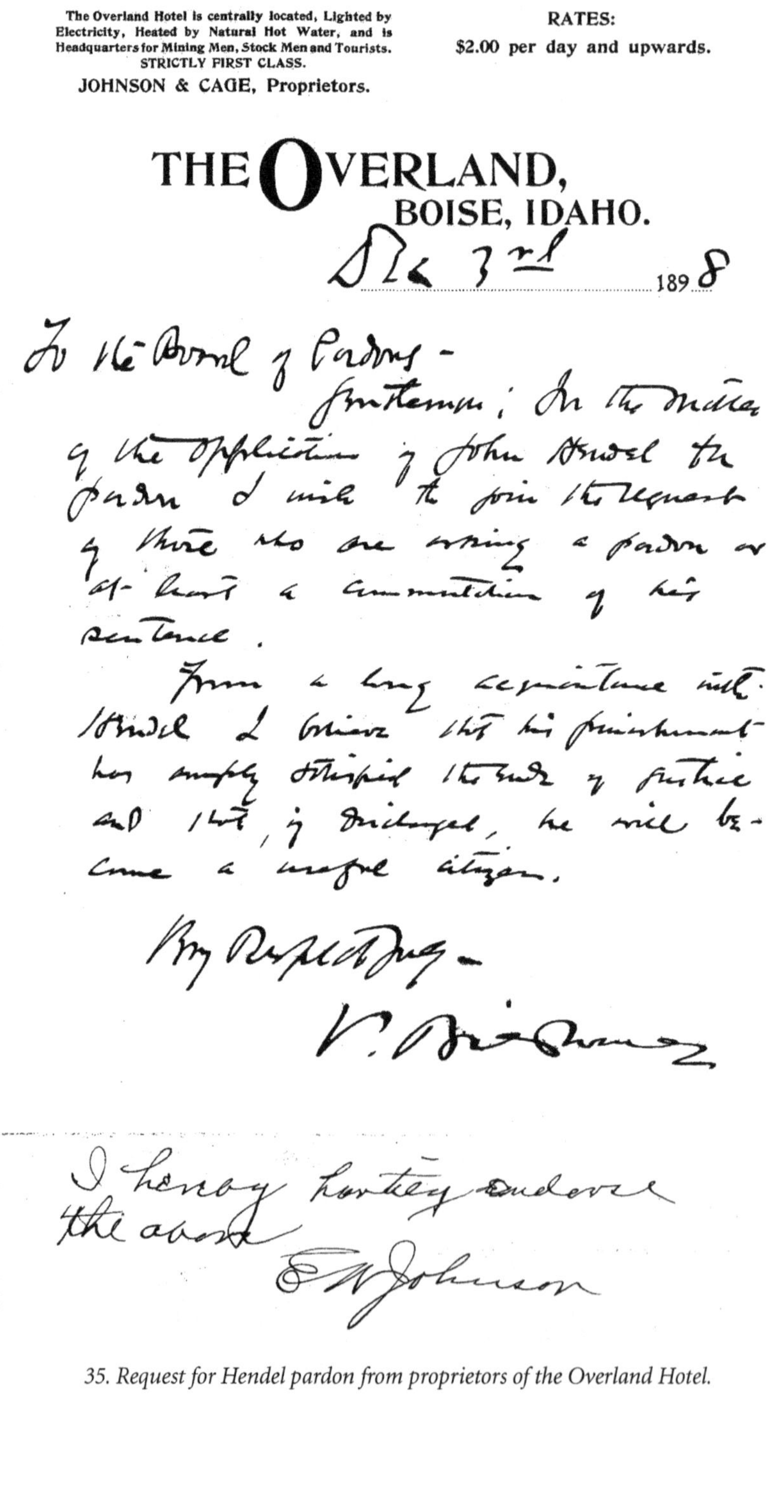

The Overland Hotel is centrally located, Lighted by
Electricity, Heated by Natural Hot Water, and is
Headquarters for Mining Men, Stock Men and Tourists.
STRICTLY FIRST CLASS.
JOHNSON & CAGE, Proprietors.

RATES:
$2.00 per day and upwards.

THE OVERLAND,
BOISE, IDAHO.

Dec 3rd 189 8

To the Board of Pardons —

Gentlemen; In the matter of the application of John Hendel for pardon I wish to join the request of those who are asking a pardon or at least a commutation of his sentence.

From a long acquaintance with Hendel I believe that his punishment has amply satisfied the ends of justice and that, if discharged, he will become a useful citizen.

Very Respectfully —

V. Bricomes

I hereby heartily endorse the above

E N Johnson

35. *Request for Hendel pardon from proprietors of the Overland Hotel.*

sheriff's office rather than a cell. Jackson locked him up anyway and then went about his official duties.

With the usual coroner out of town, Erv Johnson assumed the duties and quickly impaneled a jury for an afternoon inquest. A local physician, Dr. Figgins, was called to the scene to examine the body. He pronounced Hollstrom dead from a bullet wound to the heart and made note of all

36. John Hendel, penitentiary photo.

particulars so that he could testify to the coroner's jury that afternoon. The body was taken to Baldwin's undertaking rooms where it was laid out pending instructions from next of kin. A telegram was sent to Hollstrom's brother, a miner at the Crystal mine near Park City, Utah.

The only local newspaper, *The Wood River Times*, reported that the feeling in town was one of "intense excitement mingled with disgust." Most people felt the murder was without cause, as the Finn had been unarmed, and many voiced the long-held suspicion that Hendel had been periodically insane for years.

A reporter went to talk to Hollstrom's friends at the cabin they shared with Hollstrom opposite the brewery. The seven Finns there demanded to know why Hendel had never been sent to the state insane asylum at Blackfoot. In a classic case of blaming the victim, the *Times* reporter answered them with a lecture:

"Probably because he had not yet done anything that justified his being sent there—that gave the law a hold on him. If you or any other citizen knew him to be crazy, it was your duty to make a complaint that would have caused him to be examined and, if adjudged insane, he would have been sent there. If this had been done your friend might be alive today, the community been spared the humiliation of having such a crime committed and the taxpayers been spared perhaps thousands of dollars."

THE CORONER'S INQUEST

The impaneled coroner's jury was called into session at the brewery murder site early that afternoon and began by calling the Finns that were present the previous night and had witnessed the shooting. Their alcohol-clouded memories set the stage for the muddled legal battle to follow. John Kullas was sworn and testified that he was in the room during the shooting but was too drunk to know what was going on and did not see the shooting.

Next, another Finn, Peter Hanson, was sworn. He remembered going to the brewery about midnight with Hollstrom, Kullas, and John Carlson. Hanson remembered seeing Hendel and Roder, "the little Dutchman," with a revolver in his hand. Roder had said, "Get out of here, you sons of bitches," and pointed his revolver at them. Hanson had not seen who fired the first shot, but he remembered—erroneously, it turned out—hearing three shots being fired in quick succession, yet he could not say he had actually seen the shooting.

John Carlson was the last of the foursome of the previous night. He testified that they went to the brewery at 11 o'clock the previous night and between 3 and 4 o'clock, John Hendel told them to leave. Hendel had threatened: "If you don't go out, I will make you." After this, Hendel went to the back bedroom and returned with a revolver in his hand. Carlson said he took Hendel by the hand and told him not to shoot them. Hendel was adamant and again said: "If you don't go as fast as I want you, I will make you go." At the same time, Louis Roder went into the bedroom from the kitchen and then stood near the door with a pistol in his hand and fired. Carlson remembered Louis firing twice. Carlson did not know if the first or second shot struck Hollstrom, but he had seen John Hendel at the same time and did not see him fire a shot.

Dr. Figgins then took the stand. He testified:

"I find a gunshot wound between the 7th and 8th ribs, the ball entering the right side and passing at an angle through the middle lobe of the right lung and through the apex of the heart, penetrating both ventricles and passing out. The course of the ball being slightly upward. The wound would cause instant death."

Mrs. Hendel was next called to the stand. Whatever her motives may have been, her testimony proved to be a combination of fact and perjury. She said under oath:

There were a number of men in here, to begin with I saw nothing wrong. Everyone had a good time. The boys were spending money and willing to spend more. But about half past three this morning one of the gentlemen asked for another half gallon of beer. As they had a good deal my husband said: "You've had enough boys, and I want to close up as it is nearly 4 o'clock. You can't have the best of me so lets all take a drink." I brought the drinks. The boys wanted to sing and keep treating. My husband said no; he wanted to go to bed. There was a little man named Johnny. This little Johnny had a friend with him asleep on the table, and they bet $5.00 he could not be waked up. They tried to wake him up by rolling him over, pulling him about and tickling him in the ribs. This made him mad, and he called Johnny names. There was another half-gallon of beer ordered by them. I brought it, Johnny and his friend that had been asleep began quarreling, when John Hendel interfered, said he had never allowed such carryings on in the house and they must go outside if they wanted to fight.

　　Mr. Hendel parted them, telling Johnny his friend was stupid drunk, and he must look him up when sober if he wanted to fight. Then they had another round of drinks and cigars. The two men commenced quarreling again. Hendel got mad too and spoke roughly to them to make them go out. Lea Hollstrom had a glass of beer in his hand. I went into the kitchen, and the first I saw Hollstrom had John Hendel on the bed, in the room there, beating him with his glass. John Hendel drove him off calling, "Louis, come and help me." Louis is a sort of roust-about here. He is a butcher by trade.

Hendel came out of the room bleeding from mouth and nose, holding a handkerchief to his face. Hendel then took a revolver from under the pillows on the bed, and said he would fire a shot to scare them. He came here, stood there, within two feet of the bedroom door and fired a shot above their heads. The bullet went up there.

Mrs. Hendel then continued her testimony.

He did this to scare and did not hit anybody. There were only four of them here, scattered about the room, not in line with the pistol. I took the gun away from John Hendel and put it away in the bedroom. Just as I turned around to come out here again and as I stood there, in the door, I heard a shot fired. Lea Hollstrom turned around once or twice, in about two steps, and fell right here. I saw his eyes set at once and said: "the man is dead." When I heard the shot I saw Lea Hollstrom's coat still smoking, burning from the shot. Louis stood by him and shot him from behind, shot him in the back. He was as close as this (she held her hands about a foot apart).

Hollstrom says as he fell, "oh, oh, oh!" Louis then said: "I've fixed him." This is how it happened; only two shots were fired. The first by John Hendel to scare. The second by Louis. Louis himself said he had killed the man and that he was going to hunt up the sheriff and give himself up, and he told Sheriff Jackson on giving himself up that he had killed a man."

JOHN BRODBECK,
CITY BREWERY.

Boise, Idaho, _____ 189___

To the Honorable Board of Pardons
State of Idaho

Hon. gentlemen
                    I am pleased to
be able to speak a word for one
who is deserving and who is
in your hands for weal or
for woe - Mr John Hendel
who is now in the State penitentiary
I have known John Hendel
and have been acquainted with
him for fifteen years. He was
for four years in my Employ
in Boise City I have known
him intimately all of these years
and I know him as a good
citizen an honest Employee
always faithful to the trust
imposed in him during the
four years he was in my

37. Request from John Brodbeck that Hendel be pardoned.

A juror questioned Mrs. Hendel further and she answered that:

There was no one else in the house at that time, only myself
and Lea, John Hendel and Louis. All others ran away as
soon as John Hendel came out bleeding and showed fight. I
stood here in the door, John Hendel about two feet from me
and Louis that close to Lea and about six feet from where
John and I stood. Louis said he had killed the man and I saw
it done. I almost saw the bullets go from his gun, and saw
the man's coat burning from the powder. I looked at Lea as
he fell on his face and saw his eyes set. I said: "Oh, John, the
man is dead." The moment the shot was heard John and I
stood still, right there, in and near the bedroom door. When
my husband used forcible language to get them to go, Lea
Hollstrom said: "I won't go out, I'll kill you before I leave
the house."

   To a reporter's question, Mrs. Hendel said again that
only two shots were fired and Louis shot Lea "here"
(touching the right side, back above the lumbar region).
Replying to the coroner's question, she said:

   The revolver my husband had was handed to Sheriff
Jackson. I would certainly know it again, as it was mine. The
one Louis used we did not know he had at all. The little
fellow, after he shot Lea, went and threw it in the water closet
(toilet). Charley Sherry made him fish it out and told him to
give it to the sheriff. Charles Sherry—he can tell you a good
deal about it, as he was one of the first here, and seemed to
be cool and not excited a bit.

   Mrs. Hendel was finally dismissed from the witness stand
after this.

Sheriff Jackson was sent back to his office to get the guns from the
safe where he had deposited them. While he was gone, the jury examined the rooms and searched for possible bullet holes to try to solve

the conflicting testimony about the number of shots. They found a hole with the bullet in it in the ceiling. The coat and vest of the murdered man were looked over. The fatal bullet had entered what the tailors call the right side body of the coat, which is the part between the front and back. It had come out through the heart and stopped on the inside of the vest, tearing the lining but not the cloth of the vest. A jury man found a bullet in the sawdust on the floor, under a table, about six feet from where the dead body had been spread on a table for examination by Dr. Figgins. The bullet, it was surmised, had probably dropped when the doctor unbuttoned the vest of the decedent.

When the sheriff returned, the revolvers were examined and the bullets tried. One, the larger, fitted the larger revolver—a Navy 45 caliber, long barreled. The other and smaller bullet fitted the other revolver—a common British Bulldog, 44-caliber short barrel. The smaller bullet was badly battered and torn at the end, evidently by glancing against a rib. The coat was powder burned or charred as described by Mrs. Hendel. It was of black diagonal cloth. The jury unreservedly expressed the opinion that the bullet that penetrated the partition above the room was the larger one, out of the Colt's Navy, in the hand of Louis. The bullet that killed Hollstrom was discharged by Hendel from the smaller revolver—the British Bulldog.

One Andrew Fleming was sworn in and he identified the large Colt pistol as the gun of Louis, shown to him in the early morning. Sheriff Jackson was sworn and he identified the small gun or pistol as that taken by him from John Hendel in the bedroom adjoining the brewery that morning.

The coroner's jury felt fully satisfied. The verdict read: "We, the jury summoned to ascertain the cause of death of Lea Hollstrom, find that he came to his death by a gunshot wound caused by a gun or pistol held in the hand of John Hendel, at the Star Brewery saloon, in the town of Hailey, County of Alturas, State of Idaho, on the morning of the 17th day of March, 1893." The foreman and eight other jurors signed the verdict.

HOLLSTROM'S FUNERAL

On the 22nd, Leander's brother Sam arrived from Utah, and at 1:45 p.m. on the 23rd, the funeral took place. The cortege moved from the undertaking room to the Methodist church, where services were held. A long line of mourners then accompanied the remains to the Hailey Cemetery.

By this time, the *Wood River Times* had finally settled on the proper spelling of Hollstrom's name after several versions, and they ran his obituary.[12] He had been born August 17, 1861, at Kronaby Sahen Waza Lan, Finland, and was therefore exactly 31 years and 7 months on the day of his death. He had come to America at age 19 and soon became a miner. He had worked in Utah and then at various times in the Hailey area. He was employed in the Star Mine at the time of his death.

Leander had been a rough and tumble guy. Four years before, he had suffered a broken leg while wrestling at the Alturas Hotel, and the previous fall had sustained a severely cut wrist in a street row in front of the express office. Still, the newspaper said, he was not known to be quarrelsome and never carried firearms. Neither was he armed on the night he died.

HENDEL AND RODER IN JAIL

Hendel and Roder—the local newspaper was still calling him "Schroder," an error it took them weeks to figure out—stayed in jail. Hendel was in the "steel cell," and Roder in the "murderer's cell." Newspapers throughout Idaho reported them held without bail.[13] Neither had showed much appetite at first.[14] After the results of the coroner's jury were in, though, Roder became more hopeful and his spirits picked up. Yet he still expected to face charges of discharging a firearm that could bring a penitentiary sentence. All the first day, Hendel was in good spirits and felt no need for an attorney.

On the Saturday following the death, two local businessmen, E. Cromer and A. Wolters, called on Hendel and convinced him the matter was one of life and death. Hendel agreed to retain Norman

M. Ruick, a local attorney.[15] Ruick first wanted $1,500, which Hendel refused. Another local attorney (one with a truly memorable name), Texas Angel, was retained for $500. Ruick then reportedly lowered his fee to $1,000 and he was retained in addition. Hendel had apparently done well financially in the brewey-saloon business to be able to afford such large sums.

Later that day, some of Hendel's friends came by and suggested that he hire an attorney for Roder. Hendel said, and it was reported in the *Wood River Times*, "I killed the man, Louis don't need no attorney." Hendel relented at length, though, and hired J. S. Waters for Louis, it was reported. Later, Waters said he was not being paid and that it was Roder that asked him for representation. Be that as it may, all three defense attorneys involved had court appearances to make and the preliminary hearing was postponed for a few days.

There was a rumor in town for a while that the Finns, Hollstrom's countrymen, had taken up a collection to hire an attorney to assist the prosecution. A Finn named Sandquist had spoken to another local attorney, Mr. Brunner, but had not retained him, and if any such idea was ever held, it had been quickly abandoned.

THE PRELIMINARY EXAMINATION

The preliminary hearing for Hendel and Roder began the end of March before Probate Judge Richards in the room of the Fourth District Court. The Honorable E. Ensign appeared for the prosecution on the request of the District Attorney. Waters represented Roder, and Angel and Ruick appeared for John Hendel.[16]

The testimony was recorded, for the first time in Hailey, on a recent invention of the day—a typewriter, operated by Joe McFadden. The trial had to be slowed a bit at times for McFadden to keep up, but that was a minor problem compared to the joy of being uptodate. After the revelations at the coroner's inquest, the trial should have been an anticlimax—it was not!

Crowds stayed all day to hear the proceedings. After the prosecution presented its evidence, Roder's counsel said there was not even a suspicion against his client and he moved for dismissal.[17] The motion was promptly denied and a recess was taken until 7 p.m. to allow Judge Waters, Roder's counsel, to decide on his next move. The first day's witnesses had been Sheriff A. J. Jackson, Dr. Figgins, Charles Sherry, and "two Finns." Four or five more witnesses were left to call, but as the *Wood River Times* lamented, "If the six attorneys in the case indulge in arguments the examination might be protracted until next week."

THE SENSATIONAL THIRD BULLET

The next day, Sheriff Jackson was recalled to the witness stand for the third time.[18] Attorney Ruick asked him to examine the vest of the murdered man. Jackson felt a hard body in the lining and extracted a Colt 45 revolver bullet. The bullet was slightly broadened at the conical end, and there was, attached to it, a discolored substance which was initially thought to be clotted blood fibers or threads of dark cloth such as might have been part of the black diagonal of which the deceased's coat was made.

Opposite the rent, or bullet hole in the vest, was a blood clot and a dent in the lining that indicated the fatal bullet had stopped there. The third bullet created a sensation in the courtroom as everyone tried to crowd forward to get a view of the startling new evidence. Eventually, order was restored and court was adjourned for the noon recess. On the streets of Hailey, this new discovery was soon the major topic of town gossip.

During the noon recess, Texas Angel, Hendel's attorney, and J. S. Waters, Roder's attorney, both wandered into the local newspaper office to air their concerns. Their comments were printed in the next issue of the paper.

Waters denounced the matter: "A man who'd resort to such a contemptible legerdemain ought to be hung."

"You are quite right!" replied Mr. Angel. "If it is as you say the guilty party should be hung, because the trick might have the effect of hanging an innocent man! But the matter is straight enough. The evidence is legitimate, I have no doubt."

"Don't talk that way!" Retorted Waters. "A 45 Colts fired point blank would shoot a big hole right through a man! The bullet never went through him."

"Well the bullet that killed him went through the man's back and front and light thicknesses of cloth," protested Angel.

"I don't care who hears me," rejoined Waters. "I say that bullet never went through the man and I will back this up anywhere. I don't accuse you of doing it Angel. I believe you incapable of it. But why were those clothes twice turned over to the Probate Judge's care, and leave the bullets and guns in the hands of Jackson? Why were not the guns and all turned over, or none at all? I tell you I am not getting a nickel for my services in this case. This little fellow called on me to defend him, and I accepted as a matter of duty although he hasn't a cent or a friend or a relative in America. But I am going to have him proved innocent if it takes two years of my life."

Both attorneys then left the newspaper office. The editor was more curious than ever about the mystery bullet after hearing this exchange and he sent a reporter to the Sheriff's office after the rest of the story.

When asked where the clothes had been kept since being taken off the corpse, Sheriff Jackson answered, "I kept them locked up until I took them to court, and then the coat, vest, two shirts and suspenders were turned over to the Probate Judge. The drawers, pants and boots I kept."

Just then Attorney Ruick entered the Sheriff's office too. The reporter asked him where the clothes had been since being turned over to the Probate Judge.

"Locked up in the vault," answered Ruick, "and I saw that he got all the keys to that vault, so that he was and is, solely responsible for them."

"When did he assume charge of the clothes?" Asked the reporter to Ruick.

"Shortly after I made the discovery."

"And when did you discover the bullet?" asked the reporter blandly, trying not to dwell on the possible serious implications.

"Well, I'd prefer not to speak about that, just at present," Mr. Ruick answered, (The reporter described this comment as being delivered "somewhat curtly.")

"I'll tell you when you made the discovery, Ruick," the Sheriff joined in, winking at the *Times* reporter; "the first day of the examination, when you took the vest over to the window."

"Well, I don't care to speak about it," said Mr. Ruick.

The reporter doggedly pursued the story further and went to the chamber of Probate Judge Richards to see the third bullet personally. There he was told the Sheriff had it.

"Then I should like to get an order to the Sheriff to let me see it."

Mr. Ruick, who was now back at the court building also, jumped up and protested that the bullet should not be seen. Mr. Brunner also rushed up excitedly saying, "the prosecutor don't want the bullet seen." The reporter had not even noticed Brunner was in the room at the court until this outburst.

Texas Angel edged around and told the reporter in a very gentlemanly way: "There are things adhering to the bullet that might rub off if handled."

The reporter said he was baffled by all this and returned to the sheriff's office to ask Jackson: "Is it or is it not a fact that there are no rifle marks on the famous bullet?"

"There are scratches on the bullet," answered Sheriff Jackson, "but whether made by a rifle or not remains to be seen. Certainly it is that it has been where it got very hot, or was subjected to much friction, because there is tallow upon it."

"Thank you, sir," the reporter said, and concluded his report in the *Wood River Times* of the next day at this point.

The presence of the tallow of course might leave those who doubt the reliability of frontier criminal investigations to believe the bullet had been fired into a side of beef, possibly from a rifle, retrieved and placed in the vest lining.

That afternoon the preliminary hearing resumed and Dr. Figgins was on the stand for two-and-a-half hours of examination, cross-examination, redirect examination, and re-cross-examination, all about the mystical third bullet.[19] The third bullet was a 45, but for the coroner's inquest Figgins had fitted a 44 into the wound to show the jury what size bullet had caused it. The bullet that had made the wound figured to be much battered as it had struck a rib, or so it was believed at this point. Figgins again testified that it had struck the fifth rib, carrying away two-thirds of it and fracturing the remainder.

"The bullet shown me in Probate Court," Dr. Figgins testified, "could not, in my opinion, have passed through the body, for the reason that the bullet making the wound would have to be flattened more or less." A microscopic examination would be necessary to thoroughly examine the fibers of cloth adhering to the apex of the third bullet, he also testified.

It is certainly questionable whether the doctor could tell if the fatal wound was made by a 45 or 44 caliber. A difference of .01 of an inch would hardly change the apparent fit in a wound in human flesh, contrary to what the doctor tried to demonstrate for the coroner's jury.

In closing arguments for the defense, Judge Walters claimed again that there was not even a suspicion against his client, Roder, but he did ask for bail rather than a dismissal this time. The *Wood River Times* said a request for a dismissal would have made him appear ridiculous.[20]

The court's final decision was that the killing and use of revolvers had been proven by the prosecution. A crime of murder had been committed; under Idaho statue an accessory was equally guilty with the perpetrator of the crime. Both Hendel and Roder were bound over for trial, and this was not a bailable offense. Trial was scheduled to begin June 14.

BEFORE THE TRIAL

There was no lack of excitement during April and May as Hendel and Roder sat in jail awaiting trial. One night, just after the preliminary examination, a fellow prisoner, Mrs. Johns, who was insane, escaped from the Hailey jail. John Hendel heard the commotion and cooperated with the investigation by telling all he knew about the incident. Even without outside disturbances, John did not take well to confinement, and some of the mental instability the Finnish miners had noted began to be evident.

One evening, when told that Judge Stockslager had again refused to allow him bail and had denied a writ of *habeus corpus*, Hendel broke out in a torrent of abuse toward the judge, the officers, lawyers, and everybody in general.[21] Sheriff Jackson came in for his share of abuse, and the prisoner vilified him to his heart's content until finally Jackson said, "Look here, John. I have treated you kindly as I could, looked after you, spent a good portion of my time down here, and went to the extreme limit of the law to make you comfortable. If that does not please you and you continue to misbehave I will have to lock you up in the steel cell and refuse to allow anybody to come near you."

John quieted down upon hearing this.

The *Times* reported that the talk on the street was that, if found guilty, John would kill himself rather than serve a sentence.

Hendel had a bout of unspecified sickness about this time, but on May 11, it was reported that he was mending and would probably recover his health.[22]

THE TRIAL

On June 7th, empanelling of the jury started in the Hendel trial, which was separate from the Roder trial. Judge Stockslager was presiding. It was very difficult to get a suitable jury that had not formed an opinion on the case. Finally, miners who had not been in town during the spring and knew nothing of the case were found. On June 14, the trial began, and it lasted for five days, as the judge held court night and day to finish in a reasonable length of time. After the coroner's inquest and the preliminary examination, this all seemed an anticlimax, and the local newspaper lost interest in reporting every utterance of the event.

The main item of new evidence at the trial was about the third bullet and the wound. A second physician, Doctor Brown, joined Dr. Figgins in exhuming Hollstrom's body for reexamination on the orders of Judge Stockslager.[23]

At the gravesite, a thorough examination was made and still there was no evidence of a second bullet entering the body. The doctors cut a section of rib eight inches long from both sides of the wound and took the two sections to court as exhibits.

In court, it developed that the bullet passed out between the sixth and seventh ribs, not between the fifth and sixth, as had been the testimony at the coroner's inquest, and the bullet had not fractured any rib in the exit from the deceased. Dr. Figgins made the correction himself and admitted his initial exam had been mistaken. The jury apparently saw no great significance in this.

At 3 o'clock on Monday, June 20, the case went to the jury. In only 25 minutes, they returned a verdict of murder in the second degree.[24]

On Wednesday, the trial of Louis Roder began. This time, local businessmen made up the jury to save the mileage expense of securing miners from a distance. As the *Times* said, Roder (they had finally decided his name was not "Schroder" or "Roeder") took one look at that menacing aggregation and changed his plea to guilty of involuntary manslaughter.

Both men were sentenced the same day. Hendel got 16 years and Roder 31/2; both sentences could be halved by good behavior.[25] Sheriff Jackson took both men by train to the penitentiary at Boise the next afternoon after sentencing.

Hendel's attorney, N.M. Ruick, filed an appeal, saying the court errored on several points.[26] Namely, Hendel's request for an elisor to have charge of the jury during the trial because the sheriff and coroner "by reason of any bias, prejudice or other cause would not act promptly or impartially" was denied by the trial court. Secondly, Hendel had the right to call an expert witness to examine the mysterious third bullet. Thirdly, Hendel had the right to an expert witness to examine the paper found near the scene that may have been used as wadding and shot from a gun. The appeal was quite short, about one page.

George M. Parsons, Attorney General, responded for the state. Showing the level of 19th Century science, Parsons said an expert could not tell animal from human blood on the bullet in question anyway. The jury was allowed to examine the bullets, which the court was correct in permitting. Parsons too wrote only briefly, about one page.

Idaho Supreme Court Justice C. J. Huston wrote the opinion of the court to which justices Morgan and Sullivan concurred. There were seven exceptions Huston addressed. Among his more interesting points: "There is some evidence of a third shot being fired, but it hardly arises to the dignity of a suspicion." Huston mentions that the third bullet fitted the gun used by Roder. Roder's counsel had the right to be present at Hendel's trial and to be heard on matters, which affected Roder. The two doctors that testified about the possibility of the third bullet being the one that killed Hollstrom disagreed and the jury, rightly, made the decision.

The objection that the verdict was contrary to the evidence was not true either. Four witnesses, Field, McGarnish, Farrel, and Saunders, testified that Hendel admitted he killed Hollstrom and justified the action by saying Hollstrom had knocked him down and knocked his wife down. "Finding no reversible error in the record, the judgment of the district court is affirmed."

In February of 1894, the Idaho Supreme Court ruling upholding the verdict in Hendel's trial became public and resolved the legal question permanently.[27] Frontier justice had its quirks, but it was usually just indeed.

While the trial and the appeals were progressing, the First National Bank of Hailey filed an action in the district court on 14 July 1893 to recover $560 that Hendel owed them. They were awarded two lots in Hailey. Apparently on the 25th of October that same year, Hendel sold the lots to Sonnleitner. The matter ended up before the Idaho Supreme Court that ruled in February of 1898 that the bank's notice of conveyance from the Sheriff was so vague the property could not be identified, their claim was not substantiated, and thus Sonnleitner got to keep it.[28]

A census of the Idaho State Penitentiary in 1898 showed among the inmates' professions, one brewer.[29] Four of the inmates had been born in Germany.

In 1898, Hendel applied for a pardon and placed advertisements to that effect in several Idaho newspapers. Although listed as illiterate in penitentiary records, Hendel wrote and signed letters to several people regarding the pardons board meeting. A letter to the pardons board from Guy Bruman, who was District Attorney of the Judicial District at the time of the crime, recommended that "the sentence be commuted sufficiently to give him considering his age a hope of yet succeeding in the world."[30] There is also a record of a petition on Hendel's behalf signed by 19 citizens of Idaho, including present brewers John Brodbeck, Hendel's prior employer, and John Lemp, and former brewer John Krall.

Late in 1898, Hendel received a pardon that set his release date for January 1, 1900.[31] He had served nearly half his sentence. A few months after his release, he was running a successful saloon at Cambridge, Idaho, the then terminus of the planned railroad from Weiser to Seven Devils.[32]

Roder did not completely drop from history after his term in prison. The little Dutchman who had been framed for murder, who had only his lawyer on his side, was on the 1920 U. S. Census living in Pocatello with his wife Elizabeth, who had been born in Idaho and was 45 years old. Hendel's wife (Margette, according to penitentiary records), the lady with the immense imagination, left no trail for future historians.

N. M. Ruick, the attorney who just might have specialized in parlor tricks involving bullets that appear from nowhere, gave up his Republican affiliation and became the head of the Populist Party in Idaho in 1894, and in 1904 was made the United States Attorney for the Gem State.[33] Texas Angel moved to Boise and then to Grangeville.[34] He died in April of 1903 back at his home in Hailey.[35]

In August of 1909, Hendel was still at Cambridge, but he ran a temperance and soft drink emporium due to the local option law.[36] He ordered four barrels of beer, three cases each of wine and whiskey. Attorney Richards believed that was too much for a place selling temperance drinks. A warrant was served by sheriff Courdin for Hendel's arrest and the attachment of his goods.

In the case of State v. William Wall that reached the Idaho State Supreme Court in June 1910, the court ruled that a liquor license was required to sell liquor and that failure to have one was a misdemeanor.[37] Wall had sought to avoid this by finding a loophole in the law. The original decision was made by Judge Bryan of Caldwell in December of 1907 when he ruled the new law allowing county commissioners to refuse to grant liquor licenses was constitutional.[38] At the end of the opinion, four other pending cases with "precisely the same question involved" were listed and stipulated to follow the decision in the Wall case. One of the four was State, Appellant v. John Hendel, Respondent. Hendel was back in he liquor business and using the courts.

At the end of April 1910, the last legal saloon in Washington County, Idaho, closed.[39] Hendel could no longer sell liquor.

The brewery in Hailey was leased to Charles Sonnleitner even before the Hendel murder trial started, and he ran it for six years without ever shooting anyone. Years later, Mr. Sonnleitner wrote a brief newspaper article on the history of brewing in Hailey.[40] He remembered the shooting, but thought it had happened because of a woman. A gunfight in a western saloon over a woman might make a good tale, but in this case what we know of the truth is as strange as any fiction!

END NOTES

1   The vast majority of this chapter comes from the files of the *Wood River Times* of Hailey, Idaho, from March to July of both daily and weekly editions, during 1893. The conversations were reported in the paper as they appear here. I have invented no dialogue. The *Times* editorial style virtually novelized the event and added a little tabloid journalism for seasoning.

2 U. S. Census, 1880, Montana Territory, Madison County, p. 50. In A. D. 2000 John E. Douglas and Linda J. Brown did an extensive archaeological project on the Gilbert house.

3 *Idaho Tri-Weekly Statesman*, Boise, Idaho, 5 June 1886, p. 3, c. 1. There is a John Hendel on the 1840 U. S. Census in Pickaway, Ohio. Relationship not established.

4 *Idaho Tri-Weekly Statesman*, 17 June 1886, p. 3, c. 1.

5 Blaine County Judicial Records, Idaho State Historical Society, Microfilm reel 31, original page 35, dated 13 November 1886.

6 Blaine County Judicial Records, Idaho State Historical Society, Microfilm reel 31, original page 149, date 7 June 1887.

7 *Wood River Times,* Weekly, Hailey, Idaho, December 8, 1886, p. 3, c. 3. When Hendel arrived and began construction of his brewery he was described as an "experienced brewer and competent business man." The State Penitentiary description of Hendel states he was 5 foot 6 1/4 inches tall, 146 pounds, dark complected, with brown hair and hazel eyes, He was Catholic, a moderate drinker, and considered illiterate with only 4 years of schooling. See also *Idaho Tri-Weekly Statesman*, 9 December 1886, p. 3, c. 1.

8 *Weekly News Miner*, 5 April 1889, p. 3, c. 1.

9 *Wood River News Miner*, 14 June 1889, p. 1, c. 5.

10 *Bradstreet's Commercial Reports* vol. 87, September 1889, p. 3 of " Idaho."

11 *Wood River Times,* Weekly, 22 March 1893, p. 1, c. 2-6.

12 *Wood River Times*, Weekly, 22 March 1893, p. 3, c. 1

13 *The Elmore Bulletin*, Mount Home, Idaho, 1 April 1893, p. 3, c. 4.

14 *Wood River Times*, Weekly, 22 March 1893, p. 3, c. 4.

15 Norman Ruick was admitted to the bar in 1877 in Indianapolis and moved to the Hailey area in 1880. In 1892 he had been a state senator. He was later a Populist leader and a United States Attorney for Idaho. See Hiram T. French, *History of Idaho* (Chicago: The Lewis Publishing Company, 1914), v. 2, p. 889.

16 *Wood River Times*, Weekly, 29 March 1893, p. 1, c. 3.

17 *Wood River Times*, Weekly, 29 March 1893, p. 2, c. 5.

18 *Wood River Times*, Weekly, 29 March 1893, p. 3, c.

19 *Wood River Times*, Weekly, 29 March 1893, p. 2, c. 5.

20 *Wood River Times*, Weekly, 5 April 1893, p. 1, c. 3

21 *Wood River Times*, Weekly, 3 May 1893, p. 1, c. 5.

22 *Wood River Times*, Daily, Hailey, Idaho, 11 May 1893, p. 3, c. 3

23 *Wood River Times*, Weekly, 21 June 1893, p. 1, c. 4.

24 *Wood River Times*, Weekly, 21 June 1893, p. 3, c. 5. *Idaho World*, Idaho City, Idaho, 23 June 1893, p. 1, c. 2 and 30 June 1893, p. 1, c. 2.

25 *Elmore Bulletin*, 1 July 1893, p. 2, c. 2.

26 *Idaho Reports 4,* 1894-1896, "State v. Hendel," p. 88-98.

27 *Wood River Times*, Weekly, 7 February 1894, p. 3, c. 5.

28 *Idaho Reports 6*, pp. 21-28.

29 *Genesee News*, 14 January 1898, p. 4, c. 3.

30 The material on the pardon request is all from the file on Hendel kept by the Idaho Department of Corrections, Central Records in Boise.

31 *Ketchum Keystone*, Ketchum, Idaho, December 10, 1898, p. 3, c. 1.

32 *Wood River Times*, Weekly, June 20, 1900, p. 4, c. 2.

33 French, *History of Idaho*, vol. 2, p. 88. Ruick was also involved in the case of Harry Orchard assassinating former Idaho Governor Steunnenberg.

34 *Idaho County Free Press*, 23 December 1898, p. 1, c. 7.

35 *Idaho Daily Statesman*, 6 April 1903, p. 1, c. 1-2.

36 *Evening Capital News*, 14 August 1909, p. 1, c. 5.

37 *Idaho Reports*, 18 June 1910, pp. 300-307.

38 *Evening Capital News*, 3 December 1907, p. 1 & 2, c. 3, 4, 5.

39 *Evening Capital News*, 15 April 1910, p. 1, c.4.

40 Charles Sonnleitner, "Brewing Industry Flourished Once in Old Alturas: Expert Beer Maker Gives Some of the Salient Facts of Earlier Days," *The Hailey Times*, Hailey, Idaho, 50th Anniversary Edition, 1931, p. 16.

11

EDWARD HOSP
Dead on the Trail

EDWARD HOSP WAS APPARENTLY the first brewer in the Ruby City/
Silver City mining area of southern Idaho. In 1865, the first issue
of the long-running *Owyhee Avalanche* (Silver City, Idaho) carried
an ad for Hosp and Co.'s brewery.[1] All it said was that they were
manufacturers of lager beer in Ruby City and "respectfully request
the public to try it." Hosp was on the 1860 U. S. Census in Ashland
Precinct, Jackson County, Oregon. So he had been in the Northwest
for some time.

On the Federal Tax records of July 1865, Edward Hosp paid tax
on 10 barrels of beer brewed in Ruby City, and on another page paid
for his fermented liquor license. In October 1865, Hosp of Ruby City
brewed 7 1/2 barrels of beer; in November, 4 barrels.[2] By the next
year, the ads mentioned Andy Schrader as a partner to Hosp in the
Ruby City brewery. On the Federal records, Hosp and Shrader (sic)
paid for eight months of a brewer's license and the tax on 15 barrels
brewed early in 1866.[3] In July 1866, Schrader and Hosp (sic) paid $12
for the beer they had brewed.[4] On Federal Tax Assessment records
for September 1866, they had brewed 6 barrels and paid a brewers
reassessment, and in October of 1866, they brewed 3 barrels.[5] These
are quite small production totals.

In 1867, the brewers moved a mile or so upstream to Silver City,
as Ruby City was rapidly being dismantled. The new location was on
Jordan Street by Long Gulch. At this new City Brewery, they were
manufacturing lager, and selling wines, liquors, lager, and cigars

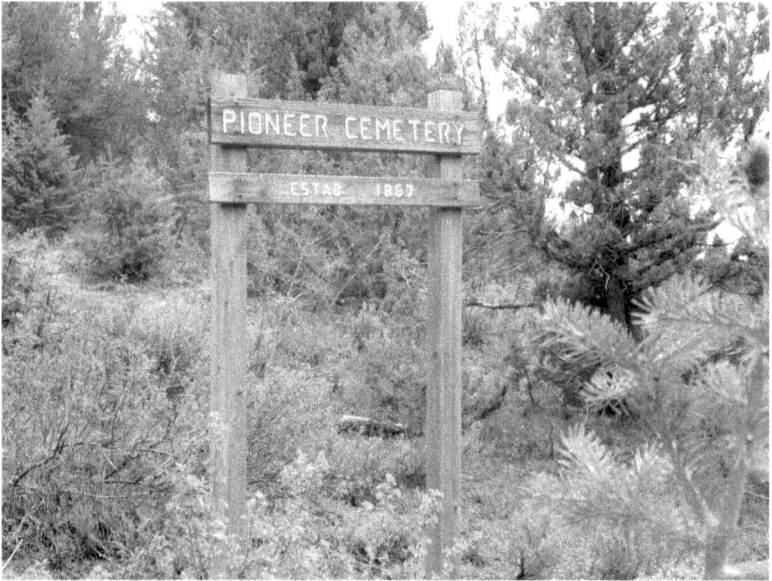

38. Pioneer Cemetery, Silver City, Idaho, where Hosp rests.

across the bar.[6] By 1869 both men had decided to move to a new gold camp in Nevada and the Silver City brewery was taken over by Nick Zapp.

In October of that year, Schrader, Hosp, and a Mrs. Westenfelter were encamped at Big Springs, some 50 miles from Silver en route to the Cope District and Mountain City, Nevada, which is just over the Idaho-Nevada border on the East Fork of the Owyhee River.[7] By stage, it was 23 hours from Mountain City to Silver City.[8] They were hauling their brewing equipment there to start a new establishment. They chose a popular camping spot for the night. Mr. Robert Griffith drove up from the south, and Charles Brumell and some others from the north, and they were immediately informed that Hosp was deathly ill. There was no physician and no medicines, but the party did all they could for his comfort until he died about 3 in the morning They decided to return the body to Silver City for burial and Mr. Griffith hauled him back in his wagon.

Hosp's friends speculated that sleeping on the ground in the open air was too much for his constitution, but no official cause of death surfaced. Hosp was German by birth, about 53 at his time of death (25 October 1869), and formally educated. It was said that he had a brother in New York who was a Catholic priest.[9] He was interred in the Pioneer Cemetery in Silver City.[10]

Schrader went on and opened his new Mountain City Brewery without his partner. Gambrinus lost a follower.

END NOTES

1   *Owyhee Avalanche*, Ruby City, Idaho, 19 August 1865, p. 3, c. 5.

2   Federal Tax Records of Idaho 1865-1866, University of Idaho Library, Microfilm reel # 558.

3   Federal Tax Records, 1865-1866, University of Idaho Library Microfilm # 558.

4   Federal Tax Records, 1865-1866, University of Idaho Library Microfilm # 558.

5   Federal Tax Records, 1865-1866, University of Idaho Library Microfilm # 558

6   *Owyhee Avalanche*, Silver City, Idaho, 30 March 1867, the ad was on p.4, c. 3, and a news report with the same information on p. 2, c. 4.

7   *Owyhee Tidal Wave*, Silver City, Idaho, 28 October 1869, p. 4, c. 3. The whole story of Hosp's death is from this newspaper story,

8   *The Elko Chronicle*, Elko, Nevada, 5 June 1870, p. 2, c. 3.

9   *Idaho World*, Idaho City, 4 November 1869, p. 3, c. 2.

10 Wilma Lewis Statham, *Owyhee County Gleanings*, 1986, p. 36.

12

JOSEPH KOENIG
Gunfight Victim

SOMETIMES A MAN'S ENTIRE LIFE is little noticed, but he escapes anonymity by a death that is long remembered. If brewer Joseph Koenig had not died in a frequently discussed August 1884 gun fight in the Sommercamp brewery in Silver City, Idaho, he would have forever been an unknown entity. Every would-be historian of Idaho has mentioned the death of Koenig, but everyone has a different version.[1] The Dewey-Koenig shoot out is one of the more famous in Western lore, mostly because of the celebrity and wealth of antagonist Colonel William Dewey, and the series of trials needed to reach a conclusion.

Koenig worked in the saloon and in the attached brewery that belonged to William Sommercamp, and he lived with his wife and small son in a house across what came later to be known as "Deadman's Alley."[2] I have found little about Koenig's earlier life, but he was a "much-esteemed member" of the Masonic Lodge.[3]

Several of the published accounts of the fight get the most obvious details wrong. Ernie White's article "Empire's End," had the affair in 1874.[4] Helen Nettleton moved the event up to 1892.[5] Interpretations were often equally imaginative. The *Owyhee Avalanche* editor during Dewey's trials was also prosecuting attorney, so he carried only brief synopses to avoid "prejudice for or against the defendant."[6] Thus, there are scant details in that readily available source. The work of Faith Fastabend (*William Dewey's Darkest Days*, Nampa, Idaho, third printing, 2006) used court transcripts—apparently for the first time—as well as newspapers and made a major contribution to knowledge of the event.

Dewey was an enterprising man who made a fortune from scratch by age 18, lost it in the search for gold in Virginia City, Nevada, and walked with a pack from that gold camp to the Silver City area, arriving in the area in 1863.[7] Michael Jordan, the legendary discoverer of gold in the Silver City area, had been Dewey's partner and he summoned Dewey to move to this new bonanza in the Owyhee Mountains. In 1871, Dewey bought the Black Jack Mine from W. B. Knott. Dewey briefly owned a store, and was an economic force in Silver City.

Dewey was a good friend with brewery-owner Sommercamp, who had financed operations on the Black Jack Mine on Florida Mountain.[8] Sommmercamp, Dewey and A. J. Stucker owned the mine jointly. Dewey was 62 at the time of the gunfight and was a new father of his fourth son. "His fourth wife, Belle—30 years his junior—had recently presented him with ... William Cornelius."[9]

Sommercamp told Dewey to help himself behind the bar when he wanted a drink. When Koenig was tending bar, he objected to

39. Washington and Deadman Alley corner, Silver City, Idaho.

Dewey trespassing in the bartender's sacred territory. Dewey said he had permission, and the matter stayed at that point until one day when Koenig got drunk and swore he'd kill Dewey if ever the man bothered him again. The night before the gunfight was a rough one in the saloon. Several fights occurred, and then Dewey came in with two other men and their noisy dispute added to the tense situation.[10]

Dewey had quite a long history of combative activities. Koenig told them both to break it up or get out. Dewey called Koenig "a cabbage eating son-of-a-bitch" and said if he'd come out to fight he would "make the cabbage back out of his ass a foot long."[11] Another witness at the preliminary hearing said Dewey called Koenig a "Dutch son-of-a-bitch." The anti-German nature of the cursing was obvious to everyone. As Julia Welch notes, anti-German sentiment was fairly rare—Indians and Chinese were the usual targets of bigotry in Silver City in that era.[12] Sommercamp came in about this time and told his bartender and his friend to both leave to prevent trouble.

The next day, about 7 a.m., Koenig went to work as bartender. Dewey came in for an early morning drink and cigar. Soon Henry Sommercamp, William's son, relieved him and Koenig went around town talking about the altercation the night before and explained to several people that while Dewey had been armed, he had not, which was the reason he did not fight. In Hasting's saloon Koenig showed the 41 caliber pistol he was carrying.

Later that morning, Koenig had his wife, her friend Mrs. Schneider, and young Willie Schneider go to the brewery with him. Inside the brewery, he had his Colt revolver on an inside shelf by the door. He fired the gun into a woodpile there to prove it was loaded. According to his wife, and the Schneider boy, who worked with him at the brewery, he practiced shooting at the woodpile behind his house. Koenig worked in the brewery all morning and drank heavily. At noon he went across the alley to his home for a nap.

That afternoon, Dewey went to Sommercamp's saloon with Sommercamp and several other men for refreshment after loading a wagon. Koenig walked into the bar room about 4 and Sommercamp

40. Deadman Alley street sign in Silver City, Idaho.

sent him to the brewery to fetch some cider and beer for the bar room. According to Sommercamp, Koenig passed Dewey and said, "I want to see you." None of the other witnesses heard the remark. Dewey's son said years later that Koenig asked his father to come to the brewery to taste some liquor he had there.[13] Idaho's most-noted writer, Vardis Fisher gave a version that Koenig offered a taste of a new brew.[14] Fisher went on to say that as they went through the dark and windowless malt room, the light of the doorway framed Dewey and Koenig opened fire. Maybe, maybe not!

Sommercamp testified at the preliminary hearing that the morning before the final fracas Koenig asked to have Dewey arrested to keep the peace and that he seemed afraid while making the request. Sommercamp told Koenig to make up his quarrel with Dewey.

Dewey with his dog went down to the brewery area and stepped over the boards nailed on the bottom of the door opening to keep out stray barley-eating hogs. Dewey was not nimble and looked down at the boards as he stepped. Koenig spoke to him and then opened fire according to Dewey.[15]

Five shots were definitely heard by witnesses, and they were fired immediately as the men went into the brewery. The first man to reach Koenig's side after the fray was told that Dewey shot Koenig just as soon as he stepped over the board at the bottom of the door. A woman who kept a boarding house nearby testified that the first shot came from inside the brewery.[16] Dewey told the same tale. Koenig had a .38-.41 Colt pistol and Dewey a .44 Webley. Initial reports that Dewey used a Sharps rifle were not true.[17] Some shots came from inside and some from outside, and therefore had different sounds. The guns also gave different sounds from each other, which created a great confusion as to who fired when and from where. Dewey claimed he fired as he retreated and only learned later that his first shot had taken effect. Koenig's two shots did not strike Dewey.

Dewey' shot struck Koenig's side and the bullet veered down and exited the body between the legs. Koenig's wife Alice may have been watching from their home, and his little son was near by, and he yelled at Dewey, "Don't shoot my papa any more."[18] Dewey hid behind a boulder in the alley and then went inside the brewery and drank a glass of water. Someone carried Koenig to his house. Dr. Belknap tended him to no avail. Joseph Koenig died about 7 p. m. that evening, 2 1/2 hours later. At first, there was a great deal of anti-Dewey rhetoric in town but it died down. At the behest of District Attorney C. M. Hays, the Grand Jury returned an indictment for manslaughter according to some sources and first-degree murder according to others, and the trial was held in September.

Koenig was buried in the Masonic cemetery and a large crowd attended. The Masons also published a tribute to Koenig: "Resolved

41. Masonic Lodge in Silver City.

42. A view of the creek that runs under the Masonic Lodge as seen from the inside.

that in the untimely death of our beloved brother, Joseph Koenig, the Lodge has lost a faithful and respected member of the fraternity, a true man, and society a law abiding and peaceful citizen."[19]

The Boise newspaper reported that Jas. L. Crutcher was in town from Silver City to employ Maj. Joe Huston to prosecute Dewey.[20] Dewey had employed R. Z. Johnson, who just happened to be in Silver City at the time, as his defense. The first examination was before Jim Wickersham, Probate Judge. Dewey was kept under guard since there was no jail in Silver City.

On September 19th, Dewey was arraigned for murder and given until the 20th to plead.[21] On the 20th, he plead not guilty and trial was set for the 22nd. Judge Broderick presided in the District Court. Over 70 prospective jurors were interviewed. The final jury impaneling took two days, and the jurors were M. R. Givens, W. R. Strickland, Arthur Pence, John Pollock, D. H. Spencer, Presley Cooper, J. C. Gough, John Frank, W. Sterling, H. T. Lord, J. Harley and R. F. Whitney. On Tuesday, 30 September, the case was argued and submitted to the jury.[22]

Prosecution witnesses included deputy sheriff Evan L. Williams, widow Alice C. Koenig, Dr. D. H. Belknap, John Hollenback, sheriff Mark Leonard, Al Meyers, and Willie Schneider. The defense called W. H. Sommercamp, George Drew, B. F. Hastings, George Stoddard,

Mrs. Mary Jordan, Miss Maggie Brady, Dr. Belknap, and Dewey took the stand in his own defense.[23] Deputy Williams testified that from the front of his stable on Jordan Street, he saw Dewey pumping bullets into the doorway of the brewery. Dewey stepped back at first and then advanced as he fired. Williams went to get his revolver and then to the scene of the crime. Williams saw Koenig's wife by his side. Williams went into the saloon and took Dewey's gun. Three shots had been fired and one shell has misfired. Dewey said "Did you take Koenig's gun too?"

"No –he's lying down in the brewery."

"Well, I had to shoot! You wouldn't let anyone shoot at you and not do anything about it!"[24]

Williams turned Dewey over to the sheriff and went to find Koenig at his home. Forty-five minutes after the clash Koenig told Williams, "Dewey shot me! Yes, he shot me in the back. He shot me just as I went through the door, as I was going over the boards!" Dr. Belknap's testimony partially contradicted this, as he claimed Koenig only mumbled unconnected phrases.

43. Altar of Silver City Masonic Lodge.

Mrs. Alice Koenig testified that she witnessed Dewey fire three times before a flash came from inside the brewery.

Dewey testified that a bullet hole in his coat and vest were not noticed until two days later. The bullet had hit his clothes but not his body.

The jury was out two nights and one day and returned a verdict of manslaughter with a recommendation of mercy.[25] The same day, Dewey was sentenced to eight years in the penitentiary. Dewey was despondent enough to take strychnine in a suicide attempt.[26] He went into convulsions and was in a very "dangerous condition" before Dr. Belknap arrived and employed his stomach pump.

When recovered, Dewey was taken to Boise to the Territorial prison. Fred T. Dubois, famous Idaho politician, was warden at the time and believed Dewey was justified in the shooting. He treated Dewey as "more a guest than a prisoner during the four or five months he was in jail."[27] Dewey had been a Congressional candidate in 1880, so the two politicos had a common bond.[28]

While Dewey was in prison, his appeal went forward, and in February of the next year, 1885, the Territorial Supreme Court granted a new trial.[29] As the case was reported in the standard legal reference books, Richard Z. Johnson filed the appeal for Dewey and it contained two grounds.[30] The second, that the court poorly

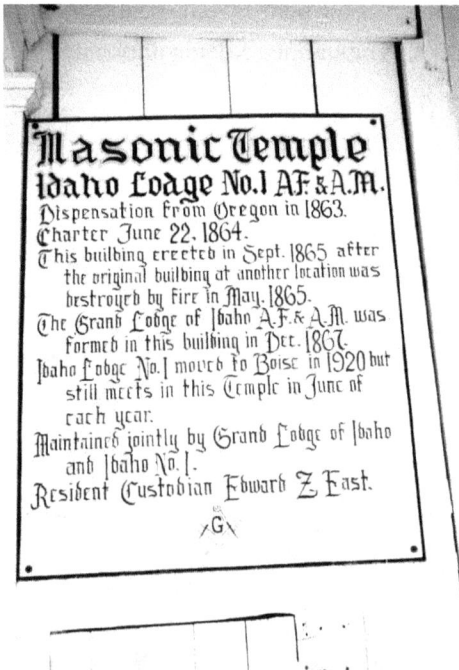

44. Masonic Lodge information from the door of the building. Koening was a Mason.

explained the concept of reasonable doubt to the jury, was ruled not to be an error. The first objection, however, which was about admitting *res gestae* statements of the deceased, Koenig, was upheld and a new trial was ordered. This objection specifically centered on the testimony of a Mr. Williams, who repeated statements Koenig made to him one-half to three-quarters of an hour after the affray ended. The Supreme Court ruled they were made too long after to qualify as part of the event. *Res gestae* means "the transaction, things done, the subject of matter." The 10-page Supreme Court decision does give some important details about the trial. Koenig spoke to Williams after Dewey had been arrested and left the scene of the fight. Under the law, the statements made as part of an event carry considerable weight if made immediately, before someone involved has time to contrive a story. Williams said he was told by Koenig that it was the first shot fired that struck Koenig, just as he went over the boards into the brewery. This was considered highly prejudicial against Dewey. The court decision was written by Justice C. J. Morgan, and concurred to by Justice J. Buck, with Justice J. Broderick, who tried the case originally, giving no opinion. The decision was handed down on 17 February 1885.

General John R. Kittrell, former Attorney General of Nevada and presently of Modesto, California, came to Silver City to assist with the prosecution in the retrial.[31] C. M. Hayes, the regular prosecutor, had studied law in the office of the defense attorney, R. Z. Johnson, and saw a potential conflict of interest. In mid-May the regional newspapers reported that 11 jurors had been found and prospects were good to get the last one impaneled and the case begun.[32] Koenig's widow and son who had moved to Baker City, Oregon, returned to Silver City in April.

The courthouse was packed with people eager to be entertained by the eloquent rhetoric of the distinguished legal minds. C. M. Hays addressed the jury for almost two hours in a review of the testimony. Not to be outdone, R. Z. Johnson spoke about the same amount of time for the defense. After these two warm-ups, General Kittrell rose for the main event. "He carried his audience with him and drew from ladies and gentlemen hot tears by his pathetic remarks and bitter invective."[33] This was supposedly Kittrell's finest oratorical performance, but it was not enough—the jury scarcely had time to look at the evidence before it returned a not guilty verdict.

Testimony about the bullets was new and seemed to indicate that a ricochet made the fatal wound. Willie Schneider had been near the brew kettle during the shooting but had seen little due to the gun smoke. He ran home after the shooting and told his mother that Mr. Koenig had shot himself. The main difference in this trial was that a reportedly reluctant witness, Maggie Brady, "who didn't want to get mixed up in that court business," now testified

45. *Deadman Alley and Washington Street.*

that it was self-defense.[34] Rafe Gibbs, Idaho historian, said the jury declared Dewey not guilty without waiting to hear any more testimony. Ernie White says the first jury ballot was 11 to one for acquittal and the reluctant juror soon changed his vote.[35] This lone juror was J. J. Connelly, according to Julia Welch's book. The spectators' "hot tears" made no difference in the outcome.

Dewey walked out a free man, but supposedly $40,000 in debt.[36] He leased the Poorman mine to wardens J. H. Richards and Dubois, and laid plans with his friend Peter Donnelly to find another mine. He indeed found a rich vein on the edge of Florida Mountain in view of Silver City and, with C. W. Moore's financing, made a fortune with the "Belle Dewey," later renamed the "Empire State."

Author Welch, who was a long-time resident and knew people alive at the time of the trial said even in the 1920s, 40 years later, people speculated that someone had been bought off. She believed that between the two trials, Silver City people rethought the situation. Dewey was a mine owner who employed many people, invested heavily in the city, and knew other capitalists whom he also enticed into making investments. Could Silver City get by without him? No matter how many tears were shed for a good Masonic brother and brewery worker, Koenig was replaceable. Dewey was a tough act to do without.

Years later, when Dewey was feuding with Boise over routes to Thunder Mountain and locations of mineral equipment, the Idaho City newspaper published an anonymous poem, which was reprinted in Boise. It seems to almost fit the Koenig altercation as well as its intended target.[37]

> Colonel William H. Dewey to Boise:
> *That band is going 'round,*
> *Old Boise dear.*
> *It will be complete,*
> *Thine isolation sweet,*
> *Never fear.*
> *And when you're dead and gone,*
> *Upon your bier*
> *Will I go o'er to drop*
> *a tear?*
> *No, nary a one,*
> *You son of a gun.*
> *To see you will be*
> *For me a jubilee—*
> *In fact enough for three,*
> *Nampa, Emmett—me.*

Neither Dewey's biographical sketch in *An Illustrated History of Idaho* nor the one in *A Historical, Descriptive and Commercial Directory of Owyhee County* mentioned Koenig nor Dewey's other notable alter-cations with Mike Rock and John Sullivan. A man like Dewey, who settled arguments with guns, cane handles, and fists, could still be accepted on the frontier. Dewey went on to make a new fortune in mining and hotels before dying in 1903 in his 80th year. He was considered a leading citizen of the state at that time. He was remembered for mining claims in Silver City and for being one of the three discoverers of the South Mountain mineral load. In 1912, his son, E. H. Dewey closed the Dewey Palace Hotel in Nampa because local option closed its bar, and made it unable to compete with hotels in Boise.[38] Mrs. William Dewey died in June of 1918 in Nampa.[39]

What happened to Koenig's wife and son? I have found only one circumstantial bit of evidence. One Joseph Francis Koenig of Dolores, Colorado, registered for the World War I draft in 1917. He was born 1 March 1875 and was a naturalized citizen. He would have been about 9 years old when his namesake Joseph Koenig was shot. Perhaps this was the little boy who yelled, "Don't shoot my papa any more," perhaps not. History recalls Brewer Koenig not for the golden brew he dispensed, but for the gray lead he received.

END NOTES

1   There is one thoroughly researched but hard to find source for these events. See Faith Fastabend, *William Dewey's Darkest Days: The Murder Trials in Silver City*. Nampa, Idaho: n. p., Third Printing, 2006. She used the actual court records as well as more easily obtained sources.

2   See the chapter on William Sommercamp for background on the brewery. The alley was originally a steep narrow extension of First Street. In 1890 Al Meyers, a teamster, killed Dan Chrisman, who had defeated him for election as constable, in that alley. William Borah defended Meyers and got a hung jury. It was Dead Man's Alley once again. See Helen Nettleton, *Interesting Buildings in Silver City, Idaho*, Homedale, Idaho, Revised Edition, 1994, p. 40.

3   Julie Welch, *Gold Town to Ghost Town*, p. 51.

4   Ernie White, "Empire's End," *Incredible Idaho*, Vol. 5, No. 3, Winter 1973-74, p. 21.

5   Helen Nettleton, *Interesting Buildings in Silver City Idaho*, (unpaginated). The early newspaper reports all misidentified Koenig as "King."

6   Julie Welch, *Gold Town to Ghost Town*, p. 45.

7   Faithe Turner, "Col. W. H. Dewey and the Dewey Palace," *Twentieth Biennial Report of the State Historical Society*, 1945-1946, pp. 129-131.

8   Vardis Fisher, *Idaho Lore: Prepared by the Federal Writer's Project of the Work Projects Administration*, Caldwell, Idaho: Caxton Printers, 1939, p. 22.

9   Fastabend, Faith. *William Dewey's Darkest Days: The Murder Trials in Silver City*. Nampa, Idaho: n.p., third Printing, 2006. p. 2.

10 Julie Welch, *Gold Town to Ghost Town*, p. 45.

11 Welch, *Gold Town to Ghost Town*, p. 45.

12 Welch, *Gold Town to Ghost Town*, p. 53, *Gold Town to Ghost Town*, p. 45.

14 Fisher, *Idaho Lore*, p. 22.

15 Fastabend, Faith. *William Dewey's Darkest Days: The Murder Trials in Silver City*. Nampa, Idaho: n.p., Third Printing, 2006. p. 5

16 Female boarding house was the euphemism for bordello used on the city maps of the day.

17 *Ketchum Daily Keystone*, Ketchum, Idaho, 8 August 1884, p. 3, c. 1.

18 *Ketchum Daily Keystone*, 8 August 1884, p. 3, c. 1.

19 Welch, *Gold Town to Ghost Town*, pp. 49-51.

20 *Idaho Tri-Weekly Statesman*, Boise, Idaho, 7 August 1884, p. 3, c. 1.

21 *Idaho Tri-Weekly Statesman*, 23 September 1884, p. 3, c. 4.

22 *Idaho Tri-Weekly Statesman*, 2 October 1884, p. 3, c. 3.

23 Fastabend, Faith. *William Dewey's Darkest Days: The Murder Trials in Silver City*. Nampa, Idaho: n.p., Third Printing, 2006. p.8.

24 Fastabend, Faith. *William Dewey's Darkest Days: The Murder Trials in Silver City*. Nampa, Idaho: n.p., Third Printing, 2006. p. 9.

25 *Idaho Tri-Weekly Statesman*, 4 October 1884, p. 3, c. 1.

26 *Idaho Tri-Weekly Statesman*, 7 October 1884, p. 3, c. 2.

27 Welch, *Gold Town to Ghost Town*, p. 48.

28 *Idaho Tri-Weekly Statesman*, 10 July 1880, p. 3, c. 2.

29 *Idaho Tri-Weekly Statesman*, 19 February 1885, p. 3, c. 1. *Boise City Republican*, Boise, Idaho, 21 February 1885, p. 1, c. 1.

30 *Idaho Reports*, vol. 2, 1881-1890, p. 83.

31 *Idaho Tri-Weekly Statesman*, 5 May 1885, p. 1, c. 5.

32 *Idaho Tri-Weekly Statesman*, 16 May 1885, p. 3, c. 1.

33 Welch, *Gold Town to Ghost Town*, p. 49.

34 Rafe Gibbs, *Beckoning the Bold*, Moscow: University of Idaho Press, 1976, p. 86.

35 White, "Empire's End," *Incredible Idaho*, Winter, 1973-74, p. 22.

36 White, "Empire's End," *Incredible Idaho*, Winter, 1973-74, p. 22.

37 *Evening Capital News*, Boise, Idaho, 28 May 1902, p. 8, c. 5.

38 *Idaho Daily Statesman*, 6 March 1912, p. 1, c. 2-3.

39 *Nampa Leader-Herald*, Nampa, Idaho, 25 June 1918, p. 1, c. 3.

13

ALBERT KRAPF

Denounced as "First Class Bilk"

ALBERT KRAPF WAS A SHOOTING star on the Idaho brewing scene: he arrived in a flash of high expectation and left under a cloud of failure and wasted potential.[1] The local press first heralded Krapf as a Cincinnati brewer of vast experience who was making an excellent quality of beer and porter at the brewery in Bonanza, Idaho, owned by Frank Gindorff.[2] He gave the *Yankee Fork Herald* crew a dozen bottles of beer that September of 1879 and won their praise for the beer and himself.[3] They even believed that they could taste a Cincinnati twang in the beer.

As summer ended and the snows of winter began to threaten in 1879, mining, and hence beer sales, slowed to a trickle and Krapf left, announcing Salt Lake as his destination.[4] As 1880 began, Krapf was back in Bonanza with tales of riding the Union Pacific all over Wyoming and Utah, and even brewing a while in Rawlins, Wyoming.[5] Krapf intended to open a brewery at the mouth of Eight Mile Creek and be in business when the spring thaw allowed a resumption of business. Krapf had bought brewery equipment and supplies and journeyed to Challis, Idaho, to give directions for their shipment from there to Custer.[6] Krapf then changed his mind and schemed to put his brewery at the Wood River mines (Hailey and Ketchum, Idaho, area), instead of at Yankee Fork. This changed again. By April, he was in partnership with John Mosler and they were in Custer grading a 60 by 18-foot spot on "the flat above Major Brookey's" for a brewery site.[7]

The brewery was to include a harbor 20 by 50 feet off of the Yankee

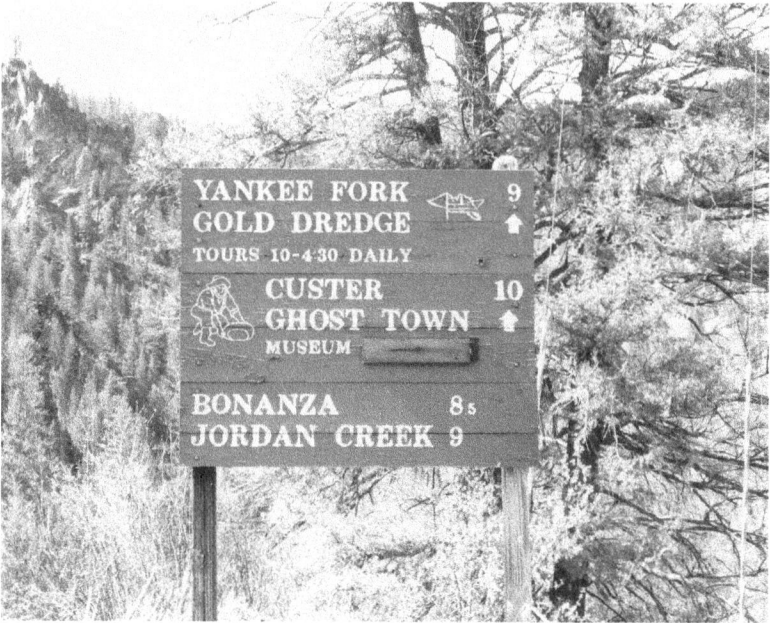

46. Yankee Fork towns.

Fork River which would "make it pleasant for visitors."[8] They opened the new Star Brewery Saloon by July 4, offering beer and cigars.[9] An early ad mentioned lager beer, bottled beer, cream ale, and porter.[10] This list indicates the influence of an Eastern brewer. It is beyond the one-style-fits-all philosophy of most small Western brewers of the time. Later that month, the local paper pronounced the beer superior to any of the imports, and a large amount was being sold for home consumption.[11] The press also said bock beer would be for sale by the middle of May, which is strange statement to make in July. Mosler and Company (the "company" in the name was Krapf) received 8,000 pounds of malt and hops in July.[12] They had big plans.

When the U.S. Census recorder for 1880 located Krapf that summer, he was 25 years old, a brewer, born in Texas of a Bavarian father and Prussian mother, and living with George Mosler and Anthony Lovett. Quickly things changed. By September of 1880, Krapf had hot-footed it out of the area denounced as a "pretend brewer," "a first-class bilk," and a "confidence man."[13] The newspaper said he owed them money, owed nearly everyone money and had treated John Mosler as "no honorable man would." I have found no more as to where he went next or what he did to invoke such rath from the newspaper editor. Albert Krapf's initial burst of light was over and there was a darkness of regrets in its place. Gambrinus must have hung his head over this disciple.[14]

END NOTES

1   Some sources spell the surname Kropf.

2   Yankee Fork Herald, Bonanza, Idaho, 14 August 1879, p. 3, c. 1.

3   Yankee Fork Herald, 4 September 1879, p. 3, c. 3.

4   Yankee Fork Herald, 18 October 1879, p. 3, c. 2.

5   Yankee Fork Herald, 3 January 1880, p. 3, c. 3. G. Fischer and Co. was the only brewery in Rawlins that year. See Bull, Friedrich and Gottschalk, *American Breweries*, p. 350.

6   Yankee Fork Herald, 7 February 1880, p. 3, c. 4.

7   Yankee Fork Herald, 3 April 1880, p. 3, c. 5.

8   Yankee Fork Herald, 1 May 1880, p. 3, c. 3.

9   Yankee Fork Herald, 3 July 1880, p. 3, c. 3.

10   Yankee Fork Herald, 17 July 1880, p. 2, c. 3.

11   Yankee Fork Herald, 24 July 1880, p. 3, c. 4.

12   Yankee Fork Herald, 31 July 1880, p. 3, c. 4.

13   Yankee Fork Herald, 25 September 1880, p. 3, c. 2.

14   An Albert Krapf applied for a Civil War pension in Texas in 1904. Our subject was possibly too young to have been in the war. This might be a relative.

14

JOHN J. MANUEL

Nez Perce War Victim

BREWING IS SUPPOSED TO BE the precursor of civilization; an urban manufacturing business that arrives on a frontier when peace with the natives has been achieved and the local settler population has progressed enough to grow the raw materials and then grown enough in population to absorb the finished product of the brewer's art. Jack Manuel's story proves that such a generalization was not the only possibility. Sometimes brewing arrived before conditions had settled down, and a brewer could face unexpected dangers and challenges.

In Warren, Idaho, in 1864, again safely in the home of her parents, 16-year-old widow Mrs. Jeanette Popham Williams, struggled to deal with her memories of the murder of her peace officer husband. She soon met John J. "Jack" Manuel, brewery owner, saloonkeeper, politician, and man of many other talents and interests and they quickly formed a strong attachment.[1]

The story quickly spread around that Manuel was engaged to the pretty little widow.[2] Mrs. George (Margaret) Popham strenuously objected to her daughter's proposed second marriage. Margaret was a diminutive woman, but held a lot of influence among the miners and was a formidable obstacle. The local Justice of the Peace, Judge C.A. Sears, was the court of first and last resort on all matters of jurisprudence, civil and criminal. To add zest to a volatile situation, the judge fell in love with the little widow too. Mrs. Popham thought he would make a better match for her daughter, and the two conspired to defeat the wishes of the happy couple by interdicting the marriage ceremony. Jack Manuel was not a man to be thwarted so easily.

He took the idol of his heart and sought out the jealous judge. Manuel said: "Judge, we have come here to be married. We are of legal age and we make the demand. It is your legal duty to perform the ceremony. I helped make you judge. You are the public servant of your constituents and you have no legal right to refuse to perform a legal duty that is demanded of you. Now proceed to make us man and wife."

The judge mildly protested, but Jack pulled his gun, and changing his pleading tone to one of command, said: "Proceed now, or I will cause a vacancy in the office and see that it is filled by a man who is willing do his duty." At this stage, Mrs. Popham burst into the office, a big revolver in her hand also. She was hunting for Manuel. She presented the gun and demanded the return of Jennie to her parents' home. At this stage, Major Sanderson, the local banker, who just happened to be passing by, entered the room and disarmed the infuriated mother. The banker also believed the judge was a public servant, so he restrained the mother, while Manuel compelled the judge to perform the ceremony that joined him for life to the woman he loved. John J. Manuel, 39, and Jeanette D. Popham Williams, 16, were united in the sight of God and man and the Territory of Idaho.[3]

John Manuel was born in Virginia in 1826; by 1850, he was still living with his three sisters, five brothers, and his father, John, and mother, Nancy, in Page County, Virginia. He moved with his family of nurture to Missouri in the early 1850s, and then in 1852 took off alone for California.[4]

In July, the 1860 U. S. Census recorded that J. J. Manuel was a miner with $700 in personal estate living in Yreka, Siskiyou County, northern California.I next located Manuel when he was still a miner impaneled on the Grand Jury of the Court of Sessions for Siskiyou County, California, in October of 1861.[5] John had apparently moved on by March of 1862, as a Mr. John Brochtlow was reportedly washing up old tailings from Manuel's claim in the western part of Yreka City when he found a solid piece of pure gold weighing five ounces plus

11 dollars.[6] The town of Yreka City paid Manuel the $10 they owed him for an unspecified reason while approving all their bills during that March of 1862.[7] He eventually went to Florence, Idaho County, Washington Territory, when the gold boom was at its loudest in 1862. By September of 1865, Jack Manuel and Co. paid federal tax on their diggings at Moore's Creek, in Boise Basin, near Idaho City, far south of Florence. Manuel later went on to Warren's Diggings, and participated in the great gold rush there by operating businesses, including a brewery, and being elected to public offices.

While his new family continued to live in Warren, Manuel was elected County Recorder for Idaho County, Territory of Idaho, and he took office 23 April 1866. His oath of office was signed by C. A. Sears, Justice of the Peace of Warren Precinct.[8] Doubtless, no revolver was needed to compel Sear's signature that time. Also in 1866, Manuel was elected sheriff. Manuel owned stock, which he wintered on Salmon River at Slate Creek at a much lower altitude than Warren.[9] Being a sheriff, brewer, and stock man simultaneously was not that unusual on the frontier, where men of talent were often pressed into service in several fields simultaneously.

On April 18, 1867, John's wife, Jeanette, then about 19 years old, gave birth to their first child, a daughter they named Julia. The next

47. Mount Idaho Hotel of Loyal P. Brown.

year, 1868, new Poppa John did not run for sheriff but was elected District Attorney for Idaho County.[10]

The Idaho City newspaper published "Sketches of Travel in Idaho" in the summer of 1868.[11] The reporter's description of Warren provided some great insights into Manuel's life there. The reporter said the people of Warren "uniformly have their time-pieces one hour fast of mean time, and this practice is maintained, so we were informed, in order to ensure the earliest commencement hour of labor in the diggings all about there, and to cause the boarding house and restaurant folks to have early breakfast for the miners. One or two reckless wags said the time was kept an hour fast so the hurdy dancers could start in at an earlier hour than the true time would show..." Beside idiosyncratic time-keeping the camp boasted 70 occupied buildings, mostly stores, saloons, shops, and tenements, a good bath house, an excellent restaurant, a barber shop, two hurdy houses, the banking house of Major Sanderson ..." On the afternoon of August 1, this traveling journalist reported that a radical congressional candidate came to Warren with S. S. Fenn, Democratic candidate for Prosecuting Attorney. "In the evening, a large meeting of the citizens of the camp and its vicinity was held in the open street in front of Manuel & Hunicut's and political speeches were made." Jack had a partner in his saloon business at this time, no doubt.

RICHSON & HANSON,   Moscow, Idaho.

48. Maggie Manuel with husband and family.

J. J. Manuel was selected to attend the Democratic Territorial Convention as a delegate from Idaho County in late April of 1870.[12] Also in 1870, Jeanette gave the family another daughter with the birth of Margaret (Maggie) on September 8.[13]

The 1870 U. S. Census located 14,999 Idaho citizens—later, the number was changed to 17,804 due to the unclear location of the Utah-Idaho border. The large populations of the gold rush had moved on, and these few remaining people had intentions to stay much longer than their predecessors; they were true settlers. The enumeration listed Manuel as a 43-year-old hotel keeper in Warren with real estate of $1,000 and a personal estate of $2,800. Both his parents were native born. Jeanette was only 21 years old. Julia A. was 2 and born in Idaho, and widower George Popham (Jeanette's father) was a steward in the Manuel hotel. About this time, Raymund Saux bought the Warren brewery from Manuel.

No photograph or drawing of Manuel's brewery has been located, but the distinct impression is that it was a small operation in the same building as his saloon. In 1872, after Warren became county seat for Idaho County, John was elected County Treasurer.

49. Pin made from Jeanette Manuel's earring.

Brewers were always considered financially trustworthy. On January 10, 1873, "J. J. Manuel and wife" sold the Idaho Hotel building in Washington (Warren) to George Church for $1,000.[14] The recorder wrote that he questioned Jeanette separately and out of the hearing of John Manuel and she freely agreed to the sale.

On 7 July 1873, R. Hurley sold J. J. Manuel 600 feet of the Rescue Gulch for $300.[15] This was a mining claim and Jack was involved with it for years. On 23 September, A. J. (Ad) Chapman sold Manuel 320 acres—along with all tools and misc.—on White Bird Creek for $1,500.[16] This was the ranch where the Manuels would soon move, and was only a few miles from the area where he formerly wintered his stock.

In the U. S. Court of Claims.

December Term, 189 *0*.

No.*3496* INDIAN DEPREDATION CASES.

John Bower - Administrator of the estate of
John J. Manuel, deceased

vs.

THE UNITED STATES, AND

The Nez Perces INDIANS.

PETITION.

To the Honorable Court of Claims of the United States:

The petition of *John Bower, Administrator of the estate of John J. Manuel deceased* respectfully represent that *he is a resident of Idaho County, in the State of Idaho, and that the said John J. Manuel was native born, and was all his life a*

citizen of the United States.

Your petitioner further states that *the said John J. Manuel* was the sole owner of the following described property, of the value as herein stated, which was, without just cause or provocation, taken or destroyed by the *Nez Perces* Indians, on or about the *12th* day of *June* 187*7*, in *Idaho* County, in the State of *Idaho (then Territory)*, and not returned or paid for, to wit:

50. *Court of Claims petition.*

The Warren community celebrated the season on the 23rd of December 1873 with a ball at the "fine hall of J. J. Manuel."[17] Five ladies were in attendance—three of which danced—and about 50 gentlemen. Women were a rare commodity. Many individuals provided music, and at 11 o'clock they had a large supper. They resumed dancing after their refreshment and continued on until four in the morning. On the 31st, they repeated the whole activity to celebrate the New Year.

In late Spring of 1873, the Modoc Indian War in California was credited by the White settlers with arousing old feelings of revenge in the Nez Perce. Supposedly, the Idaho Native Americans were neglecting their crops and riding through the country that year attending councils as never before. The long-standing problem of Chief Joseph's band clinging to the Wallowa Valley of Oregon despite illegal efforts to move them was also creating unrest and fear. The settlers' response was to organize defense companies. In Warren, Major A. H. Sanderson, the man who kept Mrs. Popham from shooting Manuel, acted as recruiting officer and soon had 119 names listed for service.[18] Future Idaho governor, Norman B. Willey, who was the de facto newspaper correspondent for the *Idaho Signal* of Lewiston, described in a tongue-in-cheek way some of the notable military neophytes of the "Washington Guards." "Sergeant Manuel answers to the call in a manner to be seen in none but the bravest of the brave, in defense of a dear and affectionate wife and loving children." The new Warren brewer, Raymund Saux, was a corporal in the force.

Former Lewiston, Idaho, and Yreka, California, brewer, Godfrey Gamble, lost ownership of the Rescue Mine at Warren in an Idaho Supreme Court decision in 1873, necessitating a corporation of local men be set up to develop the mine.[19] Alonzo Leland was the primary owner, but 26 names, including J. J. Manuel, Raymund Saux, N. B. Willey, and C. A. Sears were listed on the incorporation papers. The mine was already well developed with a main shaft, tunnels off of it, track for carts laid in the mine, blacksmith shop, boarding house, and steam-powered stamp mill. Over $74,000 had been taken from the mine by its previous presumptive owners.

That same year, Jack, Jeanette, both daughters, and Jeanette's widowed father, George, moved to a ranch on White Bird Creek several miles upstream from its confluence with the Salmon River, and upstream from the present village of White Bird.[20] The night before they left Warren their "friends (and there are many) gave him and his lady a ball."[21] The new Manuel ranch was on the traditional home of the band of Nez Perce led by Chief White Bird. They called the area La-ma'ta.[22] Other bands traditionally gathered at this area too because it was deep in a huge canyon, sheltered from harsh weather.

Manuel was reportedly in partnership with the Honorable Benjamin F. Morris in the livestock business at his new location.[23] Jeanette now lived just a few miles up White Bird Creek from her old friend, Isabella Kelly Benedict. Jeanette at last, for the first time in her life, was living far from a mining camp with its attendant noise, violence, and masculine culture. She enjoyed agrarian rhythms and values instead of those of a mining camp hotel, saloon and brewery. Morning now meant gathering eggs, not cleaning chamber pots. What a relief this must have been for Jeanette.

A letter to the Lewiston newspaper from "Fadden" described the Salmon River area in late spring of 1874, after the Manuel family had been there just a few months.[24] "On White Bird, Jack Manuel is flourishing like a green bay tree, and is making the wilderness blossom like a tulip bed. He has brought in a ditch for irrigating purposes and is now independent of rain. As one of our earliest pioneers, Jack has many friends. All wish him success and hope that now, 'under his own vine and fig tree' he will prosper as he deserves."

Meanwhile, the Rescue Mine in which Manuel owned stock was pushing forward in a seemingly ever-more-expensive fashion. Events at the mine took a bizarre turn in mid-August when the mill was "captured" one night by parties who insisted they had a claim against it.[25] The local opinion was that this was a bluff to induce the current owners to pay some of the debts contracted under the previous owner. The case went back to court.

Though temporarily out of the hotel, saloon, and brewing

businesses, Manuel was not abandoning public life. In 1875, he was elected Idaho County Superintendent of Schools. This was apparently a county level office controlling all the local school districts for this extremely physically large but sparsely populated county.[26] Manuel's obituary said he disliked public service and often refused to be re-nominated, but he certainly had a lengthy, diverse resume in that area.

In the early Summer of 1876, word of the Battle of the Little Big Horn reached settlers and Nez Perce alike in the area of the Salmon River. Any myth of the invincibility of the cavalry was destroyed. The lingering, ever-present fear in the settlers increased, while the boldness of the Nez Perce also increased.

Manuel's ranch inventory for 1877 was impressive. He had, and was continuing to add to, an extensive holding. His house was a 20 X 30-foot frame attached to a 16 X 18-foot log structure with a porch.[27] There was also a barn, granary, and corn crib. That year he had 25 acres of wheat, 15 of corn, and 20 acres of meadow. He had 137 head of cattle, four horses, 90 hogs, and between 300 and 700 chickens, depending on which copy of the inventory one accepts. That made for a lot of early-morning egg gathering. The ranch was idyllic, but the

51. Frederick Brice with Maggie on his back is confronted by Nez Perce men.

pale of possible Indian trouble cast a continual shadow over its joy.

The Manuel family, at this point, was living in two separate worlds. Their ranch with the extended family was a world of safety, calm, and plenty; the outside world had ever-more-violent interactions between the races, which presaged possible murder and war.

The first raiding party of the Nez Perce War—Wahlitits or Wahlietiits (Shore Crossing), his cousin, Sarpsis Ilppilp (Red Moccasin Tops), and his 17-year-old nephew Wetyetmas Wahyakt (Swan Necklace)—stopped at the Manuel ranch on Wednesday, June 13[28],to sharpen their knives.[28] The three young men were traveling down the White Bird hill trail from the Camas Prairie to the Salmon River, and had as yet done nothing wrong. They did not molest the Manuel family at that time, and Jack later reported that he felt no sense of impending danger.[29] The family had good relations with the Indians, and the Nez Perce were frequent visitors. The Manuel's foot-powered sharpening stone was greatly admired. This triad intended revenge, and they spilled the first blood of the war later that evening.

After Samuel Benedict was shot at his store on Salmon River and White Bird Creek the following morning, his wife Isabella and their two children that were at home, baby Addie and Frances (Frankie), fled up White Bird Creek a couple of miles to her old friend Jeanette at the Manuel ranch.[30] They passed the James Baker place, and saw Baker's body with many arrows sticking out of his back. Unbeknownst to them, Baker and the Manuel family had already been attacked.

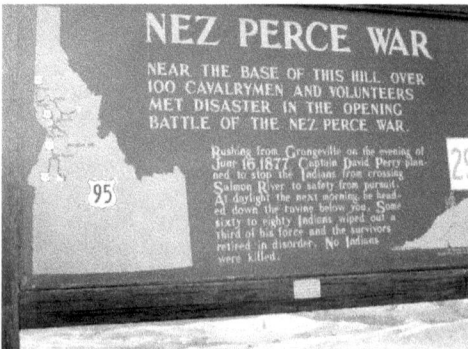

52. Nez Perce War historical sign.

George Popham told his story of the situation at the Manuel home. "I was stopping at Jack Manuel's, my son-in-law's, since last fall. The first alarm we had was on Thursday noon, when we saw the Indians go past. Soon after, Mr.

Baker came to Manuel's and told us that three Indians had shot Sam Benedict in the legs. Mr. Baker wanted to come to the prairie and inform the people, but Manuel did not deem it was safe for any of them to leave." Mr. Baker went home, and in a short time returned and intended to leave with the Manuel family. Baker, Manuel, Jeanette and children started to go down to Baker's house, and had gone a short way when the

53. White Bird Battlefield.

horses stampeded and Jeanette and son John, Jr. became separated from the others. They were confronted by about 20 Indians. They killed Baker. Mrs. Manuel fell from her horse. Manuel and daughter Maggie were both wounded and fell from their horses some distance away. They crawled into the brush to hide.

The Nez Perce took Mrs. Manuel back to the house and told her that if she would give up all the arms and ammunition they had, they would not kill them. She gave up a Henry rifle and a shot gun.

Little Maggie's memory was different and more detailed: "Our family consisted of my father and mother, sister, Julia, a baby brother 11 months old, grandfather, and myself. With the exception of my sister, Julia, who was in school in Mount Idaho, we were all home when James Baker came to the house and told us that the Indians had wounded Mr. Benedict, and that we had better flee for our lives. They suggested that we go to Mr. Baker's stone cellar, about a mile down the creek, and there leave the women while the men defended the place.

We started immediately, I mounted father's horse behind him, while mother and the baby took another animal. Grandfather remained at the house. We had proceeded about half a mile on our journey when, looking to a hill we had descended, I saw several Indians coming toward us on the run, yelling and whooping at the top of their voices.

"The Indians are coming," I said to father. Just as the Indians appeared, the horses we rode became frightened at the noise and stampeded, separating father from mother. The Indians opened fire on us with arrows, the first arrow striking my left arm near the shoulder. An arrow struck me in the back of the head and glanced and pierced my father's neck. An Indian who had only two cartridges, as we learned, fired at father, at the same time, and shot him through the hips. A second bullet burned one of his ears. Father was also wounded between the shoulders by an arrow. The wound through the hips caused him to fall from the horse, dragging me with him. Our horse had taken us to the top of the hill before we fell from the saddle.

Father saw that our only chance was to roll down the hillside into the brush, and this we did, meanwhile undergoing rock throwing of the Indians. One rock broke my father's little finger, and another struck me on the forehead. The redskins were afraid to follow us, doubtless thinking that father still had his pistols. Very foolishly, we had left all weapons and ammunition at the house, with the idea of showing the Indians we might meet that we were peaceable."[31]

The attackers lost interest and left the area. Jack remained hiding in the brush, scarcely able to even crawl. Grandfather Popham found them and took Maggie back

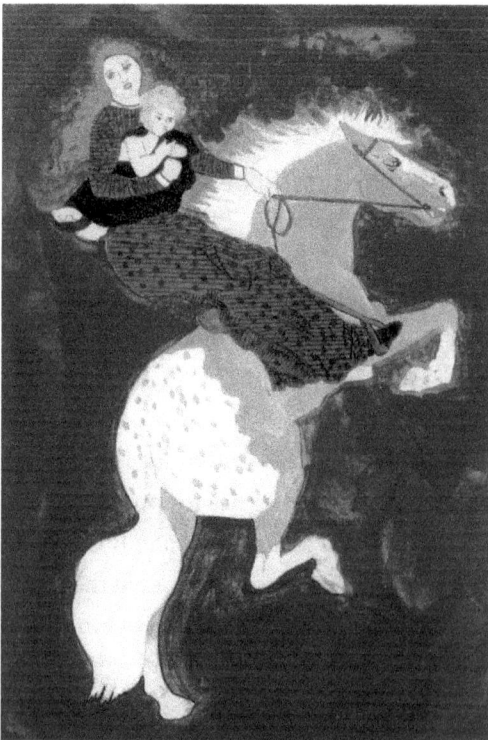

54. Painting of Jeanette trying to flee with John Jr. by Liz Hess.

to the ranch house to be with her mother and brother. The family went from the house to the brush and back again over the next day and a half as they tried to avoid any Indians riding by.

All accounts agree that the Manuel house was burned Sunday morning, June 17. The details of how and why remain elusive. Jeanette and her son were never again seen after that night. The mystery of her disappearance remains to the present day.

Throughout her life Maggie kept a piece of jewelry made from an earring recovered from the ashes of the house and found, supposedly, in conjunction with a piece of skull bone. It was later made into a pin and is still owned by family descendants. In the version of of the story historian Defenbach wrote, the house was described as logs lined with lumber which "must have made a very hot fire" (which cremated Jeanette's body?)[32]

Contemporary writer Duncan McDonald made the most detailed accusations, and they were based on interviews with men who claimed to have been there. He claimed that Mrs. Manuel was hiding in the upstairs loft when the Indians burned the house.[33] After the war, the *New Northwest*, of Deer Lodge, Montana, commissioned him to go to Canada and spend time with the Nez Perce who had escaped there, and then tell the story of the war from the Indian viewpoint. It is unclear just who he talked to and how close to the events those informants really were.

He wrote, "The other white woman was burned in a house with her child. When her husband and others were murdered by the Nez Perces, she went upstairs. The Indians say they did not see her at the time of killing the men. When the Indians got possession of the house, Joseph, Jr. [Chief Joseph] was present.

55. *Monument to soldier who fell at White Bird. Recent research indicates this person died years after the battle.*

He was sitting at one side of the place smoking his pipe. He was asked by the warriors what should be done—whether they should set fire to the house or leave without destroying it. All this time, the woman and child were upstairs, but the Indians say they did not know it. Young (Chief) Joseph answered, "You have done worse deeds than burning a house. You never asked our chiefs what was best to be done. You have murdered many men and not asked advice of your chiefs. You can do as you please about the house."

"Some of the young men lit a match and set fire to the building. They then went back a little and sat down to watch it burn. They were suddenly startled by the piercing screams of a woman in the second story if the house. Young Joseph ordered them to put out the fire. The young Indians ran down to the water, filled their hats, threw it on the flames, and tried every way they knew to extinguish the fire and save the woman. But it was too late. She and her child perished.

The same young warriors who were with Joseph, Jr., at the time told me that when he left the place, Joseph held down his head for a long time and, at last looking up, he said they had done very wrong in burning the woman, that he was very sorry, that he had believed the house empty.

The burning of this poor, harmless woman looks very bad for the Indian side. Still, there is some blame that should attach to the white man. The white man does wrong in allowing Indians to have whiskey. It is easy to reply that the Indians take the whiskey away from them by force, but there are many whites who are ready to sell

56. Monument to the Nez Perce War.

whisky to them in time of Indian wars."[34]

One important detail was that the Manuel home was only one story high. The part about carrying water in hats seems strange since the Manuels' had a well in the yard and the creek was some distance away. Why would the Nez Perce men carry water in their hats instead of go inside and try to rescue Jeanette if rescuing her was their goal? Whoever related this story to McDonald seemed to be trying to partially exonerate the Nez Perce rather than tell a factual story. Apparently, McDonald's main source was his relative by marriage Chief White Bird himself.

Manuel was listed with the dead in the Lewiston newspaper on June 23.[35] On June 29, the report came out that Jack Manuel was not dead. Reports in Portland and other points contained a report on June 30.[36] This did not name Jack Manuel but said, "We found and brought into camp one of the settlers, reported dead after the massacre on the Salmon River. He is wounded in two places and almost starved. He has now a fair prospect for recovery." The Lewiston newspaper said "J. J. Manuel was found wounded, in the hips and between the

57. Manuel homestead area.

shoulders, secreted 13 days after being wounded and subsisted on turnips and berries, thinks he will recover."[37]

Manuel told a harrowing tale.[38] The first night after the attack (Friday 15 June) Manuel had played dead and two Nez Perce spread their blankets within twenty feet of where he lay. Jack heard their breathing, but was so badly wounded he was unable to move. In the morning (Saturday 16 June), they took a drink of whiskey from a bottle they had and moved away. Jack made a superhuman effort and crawled further into the brush. The braves returned and discovered his warm blanket but did not find him. After five days, when everyone had left the area, Jack was able to reach the arrowhead in his neck, and with the aid of a hunting knife, pull it out himself. He treated the wound with a homemade compress of horseradish leaves.

In September of the year of that hateful war, while the Nez Perce continued to try to reach Canada, widower Jack Manuel sold his ranch to L. P. Brown, who intended it for sheep pasture.[39] Manuel then moved to Mount Idaho with his daughters and returned to the saloon business. He was broken physically and spiritually and never regained his earlier vigor. He was alone and had two young daughters to raise. Nevertheless, this was an ideal time for a move to Mount Idaho, which experienced its greatest growth and prosperity during those next few years.[40]

There was talk later that year, after the war ended in October, of sending Manuel to Leavenworth, Kansas, where many of the Nez Perce combatants were being held, to see if he could identify the man who killed his wife. Since he never went, it seemed he had not been a witness to the burning of his house.[41]

A legend from Mount Idaho seems to describe Jack Manuel. "After the war, a man [unnamed] living in Mount Idaho whose wife and baby were among the victims of the war threatened to shoot the first Indian who came to Mount Idaho. In Kamiah lived a dear old Indian called "Indian Billy Williams" who was the historian of the tribe. He loved the Mount Idaho people and was very eager to see them, but hearing about the threats to shoot any Indian going there, he hesitated for a long time. Every day he would pray for his Mount Idaho friends, and one day he said he must go to see them, "If they shoot me, all right." With

58. James Baker's grave.

a prayer on his lips, he started up the hill. As he came to the top of the hill to enter the town, a man shouted that there was an Indian coming. The man [Manuel?] who had made the threats had his gun raised ready to shoot when another man ran up and grabbed it down, saying it was Indian Billy and "We can't shoot Billy." Everyone was glad to see him."[42]

In 1887, there was a report that Jack Manuel was reopening his Mount Idaho saloon, after some disruption of business, with a fine stock of imported liquors and sundries.[43] Two years later, he sold out to Frank McGrave and retired.[44] He was 63 years old at the time. Manuel was one of six men appointed to set up the Idaho County Pioneer Association in July of 1887.[45]

In May of 1888, J. J. Manuel filed a claim for Indian Depredations with the United States Court of Claims. This court had been set up to hear and pay claims resulting from the Indian wars. They were to make recommendations to Congress and Congress would then have the ultimate financial decision. Hundreds of claims had been filed, but the court claimed the proofs were weak. This was an attempt to provide some substantiation.

A complete inventory of the ranch was given and the facts were attested to by Manuel, George Popham, Charles Rice, Benjamin Morris, and other neighbors. The claim totaled $8,298.50. In the case of Wolvertons, No. 923, the court determined Joseph's band was not in amity with the U. S. on June 14, 1877. Based on this decision, they ruled in the Manuel case that "under Chief Joseph and his allies," by whom the "alleged depredation was committed, if at all, were not in amity with the United States on

59. John J. Manuel's grave.

June 14, 1877 and therefore the claim should not be paid, and the petition dismissed." This was an absurd and insulting finding. The vast majority of these claims filed were dismissed for some reason.

Jack died peacefully at home just after Christmas in 1889. In early 1890, J. J. Manuel was also laid to rest by the family headstone.[46] A Memoriam Resolution was published in the *Idaho County Free Press* by Mt. Idaho Lodge No. 7 of the I.O.O.F. (Odd Fellows) which called him an "active and useful member" and extended sympathies to his family. As his obituary so aptly philosophized: "Time is a stern iconoclast and everything touched by its pallid hands reverts back to the dust from which it sprung." By this time, Maggie was married to W. W. Bowman, and Julia was Mrs. W. N. Knox of Goldendale, Washington.[47] A headstone had been erected at the Mount Idaho cemetery memorializing Jeanette Manuel, although her body was apparently never buried beneath it. Jack's name was put on the other side of the stone. Many other victims of the war were also buried in that beautiful spot in the pine forest.

Manuel's days as a brewer in Warren seemed to be part of an ancient other-worldly past by this time.

END NOTES

1   For a complete look at Jeannette Manuel's life see Ronnenberg, Herman, *Jeannette Manuel, The Life and Legend of the Belle of Fabulous Florence.* Troy, Idaho. HWR Publishing, 2009.

2   *Florence Miner*, Florence, Idaho, 8 January 1898, p. 3, c. 2-3.

3   The first miner's laws were adopted in "Warren's Discovery" on 22 July 1862 according to *Washington Statesman*, Walla Walla, 16 August 1862, p. 1, c. 3. The story of the wedding is from *Florence Miner*, 8 January 1898, p. 3, c. 2-3..

4   On the 1850 U. S. Census John Manuel, age 23, lives with his father John and Mother Nancy and his 3 sisters and five brothers in District 49 of Page County, Virginia.

5   *Yreka Weekly Journal*, Yreka, California, 10 October 1861, p. 3, c. 2.

6   *Yreka Weekly Journal*, 26 March 1862, p. 3, c. 2.

7   *Yreka Weekly Journal*, 2 April 1862, p. 2, c. 4.

8   The original document is in the Manual family collection of Jennie Byington in Pomeroy, Washington. Photocopy in possession of the author.

9   Helmers, Cheryl. *Warren Times, A Collection of News About Warren, Idaho.* Wolfe City, Texas: Henington Publishing Co., 1988. No page numbers.

10 Helmers, *Warren Times,* no page number.

11 The report which follows is from the installment of *Semi-Weekly Idaho World,* Idaho City, Idaho, 29 August 1868, p. 3, c. 1 & 2.

12 *The Capital Chronicle,* Boise, Idaho, 30 April 1870, p. 3, c. 1.

13 Helmers, *Warren Times,* no page number. This source said she was born on the 7th. The family genealogy said the 8th.

14 *Idaho County Deed Book,* number 2, pages 155-6.

15 *Idaho County Deed Book,* number 2, page 174-5.

16 *Idaho County Deed Book,* number 2, page 170.

17 *Idaho Signal,* Lewiston, Idaho, 11 January 1873, p. 1, c. 3.

18 *Idaho Signal,* 7 June 1873, p. 2, c. 2.

19 *Idaho Signal,* 12 July 1873, p. 1, c. 2-5.

20 Helmers, *Warren Times,* no page number. In a 1944 interview Maggie Manuel Bowman said her father was going to go to Chicago when he left Warren but changed his mind.

21 *Idaho Signal,* 11 October 1873, p. 2, c. 2.

22 Bob Painter, *White Bird: The Last Great Warrior Chief of the Nez Perces.* Fairfield, Washington: Ye Galleon Press, 2002, p. 3. Author Painter grew up on a ranch on White Bird creek.

23 *Illustrated History of North Idaho,* 1903.

24 *Idaho Signal,* Lewiston, Idaho, 30 May 1874, p. 2, c. 4 & 5.

25 *Idaho Signal,* 22 August 1874, p. 2, c. 4.

26 Helmers, *Warren Times,* no page number. The former Manuel ranch was a point of reference on the self-guided tour that followed the old highway down White Bird grade just off of highway 95. It was a tour stop number five in the mid-1990s. At present there is a self-guided hiking trail at the site of the White Bird Battle, up the road from the old Manuel ranch.

27 Court of Claims Records, group 123, Case 3496.

28 Wilfong, Cheryl. *Following the Nez Perce Trail: A Guide to the Nee-Me-Poo National Historical Trail with Eyewitness Accounts.* Eugene: Oregon State University Press, 1990. p. 8, 78. There are numerous transliterations of the native names in different sources.

29 McDermott, John. *Forlorn Hope.* Boise: Idaho Historical Society, 1978 p. 5.

30 Grant and Mary were in school at Mount Idaho just as Julia Manuel was.

31 McWhorter, L. V. *Hear Me My Chiefs: Nez Perce History and Legend.* Caldwell, Idaho: Caxton Printers, 1986. pp. 213-4. Wilfong, *Following the Nez Perce Trail,* p. 79. She broke her arm in the fall from the horse and had a facial scar all her life.

32 Defenbach, Byron. *Idaho the Place and Its People, A History of the Gem State from Prehistoric to Present Days.* 3 Vols., Chicago: American Historical Society, 1933, Vol.I, p. 418. The original reporter heavily edited Maggie's words.

33 Duncan McDonald, "Goaded to the War-Path," *The New Northwest* (Deer Lodge, Montana) 21 June 1878, p. 2. McDermott, *Forlorn Hope,* p. 4n. A bit of the background of the author helps to explain his outlook and qualification for doing this research. See William S. Lewis, "Spent Boyhood Days at Old Fort Colville," *Spokesman-Review,* and William S. Lewis, "Indian Mounds of Spokane Country Unique: Angus Macdonald Told of Donation Feast Custom—Stories of long Ago," *The Spokesman-Review,* 19 September 1920, Section II, p. 2. Duncan's father Angus was the agent of the Hudson Bay Company at old Fort Colville from 1852-1871, and in all spent 60 years trading with the northwest Indians. Duncan's mother was half Nez Perce and half French/Iroquois. He knew the Indians he was contacting.

34 Laughy, Linwood. *In Puruit of the Nez Perces: The Nez Perce War of 1877 as Reported by Gen. O. O. Howard, Duncan McDonald,Chief Joseph.* Kooskia, Idaho: Mountain Meadow Press, 1993.p, 239-40. Duncan McDonald, "Goaded to the War-Path," *The New Northwest* (Deer Lodge, Montana) 21 June1878, p. 2.

35 *The Teller,* Lewiston, Idaho 23 June 1877, p. 1, c. 3.

36 *Eureka Daily Republican,* Eureka, Nevada, 29 June 1877, p. 3, c. 2 & 3.

37 *The Teller,* 30 June 1877, p. 3, c. 2.

38 *Idaho Tri-Weekly Statesman,* Boise, Idaho, August 4, 1877, p. 2, c.3.

39 Helmers, *Warren Times,* no page number. *Idaho Tri-Weekly Statesman,* 27 Sept. 1877, p. 2, c. 2. Brown also bought the Stanard steam flouring mill from John McPherson at the same time.

40 Elsensohn, Sister M. Alfreda. *Pioneer Days in Idaho County.* 2 Vols., Caldwell, Idaho: Caxton Printers, 1947, 1951. p. 17.

41 Helmers, *Warren Times,* no page number.

42 Frances Bodine, *Mount Idaho History, Idaho County Voices: A People's History from the Pioneers to the Present,* Idaho County Centennial Committee, 1990, p. 130.

43 *Idaho County Free Press,* Grangeville, Idaho, 17 June 1887, p. 1, c. 6.

44 *Idaho County Free Press,* 31 May 1889, p. 1, c. 6. By 1890 McGrave owned the Bank Exchange saloon in Grangeville.

45 *Idaho Tri-Weekly Statesman,* 30 July 1887, p. 1, c. 4.

46 His obituary in the 3 January 1890 issue of the *Idaho County Free Press* gives many details of his life. Jeanette and John are respectively in row 9, plot 213 and 214, block D-1 of the cemetery. George Popham is in row 9, plot 215, block D-1.

47 On the 1870 Census was J. Manuel, age 74 and his wife Nancy Manuel age 75, both born in Virginia and living in St. Charles County, Quivre, Flint Hill post office, Missouri. Federal *Population Schedule,* page 167, image 23 of 80. These were Jack's parents.

15

RUPERT MAXGUT

Gunfight Victim

F. M. Brown was washing the blood from his face and hands in the saloon across the street from his boarding house when Rupert Maxgut, his landlord, walked over, approached Brown, drew his revolver, and fired. Maxgut missed, but Brown's answering shot went through the former brewery manager's lungs. A long and unpredictable road took Maxgut from being the respected brewery boss of Boise to the cemetery of Goldfield, Nevada.

When Butte, Montana, brewer Henry Muntzer finally closed the deal to buy John Brodbeck's Boise, Idaho, brewery in early 1901, he immediately said that Rupert Maxgut would be his manager.[1] Maxgut had the proper background. Before moving to the Northwest, he had married Lina John at San Francisco in 1888.[2] He was in the Tacoma, Washington, directory by 1891 listed as Robert (sic) Maxgut, an engineer at Scholl and Huth Brewery who roomed at 2327 Tacoma Avenue.[3] Soon after, Maxgut worked at the Claussen-Sweeney Brewery in Georgetown, Washington—later, in 1892, it was incorporated into Seattle Brewing and Malting Company, which became famous for its Rainier brand.[4]

Maxgut was not in the Butte, Montana, City Directory in 1896, but was listed as a brewer for the Centennial Brewery by 1898, which gives an idea of when he arrived in Montana. Henry Muntzer owned the rival Butte Brewery but the men met and admired each other's abilities. The Centennial had been started in 1876 by Leopold F. Schmidt and partner Raymond Saile. Then, Schmidt sold it to Henry Mueller after moving to Tumwater, Washington, to start Olympia Brewing. The Centennial's secretary-treasurer was Louis Best of the family that founded Pabst Brewing in Milwaukee.[5] In 1905, Centennial's slogan was "A Million Glasses a Day-Someone Must Like It!"[6]

On the 1900 U. S. Census, Maxgut was in Silver Bow County (Butte area), Montana. He was 36, having been born on 25 January 1864.[7] His wife, Helen M., was 35, having been born in October of 1864. Apparently, this was his second wife. I don't know what happened to Lina.

BOISE SOJOURN

When Rupert and his wife arrived in Boise from their previous home in Butte, all of Boise was alerted.[8] A reporter from *the Idaho Capital News* identified Rupert Maxgut as the manager of Muntzer's new $50,000 brewery plant when he received a tour in March of 1901.[9] Maxgut was soon known around Boise as "Max."[10]

In April of 1901, Maxgut secured a one-year, Ada County liquor license, with H. M. Hughes and John Nagel as sureties, for the brewery's retail establishment.[11] The Rocky Mountain Bell Telephone Company listed all its subscribers in the *Evening News* in April of 1901.[12] Idaho Brewing Company, R. Maxgut, phone number 25A, was listed. In May, Maxgut went up the mountains to the Boise Basin area to drum up business. He was going to visit the various towns in the Basin and return to Boise through Pearl.[13] His manager job involved many diverse daily activities.

Among the new brewing devices Maxgut had to brag about was an improved water filter, first introduced in Germany but "now installed in all the largest breweries of

60. Maxgut's saloon entrance.

this country, but a little too expensive for the smaller class of breweries."[14] He sent water samples to Milwaukee for testing by Professor

61. Centennial Brewery, Butte, Mt.

Ernest Hantke, the head of the Hantke's Brewers' School and Laboratories of Milwaukee. Hantke's report was translated from German to English and published in the *Evening Capital*.[15] He said Boise's H_2O was clear, colorless, tasteless, and odorless; decidedly alkaline, little if any sediment, little organic matter or sand, only harmless bacteria present. There was a complete list of everything found in the water. Hantke recommended gypsum be added at the rate of one ounce per 10 barrels of water to make it hard enough to acquire flavor and sweetening in the brewing process.

Maxgut was also pursuing business in Nampa during a brief trip in August of that year.[16] Shortly, Muntzer was back in Boise to approve erection of a new five-story brewery building on the Idaho and Sixth corner.[17] By the end of September, the brewery was making extensive improvements to the bottling department too, and rumors were that a new two-story brick building on the corner of Seventh and Idaho was under consideration.[18]

Brodbeck's old plant had not proved adequate for the new century. The brewing company was listed as the 38th richest property owner in Ada County that August with a value of $20,944.[19] In early October, the brewery had a large force of men constructing a "mammoth cold storage building" at the brewery site of Sixth and Idaho streets. The 75 barrels per day capacity had increased enough to demand

62. Centennial Brewing Company.

more storage. The new facility would be able to hold 25,000 barrels.[20] Tom Finnegan had the contract for the brickwork. By November, the value of the brewery had a new estimate of 50 to 60 thousand dollars.[21] Steel beams for the building arrived about that time for the expanding construction.[22]

In September of 1901, several men met with the Boise City Council to see if a license could be procured for beer sales at the State Fair.[23] The German village at the fair had to have beer and wine to go with the Limburger cheese, sauerkraut, and weinerwursts. Maxgut spoke to the council and said if a liquor license was needed, some provision should be made to procure it. The council decided to grant a regular license, and after the fair a rebate on unused time was possible.

On New Year's Day of 1902, the *Evening Capital News* ran a special edition on Idaho business and gave the brewery a large article with a four-column drawing of the establishment.[24] "Coming here from Butte, Mont., in the present year, Rupert Maxgut with the shrewd foresight of the successful manufacturer, saw in Boise the coming great city of the intermountain region and decided to 'pitch his tent in our midst'. Rupert Maxgut, the popular gentleman who manages the affairs of the big Boise concern is secretary and treasurer."

One way Maxgut was increasing brewery business was to sign the bonds for saloonists. He and liquor retailer Leo Grunbaum signed for T. A. Clark of Meridian at the end of 1901.[25] This was a common practice throughout America. It created a semi-tied house where only

63. Maxgut's saloon in 21ˢᵗ Century.

Maxgut's brand would be carried.

At a meeting of Boise capitalists in January of 1902, Maxgut was among those who spoke of the need for road building. He said he realized the importance of a road to

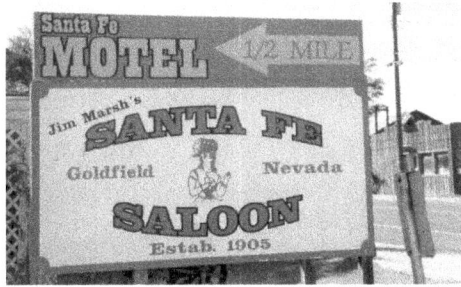

64. *Sign directing visitors to the Santa Fe Saloon.*

Thunder Mountain and the Idaho Brewing Company, which he managed, was prepared to donate $1,000. [26] He said that when he came to Boise, he was advised that there was no market for beer, but he had been expanding his sales territory at a rapid rate.[27] It would benefit Boise and his business to build the road, and every day it was put off, Boise was losing ground. A week later, he repeated his boast at another meeting.[28] "Build the road. My check is ready for $1,000," he said.[29] Both local newspapers then temporarily assigned Rupert the given name of "Emil," for reasons unknown. He indeed donated $1,000 on behalf of the brewery to the Thunder Mountain road fund in April.[30]

In February of 1902, Maxgut went to Glenn's Ferry and Mountain Home for a business trip.[31] Before he could depart, he was among the 10 men on the committee to organize a German social event at the Grand Army of the Republic Hall in Boise.[32] The committee members were John Lemp (brewer), John Brodbeck (former brewer), Charles Leyerzapf, General John Green, Rupert Maxgut (brewery manager), John Nagel, Louis Koehler (former brewer), M. Klinge, Ben Kury, and August Mortiz. They sent out a call for all Germans of Boise to join them at the Grand Army of the Republic Hall for a social.[33] Dancing and speechmaking in the German language were the order of the day.[34] Refreshments were served at intervals throughout the evening. John Lemp made a short address in which he spoke of the pleasure it gave him to see the German citizens all gathered together after so many years, and he hoped the gathering would be the first of

65. Across the street from Maxgut's saloon.

many to be held in the future. Rupert Maxgut then spoke with a well-received talk, followed by a humorous recitation by Mrs. Heuschel and C. E. Kaufer. Maxgut was definitely a member of the German community of the city.

In the magazine *Western Progress*, in a special issue devoted to Idaho, Rupert Maxgut was listed as the Secretary-Treasurer of the Idaho Brewing Company and described as "eminently well fitted for his important position as he possesses excellent business capacity, is up with the times, and enjoys the good will and esteem of the entire community."[35] He remained busy with all his work.

Maxgut went to Portland for a brief visit in March.[36] On the first of April, the German Society of Boise gave an evening of fine entertainment with Rupert Maxgut as master of ceremonies.[37] Later in April of 1902, he had a force of men installing a set of wagon scales in front of the brewery warehouse on Sixth Street between Main and Idaho.[38] Maxgut was also traveling the area—such as a trip to Owyhee County in June—drumming up business.[39] Maxgut was in addition a member of the committee to build the wagon road to Thunder Mountain, and his brewery had paid up their $1,000 donation.[40] At the public meeting to discuss routes and prices for the proposed road, Mr. Maxgut asked if Idaho City intended to give anything for the construction.[41]

The *Statesman* conducted a survey of the opinions of businessmen about what paving material should be used on the streets of Boise.[42] They quoted Rupert Maxgut: "I have not given the matter any attention. What suits the others will be all right."

In May, the Thunder Mountain road question was again in the news. Maxgut did not attend this meeting. A confidential friend said that Maxgut pledged the $1,000 with the distinct understanding that the road would go through Bear Valley. He was opposed to the route selected and would protest the contract with John Pilmer and Company.[43]

That July of 1902, the Idaho Brewing Company filed articles of incorporation. Stock was fixed at $2,000,000 and its purpose was to engage in mining, milling, purchase or acquire mines, power plants, roadways, railways, stores, buildings of any kind. Among the six directors for the first year was Rupert Maxgut.[44]

A special business supplement to the *Evening Capital News* in August of 1902 discussed the brewery and Maxgut.[45] It said that in a few weeks, the company would begin erection of its new brew house and offices—the highest building in Boise—at the corner of Idaho and Sixth streets. Maxgut had met with phenomenal success and shipped beer out of Boise in a 125 miles radius. Their cellars were capable of aging 35,000 barrels of beer. They also corked a high grade of bottled beer called "Capital" for family use. When the addition was finished they intended to brew Lager, Culmbacker, Naortzen, Hofbrau, and other dark beers. The capital of the business had increased from an initial $50,000 to $125,000.

A. J. Volk received a liquor license in September of 1902 to conduct business in the room formerly used by the Ada County Abstract

66. Maxgut's saloon.

Company on Main Street.[46] Maxgut was one of the two sureties on his bond.

The Sons of Herman Lodge held a Christmas night social event in 1902 with Rupert Maxgut as the master of ceremonies who "saw to it personally that everybody had a good time."[47] There was a Christmas tree, presents for the kinder, "no end of refreshments, and dancing until late." Soon after this, Maxgut was laid up with rheumatism for two weeks.[48] He must have overdone the celebrating.

In March of 1903, Mr. and Mrs. Maxgut left Boise to see Europe.[49] They were going first to Milwaukee to see his relatives, and then on to Germany. They expected to be gone two or three months.

When the Maxguts returned in July, Rupert gave a scathing report on conditions in the Fatherland.[50] They visited old friends and relatives and enjoyed it very much, but "he was glad beyond measure to feel the land of his adopted country once more beneath his feet." He said most Germans were poor in the extreme and subsisted on fare that no American of any class would eat. He would not feed his dog what some of the Germans ate. It was painful to see how they try to make ends meet. Meat was a luxury seldom enjoyed and they did not even have vegetables in variety or abundance. "There was more meat thrown away in New York," said Mr. Maxgut, "than the entire German empire ate."

He also said that if people from abroad who are dissatisfied with conditions here should go back home and look around, then "they would be glad enough to get back to the land where people have an opportunity to secure good wages for honest work, and where there is an abundance of good food for every man who is willing to turn his hand over for it."

As secretary and treasurer of the Idaho Brewing Company, Maxgut signed an agreement with the union to make the brewery a union company, employ no one except union members, and abide by union rules. "This was brought about without any strike or ill feeling of any kind."[51]

MAXGUT LEAVES BOISE

Maxgut left the Boise scene and the brewery with little announcement, and his whereabouts were not obvious for some time. However, in September of 1904, a birth announcement in the newspaper said that on August 23, a 12 pound daughter was born to Mr. and Mrs. Rupert Maxgut in Prescott, Arizona.[52]

Maxgut was in Goldfield, Esmeralda County, Nevada, running a saloon and rooming house by 1907-08. I don't know if he was involved with the brewery there, but suspect he was not. Robert (sic) Maxgut was listed on the U.S. Census for 1910 in Esmeralda County, Goldfield Precinct Three.[53] Goldfield, one of the largest and fastest growing gold camps in the history of the West, had the Goldfield Brewing Co. from 1905 to 1908, and the Consumers Brewing Association, with its "High Grade" beer from 1908 to 1911.[54] The Goldfield brewery had steam beer that reportedly tasted rather peculiar. They had a European beer garden where girls from the tenderloin used to congregate early in the evening.[55] In March of 1912, the local brewery was owned by the Reno Brewing Company but was not in operation. A. Mantel was their company representative in Goldfield and he talked of reopening the brewery during the warm months of 1912.[56] Liquor stores, such as the California Winery, retailed beer all the way from St. Louis.[57] Max Stenz, Munich native, one-time associate of Riter's Elite, and later owner of the Carson Brewery was a "leading industrial figure" in Goldfield.[58]

The Santa Fe Saloon was established in Goldfield, Nevada, in 1905 by Hubert (sic) Maxgut, according to their Internet business site nearly a century later.[59] He was killed in a shootout 27 August 1912. The business name-drops with stories of early patrons Jack Dempsey and Virgil Earp. Nearly a century later, in 2010 C. E., it claimed to be the oldest saloon in continuous operation in central Nevada with no end in site. I visited it in the summer of 2002 and saw a vigorous business with an emphasis on its storied history.

The story of Maxgut's untimely death that reached Boise in 1912 described the event in abbreviated form as a pistol duel.[60] Maxgut and a miner, J. H. Brown, engaged in fisticuffs in which Brown was

bruised and beaten. J. H. Brown was washing the blood from his face
and hands when Maxgut approached, drew his revolver, and fired.
Maxgut missed, but Brown's shot went through the saloonist's lungs.
Maxgut left a wife and daughter.

In Goldfield, the story was much bigger and more detailed than
either of these versions would indicate.[61] At 7 p.m. on August 27,
Maxgut, proprietor of the Santa Fe boarding house and saloon at
Fifth Avenue and Myrtle Street, was shot through both lungs at the
Fifth Avenue Saloon across the street from his business. F. M.—not J.
H.—Brown was a boarder at Maxgut's, and had been a miner at the
Merger mines. That night's problems began at the boarding house
dinner table. Brown had left in a huff an hour before the final altercation because Maxgut accused Brown's friend, Jim Hudson, a
blacksmith, of acting in an offensive manner toward a little girl in
the neighborhood.

About an hour later, they met again on the street and renewed their
wordy war. As both men grew vituperative and noisy, Mrs. Maxgut
and several other people came out of the boarding house to the scene.
According to bystanders and Brown, Maxgut got past his wife and
struck Brown a crushing blow to the nose followed by two others to the
head. Brown then struck at Maxgut, but the bystanders separated them.

Bleeding profusely from two cuts on his face, Brown went to the
saloon across the street and got a washbasin and water from the
proprietor, Mr. Cris Tenklesen. Brown put the basin on a chair at
the far western end of the bar counter. As he washed himself, he was
distracted by Tenklesen hurrying from behind the bar. Brown looked
up to see Maxgut, his pistol clutched in his right hand and his left
hand steadying the aim of the weapon, looming in the doorway.

Brown and Tenklesen both dropped suddenly and the bullet from
Maxgut whizzed between them and buried itself into the wall. Mrs.
Maxgut ran into the room at this time. Brown straightened up and
while Maxgut was trying to control his nervousness and aim for a
second shot, Brown shot quickly without aiming. With a scream, Mrs.
Maxgut threw herself between them, but a fraction of a second too

late to save her husband. Brown's bullet struck the former brewery manager's right side, pierced both lungs, and came out just below the heart. Several bystanders caught Maxgut before he dropped, and they took him across the street to the boarding house. Brown put his gun back into his pocket, told Tenklesen to phone for the sheriff, and then calmly continued to wash his bloodstained face.

Deputy Sheriff Bogard and Rod Armstrong, a miner, who was working some claims of his own north of the camp and who was a neighbor of Bogard's, were in the sheriff's office when the summons came. Both hastened to the scene in a taxi and found an animated group around Brown, who was trying to explain the reason for the shooting. Bogard place Brown under arrest and Brown handed over his pistol without incident. Bogard left Brown under Armstrong's control and went to see about getting Maxgut to the hospital. Dr. J. L. McCarthy was already attending to Maxgut, and Bogard helped him put Maxgut into a taxi. Maxgut was conscious on the way to the hospital but unable to speak.

The gun carried by Brown was a Colt and that used by Maxgut an old make of 38-caliber. The hammer was down on the unexploded shell in both men's guns, showing that Maxgut did not have time to pull the trigger a second time before he was felled by Brown's bullet.

Brown, who allegedly was fired from the Merger mine a week before along with several other men for intoxication, spoke freely to the *Tribune* about the incident and maintained he was fully justified in taking the action he did.

"I had nothing against Max until he began to talk against Hudson. 'Hutch' as I call him, is a friend of mine, and I know that the things Max said against him about abusing little girls, and all that sort of business was all rot. I did not have any idea in the world of killing Max. I did not even take aim. I was going to the first show at the Exchange last night when Max stopped me and began to abuse me about 'Hutch.' Then Mrs. Maxgut got in between us, and using his wife for a shield, he hit me three times. I could not stand it any longer, so I punched back. Then we were separated, and I went over to the saloon to wash up.

I carry the gun because several years ago in Missouri I got in trouble with a family by the name of Smith, John Smith, one of the sons, accusing me of wronging his sister. I came out here to escape being killed by them, but I was told only a few days ago that John Smith is still on my trail, and may be hanging around here now in wait for me. I did not wrong his sister, but he and some of his brothers took an oath they would 'get' me and I know they are still after me. That is the reason I carried the gun when I started for the show last night."

Deputy Bogard's statement to the press was: "Brown was at the west end of the bar cleaning the blood off his face when I arrived, 'Give me that gun, Brown,' I said, and he handed it over. Then I took Maxgut to the hospital, then came back in the taxi and took Brown back to the lockup. The sheriff was here when we arrived and he had a talk with Brown."

The previous Thursday, five days before the shooting, Maxgut went to the District Attorney and stated that Hudson and two other men were insulting little girls in the neighborhood, and had actually abused some of the children in an obscene manner. Walsh said he advised Max to have Hudson and the others arrested, but Maxgut declined to swear to a warrant, fearing the publicity might hurt the children. He asked Walsh if the men could not be driven from town, but Walsh advised him that no man could be driven from town unless given a proper hearing. Then Maxgut left promising he would consider the matter of swearing out a complaint against Hudson.

Maxgut was remembered as prominent in Moose circles and that lodge would have charge of the services over the remains, which would be at 2 p. m. on Friday the 30th of August from Dunn's funeral parlor. Internment was to be in the Moose Lodge plot in the cemetery. Maxgut was insured for $5,000.

67. Goldfield, NV, Cemetery.

Doctors McCarthy and Wheeler conducted a post mortem. Justice Barnes, acting as ex-officio coroner, held the inquest. Witnesses to the shooting that were summoned to testify were Jack Roache, Tom Eden, Bob Darty, D. Duboce, C. D. Stauffer, O.C. Bouz, G. A. Miller, Cris Tenklesen, and Louis Schultz.

Brown had lived in the district for about two years, and in the state for a considerably longer period. He had two mining claims near Lida, which he frequently visited. Maxgut was remembered as a pioneer in the camp, coming there in the early bonanza days.

Brown retained H. V. Morehouse of the law firm of Thompson, Morehouse, and Thompson that afternoon as his attorney. No complaint against Brown was sworn out that first day.

At 7 a. m. the next morning, Rupert Maxgut died at the hospital.

The following day, the results of the preliminary examination were published.[62] Declaring the evidence submitted in the preliminary examination was not conclusive enough to demand the binding over of the defendant to the grand jury, Justice Barnes yesterday released F. M. Brown from custody. All the witnesses, including Mrs. Maxgut, testified that Maxgut fired the first shot, and most of them stated that Brown departed for the Fifth Avenue Saloon after the fistfight with Maxgut. A clear case of self-defense was established.

District Attorney Walsh, acting upon information he had received in the past few weeks regarding the mistreatment of little girls by men in the vicinity of Fifth Avenue and Myrtle Street, said he was prepared to make an exhaustive report on the matter at the next meeting of the grand jury to be held in the near future. The district attorney had arranged an appointment with J. A. Thein, one of the parents whose little girl allegedly was an intended victim. After the Maxgut funeral, it was thought probable that Mrs. Maxgut would also be included in the conference, the purpose of which was to devise ways and means of preventing repetitions of the outrages. Mr. Thein would not commit himself on the matter of swearing out a warrant against any of the men charged until he had discussed the matter with Mrs. Maxgut and others of his neighbors.

Since the expose' of the conditions existing in the district in question, neither the sheriff's office nor the district attorney had received a single complaint. It was understood, however, that one of the men against whom suspicion was directed was still in the camp. The talk of a vigilance committee lacked an authentic source, but it was expected that this and other matters would be fully brought out in the grand jury deliberations.

The funeral of Maxgut took place that afternoon with the lodge of the Moose in charge. It was understood that Brown the slayer has forsaken the camp for the Lida where he had mining interests.

Another large article in the *Tribune* the day after the killing explained the "Reasons Back of the Tragedy."[63] The newspaper directly said the shooting was the climax of a long series of alleged attacks on little girls in the neighborhood by men well known in the district, and "in which attacks Brown was indirectly implicated ..." The evidence given at the coroner's inquest yesterday afternoon showed that Brown, the slayer of Maxgut, had on several occasions driven small girls away from the vicinity of his shack on Fifth Avenue, because of rumors that his roommate, Jim Hudson, had acted in an indecent manner toward the little Maxgut girl and several other children of like age in the neighborhood. Brown, not desiring any such imputation to be directed against him, chased the children off the premises. Brown and Hudson, who was said to have fled to parts unknown immediately after the shooting, were fast friends, having rented the shack several months ago in order to be convenient to their work in the Merger mines.

Suspicion had been directed against Hudson, a bartender in the Fifth Avenue Saloon, and an unknown man for some time. It being claimed that the three men enticed the small daughters of Maxgut and J. A. Thein, an employee of the Consolidated Mill living in the neighborhood, and acted in an obscene manner toward them. Both Nichols, who was a witness at the inquest, and his daughter vehemently denied these charges, saying that the only man who had anything to do with the girls was Hudson, and he merely played with them in an entirely inoffensive fashion whenever they came around. The Nichols girl was

11 years of age, and told a story that does not seem to be prompted by intimidation on the part of Hudson or any other person.

Maxgut and Thein, while desiring in every way to avoid the publicity of bringing the alleged assaulters to trial, told somewhat different stories when they waited on District Attorney Walsh In the presence of Sheriff Ingalls. Then Maxgut charged Hudson, Dominick Duboce and a stranger, whose identity was obscure, with illicit conduct toward his daughter, and other children in the neighborhood. Walsh expressed his willingness to swear out a complaint, but Maxgut asked if the matter could not come up before the grand jury and be disposed of in that way. Thein then asked if he could not have his daughter testify in the presence of her mother before the grand jury, but Walsh said the presence of any person other than the witness could not be

68. Maxguts' grave, Goldfield, NV.

allowed in the jury room. The fear was then expressed that the little one, being only 5 years of age, would not be able to tell a lucid story. Walsh said he left the proposition of swearing out a warrant directly up to the men, but they were wary of such a move and finally left. That night, Walsh waited on Maxgut in the Santa Fe Club, and told him the grand jury would take the matter up at its next session. Then the matter was apparently dropped for the time being.

Duboce and Mrs. Maxgut were both on the stand in the inquest, but did not touch on the matter of the little girls being approached. The inquest lasted two hours, the jury at that time fixing the cause of death as a pistol wound, and exonerating Brown from all blame. Judge Barnes expressed the opinion that it was optional with the district attorney to release Brown or demand a preliminary examination. Both Walsh and Senator Morehouse, who represented Brown, stood for the examination, conducted that afternoon. It was expected to end in the release of Brown from custody.

District Attorney Walsh and other authorities were inclined to take exception to the attitude assumed at all times by the Fifth Avenue residents whose little girls had been approached. It was said that the alleged assaults had been going on for over a year, but despite this, the people most interested avoided the courts and the press in the hope that the thing might blow over. "They wanted me to drive the men out of town without a trial or a hearing of any kind," declared the District Attorney. "They were anxious to have the authorities act without warrant of any kind in order to avoid the publicity that they would have stirred up had they acted on their own accord. We were at all times ready to proceed along legal lines, but they would not back us up."

It developed that the direct cause of the shooting was the eviction of Brown from Maxgut's boarding house a few hours before the tragedy on account of an overdue board bill. Brown thereupon went to Mrs. Nichols and secured money enough to meet the bill from her, giving her his promise that he would pay her back as soon as he secured work in the mines. Brown declared that he would board with Mrs. Nichols thereafter, and went to give Maxgut the money due him. After the transaction, the men met on the street in front of Maxgut's place, and the quarrel was precipitated by the mention of Hudson's name.

The local newspaper announced that the funeral of Maxgut would take place the next afternoon from Dunn's Funeral Parlors, thence to the Sacred Heart Catholic Church, where Rev. James Dermody would conduct services. A delegation from the Moose Lodge would be in attendance, that organization being in charge of the arrangements. The internment would be in the Moose plot of the local cemetery.

69. Maxgut tombstone.

On September first, more information was published under the headlines "Girl's Annoyers to Be Prosecuted: Indignant Parents to Force an Investigation-Maxgut Funeral."[64] The witnesses to the shooting appeared before Judge Barnes to verify their testimony from the previous day. J. A. Thein, one of the witnesses, said before the court session that the parents of the little girls who had been annoyed by men in the vicinity of Fifth Avenue and Myrtle Street were to make a thorough investigation of the matter through the district attorney's office. "We are going to get to the bottom," declared Thein. "We have arranged for a meeting with the district attorney previous to the meeting of the grand jury, and we hope that the action taken by that body will put an end to all further complaints and mete out punishment to the real offenders. We are all interested in this matter, and we intend to have justice done as speedily as possible."

The funeral of Maxgut occurred the previous afternoon, and was one of the most elaborate ever held in the camp. The Moose band was in attendance, and 50 or more of the lodgemen turned out. From business manager to gunfight victim was an unexpected odyssey for Maxgut.

Maxgut's grave is just beside the lane through the cemetery and is surrounded by beautiful stones. The Sante Fe Club, a saloon with a Laundromat and motel is at the original site. Along with the other historical artifacts, the newspaper clippings of their former owner's death are tacked on the wall. Goldfield is not quite a ghost town but it is a shadow of its glory days.

A former Idaho Disciple of Gambrinus rests in the sandy soil of a western Nevada cemetery.

END NOTES

1   *Idaho Daily Statesman*, Boise, Idaho, 3 January 1901, p. 8, c. 1. Rupert is nearly the only person known in America with his sir name. A Johann Maxgut is listed as immigrating from Wuerttemberg to America on 15 March 1836. The age makes him a possible father to our subject.

2   Wedding listed in the *San Francisco Call* newspaper vital records, 1869-1891, Internet.

3   MyFamily.com. Internet site.

4   Seattle City Directories of 1889 and 1890 listed Maxgut. W. J. Rule started the Claussen-Sweeney Brewery in 1884 in what is now south Seattle. In 1884 the company reorganized with German brewmaster Hans J. Claussen.

5   David F. Slade, "History of the Billings Brewing Company," masters thesis, University of Montana, 1971, p. 9.

6   Steve Lozar, "1,000,000 Glasses a Day: Butte's Beer History on Tap," *Montana, The Magazine of Western History*, vol. 56, no. 4, p. 47.

7   His tombstone in Goldfield, Nevada, has birth and death dates on it.

8   *Idaho Daily Statesman*, Boise, Idaho, 14 January 1901, p. 4, c. 2.

9   *Idaho Capital News*, Boise, Idaho, 8 March 1901, p. 4, c. 2. 9 March 1901, p. 1, c. 3.

10 *Idaho Daily Statesman*, 1 September 1912, p. 1, c. 2

11 *Idaho Daily Statesman*, 22 April 1901, p. 4, c. 3.

12 *The Evening Capital News*, 30 April 1901, p. 3, c. 1-4.

13 *Evening Capital News*, 7 May 1901, p. 6, c. 1. 10 May 1901, p. 1, c. 7.

14 *Evening Capital News* 14 June 1901, p. 4, c. 3 & 4.

15 *Evening Capital News*, 14 June 1901, p. 4, c. 3 & 4.

16 *Evening Capital News*, 6 August 1901, p. 6, c. 1.

17 *Evening Capital News*, 28 August 1901, p. 6, c. 3

18 *Evening Capital News*, 28 September 1901, p. 6, c. 1.

19 *Idaho Capital News*, Boise, Idaho 15 August 1901, p. 5, c. 5-6. *Idaho Daily Statesman*, 10 August 1901, p. 5, c. 1-2.

20 *Evening Capital News*, 5 October 1901, p. 1, c. 1. The building permit was listed in the same paper on 4 October 1901, p. 1, c. 1.

21 *Idaho Capital News*, 14 November 1901, p. 5, c. 1.

22 *Idaho Capital News*, 21 November 1901, p. 3, c. 6

23 *Idaho Daily Statesman*, 10 September 1901, p. 5, c. 3-4.

24 *Evening Capital News*, 1 January 1902, p. 10, c. 1-6.

25 *Evening Capital News*, 21 January 1902, p. 6, c. 2.

26 *Idaho Capital News*, 23 January 1902, p. 2, c. 7. *Idaho Daily Statesman*, 21 January 1902, p. 5, c. 2-3

27 *Idaho Daily Statesman*, 21 January 1902, p. 5, c. 2-3. *Evening Capital News*, 21 January 1902, p. 1, c. 7.

28 *Idaho Capital News*, 30 January 1902, p. 2, c. 7.

29 *Idaho Daily Statesman*, 23 January 1902. 25 January 1902, p. 3, c. 4.

30 *Idaho Daily Statesman*, 12 April 1902, p. 5, c. 1.

31 *Idaho Daily Statesman*, 4 February 1902, p. 5, c. 4.

32 *Idaho Daily Statesman*, 10 February 1902, p. 5, c. 4. *Evening Capital News*, 10 February 1902, p. 6, c. 1.

33 *Idaho Daily Statesman*, 10 February 1902, p. 5, c. 4. *Evening Capital News*, 10 February 1902, p. 6, c. 1.

34 *Idaho Daily Statesman*, 12 February 1902, p. 5, c. 2.

35   "Idaho Brewing Company," *Western Progress*, no. 17, Chicago, April 1902, p. 62.

36   *Evening Capital News*, 8 March 1902, p. 8, c. 2.

37   *Evening Capital News*, 2 April 1902, p. 6, c. 4.

38   *Idaho Daily Statesman*, 29 April 1902, p. 6, c. 2.

39   *Idaho Daily Statesman*, 29 April 1902, p. 6, c. 2.

40   *Idaho Daily Statesman*, 8 June 1902, p. 5, c. 1.

41   *Evening Capital News*, 14 May 1902, p. 1, c. 6-7.

42   *Idaho Daily Statesman*, 14 June 1902, p. 6, c. 2.

43   *Evening Capital News*, 17 May 1902, p. 8, c. 3.

44   *Idaho Daily Statesman*, 27 July 1902, p. 8, c. 2.

45   The Evening Capital News: Mid-Summer Supplement, 30 August 1902, p. 11, c. 4-5.

46   *Idaho Daily Statesman*, 18 September 1902, p. 3, c. 4.

47   *Idaho Daily Statesman*, 26 December 1902, p. 5, c. 4.

48   *Idaho Daily Statesman*, 13 January 1903, p. 5, c. 4.

49   *Idaho Daily Statesman*, 18 March 1903, p. 5, c. 4

50   *Idaho Daily Statesman*, 11 July 1903, p. 5, c. 4.

51   *Idaho Daily Statesman*, 27 July 1903, p. 5, c. 2

52   *Idaho Daily Statesman*, 10 September 1904, p. 5, c. 2. *Evening Capital News*, 10 September 1904, p. 5, c. 2. This paper said they were living in Phoenix, not Prescott.

53   MyFamily.com. Internet site.

54   Van Weiren, Dale P. *American Breweries II*, West Port, Pennsylvania, 1995, p. 201.

55   Sally Zanjani, *Glory Days in Goldfield, Nevada* Reno: University of Nevada Press, 2002, p. 48-49.

56   *Goldfield Daily Tribune*, 21 March 1912, p. 3, c. 6.

57   *Goldfield Daily Tribune*, 3 January 1912, p. 2, c. 6 & 7.

58   Eric N. Moody and Robert A. Nylen, *Brewed in Nevada: A History of the Silver State's Beers and Breweries*, Carson City: Nevada State Museum, 1986, p. 15.

59   Internet site. Santa Fe Saloon and Motel, Fifth Avenue, Goldfield, Nevada

60   *Idaho Daily Statesman*, 1 September 1912, section I, p. 1, c. 2. Reports around Nevada echoed this abbreviated report. See *Nevada State Journal*, (Reno) 28 August 1912, p. 1, c. 1.

61   *Goldfield Daily Tribune*, Nevada, 28 August 1912, p. 1, c. 1 & 2.

62   *Gold Field Daily Tribune*, 30 August 1912, p. 1, c. 7.

63   *Goldfield Daily Tribune*, 29 August 1912, p. 1, & 4, c. 4 & 5

64   *Goldfield Daily Tribune*, 1 September 1912, p. 1, c. 5.

16

JOSEPH M. MISSELDT
Accident or Suicide?

JOSEPH MISSELDT WAS A LARGE MAN with a large impact on Idaho brewing history, particularly during the 1870s in Boise. The record of his early life remains a bit spotty, but he was born in Prussia about 1833.[1] In 1854, he was in California driving a beer wagon around Moquelumne Hill, Calveras County, and a mule team between Stockton and that place.[2] He was regarded there as an industrious, enterprising, and prosperous citizen.

He came to Boise in 1868 and entered into partnership with baker-brewer-orchardist John Krall in the brewing business.[3] On 14 October 1868, Misseldt paid Krall $2,133.38 with a like amount due in 18 months for lot 5 of block 4 of Boise and the brewery thereon.[4] On 26 August 1870, Joseph "Missal" paid Krall $500 for half of the John Krall brewery and lots 4 & 5 of block 4. Co-owner Mrs. John (Barbara) Krall signed the deed with a mark. The same day, Moses Moritz paid Krall $2000 for half of the brewery.[5] In August of 1870 Krall and Misseldt announce the dissolution of their partnership in the brewery and saloon. Krall kept the collection rights on debts others owed them and Misseldt kept responsibility for the debts they owed to others. "John keeps the old stand, and 'Yoseph' and Mr. M. Moritz will shortly re-open the City Brewery stand."[6] Misseldt was briefly in this partnership with Mr. Moses Moritz.[7] In the business directory published in the *Boise Weekly News* in 1870, only John Lemp's brewery and this one were still in business compared to the many small ones in the early 1860s.[8]

The First advertisement for the new brewing partnership read: "City Brewery Saloon, opposite Curtis Block, Boise City, Idaho Territory. Fine wines, liquors and cigars of the best brands constantly on hand. The best of lager beer, in kegs or in bottles, always ready to be delivered to families in or near the city at short notice. Moritz and Misseld [sic.]."[9] Just a week later, they announced a reduction in the price of lager from $5 to $4 per keg, and bottled beer was $3 per dozen bottles.[10] A very similar ad that emphasized the delivery of beer to families was in the *Idaho Democrat* from September 14 through December of that year of 1870.[11]

Misseldt, Mrs. Agatha Misseldt, and Moses Moritz apparently did not pay John Krall, and he sued them.[12] On the 17th of October, the sheriff was directed to sell their property for the debt. On November 11, the sale was held. Krall purchased the half interest in lot 5 block 4 for $600. On 9 February 1872, Joseph Misseldt paid $775 to Krall and Mrs. Barbara Krall for a half interest in lot 5 of block 4. He apparently owned the entire brewery after this transaction.

By early 1872, there was a comical report in the *Statesman* that since there was no ice on Cottonwood Creek, Joe was going to fill his icehouse with water, cork it up, and let it freeze.[13] He already had one icehouse filled. By

BOISE BREWERY AND SALOON

Main street, opposite Overland House,

John Lemp, Proprietor

KEEPS CONSTANTLY ON HAND THE finest and best brewed

LAGER BEER!

Wines, Liquors and Cigars.

Everything kept is first-class in quality, and those who favor me with a call can rest assured that they will not be disappointed in their expectations. **JOHN LEMP**
Boise City, Dec. 9 1868. tf

CITY BREWERY!

AND SALOON

Main street, next door below Statesman Office.

JOS. H. MISSELD, Proprietor.

WILL KEEP CONSTANTLY ON HAND the best brewed LAGER BEER, to be sold by the bottle, quart, gallon or keg. Will also deliver anywhere in the city.

Having opened this popular Saloon, we respectfully solicit the patronage of the public.

Everybody give us a call.
JOS. H. MISSELD

70. Misseldt Brewery saloon ad.

March of 1872, he was advertising his fermented wares at the City Brewery and Saloon on Main Street, next to the *Statesman* office.[14] This proximity may explain the good relations he always seemed to enjoy with the local press.

In May of 1872, brewer and Turnverein officer Christ Sans sued brewer Joseph Misseldt. The cause was delivered without arguments and the case taken under advisement briefly. I suspect this involved unpaid wages that Sans was due. In a non-jury trial, Mr. Sans received $70.25 in coin by the ruling of Judge M. E. Hollister and Misseldt also had to pay $66.95 in costs.[15]

In May the *Statesman* described Joe as a practical brewer who gave "his personal attention to the manufacture" and "never has bad beer."[16] In fact, they believed it the best ever brewed in Boise—a bit of a slap at John Lemp's competing brew. During July, the press said that the soldiers at Fort Boise were holding a camp meeting at Joe Misseldt's brewery.[17] They did love his brew.

The yearly ice cutting ritual was always good for a bit of press coverage. In 1873, he again filled the icehouse with ice, and then the newspaper printers with beer. The *Statesman* commented: "The boys think it a great blessing to have the printing office located in such close proximity to a brewery, especially when the brewer is such a generous soul as Joe Misseldt."[18]

Joe put an addition on his house in 1873. He wanted to buy the adjacent lot and raise a new brick home, but the land was unavailable so he settled for a frame addition.[19] He soon had the saloon at the brewery repapered and painted too.[20] He had his

71. *Misseldt portrait.*

beer cellar available for those who wanted to cool off, he joked, and a nice lunch available to assuage the pangs of hunger.

In September, Joe won the foot race for the over 200-pound competitors by default when no other runners showed. The local paper said, "Jo's athletic proportions no doubt frightened the others off."[21] This was a not so subtle poke at Joe's massive girth. That October, he purchased the lot between the *Statesman* and his brewery for future use.[22] The site had been a carpenter's shop, which Misseldt tore down. He also made additions and improvements to the brewery itself that fall. The year wore on, and by December it was ice-cutting time again. That year he got permission from the quartermaster at Fort Boise and cut ice from a pond near the garrison.[23]

In January 1874, Joe went to the *Statesman* office to apologize for forgetting them on New Years, and gave them a barrel of beer.[24] In February, Joe built a new cellar to keep additional ice. The *Statesman* said he would "keep his peer so cold dis summer dut it will melt in your mouth just like a lump of sugar."[25] In May, he built a new sidewalk in front of the brewery.[26] Also that summer, there must have been a little trouble with prohibition forces. The *Statesman* predicted the crusaders would arrive at Misseldt's about the time the paymaster arrived at Fort Boise.[27] Joe seems to have been a man of good humor. He once jested that his beer was feminine and that was why the guys like him "so goot."[28] In July of 1875, Joe hauled dirt into the alley by the brewery to divert the water from flowing into his beer cellar, and soon he was digging yet another beer cellar on his endless scheme of improvements.[29] He reportedly said he had to keep water out of his

72. *Misseldt home.*

beer cellar because "he don't vant his peer too vet."[30] By November, it was time for a new barn in the alley behind the *Statesman* office.[31] At Christmas, the press reported their "fat neighbor" Misseldt had received an anonymous box of cabbage leaves under his tree. Joe proposed to reciprocate—if he could identify the donor—with blood sausage, liver sausage, and headcheese once he killed his porkers.[32] Joe seems to have raised swine as a sideline. Spent grain from a brewery makes excellent hog feed, and many brewers raise hogs.

Joe's efforts with the fire department were only rarely mentioned in the press, but at the Fireman's Ball in June of 1876 he was listed as one of the firemen in uniform.[33]

Misseldt also had an interest in horses, mules, and racing. In September of 1876, there was a harness race between Misseldt's brown "Moole" against

73. Misseldt home.

G. W. Sayre's red mule and any other would-be challengers.[34] This was a one-mile race with a first prize of $50 and a second prize of $25.

Before the elections of 1876, Joseph sent a missive to the *Statesman* so cryptic that even a professional historian might have trouble explaining it. Under the headline "Ho! for Salt River" he addressed the editor thus:

> Knowing the necessity of a good substantial craft to convey the defunct candidates up salt river after our next election, I have purchased the gallant monitor (Melvina.) I have thoroughly repaired the gallant craft of all the rotten plank, and caulked and pitched her to prevent leakage, as well as supplied her with all the munitions of defense, with two additional parrot swivel guns and a skillful pilot to navigate her and keep her clear of Mormon's threatening reefs and would dash her asunder. She will be launched today in front of my saloon and anchored by her two best bowers and stayed by two quarter sheet anchors. Captain John Mopps will be placed in command until sunset on the day of

election. She will be launched at 3 O'clock and 30 minutes
P.M. under the gallant display of our national flag and
marine pennants of our country, and a national salute from
our best gun.[35]

Not only was his hyperbole running away at this point, but his
"mooles" ran away that week, but without damage.[36] As April of
1877 approached, everyone was awaiting the hot weather and the
lager beer season. Two reporters said Joe's beer "illuminated their
diaphragms with iridescent scintillations and rainbow colored cor-
uscations," and they pronounced the lager "es muy buena pour le
stomjack."[37] At that time Misseldt advertised new reduced prices:
$2.50 per keg, $2.50 per dozen bottles, 25 cents per quart or $1.00 per
gallon.[38] One newspaper item of 1876 merely said "Joe Misseldt took
a drink of water yesterday."[39] That was rare news indeed.

Misseldt was among a group of men who met to volunteer for the
Nez Perce War in 1877.[40] Joe never got physically involved, but provided
the use of a one of his horses to the military, which was duly acknowl-
edged by Chief of Scouts Orlando Robbins in his report to Governor
Brayman.[41] Perhaps that was just as well for Joe, by then he had reached
a girth that led the press to joke that he can't go swimming because
"all the water goes out of the pond when he goes in."[42] That summer
Misseldt had a new house built at the corner of Idaho and 6th Street.[43]
The foundation walls were three feet high and made of brick, the handi-
work of James Flanagan.[44] The upper portion was to be wood from the
lumber mills of Rossi and Karcher. George White did the carpentry on
the 1 1/2 story, 12 by 36-foot structure with the adjoining 11 by 16-foot
cellar. Misseldt was not fated to enjoy the new home for long.

Fred Bekeart, the carpenter, constructed a pump to drain the water
from Joe Misseldt's cellar. This was not only a simple and powerful
contrivance, but also an ingenious one. It would throw a steady stream
of two or three gallons at least. The press said, a pump after this
fashion would be a splendid thing to clean out wells.[45]

In January of the next year, Joe put a picket fence around his house and began plowing up the yard to be ready to plant trees, shrubbery, and gardens.[46] The *Statesman* praised Joe for his vast amount of work endeavoring to make his home one of the prettiest in town. About this time, there was a theft at the brewery stables by a culprit who took half a set of harness. The press speculated that he would either return them or come back and steal the other half.[47]

Joe's happy, successful life came to an unanticipated end just after this, in February of 1878. One day, brewer Misseldt could not be found, and after checking all around it seemed no one had seen him since the previous afternoon. For some reason, Mr. George White looked in the brewery well, which was in a shed by the brewery. He found Joe's body.[48] There was at least five feet of water in the well and no part of the body was less than 18 inches below the surface.[49] Mr. White believed it an accident, but some speculated that it was suicide.[50] Being such a large man, there was no way he could get out of the well when he fell in headfirst.

The funeral was the next day and orchestrated by the fire department. Reverend Stratton of the Presbyterian Church conducted the service, and a large group of citizens accompanied the remains to the cemetery.[51] Misseldt was buried at Pioneer Cemetery in Boise. His metal plaque reads: Joseph M. Misseld/ Died Feb. 4, 1878/At age 45 Years."

Joseph's will, dated 7 February 1876, two years previously, left everything to his wife and named her executrix.[52] The will was filed on 14 February, and testimony filed on 28 February. A second copy of the will was filed late and finally, on 21 September, the will was admitted into court.

Within a month, the City Brewery with its stock and fixtures was for sale or rent.[53] John Brodbeck of Idaho City brewing fame, who was also the former treasurer of Boise County, quickly traveled to Boise to look.[54] Soon the agent for the sale, Thomas Cahalan, Boise attorney, told the press Brodbeck had indeed bought the property.[55] In November, the widow Misseldt advertised her home for sale.[56] R. Z. Johnson, esquire, of Silver City purchased the Misseldt home on

74. Misseldt grave marker.

6th and Idaho, and became a Boise resident.[57]

On the 1880 U. S. Census, Agatha Misseldt was 54 and lived alone, keeping house. Just over three years from her husband's death, on 24 April 1881, Agatha married Charles W. Roth at the residence of the clergyman A. J. Joslyn.[58]

By 1888, Agatha was again known as Mrs. Misseldt when she was elected to the executive board of the Women's Relief Society.[59] What happened to cause this, I don't know.

Mrs. Misseldt died on 15 December 1898 at the home of her daughter, Mrs. Peter Sonna.[60] She was described as a 30-year resident of Idaho who lived with Mrs. Sonna, her only surviving child. The cause of death was listed as heart failure brought on by rheumatism. She was lauded as a warm friend of the poor who worried about them, not herself, at the end of her life. She was buried in the Masonic cemetery and the service was officiated by Rev. Sharp of the Adventist Church. She was 73 years old.

In 1904, the Pioneer Association of Boise displayed an early bird's eye view map of Boise. Surrounding the map were drawings of houses, and the *Statesman* mentioned that among the houses still standing was that of Mrs. Misseldt.[61] Joe's legacy was not forgotten.

A rambling reminiscence by James H. Twogood in 1908 said of Misseldt: "and old Joe-he, too was a character. He was a member of the volunteer fire department. He owned a span of ponies and his happiest days were spent in driving the ponies up and down Main Street."[62] Joe was another disciple of King Gambrinus who had a tragic and mysterious end to his life.

END NOTES

1   *Idaho Tri-Weekly Statesman*, Boise, Idaho, 7 February 1878, p. 3, c. 3. The name is spelled without the "t" in many sources, including his tombstone plaque.

2   *Idaho Tri-Weekly Statesman*, 7 February 1878, p. 3, c. 3. James H. Hart of

Boise during 1878 remembered knowing Misseldt there at that time

3   *Idaho Tri-Weekly Statesman*, 10 September 1870, p. 3, c. 3.

4   Ada County Deed Book 3, p. 286-7.

5   Ada County Deed Book 4, pp. 136-143.

6   *The Capital Chronicle*, Boise, Idaho, 31 August 1870, p. 3, c. 1. p. 2, c. 3.

7   *Idaho Tri-Weekly Statesman*, 13 September 1870, p. 2, c. 4.

8   *Idaho Tri-Weekly Statesman*, 13 September 1870, p. 2, c. 4.

9   *The Boise Weekly News*, Boise, Idaho, 1 October 1870, p. 2, c. 6.

10 *The Boise Weekly News*, 8 October 1870, p. 3, c. 3.

11 *The Idaho Democrat*, Boise, Idaho, 24 December 1870, p. 1, c. 3.

12 Ada County Deed Book 4, pp. 505-508.

13 *Idaho Tri-Weekly Statesman*, 20 January 1872, p. 3, c. 1. *Idaho Daily Statesman*, 14 January 1912, Section II, p. 3, c. 3. Forty Years Ago Section.

14 *Idaho Tri-Weekly Statesman*, 10 March 1872, p. 1, c. 2.

15 Judgment Records, Ada County, microfilmed records, Idaho State Historical Society. 13 May 1872.

16 *Idaho Tri-Weekly Statesman*, 28 May 1872, p. 3, c. 2. *Idaho Daily Statesman*, 26 May 1912, Section II, p. 3, c. 2. Forty Years Ago Column.

17 *Idaho Daily Statesman*, 28 July 1912, Section II, p. 4, c. 3. Forty Years Ago column.

18 Quote from *Idaho Tri-Weekly Statesman*, 6 February 1873, p. 3, c. 2. Another mention of the ice harvest was 30 January 1874, p. 3, c. 2.

19 *Idaho Tri-Weekly Statesman*, 10 April 1873, p. 3, c. 1.

20 *Idaho Tri-Weekly Statesman*, 15 May 1873, p. 3, c. 1.

21 *Idaho Tri-Weekly Statesman*, 30 September 1873, p. 3, c. 2.

22 *Idaho Tri-Weekly Statesman*, 11 October 1873, p. 3, c. 2.

23 *Idaho Tri-Weekly Statesman*, 23 December 1873, p. 2, c. 1.

24 Arthur A. Hart, "Joe Misseld, German Brewer Knew How to Make the Papers," *Idaho Statesman*, 26 December 2006.

25 *Idaho Tri-Weekly Statesman*, 17 February 1874, p. 3, c. 1.

26 *Idaho Tri-Weekly Statesman*, 12 May 1874, p. 3, c. 1.

27 *Idaho Tri-Weekly Statesman*, 11 July 1874, p. 3, c. 2.

28 *Idaho Tri-Weekly Statesman*, 27 May 1875, p. 3, c. 1.

29 *Idaho Tri-Weekly Statesman*, 15 July 1875, p. 3, c. 1. 20 July 1875, p. 3, c. 1.

30 *Idaho Tri-Weekly Statesman*, 15 July 1875, p. 3, c. 1.

31 *Idaho Tri-Weekly Statesman*, 18 November 1875, p. 3, c. 1.

32 *Idaho Tri-Weekly Statesman*, 28 December 1875, p. 3, c. 1.

33 *Idaho Tri-Weekly Statesman*, 10 June 1876, p. 3, c. 3 & 4.

34 *Idaho Tri-Weekly Statesman* 28 September 1876, p. 3, c. 1.

35 *Idaho Tri-Weekly Statesman*, 17 October 1876, p. 3, c. 2.

36 *Idaho Tri-Weekly Statesman*, 17 October 1876, p. 3, c. 3. Joe, if he was indeed

the author of this letter, seemed to write much better than his speech was quoted, for at least there was no accent apparent here.

37 *Idaho Tri-Weekly Statesman*, 28 April 1877, p. 2, c. 4.

38 *Idaho Tri-Weekly Statesman*, 3 May 1877, p. 3, c. 5.

39 Arthur A. Hart, "Jolly German Ran Brewery," *The Idaho Statesman*, 2 October 1972, p. 10-A, c. 1.

40 *Idaho Tri-Weekly Statesman*, 21 June 1877, p. 3, c. 2.

41 "Nez Perce War Letters," Orlando Robbins to M. Brayman, July 7, 1877. Fifteenth Biennial Report of the Board of Trustees of the State Historical Society of Idaho, 1935-36, p.p. 109-111.

42 *Idaho Tri-Weekly Statesman*, 19 June 1877, p. 3, c. 3.

43 *Idaho Tri-Weekly Statesman*, 23 August 1877, p. 3, c. 1.

44 *Idaho Tri-Weekly Statesman*, 6 September 1877, p. 3, c. 1

45 *Idaho Tri-Weekly Statesman*, 7 August 1877, p. 3, c. 3. A drawing of the Misseldt house is on a sketch of Boise of that era which shows the town in the middle with a border of business and dwelling houses. This was after Joe's death as a sketch of the city brewery on the same drawing shows John Brodbeck as the owner. Brewer John Lemp's impressive house was also depicted.

46 *Idaho Tri-Weekly Statesman*, 31 January 1878, p. 3, c. 1.

47 *Idaho Tri-Weekly Statesman*, 2 February 1878, p. 3, c. 3.

48 *Idaho Tri-Weekly Statesman*, 7 February 1878, p. 3, c. 3.

49 *Idaho Tri-Weekly Statesman*, 7 February 1878, p. 3, c. 1.

50 *Idaho World,* Idaho City, 8 February 1878, p. 3, c. 2.

51 *Idaho Tri-Weekly Statesman,* 7 February 1878, p. 3, c. 5.

52 Photocopy of the will and probate records. Probate Court. Ada County, Idaho. There are two difference copies of the will, one from February and one from September.

53 *Idaho Tri-Weekly Statesman*, 8 March 1878, p. 3, c. 2.

54 *Idaho Tri-Weekly Statesman*, 16 March 1878, p. 3, c. 3.

55 *Idaho Tri-Weekly Statesman*, 26 March 1878, p. 3, c. 2.

56 *Idaho Tri-Weekly Statesman*, 20 November 1880, p. 3, c. 1. The newspaper ad (p. 3, c. 3.) described the house as half brick and half wood, with 4 rooms, well and fruit trees. She was asking $1,200 with furniture and $1,000 without.

57 *Idaho Tri-Weekly Statesman*, 28 November 1878, p. 3, c. 1.

58 *Idaho Tri-Weekly Statesman*, 26 April 1881, p. 3, c. 2. In the 1880 Census Agatha was listed as 54 years old, born in Austria of Austrian parents.

59 *Idaho Tri-Weekly Statesman* 9 November 1888, p. 3, c. 2

60 *Idaho Daily Statesman*, 16 December 1898, p. 6, c. 1-2.

61 *Idaho Daily Statesman*, 20 October 1904, p. 5, c. 3-4.

62 *Idaho Daily Statesman*, 6 December 1908, Section II, p. 5, c. 3 & 4. Mr. Twogood went on to say that Misseldt "built a handsome residence on the corner of Sixth and Main Street, which he later sold to R. Z. Johnson."

17

ALOIS RIID

Bizarre Death of a German Patriot

LOUIS, AS HE WAS KNOWN, was an enigma inside a mystery surrounded by a question mark.[1] I recovered nothing of his early life. Alois Riid arrived in Idaho City during the turbulent early boom days and worked a while at the Pacific Brewery.[2] Messers. Friend, Cunningham & Co. owned the Pacific Brewery in 1864; Zeile & Summers took over later in 1864, and by early 1865 Ignas Huber owned it.

By May 1865, Riid had purchased the brewery as witnessed by his paying a Federal fermented liquor fee; in July 1865, he was listed as a brewer in Idaho City and continued on the federal records paying taxes on his brew for the next few years. For instance, in November of 1866, Riid and Co. paid for brewing eight barrels of beer according to Federal Tax assessment records.[3] Less than a month after, rival Idaho City brewers Herman Fischer and William Meydenbauer dissolved their brewing partnership.

The great Idaho City fire of May 1867, one of three great fires in the town's early days, changed the dynamics of the owners and competitors in the brewing business. After the fire, Fischer announced that he had sold his interest to Louis Riid and John Brodbeck.[4] Riid then went into business with William Meydenbauer and Brodbeck in the Miner's Brewery, apparently while still operating the Pacific.[5]

Meydenbauer and Riid's Miner's Brewery, Bakery, and Saloon was listed as one business quickly being rebuilt and ready to open after the great fire flattened much of the city.[6] They next bought out Herman Fischer, half-owner of the Miner's Brewery and Bakery, and then were

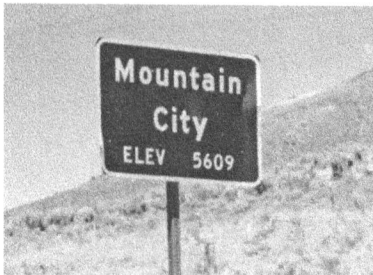

75. Mountain City, NV, sign.

back in business at the different brewery.[7] In another story on June 8, the newspaper confirmed that Riid had bought out Fischer.[8] The first new ad for the Miner's Brewery and Bakery mentioned only Meydenbauer and Riid who had the "intention of sustaining the reputation of the house."[9] Brodbeck may have left the partnership or the newspaper merely failed to mention him. He reappeared later.

In November of 1867, they advertised Russian caviar and Swiss and Holland cheeses. They delivered a gift basket of caviar, bread, cake, Swiss cheese and champagne as well as "something stronger to help it all down" to the newspaper crew and won their praise.[10] As the end of 1867 approached, the newspaper gave more details of what was available to properly celebrate New Year's Day. "They (the brewery) have a splendid lot of rich and handsomely ornamented pound, fancy and fruit cakes, of their own making, and all kinds of confectionery, dried fruits, canned oysters, peaches, &c; and the finest German and Swiss cheeses, Russian caviar, and any quantity of excellent lager, or rare wines and finest liquors to refresh the inner man. Pay their well known establishment a visit."[11] These wares indicate a high level of sophistication and wealth in their customers. New Year's Eve and Day, as 1868 arrived in Boise Basin, was a wondrous moveable party at many locations including the Miner's Brewery and Bakery.[12]

In March 1868, the local newspaper said that Meydenbauer and Riid had opened cases of wines and liquors of prime quality and "to praise the quality of their own brew of lager is simply unnecessary, because everybody who drinks that style of thirst slaker hereabouts is perfectly aware of its excellence."[13]

The Good Templars, an anti-alcohol group contemptuously known as Water Tanks, made some strange impacts on the brewing business as the fad of membership swept the gold camps.

"A novel spree-We learn that even the Tankists yet cling to that frequent ebullition of ripe civilization known among the topers as a spree. But we had better tell at once just how they do it: A reliable informant tells that a few nights ago, in rejoicing over some Tankite victory, a number of the members repaired to Meydenbauer & Riid's Miner's Brewery, there called for five pounds of peanuts and a big bucket of cold water, all of which was placed upon a large table for them in a short time. Around the board this festive crowd gathered, and vigorously began the attack. As disappeared the huge pile of bread before Gourmand, and the small lake before Guzzler, in the fairy tale of Fortune, so disappeared the huge pile of peanuts and the big bucket of cold water, that very frigid, arctic night, before that virtuous and soft shelled, hydropathic party of Tanky revelers. They cracked their nuts and their jokes, and draughts of water and of social inspiration went down together. And to wind up all, sweetly as could be, the whole party ordered a dessert of candy, 'all sorts,' of which about four pounds was made to sugar the queer spree over. The effect of this spree on Maydenbauer [sic] & Riid's brewery we are not disposed to tell. He is not a Templar. What effect it had the next day on those who participated in it, we may never be able to ascertain. But the spree, while it lasted, put squirrels and cattle and the sugar-toothed children far out of sight. We should prefer an old style spree."[14]

The brewery was also a bakery with pies, cakes, bread, etc. as well as a saloon with "prime quality wines and liquors."[15] Those liquors had to come all the way from San Francisco and by team from the closest steamboat shipping spot at Umatilla, Oregon, on the Columbia River.[16] For example, the Miner's Brewery of Meydenbauer and Riid received a large stock of liquor from San Francisco via teams from Umatilla in May 1868.[17] One special treat was genuine English stone ale.[18] In a week the stone ale was sold out, but they refilled the bottles with their own beer.[19] Archaeologists of mining camps should note this custom. Their saloon was called the Gambrinus and was $12.56 delinquent in taxes in November of 1868.[20] The brewery gave another community service. They provided free wagons and horses to take the local children to a picnic outside of town.[21]

In January 1869, the dissolution of the Meydenbauer and Riid part-nership in the Miner's Brewery and Bakery was announced with debts to be paid to the new firm of Riid and Brodbeck.[22] John Brodbeck, a Swiss native destined to be one of the biggest names in Idaho brewing, became Riid's partner.[23] By February 4, 1869, the newspaper ad for the Miner's Brewery said Riid and Brodbeck proprietors.[24] Other ads said, "The bar is always attended to by competent persons."[25] They advertised their steam beer as well as lager.[26] In May of 1869, a newspaper report said the partners had renovated and refitted their saloon.[27] They were still operating a bakery too. That August, Nicholas Haug was added to the firm and its name was changed to Riid and Company.[28] Riid, Brodbeck, and Haug next bought the Idaho Brewery in Idaho City and kept both it and their old Miner's Brewery open.[29] As Christmas of 1869 approached, Riid & Co. at the "Miner's Brewery and Bakery have a fine assortment of candies, cakes, nuts and confectionery, generally suitable for Christmas."[30] Lager beer remained their main product.[31]

FRANCO-PRUSSIAN WAR

Political and regal machinations in Europe in 1870 would prove to have unpredictable repercussions in Idaho and in the life of Alois Riid. First, Spain's Isabella II abdicated the crown. It was offered to Prince Leopold of Prussia, but Kaiser Wilhelm I, as head of the House of Hohenzollern, persuaded him to refuse it. The French were terrified that a Spanish-Prussian alliance would upset the balance of power. France's Napoleon III wired Wilhelm demanding a letter of apology and assurance that Leopold would not accept any future offer from Spain. Prussia's Count von Bismarck made the telegram public to show that Napoleon had tried to humiliate the Kaiser and that Wilhelm had refused the demands. On July 19, France declared war on Prussia and invaded the Saar Basin while Prussia sent three armies to invade France.

Most experts thought France had the greatest army in the world, Emperor Napoleon III was the greatest threat to peace and stability, and the Prussians were in for a very difficult time. The war seemed to have given the Boise Turnverein an issue with enough power to cement the new German American organization solidly together, and all over Idaho, Germans and Frenchmen opposed each other in solidarity with their warring homelands. The Boise newspaper said "it will be seen that the Germans of Idaho are not behind their fellow citizens of the eastern cities in sympathy for their kindred in the struggle through which they are now passing."[33]

In August of 1870, there was a major announcement in Idaho City that "Louis Reid" had started for the Fatherland to join the Prussian army. The newspaper wished "to see him return safe and sound when the war closes."[34] He would take stagecoaches south to Nevada and then take the Union Pacific east for connections on an Atlantic port. Far sooner than the close of the war news came about Riid's journey.

On August 11, the Idaho City paper carried an amazing story.[35] A letter from newspaper editor, Mr. Yates, in Mountain City, Nevada, explained that before reaching Mountain City, Riid had jumped from the stagecoach on which he was riding two or three times but each time the driver persuaded him to get back in.[36] Finally, early in the morning, about three miles from town he jumped out again and ran down a gulch and could not be located. In the afternoon, long after the stage arrived in town, deputy sheriff L. Jackson went out to search for him and found him in a dying condition. He expired shortly. Among the effects found on Riid was a certificate from Charles De La Baume, secretary of the M. Company at Rocky Bar and signed by a Mr. Leonard of that office. This was so he could get funds back East. He also had a ladies watch, enameled and set with diamonds with a chain attached. In addition he had two gold bars, made by Dickinson of Idaho City, worth $1,400 and $988, another small gold bar also made by Dickinson, and $40.50 in coin. He had an address supplied by Nick Haug for some people in Germany for him to see. Riid's money was put

76. Mountain City main street.

in trust in the bank of H.M. Grant and an inquest by Justice Steinburn was scheduled. Yates wrote similar letters to John Brodbeck and Louis Wilhelm of Idaho City. Brodbeck left for Mountain City to see what he could do for his old friend and partner.

The Mountain City newspaper is not extant but the papers of Elko, Nevada, which was just down the stage line 70 miles, carried the story from their own perspective. The *Chronicle* labeled him an insane man and said he ran into the willows on the Owyhee River, which made him difficult to find.[37] A Mr. Cutler accompanied Jackson when Riid was found. Riid died a few minutes later, but not before he turned his money over to them. The paper said he was reportedly worth $20,000. The Masonic order of Mountain City buried their fellow Mason according to their rites.

The Elko Independent referred to the incident as a melancholy death.[38] They said that when the body was brought to town, an inquest was held and the ruling was that death was caused by "congestion of the brain, caused by exposure." An interesting addendum from this source was that his valise had not been found. They mentioned that he also had a valuable watch and chain. Many friends and Masonic brethren recognized his body. Mountain City must have had a large contingent of former Idaho City residents.

When Brodbeck arrived, the estate questions were also covered in the Nevada newspapers.[39] The Elko *Chronicle* said Brodbeck found Riid's money deposited in the bank at Mountain City. Brodbeck was representing Mr. Lauer, who was the administrator of the estate back in Idaho, and claimed the right to take possession. The question was whether it

77. Owyhee River just outside of Mountain City, NV.

could be taken back to Idaho without going through a long legal process. Deputy Sheriff Lycurgess Jackson felt he had the right to give it to Brodbeck since he had received it from Riid before his death. The newspaper hoped the money could be returned without doing "violence to the law."

They went on to say that their acquaintance with Mr. Brodbeck and knowledge of his business affairs indicated he is "incapable of claiming anything that does not properly belong to him; and that he is perfectly responsible, morally and legally, for many times the amount in question." They went on to say the Elko County authorities were right to be guarded in their actions.

Two weeks later, Brodbeck was back in Idaho City and he explained all he knew in the *Idaho World*.[40] John thought that Riid could have been saved if someone had gone for him more quickly. Riid had wandered around in the sun all day without a hat. The Public Administrator of Elko County had taken charge of the money Riid carried, but Brodbeck expected administrative expenses to take most of it.

Riid had seemed perfectly normal, sane, and healthy when he left Idaho City. What caused his problem? Stress due to the trip or the anticipated military service at its end is a possible cause. Was he perhaps poisoned by the food or drink on the trip, or just irrational from the exhaustion of riding all night in the dusty, bumping conveyance? I know nothing of his family history, his age, or background, and this story of jumping from the stage and dying strains credulity. Auf Wiedersehn, mein freund!

END NOTES

1   Though few sources are available, Riid's name is variously spelled Rud, Reid, Ridd, and he was usually called Louis, not Alois. In August 1865 he brewed 15 barrels of beer; in September 1865 Riid paid tax for brewing 8 barrels; In October of 1865 he paid Federal tax on 6 barrels of beer brewed, and on the February 1866 records he brewed 4 barrels of beer to pay tax on, in March, 5 barrels, and on the May 1866 records Reid (sic) brewed 7 barrels of beer, and he also paid his retail liquor and brewer licenses. On the June 1866 Federal Tax records Rudd, L3. (Sic) paid on 8 barrels of beer brewed. In July he paid tax on 10 barrels brewed. In August he paid for brewing 12 barrels of beer. In September of 1866 the Pacific Brewery brewed 9 barrels of beer. In October 1866 he paid on 11 1/2 barrels, and in November of 1866 Riid and Co. paid for brewing 8 barrels of beer on Federal Tax assessment records. See Federal Tax Records, 1865-1866, University of Idaho Library Microfilm # 558

2   *Idaho World*, Idaho City, Idaho, 8 June 1867, p. 3, c. 1

3   Federal Tax Records, 1865-1866, University of Idaho Library Microfilm # 558.

4   *Idaho World*, 12 June 1867, p. 3, c. 3.

5   *Idaho World*, 23 November 1867, p. 2, c. 4. This advertisement was one of the first mentions of the brewery with Meydenbauer having Riid as a new partner.

6   *Idaho Semi-Weekly World*, Idaho City, Idaho, 8 June 1867, p. 3, c. 3.

7   *Idaho World*, 25 May 1867, p. 3, c. 2.

8   *Idaho Semi-Weekly World*, 8 June 1867, p. 3, c. 1.

9   *Idaho Semi-Weekly World*, 12 June 1867, p. 3, c. 4.

10 *Idaho World*, 23 November 1867, p. 3, c.1.

11 *Idaho Semi-Weekly World*, 28 December 1867, p. 3, c. 1.

12 *Idaho World*, 4 January 1868, p. 3, c. 1.

13 *Idaho World*, 4 March 1868, p. 3, c. 1.

14 *Idaho World*, 5 February 1868, p. 3, c. 1.

15 *Idaho World*, 4 March 1868, p. 3, c. 1.

16 *Idaho World*, 27 March 1868, p. 3, c. 1.

17 *The Idaho Semi-Weekly World*, 27 May 1868, p. 3, c. 1.

18 *Idaho World*, Idaho City, 1 August 1868, p. 2, c. 3, p. 2, c. 3. and p. 3, c. 1.

19 *The Idaho Semi-Weekly World*, 8 August 1868, p. 3, c. 1.

20 *Idaho World*, 21 November 1868, p. 3, c. 4.

21 *Idaho World*, 30 May 1868, p. 3, c. 1.

22 *Idaho World*, 28 January 1869, p. 2, c. 5.

23 *Idaho World*, 4 February 1869, p. 3, c. 1.

24 *Idaho World*, 4 February 1869, p. 2, c. 5.

25 *Idaho World*, 18 March 1869, p. 3, c. 5.

26 *Idaho World*, 1 July 1868, p. 2, c. 1.

27 *Idaho World*, 20 May 1869, p. 3, c. 2. The saloon sat opposite the Good Templar Hall on Main Street.

28 *Idaho World*, 28 October 1869, p. 4, c. 3.

29 *Idaho World*, 30 September 1869, p. 3, c. 3.

30 *Idaho World*, 23 December 1869, p. 3, c. 2.

31 *Idaho World*, 5 May 1870, p. 4, c. 3.

32 *Idaho World*, 23 December 1869, p. 3, c. 2.

33 *Idaho Tri-Weekly Statesman*, Boise, Idaho, 13 August 1870, p. 3, c. 1.

34 *Idaho World*, 4 August 1870, p. 3, c. 2. The Franco-Prussian War was at hand.

35 *Idaho World*, 11 August 1870, p. 2, c. 3

36 Yates must have been the editor of the *Weekly 6 Shooter*, which published from September 1869. Unfortunately none of these papers are known to be extant.

37 *The Elko Chronicle*, Elko, Nevada, 7 August 1870, p. 3, c. 1.

38 *The Elko Independent*, 10 August 1870, p. 3, c. 1.

39 *The Elko Chronicle*, 14 August 1879, p. 3, c. 1.

40 *Idaho World*, 25 August 1870, p. 3, c. 1. See also *Idaho Tri-Weekly Statesman*, Boise, 27 August 1870, p. 2, c. 2.

18

LOUIS RODER

Accessory to Manslaughter

RODER SEEMED DESTINED to be one of those part-time brewery workers who completely escaped the historical record. He was a trained butcher, but found employment at John Hendel's brewery in Hailey. If the people in Hailey knew him at all, they found his name confusing. Was it Roder, Roeder, or Schroder?

Just before 4 a.m. on March 17, 1893, a commotion spread through the night owls of Hailey—a murder had just been committed in John Hendel's brewery.[1] Roder's comfortable anonymity ended. Sheriff A. J. Jackson was awakened and he bolted from bed and ran to the scene. Leander Holstrom was dead. Roder and his boss, Hendel, were still on the scene and each admitted firing a shot from his revolver. Jackson arrested them both and took them to the county jail.

Most of the account of the trail centered on Hendel, but Roder was considered an accomplice. At the Coroner's Inquest, Holstrom's drunken friends were clueless about details they should have witnessed and Hendel's wife was proved a liar.

John Carlson was one of the foursome of the previous night that had included Holstrom. He testified that they went to the brewery at 11 p.m. the previous night and between 3 and 4 a.m. John Hendel told them to leave. At the same time, Louis Roder went into the bedroom from the kitchen and then stood near the door with a pistol in his hand and fired. Carlson remembered Louis firing twice. Carlson did not know if the first or second shot struck Holstrom, but he had seen John Hendel at the same time and did not see him fire a shot.

State Penitentiary, Boise City, Idaho.

DESCRIPTION OF CONVICT.

Registered No. *340*   When Received *June 29th, 1893*

Name *Louis Roder*   Alias

County *Alturas*   Term *May*

Crime *Involuntary Manslaughter*

Sentence *Three (3) years of Six (6) months*

Age when received *35* years   Born in *Germany*

Legitimate occupation *Butcher*   Served apprenticeship *yes*

Height *5* feet, *3¾* inches. Complexion *Light* Weight *135*

Color of Hair *Brown*   Color of Eyes *Blue*

*Conjugal Relations: ~~Single. Married. Separated. Widower.~~ Has ~~Child~~

*Domestic Relations: Father living *No* Died when prisoner was *14* years old

    Mother living *No* Died when prisoner was *26* years old

    Prisoner left parents' home when *23* years old.

Religion: Has had religious instruction *yes* Attended Sunday School *yes*

  In what church *Lutheran* Member of what church now *Lutheran*

*Education: ~~Illiterate. Can read. Can read and write.~~ Common school education.

  Higher school and collegiate education. Attended school *7* years.

*Habits of Life: Abstinent. Moderate drinker. Intemperate.

Former imprisonment: *None*

Name and address of nearest relative: *Herman Medders*
Fistleburgh Germany

GENERAL REMARKS:

Peculiarity in build and feature:

Condition of teeth: *Good*

Beard worn when received: *Mustache*

Size of boot worn: *7*

India ink marks, scars and deformities: *1 Scar over right eye about ½" long. Scar on right hand ½ in. long in palm. Several small ones on back of left hand.*

Property found on convict: *$3 75/100 cash*

78. Roder's convict description document.

Peter Hanson was sworn in. He remembered going to the brewery about midnight with Holstrom, Kullas, and Carlson. Hanson remembered seeing Hendel and Roder, "the little Dutchman," with a revolver in his hand. Roder shouted, "Get out of here, you sons of bitches!" and pointed his revolver at them. Hanson had not seen who fired the first shot but he remembered—erroneously, it turned out—hearing three shots being

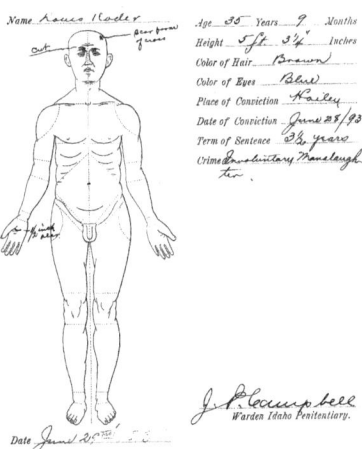

79. Roder's biometric chart from penitentiary, front.

fired in quick succession, yet he could not say he had actually seen the shooting.

Mrs. Hendel then gave her testimony. *He [Hendel] did this to scare and did not hit anybody. There were only four of them here, scattered about the room, not in line with the pistol. I took the gun away from John Hendel and put it away in the bedroom. Just as I turned around to come out here again and as I stood there, in the door, I heard a shot fired. Lea Holstrom turned around once or twice, in about two steps, and fell right here. I saw his eyes set at once and said: "the man is dead." When I heard the shot I saw Lea Holstrom's coat still smoking, burning from the shot. Louis stood by him and shot him from behind, shot him in the back. He was as close as this* (she held her hands about a foot apart).

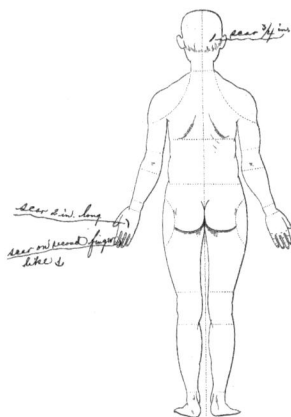

80. Roder's biometric chart from penitentiary, back.

Holstrom says as he fell, "oh, oh, oh!" Louis then said: "I've fixed him." This is how it happened; only two shots were fired. The first by John Hendel to scare.

OFFICE OF

Alturas Saddlery Co.

(Successors to H. R. Plughoff.)

MANUFACTURERS OF AND DEALERS IN

Harness, Saddles, Collars, Whips, Boots, Shoes, Trunks and Valises, and Fur Goods of All Kinds.

Hailey, Idaho, _July 1st_ 1894

To the Hon Board of Pardons
Boise City.
            Gentlemen,
In the matter of application for pardon
of Louis Roder. Think he has been
Sufficiently punished for Crime
Committed. And the ends of justice
have been satisfied. And think if
your Honorable Body should grant
this petition. That he will become
a good Citizen.
            Yours Very Truly
            H. R. Plughoff
Chairman Board Co Com's
Alturas. Co. Ida.

81. Alturas Saddlery pardon support letter.

The second by Louis. Louis himself said he had killed the man and that he was going to hunt up the sheriff and give himself up, and he told Sheriff Jackson on giving himself up that he had killed a man."

The coroner's jury easily decided the fatal shot was fired by Hendel's gun and the bullet cut out of the ceiling was from Roder's.

Hendel and Roder—the local newspaper was still calling him "Schroeder," an error it took them weeks to figure out—stayed in jail. Hendel was in the "steel cell," and Roder in the "murderer's cell." Newspapers throughout Idaho reported them held without bail.[2] Neither had showed much appetite at first.[3] After the results of the coroner's jury were in though, Roder became more hopeful and his

82. *Application for Pardon.*

spirits picked up. Yet he still expected to face charges of discharging a firearm, which could bring a penitentiary sentence. All the first day, Hendel was in good spirits and felt no need for an attorney.

The preliminary hearing for Hendel and Roder began the end of March before Probate Judge Richards in the room of the Fourth District Court. The Honorable E. Ensign appeared for the prosecution on the request of the District Attorney. Waters represented Roder, and Angel and Ruick appeared for John Hendel.[4] After the prosecution presented its evidence, Roder's counsel said there was not even a suspicion against his client and he moved for dismissal.[5] The motion was promptly denied and a recess was taken until 7 p.m. to allow Judge Waters, Roder's counsel, to decide on his next move.

In closing arguments for the defense, Judge Walters claimed again that there was not even a suspicion against his client, Roder, but he did ask for bail rather than a dismissal this time. The *Wood River Times*

LAW OFFICE
—OF—
F. M. Bruner.

Hailey, Idaho, June 29th 1894,

To the Hon. Board of Pardons,
State of Idaho.
Gentlemen,

In the matter of the Application of Louis Roeder now serving a term in the Idaho Penitentiary for Involuntary Manslaughter, alleged to have been committed in Altura, Co. on Mar, 17th 1893, I would respectfully represent to you, that I am fully convinced that the ends of Justice, in said matter have been more than met, so far as said Roeder is concerned, I would further say that I conducted the entire prosecution from its inception to the close, and am fully conversant with the case, and firmly believe that Louis Roeder should be pardoned, and restored to citizenship,

Very Respectfully,
R. M. Bruner,

83. R. M. Brenner letter in support of pardon.

said a request for a dismissal would have made him appear ridiculous.[6]

The court's final decision was that the prosecution had proved the killing and use of revolvers. A crime of murder had been committed; under Idaho statue an accessory was equally guilty with the perpetrator of the crime. Both Hendel and Roder were bound over for trial, and this was not a bailable offense. Trial was scheduled to begin June 14.

On June 7, empanelling of the jury started in the Hendel trial, which was separate from the Roder trial.

At 3 p.m. on Monday, June 20, the case went to the jury. In only 25 minutes, they returned a verdict of murder in the second degree against Hendel.[7]

On Wednesday, the trial of Louis Roder began. This time, local businessmen made up the jury to save the mileage expense of securing miners from a distance. As the *Times* said, Roder (they had finally decided his name was not "Schroder" or "Roeder") took one look at that menacing aggregation and changed his plea to guilty of involuntary manslaughter.

Both men were sentenced the same day. Hendel got 16 years and Roder 3 1/2 years. Both sentences could be halved by good behavior.[8] Sheriff Jackson took both men by train to the penitentiary at Boise the next afternoon after sentencing.

An appeal was made. Idaho Supreme Court Justice C. J. Huston wrote the opinion of the court regarding the appeal to which Justices Morgan and Sullivan concurred. There were seven exceptions Huston addressed. Among his more interesting points: "There is some evidence of a third shot being fired, but it hardly arises to the dignity of a suspicion." Huston mentions that the third bullet fitted the gun used by Roder. Roder's counsel had the right to be present at Hendel's trial and to be heard on matters that affected Roder. The two doctors that testified about the possibility of the third bullet being the one that killed Holstrom disagreed, and the jury, rightly, made the decision. Appeal denied.

At the penitentiary in Boise, Roder's description listed him as 35 years old, born in Germany, 5 foot 3 ¼ inches tall, 7 years of education, Lutheran religion, with good teeth and a moustache, and his nearest relative was Herman Meddrks (sic), in Fisleburgh, Germany. He had $3.75 on him when incarcerated.[9]

In July of 1894, Roder applied for a pardon. A notice to that effect had to be published in the newspaper and a formal application made. Apparently he was denied that year and he applied again

OFFICE OF
GEO. W. RICHARDS,
Probate Judge and Supt. of Schools,
ALTURAS CO.

Hailey, Idaho, June 28 1892

To the Hon Board of Pardons
                    Gentlemen.
    Louis Roder. who will apply to your Hon Board. at its next Session. for a pardon. had his preliminary Examination before me. and taking all the testimony adduced. I was satisfied that the said Roder. had no intent to commit a crime. but shot off his pistol to scare away the parties. While I do not uphold him in such an act I think he has been sufficiently punished for what he did. and would recommend his pardon
                Respectfully Yours
                    Geo. W Richards
                    Probate Judge
                    Alturas Co. Idaho

84. Geo. Richards' letter in support of pardon.

in 1895. He failed to have all the papers he needed at that time and applied again in March of 1896. Even the prosecuting attorney in the case wrote on his behalf. Dozens of local business owners signed a petition on his behalf. He was at last released just short of the completion of his sentence.

Roder did not completely drop from history after his term in prison, but he was little noted. The little Dutchman who had almost been framed for murder, who had only his lawyer on his side at one point, was on the 1920 U. S. Census living in Pocatello with his Idaho-born wife, Elizabeth. Roder's brief servitude to Gambrinus nearly ruined his life.

END NOTES

1   *Wood River Times* Weekly, Hailey, Idaho, 22 March 1893, p. 1, c. 2-6. See Hendel's biography in this volume for more details regarding the homicide.

2   *The Elmore Bulletin*, Mountain Home, Idaho, 1 April 1893, p. 3, c. 4.

3   *Wood River Times*, Weekly, 22 March 1893, p. 3, c. 4.

4   *Wood River Times*, Weekly, 29 March 1893, p. 1, c. 3.

5   *Wood River Times*, Weekly, 29 March 1893, p. 2, c. 5.

6   *Wood River Times*, Weekly, 5 April 1893, p. 1, c. 3

7   *Wood River Times*, Weekly, 21 June 1893, p. 3, c. 5. *Idaho World*, Idaho City, 23 June 1893, p. 1, c. 2 and 30 June 1893, p. 1, c. 2.

8   *Elmore Bulletin*, 1 July 1893, p. 2, c. 2.

9   Penitentiary Records, Louis Roder, Idaho State Historical Society.

19

WILLIAM SLAGLE
Suicide

WILLIAM SLAGLE LEFT his brother and his home in Knight's Landing, Yolo County, California, to locate at Silver City in southwest Idaho in that mining camp's salad days.[1] He was a carpenter by trade and presented himself initially as a "sober and industrious citizen," according to the local newspaper. In late summer of 1866, he joined John Williams in a partnership to operate the Miner's Brewery on Washington Street in Silver City.[2] Williams had briefly been partners with John Grete, and these two had only opened the business at that location in June.[3] Perhaps Slagle did some of the carpentry on the new brewery and met Williams that way; there is no evidence.

Ironically, the first ad for the brewery with the partnership of Williams and Slagle appeared in the local newspaper, the *Avalanche*, in October 1866, almost a month after Slagle's death.[4] Slagle was in a cabin near the N.Y. & O. Mill, opposite Ruby City about a mile from Silver City, in the forenoon of Tuesday, 11 September, when he shot himself through the brain. According to the *Avalanche* this happened "while in a state of mental derangement brought on by too free use of alcoholic liquors."[5] This quiet, intelligent man had only been a "victim of the demon intemperance" the last few weeks of his life, according to the news story.

Justice Miller of Ruby held an inquest on the body the next day and found in accordance with the suicide the newspaper described. Slagle was buried in the Ruby City Cemetery that afternoon. This was the second Ruby City Cemetery which had been started that March.[6]

The local paper requested that the Sacramento, California, newspaper carry the obituary to inform his former acquaintances of his death.

Early in January, Williams bought Slagle's interest in the business, apparently from whoever administered the estate. Slagle had a very brief sojourn as an Idaho brewer. There is certainly not enough known to realistically attribute his final depression to the brewing business or even to alcohol.[7] Such a short-time problem may have indicated severe depression, which he was self-medicating with an unusually large alcohol intake, rather than derrangement brought on by liquor that could not work that fast. Slagel's servitude to King Gambrinus was too short to properly age a single barrel of lager beer.

END NOTES

1   Don Jamison, *By My Own Hand I Perish: Suicide in the Owyhee Mining Camps,* p. 12. Jamison quotes the *Owyhee Avalanche,* Silver City, Idaho, of September 1866.

2   *Owyhee Avalanche,* 16 October 1866, p. 1, c. 4

3   *Owyhee Avalanche,* 9 June 1866, p. 3, c. 2, and p. 2, c. 4.

4   *Owyhee Avalanche,* 16 October 1866, p. 1, c. 4.

5   Jamison, *By My Own Hand,* p. 12.

6   Statham. Wilma Lewis. *Owyhee County Gleanings.* Boise, Idaho: The Idaho Genealogical Society and the Idaho Historical Society, 1964, 2nd printing, Copyright 1986. P. 38.

7   One Dell F. Slagle, widow of William H. Slagle ran a lodging house in Portland, Oregon according to the city directories of 1890-91. Maybe this was William's widow or other relative. No wife was mentioned at the time of his death.

20

JAMES SMITH
Suicide

THERE WAS NEVER A BREWERY with a federal permit in Elk City, Idaho, but apparently there was an unlicensed one there in the early 1860s. The oldest records in the probate court at Lewiston, Idaho, relate to the death of one James Smith.[1] On 29 January 1865, Smith, a German brewer, committed suicide at Elk City by shooting himself through the head with a rifle. Fifteen residents of the mining town signed a petition to E. S. Sprague, Probate Judge, asking that Godfrey Sarter be appointed administrator because he spoke both German and English and was acquainted with the friends of the deceased. There was another paper in the probate records directing the administrator to sell the property, consisting of liquors, cigars, and malt for brewing. This leaves little doubt that Smith ran a saloon and did his own brewing. Incidentally the Probate Judge charged $27 for docket fees and signing the papers, etc.

Elk City was founded by prospectors who headed up the south fork of the Clearwater under the leadership of Capt. L. B. Monson. The fact that this was Nez Perce land was irrelevant to the gold hungry. By September of 1861, a town site was laid out and over 20 log buildings constructed in anticipation of a great winter snowfall. By that next spring of 1862, there were five saloons and two hotels.

At the height of the gold rush there, in 1861, there were 2,000 miners in the area and six saloons to meet their hydration needs.[2] Certainly, this was too remote a spot to successfully ship in any suitable quantity of beer. Brewing on a small scale seemed a likely business concept. When gold was found at Florence that same year, all but 50 or 75 miners moved on. Smith's brewing business may have been irreparably hurt, and this could have led to his despondency. Elk City, depleted by 1862, never became a ghost town, and remained a viable settlement into the 21st Century. Brewer Smith had been forgotten until now.

END NOTES

1 *Coeur d'Alene Press*, Coeur d'Alene, Idaho, 2 September 1905, p. 1, c. 5.
2 Merle Wells, "Rush to Idaho," Bulletin # 19, Moscow, Idaho: Idaho Bureau of Mines and Geology, 1958.

21

J. L. G. SMITH
Victim of Spousal Homicide

JOHN LAWSON GREEN SMITH was a brewery worker and owner for a short period of his troubled life. He might qualify as the poster boy for dysfunctional family men; yet if he had not died as he did, no one would know of this today. Let's go back to the earliest record of his life, the 1870 U. S. Census.

"Shanghai " Smith, as he was nicknamed, was born in Maine in 1831, his wife Margaret was born in Missouri in 1841, son Pitt was born in Wisconsin in 1854, Katie was born in Washington in 1859, and Charles was born in Washington in 1860.[1] This family had another son later, named Willie. Smith already had two other children from a previous marriage to Mary Hamilton.[2] According to the records in Maine, J. L. G. was born on 30 June 1831, the son of John and Martha Ann Green Smith.[3] This highlights Smith's wandering before he reached Boise and became an employee in the Central Brewery and Bakery, Main and 6th & 7th Streets, in 1865.

His biographical sketch in Elliot, *History of Idaho*, 1884 read:

"John Lawson Green Smith is the proprietor of the Hailey Hot Springs. The curative properties of these springs are well known and are rapidly growing in favor among invalids, a number of whom have been greatly relieved or entirely cured by their use.

Mr. Smith has had a career full of excitement and adventures; such as accompany a pioneer life in the Western wilds. To see him superintending his business about the springs, or looking after the comfort of his passengers and guests on the crowded bus to and from the springs, or accommodation at the springs, for those who visit it daily for health and pleasure, at all seasons, who would think he was born Westerner, full of the enterprise of the Pacific Coast. But, however much his manners may tell of the pioneer life, his business is conducted on the most substantial basis. Before he ever expended a dime on the springs, or lifted a spade for their improvement, he thoroughly satisfied himself that the springs, now well know as the Hailey Hot Springs, possessed virtues which would be valuable, not only for cleanliness and pleasure, but also as a restorative for suffering. As a consequence they are visited by people from every part of the Union. The Oregon Short Line Railroad has made the springs accessible to the outside world, running as it does within two miles of the springs.

At the terminus (Hailey), Mr. Smith meets his guests with an easy-riding carriage, and the drive to the springs is soon accomplished. This man, who his neighbors term Alphabetical Smith, was born away down in Maine, and has grown much longer than his name, standing six feet one inch in his stockings.

His mother, who first taught him the principles of honor and courtesy which characterize his management of the famous establishment for the sick and suffering, at Hailey, was a devout and pious woman, setting a good example before her son, and, when necessary, compelling his sometimes wayward steps to follow her example.

When he was a lad of twelve years she lost her husband, and he became the guiding star of her hope and affections. Thus early did he learn to sympathize with sorrow and suffering, and became the stay and support of her widowhood. Leaving the checquered scenes of his childhood, at the age of nineteen years he came to California, by way of Panama, in the steamship *California*.

With the ardent affection of an earnest young man, he could not long lead a single life. He wooed and won Miss Mary Hamilton, in Camptonville, California. He built the first fence in Santa Rosa, and turned his attention to freighting and ranching, or any work where he could be useful. Not content with California, he led the van of civilization in Washington Territory. He followed mining excitements, always having his family with him, until the death of his wife.

In 1879 he again married, this time Miss Maggie Agnew, who still stands faithfully by his side, dispensing the hospitalities of the Hailey Hot Springs, spreading light and comfort where ever her footsteps lead. By this union his already large family has been increased by the addition of three boys and a girl.

After years of hardship and toil in frontier countries, Mr. Smith has now a home near the young and enterprising city of Hailey, which promises only comfort, peace, and plenty during the remainder of his years. He intends erecting a large and commodious hotel next spring (1884), and otherwise beautifying the grounds for the pleasure and comfort of his guests, as the popularity of the springs is steadily increasing.

In this region where fortunes are made almost in a day by the discovery of rich lodes of galena ore, and where the intense eagerness in the race for wealth characterizes every class in society, this place is growing in its beauty and attractiveness. Here may be found rest and quiet away from the bustle and clamor of business, where the sick may find health, and the tired and worn refreshment.

The name of Smith, renown in history, here receives a new luster by the establishment of a successful institution in a time of peace."[4]

This was only part of Smith's life story. The problem with these sketches was that the subject supplied all the "facts," while the writer used all his power to put a positive spin on everything. J. L. G. apparently became a co-owner with Mr. Young in the Boise Central Brewery, because in July of 1865, they were co-listed as Federal Tax payers, and in August of 1865, they brewed 14 barrels of beer; in September of 1865, Smith and Young paid their Federal fermented liquor tax; in October of 1865, Smith & Young brewed six barrels, and in November of 1865, Smith and Young paid Federal tax on the two barrels of beer brewed.[5] A report about Smith from August 1865, during his days as a brewer, told an interesting tale.

> "Mr. J. L. G. Smith, a resident of Boise City, was dangerously wounded a few days ago, by some person unknown. It appears that Mr. Smith (who keeps a saloon) had retired to bed after closing his house and hearing someone at the back door, he arose and opened it. The first thing that met his view was a pistol leveled at his heart. His presence of mind not deserting him, he raised his hand quickly, and elevated the murderous weapon so far that the ball (which was fired instantly) entered a little below the collar bone, and lodged under the shoulder blade from whence it has since been extracted. The weapon was so close that it burnt his face and neck, also his hand, which was slightly wounded. He is doing well."[6]

I found nothing else about this incident.

In November of 1866, Smith was a Boise member of the Committee of Invitation for the Grand Ball held at Hart's Exchange in Boise.[7] He obviously had some local status.

In March 1867, J. L. G. Smith entered his cream horse, "Pigeon," in the annual races and won the race in 2:2 by defeating J. Wayatt Gray's mare, "Nannie Hunt," and S. Owens bay, "Curley."[8] This was the big racing event in Boise that year. In such races up to $10,000 dollars often changed hands.

On 24 June 1869, J. L. G. Smith paid M. A. Devers & Wife $475 for lot 7 of block 33 in Boise City. On June 26, only 2 days after, he sold it to E. Raymer for $500, a $25 profit.[9] By the 1870, Census he was recorded as a common laborer with $1,500 in real estate and $1,500 in personal estate-not a paltry accumulation.

In July 1870, the Ada County Jockey Club, which arranged the races in which Smith entered horses, named Smith one of eight vice-presidents.[10] Smith also served on the coroner's jury that declared the death of George W. Matthews a suicide by laudanum in November of 1870.[11] Shanghai was serving Ada County well.

Shortly after this, he invested in a toll road to Idaho City, moved to the halfway house, and seemed to prosper. By 1873, he was noted for building a new bridge over Moore's Creek along his road.[12]

In September of 1877, Smith wrote to the *Semi-Weekly Idahoan* a vague missive.[13] Under the date of September 26 he wrote: "Friend Jud: $1,000,000 or half of my toll road reward for the red-headed boy my wife lost in the city the other day. Tell Paxton to wait till night and he can find him by his head light." The *Idahoan* editor said he did not comprehend the meaning so he went to Mr. J. D. Agnew for enlightenment. Jim Agnew explained,

"Mr. Smith's little boy, on a visit with his mother down here, strayed off last Sunday and became lost. Lewis, of the Express office, found the waif, and thinking from the brand it belonged to Mr. Jas. Mullany, conducted it to his residence. Jim Mullany examined it well and was in doubt, but to be sure about the matter he ordered a round-up and counted noses. And discovered it wasn't his. In the meantime a thorough search for the lost child was in progress, and it was finally picked up and restored to its distracted mother. We take great pleasure in informing friend Smith that his wife and little one left here for home all right, and have no doubt safely reached there. And you will most likely have your hair pulled for furnishing this item."

In 1877, when J.L.G. came to Boise to pick up his son who was recovered from diphtheria, he was described as the Idaho (City) road man.[14] He was well known. In 1878, J. L. G. Smith built a new grade up Moore's Creek as to avoid the Minnehaha and Thorn Creek hills. His road "is said to be an excellent road on a regular grade and shortens the distance about 4 miles and about two hours in time with light teams."[15] In late November of 1879 Smith advertised for sale his toll road between Idaho City and Boise.[16] When he visited Boise the next month, he reported it was 20 degrees below zero when he left home.[17] With no quick sale made, in 1880, Smith thoroughly repaired the road and rerouted it up Moore's Creek so the heavy grades were avoided and there were no sharp turns to distress teamsters.[18] He finally sold the road to the famous John Hailey, stagecoach king and future historian, in December of 1880 for $3,500.[19]

Margaret Smith sued J. L. G. Smith for divorce in October 1881, but changed her mind apparently.[20] Her attorney, F. E. Ensign moved that the case be dismissed by mutual agreement of the parties. This was a foreshadowing of things to come.

In 1881, Smith took ownership of the Hailey Hot Springs and moved to the Wood River area. In July of that year, the *Statesman* described him as "the owner and proprietor of the Warm Springs, in Croy's gulch, a mile and a half west of Hailey, Wood River."[21] By 1883 there was a new ladies swimming pool there, which featured a red hot stove in the dressing room, and floats for non-swimmers in the pool.[22] Smith was also planting 74 Balm of Gilead trees around the hot springs. Medicinal

85. Hailey Hot Springs.

plasters were commonly made from the gum of the tree and it was also chewed for a supposed beneficial effect. By July, he advertised the fare for the mile and half ride from Hailey to the springs as 25 cents and baths 50 cents.[23] The R. G. Dun Mercantile List of 1883 listed J. L. G. Smith, Hot Springs and saloon, in Hailey (p. 107). In 1885 there was a report from Hailey that Smith was looking well but not feeling well.[24] Son Willie, who was born after 1870, was reportedly thrown from a bucking horse, badly bruised and his right wrist dislocated.[25] In November of 1885, the family moved to town for the winter and lived in the house formerly occupied by the family of ex-District Attorney Bruner.[26]

In 1888, the long-standing but little-known family trouble surfaced. The headline in the *Wood River Times* said: "J. L. G. Smith Dead. His Wife Literally Blew His Brains Out."[27] The newspaper tried to present every detail. About 4:30 in the afternoon, Margaret Smith "shot the top of the head" off her husband, killing him instantly.

> "The victim's brains were splattered all over the ceiling and two walls of the room in which the tragedy occurred, and he fell to the floor, dead. The ball was from a Sharp's rifle, 45-70 caliber; it entered just above the left temple, breaking off a piece of skull probably two inches wide by four long, passing out at the back of the neck and imbedding itself in the east wall of the log building at a height of about seven feet. As the deceased fell to the floor his brains dropped out, and he lay there in a pool of about two quarts of blood and brain-matter when the people attracted by the news reached the house."

Immediately after the shooting Mrs. Smith put on a wrap and hat and walked rapidly down to Wertheimer's store where she saw Dr. McKay, and asked him to go up to the house, about half-a-mile distant, and see if he could help her husband any.

She then walked to the District Attorney's Office to give herself up.

At this time no one who she met knew of the occurrence; but as she was crying as she went all who saw her surmised that her husband had been beating her again, and she was on her way to have him arrested.

The District Attorney received her statement. She said, in substance, that her husband began abusing her again, and that she shot and possibly killed him. A complaint of murder was thereupon made against her.

THE ONLY WITNESS

It is stated that the only witness of the affair was a boy 17 years old, son of the parties; and this reporter is informed that he told Charles Haupt and others that his father was abusing and beating his mother; that he twice stepped between them to protect his mother; that his father made a dash for his mother again, but that before he could reach her she up and shot him.

THE SAD PROBABILITY

This version is generally accepted as probably true. Deceased and his wife lived in almost constant turmoil. He was much given to strong drink, and was an exceedingly ugly customer to meet at such times, as he seemed to rely upon his Herculean strength to indulge his bullying disposition.

About a year ago his life policy in the Equitable was canceled on his account, and only a few months ago he brutally beat his wife— for which offense he was severely reprimanded by Probate Judge Lemmon, besides being fined $80."

The next day the newspaper had time to put together even more coverage.

All the following stories are directly quoted from the newspaper accounts cited.

86. Idaho City Toll Road historical sign.

The Tragedy

Evidence Elicited at the Coroner's Inquest To-day.

William Smith, the only eye-witness of the shooting, testified—Deceased was drunk, abusive, and violent, and was fought off repeatedly—He drove his wife and child out into the yard, broke some crockery, and threatened to burn the House down.

The inquest into the death of J. L. G. Smith was held in the Probate Court at 10 o'clock this morning, before Dr. N. J. Brown, the coroner, and a jury composed of E. H. Porter, A. J. Jackson, Orrin Porter, T. J. Kingsbury, Charles Haupt, Charles Nelson, Gus Morrison, George Robertson, and J. L. Cederholm.

Angel & Sullivan and N. M. Ruick appeared in behalf of Mrs. Margaret Smith, the defendant, and District Attorney Roberts appeared for the Territory.

William B. Smith, aged 17, was the first witness sworn. He testified as follows: I am the son of J. L. G. Smith; was in the house where the tragedy occurred, about half past 4 o'clock yesterday afternoon. Came to the house in the morning, about 6 o'clock, and stayed for breakfast, at about 8. Then went down to Mrs. Louck's house to nurse a patient who was sick of pneumonia. During the day—about half-past 9—went back home and to bed. Stayed in bed three hours, got up at half past 12. Went down to see how the patient was. Lingered around town a little while, and came back; must have got home about half-past 1; his father was not there at the time; he came about half-past; witness' mother, and himself were present when the shooting took place. Shortly before the shooting Mrs. Smith went to Brown's a neighbor living on the same block. She remained away two or three minutes, then returned. And went into the front room. During Mrs. Smith's absence the deceased chased witness around the house and out in the yard. Deceased came home in a buggy, drove to the barn, in the alley; he threw the lines out and began unhitching. Witness went out of the front room to help him unhitch; witness did up the line on the near horse, but his father, instead of doing up the line on the off horse, left it down; they then started for the stable, the father leading; his horse stepped up, and ran away. All this time the deceased was cursing and using all the bad language any man could use. Deceased caught his horse; and started to lead him to the stable—cursing all the time. Witness had not spoken a word to him up to this time. Deceased was pretty well intoxicated, and could not walk very straight. After horses were unhitched witness and deceased went into the stable, both then went into the house, and stayed there; deceased then went out three or four times, but not exceeding a minute at a time. Deceased must have been in the house, the last time, two or three minutes before the shooting took place. When the defendant returned from Brown's the deceased was in the kitchen; when he was shot he was in the front room, standing right by the head of the lounge, or, rather, moving; witness' mother shot him with a rifle. [A Sharp's rifle shown witness] That is the gun; it is a 45-70 hammerless Sharp. William Brock owns the gun; it has to be loaded each time after firing. Witness took the gun to his father's house; he borrowed it from William Brock about three months ago, to go to Snake River hunting deer. When the difficulty commenced the gun was standing either behind the door, or in the closet about three inches from the door; witness used the gun about two weeks before, to shoot at a crow, and left a cartridge in it; the crows were on the flat, near the house where the tragedy occurred; witness took two shots at them, and intended to take another, he therefore re-loaded the gun, but as he did not shoot, he left the cartridge in it. Just before the shooting deceased threatened to strike her at different times, and also attempted to; witness pushed him off five or six times, and Mrs. Smith ran into the bedroom, deceased rushed the door, and kicked it open in; opening it slammed against her, throwing her against the foot of the bed; she caught her balance and straightened up; after she got straight he caught her by his left hand, about the center of her right arm, in the attitude of striking; before he could strike witness caught deceased's arm and pulled him back out of the door; deceased bumped his head on the door and this made a scar on the right cheek-bone; he then attacked witness for doing so, but the latter, instead of fighting pushed him off at arm's length; deceased thereupon swore that he would clean them out, and proceeded to attempt to do so, but witness succeeded in retreating until the stove stood between witness and

J. L. G. SMITH DEAD.

HIS WIFE LITERALLY BLEW HIS BRAINS OUT,

And Spattered Them Over the Ceiling, Walls, and Floor—How the Shooting Occurred.

deceased, the former standing in the bedroom door, and the latter on the east side of the stove. Deceased then backed up against the east wall, witness facing him, but on the other side of the stove, and he [deceased] made another attempt to attack witness' mother; this must have been the seventh attempt—and as he was going to make the attack he advanced with clenched fist, in somewhat of a crouching attitude and as he did the defendant took up the gun and as deceased had made about three steps, SHE FIRED, Deceased had then got to about the center of the room. As Mrs. Smith fired deceased fell backward; he had nothing in his hand, that witness could see, when he advanced toward his mother; deceased said: "I will clear you both out!" just as he started. Deceased was moving when the shot was fired; when the shot struck him his knees began to bend first, before anything else, and he fell with the right leg partly under him and caught under the leg under the head of the lounge. Witness straightened the deceased's legs, because the right leg was in a kind of a cramp—he did this to make deceased more comfortable; witness supposed him dead. He [witness] had had considerable difficulty in keeping his father from his mother, as deceased was stronger than he. When the shot was fired, witness was standing on the opposite side of the stove, from his father, in the front room; did not see his mother reach for the gun. When the fatal shot was fired, his mother was standing just inside the threshold of the bedroom. When witness' father fell his mother did not say anything that he can recollect; she went to his head, and looked at it; she put on her shawl and hat, and started down; witness went over to Brown's to get Uncle Johnny West, and said to him to come over and stay with his father while he went down town; witness returned home, and from there down town to see some friends; met Dr. MacKay at Wertheimer's store, and also the defendant. [Fur cap shown.] This is the cap deceased had on when he was shot; does not know whether or not deceased had the visor in front, in the usual way. When deceased advanced toward his wife, witness should judge he tottered some, from the way he walked when he first came home; when running witness out of the house could not say whether he was steady or unsteady as witness did not look back; he just run to get out of the way.

Questions by Charles Nelson, a juror: At the time your father was advancing toward your mother the last time, couldn't you have stepped in and interfered as you had done previous?

Answer: I might have done so but it would have done no good. I had done this so much that it tired me out, and I was afraid to—afraid I could not get away.

Q: (By same juror)—What position was your mother in at the time he was advancing toward her?

A: she was standing up straight.

Q: Was she close by the gun at the time?

A: Yes sir, she was.

Q: Why was the gun standing there at the time, loaded?

A: Because, as I told you before I was going to shoot crows and did not take the cartridge out.

Q: She knew the gun was loaded or not?

A: As to that I could not testify.

Questions by Orrin Porter, another juror: How near were you to your mother when she fired the shot?

A: About four or five feet.

Q: She stood in the bedroom?

A: Yes sir.

Q: Could you see her from where you stood?

A: If she had held her arm out from her body, I might have seen her arm, that's about all.

Q: Did you see the gun when she had it in her hand, just before she fired?

A: I saw the gun just as it went off.

Q: (By Juror Nelson) If you wanted to, you or your mother both—if you wanted to leave the house, at the time for this fuss—couldn't you have left the house without any shooting?

A: We could have left the house but if we had I think he would have executed his threats, which were burning down things that he ever had destroyed. He had already broken up one teapot.

Q: (By juror Cederholm.)—Did you ever see your mother handle this gun before the time she was shooting?

A: I did not.

Q: (By Juror Nelson.) Do you consider that you and your mother both were in danger of your life at the time?

A: Yes sir. I do.

Q: (By juror Jackson.) —Did you hear your mother threaten your father—make any threats of any kind—before the shot was fired?

A: No sir; I did not.

Q: Did your father make any threats to kill you or your mother?

A: He said he would clean us out. He said at the springs, a few days before—[interrupted by the District Attorney.]— "You needn't mind about that."

Q: (By juror Jackson.)—Did you ever explain to any one else in her presence, so that she knew how it worked?

A: No, sir.

Q: Did you ever explain to any one else in her presence, so that she knew how the gun worked?

A: I don't know if she knew how the gun worked, from my
instructions, or not, but I did show my little brother how it
worked. Whether she was present or not, I don't know.

At 12:45 the further hearing was adjourned for one hour, to meet in
the District Courtroom.

AFTERNOON SESSION

Every seat in the District Courtroom was occupied, several ladies being among the audience, when Coroner Brown called the assemblage
to order.

Dr. D. W. Figgins sworn: Am a physician and surgeon. Made a
post-mortem examination on the body of J. L. G. Smith, this morning,
between 9 and 10 o'clock. The cause of his death was a gunshot wound
about two inches above the left eye, running directly back in a straight
line, the ball penetrating the frontal bone, passing through the entire
left lobe of the brain, passing out between the occipital and the parietal
bones, as near as witness could make out from the shattered condition of the bones; and absence of some parts. His opinion is that it
caused instant death. Witness found some powder marks over the
face and forehead, and a gash or slight cut at the lower corner of the
right eye. Witness removed one or two small bones from the head of
the deceased. Judging from the powder marks on the face and from
the edges of the bone in front, deceased came to his death from a shot
directly in front. [Witness produces a few small pieces of bone.] These
bones are from different parts of the left side of head of deceased. [In
obedience of instructions witness marks the pieces of bone.] The piece
marked X comes from the frontal bone, directly over the left eye. The
piece marked 1 comes from the occipital, adjoining the frontal; the
piece marked 2 of the occipital and left parietal. The smaller fragment
from the same. What witness would judge to be the entrance by a
portion of the frontal bone, showing that it had been broken from
without inward; portion of occipital broken from within outward;

in entrance of flesh wounds the opening is smaller than the exit. In order to have made the powder marks witness cannot say positively how close the gun must have been to deceased's face, but he presumes about five or six feet.

Question by Juror Jackson: From the range of the ball, would not the gun have to be on the level?

Answer: I should judge that it would not be due to the position that the head might be in.

THE VERDICT

After being out about one hour, the jury returned the following verdict:

We find that the deceased was named J. L. G. Smith, a native of the United States; that he came to his death on the second day of April, 1888, by having been shot with a rifle in the hands of Mrs. Margaret Smith, his wife, and that we believe the same intentional.

NOTES

J. L. G. Smith's remains were removed to Schwamb's undertaking rooms, about half-part 7 o'clock last evening; when they will be sent to Boise for internment.

Mrs. Margaret Smith, the woman who did the shooting, spent last night in the bedroom formerly used by the deputies, in front of the jail, in the basement of the courthouse. She was quite composed, at least when anybody besides the members of her family was around. Her daughter—a young lady about 15 years of age—spent the night with her.

Public sentiment in this community is divided on the question of the defendant's guilt or innocence; and a newspaper man should be careful to abstain from publishing anything that might prejudice the case of any accused. For this reason the Times expresses no opinion on the case.[29]

THE SMITH TRAGEDY.

Funeral of the Victim Postponed—Mrs. Smith in Jail—Her Preliminary Examination.

Mrs. Margaret Smith, who killed her husband by shooting "the top of his head off" with a Sharp's rifle, last Monday afternoon, is still kept in the rooms occupied by the Sheriff, in the basement of the courthouse, before the room at present fitted up as the Sheriff's office was made. Her daughter spent last night with her, and will probably continue to sleep with her until Mrs. Smith's case shall have been inquired into by the grand jury. At 10 o'clock next Monday morning she will have her preliminary examination in the Probate Court—or, at least, she will be offered a preliminary examination according to the law. It is not unlikely, however, that her attorneys may advise her to waive examination; in which case she will be held to appear, without bonds, the offense with which she is charged not being bailable.

A rumor was current today that Willie Smith, the only witness of the tragedy, was to be arrested on a charge of having been an accessory before the fact; but on inquiry at the Probate Court the rumor was ascertained to be without foundation. The Probate Judge admitted, however, that some citizens had urged the placing of Willie Smith under bonds to secure his attendance when wanted; but as the law bearing on such cases had not been complied with, no such action could be taken.

The funeral of J. L. G. Smith, the victim, which was to have taken place today, was postponed until tomorrow at half past 12 o'clock, in order to give Charles Smith, second son of the deceased, an opportunity to attend. Charles Smith is settled at Solder, on Camas Prairie; and news of the tragedy could not, therefore, have reached him until last evening. By leaving immediately on hearing it, he could not reach here before the evening owing to the condition of the roads.

Fully a score of ladies of this city called on Mrs. Smith at the jail today. They found her quite composed, and evidently satisfied that she had acted in self-defense.

WOOD RIVER TIMES

HAILEY. IDAHO.

THURSDAY...........................APRIL 5, 1888

J. L. G. SMITH'S FUNERAL.

It took Place this Afternoon—Deceased's Wife Permitted to View the Body.

J.L.G. SMITH FUNERAL[31]
IT TOOK PLACE THIS AFTERNOON—DECEASED'S WIFE PERMITTED TO VIEW THE BODY.

The funeral of J. L. G. Smith took place this afternoon, the Rev J. W. Maxwell conducting the services. At their conclusion the funeral cortege left Schwab's undertaking rooms and proceeded to the Hailey depot, where the corpse was turned over to the care of Dr. Mackay, who will escort it to Boise, accompanied by Willie Smith, eldest son of Mrs. Margaret Smith and third son of the deceased, and by Miss Mollie, eldest daughter of Mrs. Margaret Smith and the deceased.

Charles Smith, second son of the deceased by his first marriage, came in from his ranch at Soldier, Camas Prairie, last evening, and attended the funeral—which was numerously attended by citizens afoot or in carriages.

Mrs. J. L. G. Smith requested, and was granted, permission to take a last look at the corpse; and about half-past 12 she left the jail in company with her son Willie and her two nieces—the little Agnew girls—and walked up First Avenue to the undertaker's, where all were in the meantime excluded, except the four persons of her party. She then returned to jail, the sheriff having, as in duty bound, kept an eye on her from the jail to the undertaker's and back again.

Pitt, eldest son of the deceased, has not been heard from since the deplorable affair. He and his uncle, James Agnew, brother of Mrs. Smith, were at Silver Mountain at last accounts, and they expected to reach Boise in time to attend the funeral."

THE SMITH CASE
PRELIMINARY EXAMINATION OF
THE WIFE OF THE DECEASED.

The Charge of Murder in the First Degree—Testimony of the Coroner, Dr. Figgins, and Others—A Bloody Hammer in Evidence.

The preliminary examination of Mrs. Margaret Smith, on a charge of murdering her husband, J. L. G. Smith, proprietor of the Hailey Hot Springs, began at 10 o'clock this morning, in the District Courtroom, before Probate Judge Lemmon.

The defendant appeared in court accompanied by Willie, her eldest son, and by Messrs. N. M. Ruick, Texas Angel, and I. N. Sullivan, her attorneys.

District Attorney Roberts appeared for the prosecution.

Dr. Figgins was the first witness called.

Mr. Ruick asked if these were all the witnesses to be called by the prosecution? If so, the rule in relation to the absence of witnesses would not be enforced.

The District Attorney said he wanted Dr. Brown and William Smith called.

"What is your full name, Mrs. Smith?" Asked Judge Lemmon.

"Margaret Francis" the prisoner replied in tremulous tones.

Dr. Figgins took the stand.

I. N. Sullivan, of counsel for the defense, asked if any further witnesses were to be called?

"C. V. Haupt," answered Judge Lemmon.

Dr. Figgins, Dr. Brown, and John West were then sworn.

Dr. Figgins (the witness) made the post mortem on the body of J. L. G. Smith, deceased, at Schwamb's undertaking rooms April 3rd; deceased died of a gunshot wound in the head—in the left lobe, the ball penetrating the frontal bone about two inches above the entire left lobe of the brain passing out about the line of the occipital and parietal bones, as near as I could make out from the shattered condition of said bones; in my professional opinion death was instantly caused by the wound described; from the marks of lead I found on some pieces of bone, I judge the wound was caused by a rifle ball.

I. WERTHEIMER SWORN

The 2nd of April was in his store; Mrs. Smith was there several times—about 3 o'clock in the afternoon and again about half-past 4 or 5. When she first came there was nobody there. Mr. Ruick came in while Mrs. Smith was talking to him. She asked if Dr. Figgins was upstairs. I said I don't think he was. She went out, and shortly after came back—she probably went upstairs in the meantime. When she returned she told me she wanted me to go to the sheriff's office. I asked what for? She answered that she had killed her husband—had killed Smith.

> Mr. Ruick: You did not accompany Mrs. Smith to the Sheriff's office?
> A: No Sir.
> Q: Who did?
> A: Dr. McKay.
> Q: Did she, or did she not start in the direction of the Sheriff's office when she left your store?
> A: I don't know; I didn't notice which way.

DR. BROWN SWORN

Am a physician and surgeon, and Coroner of Alturas County. About 5 o'clock p.m., April 2nd, went to the Smith dwelling, having heard, through a messenger, that there had been a shooting at the house and that Mr. Smith was seriously injured. Mr. John West, Mr. Tatro, and several others were present when I arrived there. Mr. Smith was dead, and lying flat on his back in the northeast room of the house, his head in a northeasterly direction. His head was about two feet from the northern wall of the room. Deceased had been wounded about the left side of the vertex of the skull, the ball penetrating about two inches above the left side of the left orbit. In my opinion death resulted instantaneously from the wound. Deceased fell just where he was shot, or nearly so. When shot deceased was inclining forward—or his head was—in my opinion. Saw the bullet with which this wound was supposed to have been inflicted sticking in the wall near the top of the ceiling and had A. J. Jackson take it out for me. [Producing a bullet.] Here it is. [Bullet introduced in evidence.] On the floor found several pieces of the bones of the skull, a large quantity of blood, also brain-matter, and a fur cap with a bullet-hole through it. Found a Sharp's rifle in an adjoining bedroom. [A fur cap handed witness.] This is the cap. [A rifle handed witness.] This is the gun. [Cap and gun admitted in evidence.] Casually examined the face of deceased. Did not see any powder-marks upon it. They might have easily been overlooked, the face being bloody and dirty. From observation and reading. I think the face would have been safe from powder burns at a distance of 15 or 18 feet. Assuming that there were no powder marks on the face, or flakes that might have been blown away by a strong wind, the deceased must have been 20 feet away.

AFTERNOON SESSION

John West sworn: Was at Andy Brown's when the shooting occurred—140 or 150 feet from the Smith dwelling. Saw deceased come home that afternoon, about 4 o'clock. From where witness stood could see but could not hear what was said. Deceased was running the boy around the house and barn. About 4:15 Mrs. Smith came over and asked me to get Mr. Tatro to arrest Smith. I said I would. She started toward the house, when I called out that she had better go down town to swear out a warrant, as Mr. Tatro could not act without it. She said she would, and went back to the house. About three minutes later I heard a report of a gun; and immediately Mrs. Smith and Willie came out, and Willie came over and said, "Ma shot pa, and I'm afraid she's killed him." He left me to go down town to ask some one to come up. Was looking toward the kitchen door when Mrs. Smith and Willie came out. Saw some blood on Willie's hands and face; it might have been something else. Thinks the door was shut when she came out. About a minute after they came out Willie came right over to witness and told him about the shooting. Witness went right over to the house with Willie. Found the dining room and sitting room doors closed. Opened them, and saw Mr. Smith lying on the floor, on the north side of the stove, lying very strait [sic] on the back. The bedroom door was open; the north door was locked; this last was about seven feet from the bedroom door. Did not see the rifle until after the Coroner came up; it was setting inside the bedroom, behind the door. After the shot was fired I heard what seemed as though it was some bad language. [Objected to by defense. Objection sustained.]

District Attorney: You can state, if you know, what was said by Mrs. Smith, immediately after the shooting.

Witness: I don't know; I heard something—she might have said something—but I could not understand.

[The prisoner rocks nervously in her chair and is evidently about to protest that she did not say anything. Her son restraining her.]

District Attorney.—What did you understand the words to be?

[Objected to. Objection sustained.]

The witness being directed to answer to the first question above stated, said: "The way I understood what Mrs. Smith said, I would not swear to it."

Q: (By District Attorney.)—How far were Mr. Smith's feet from the bedroom?

A: Between eight or nine feet—it might be less, and it might be more.

Witness noticed a hammer upon the table in the bedroom; noticed blood on the pole of it; does not know where the hammer is now. Searched for it that day, to give to the Coroner, but could not find it. This must have been 15 minutes later. The house was then full of people. After the shooting Mrs. Smith came right out, and started off toward the schoolhouse, just as if nothing had happened.

Adjourned till 10 a.m. tomorrow. [The impression prevails that the defense will seek to have the prisoner admitted to bail pending action by the grand jury. As this would have the effect of reducing the charge against her the prosecution will probably object; on the ground that murder is not a bailable offense.—Rep.]

The Smith Case[33]
PRELIMINARY EXAMINATION OF THE WIFE OF THE DECEASED

The evidence all in. The arguments to be heard Thursday morning, at Ten o'clock.

The preliminary examination of Mrs. Margaret Smith for killing her husband J. L. G. Smith, the 2nd instant was resumed this morning in the Second District Court, before Probate Judge Lemmon.

Charles Haupt sworn: Is a saloonkeeper and resides in Hailey. Was acquainted with deceased, and is acquainted with defendant.

Q: By District Attorney.—About the 8th or 10th of March lat, did you have a conversation with the defendant during which she made threats against the life of deceased? [Objected to, because "leading" Objection sustained.]

Q: You can state if, about the 10th of March last, you had a conversation with this defendant; and if so, you can state what that conversation was?

A: On or about the 8ᵗʰ of March Mrs. Smith drove very fast or the team ran away—I couldn't tell which; Mrs. Smith made the remark: "There goes the old fool again; I wish them horses would break his neck. I wish to God they would kill him." I then said: "Mrs. Smith, you don't mean that—do you? You don't want your husband killed?" While saying this I walked to the front porch; she followed me right to the door, and answered: "Yes, I do mean it! It will save me or somebody else the trouble of killing him, some time."

RECESS FOR A FEW MINUTES

Mrs. J. R. Wilson sworn: Resides in Hailey; is acquainted with the defendant. During November or December last had a conversation with Mrs. Smith; remembers some of it. Pretty soon after Mrs. Smith came to her house she spoke about Mr. Smith being drunk again. She said she came very near shooting him, the other day. Witness said: "Mrs. Smith don't do that!" She said: "I will!" Witness said: "Don't you know they'd take you and put you in prison, if you was to do that? And what would become of your children?" She said: "No, they wouldn't bother them."

Mrs. Margaret Brown sworn: Resides about a block or a half from the Smith dwelling. Mrs. Smith was at her house the afternoon of the 2ⁿᵈ instant, between 3 and 4 o'clock. She came over and inquired for Mr. West, she also wanted him to go after Mr. Tatro; witness came out and asked her what she wanted with him? She said she wanted Mr. Tatro to come and arrest Mr. Smith, witness asked her if he was drunk? She answered "He's always that." Witness answered, "That's too bad." She said, "Yes, I've stood it for 12 years and can't stand it any longer." She then went over and just as she went in witness had in the mean time gone to the back part of her house, and was looking through a window by the kitchen door. Went after Tatro. Then witness heard a shot and groans. It was one or two minutes after they went into the house; can not say whether she heard the groan first or the shot, remained at the kitchen window, and saw Willie come out and wash his hands, his mother was with him, she talking to him but witness could not hear anything she said: Willie was endeavoring to wash blood stains off his hands, did not notice any stains on any other portion of his person. Mrs. Smith then turned into the house, in the sitting room, after her hat; she then came out and started to town. While Willie was washing his hands in a tin basin.

Q: Did he get the basin himself, or did somebody hand it to him? [Objected to; Objection sustained.]

Q: Where did he obtain that basin?

A: From inside of the kitchen door. Cannot say whether there was water. [Question objected to as shading." Objection sustained.] When Mrs. Smith came to the kitchen door she had on a large kitchen apron, with sleeves. It was a light colored apron. When she started to go down town she did not have that apron on.

Cross-examined. Is acquainted with W. C. Tatro.

Q: (By Mr. Ruick)—Is he, or is he not an officer in this town or acting as such? [Objected to as not the best evidence and immaterial. Objection overruled.]

A: Yes sir; he is acting as such.

Q: (By Judge Lemmon.) —Mrs. Brown, how long after you heard the shot and groans was it until you saw Mrs. Smith and Willie come out the kitchen door?

A: I could not exactly say, but everything was quiet in the sitting room when they came out. I don't suppose it was more than a minute after the shot.

The prosecution rests.

Recess until 2 o'clock.

AFTERNOON RECESSION

Dr. Figgins recalled (for the defense)—Conducted the post mortem at the request of Dr. Brown, Coroner of Alturas County, April 3rd, between 9 and 10 o'clock, a.m.; counted 19 grains of powder that had been blown in to the skin of the face; they were thoroughly imbedded in the face of deceased, as he had been thoroughly washed by the undertaker.

William Smith sworn: Is a son of J. L. G. Smith, deceased, and of Margaret F. Smith, the defendant in this case. The 2nd of April, this year, in the afternoon, was present when the difficulty occurred between his father and mother which resulted in death of the former. In the morning, about 6 o'clock, witness came home from Mrs. Lopuck's house, and stayed until breakfast—about 8; he then went down to Mrs. Louck's house again, to relieve a person who had sat all night; stayed there a while, until young George W. Faylor came to his assistance; he then went home. This was about half-past 9 in the morning. Went to bed and got up about half past 12, went down town, came back about 2. There was no one home when he came back. Stayed around for a while, built a fire. By this time my mother had come back; Andy Brown came over after some potatoes; I went into the house; and my mother followed me; went into the sitting room; my mother looking out the kitchen window saw my father coming home with the buggy. She came into the front room, and told me to go and help father with the team. I went out, and unhitched one tug. By this time my father had unhitched three; I took the inside checks, my father the inside. And I did up the line on the near horse; the line on the off horse was left down, my father not doing it up. We started to lead our horses into the stable—he going first. His horse stepped on the line that was dragging, threw up his head and ran away. All this time my father was cursing my mother, myself, and the rest of the family. Father's horse ran around back of the barn. I led my horse to the front of the barn door, father ran back of the barn and caught his horse. I let him go in first, as usual, then followed in with mine. Father then went out back of the barn, stood there cursing myself and all of us, while I was unharnessing the team. When I got through I went to the house, my father following. He then began cursing my mother, who had not spoken a word to him yet until he went out of the house and came back. I then told him I didn't want him to curse me or my mother—or something to that effect. This seemed to enrage him all the more. He advanced, swore at my mother, as if getting ready to strike her. I jumped between, and interfered. He seemed to get madder at me, and attacked me. I ran around the stove, to get out of his way. I did this two or three times. He stopped, and went out in the yard, but soon came in throwing three newspapers and a bill from Swift and Regan on the floor, saying: "Look at the bills I've brought in!" After that he again advanced toward my mother. I interfered. He made another attack on me for doing so. I kept out of his way the best I could. He went out into the yard again, came in and pulled his coat off, and swore he would clear us out. He made another attempt to fight, I interfered again. He then went out into the dining room where he laid his coat, came into the room and my mother went over to Brown's; my father chased me out into the backyard and around the buggy, I then saw my mother coming back. She went in; my father started in as soon as he saw her, and followed her into the front room. She went into the bedroom, and started to close the door, which she got almost or quite closed when my father kicked it open; in kicking the door struck my mother with such force that it staggered her back against the foot of the bed. She straightened up and caught a gun; my father caught her right arm with his left hand, just as she got straightened up. He raised his arm in the attitude of striking; I caught his arm and saved him from striking; in getting back through the door he struck his right cheekbone on the side of the door, peeling the skin off the bone. He then made another attack on me; I got out of his way by running out in the yard, till he stopped chasing me; he came back into the house, and started striking mother; I interfered again; he backed up against the side of the wall, and said some words I didn't exactly understand, but I understood some of them: These were "I'll clean you out!" He then started toward my mother again. At this time I went on the opposite side of the stove from him; after he advanced toward my mother about three steps, mother fired, my father began to fall, his knees bending first, and the rest of his body came to the floor. I went to his head, and lifted it up, went to his feet and took the right foot out from under the lounge, as it seemed to be cramped. My mother went to his head, and said: "He is dead!" She went and put on her rubbers, hat and shawl, and started down town to give herself up. I started down town; the first person I saw was, Uncle Johnny West. I said I was going for Dr. Figgins. We went over to the house to look at father. He stammered out these words: Go down to Wertheimer's store and tell him to come up. I went to Wertheimer's store; and there I met my mother, Dr. McKay, Mr. Ruick, and Mr. Wertheimer; by this time they knew what was the matter, and I went out of the store with my mother and Dr. McKay down to about opposite the Bank. I then turned back, left my mother with Dr. McKay, and started toward home. The streets were alive with people aware of the accident; every body that I could see was running. I went straight in the house, some coming and some going.

Q: (by Mr. Ruick) What had you been doing at Mrs. Louck's during the night between the 1ˢᵗ and 2ⁿᵈ of April?

A: I was sitting up with a friend and a brother, in a Good Templar's house; he was sick with pneumonia.

Q: What was your father's condition as to sobriety the afternoon of April 2ⁿᵈ?

A: He was slightly intoxicated—about enough to be at his best.

Q: How many children has your mother, besides yourself?

A: She has three.

Q: All younger than yourself?

A: Yes, sir.

Q: At the time he pulled off his coat in the house, what coat did he pull off?

A: His every day dress coat.

Q: When, if at all, did he put that coat on?

A: He put it on shortly after he took it off.

Q: Please state the names, and the language which he used at the time you mentioned when he was in the front room, and at other times after he came home?

A: He said: "You d—d old bitch," "You d—-d old son of a bitch," "You d—d old whore," and referring to me, called me a "God d—d son of a bitch," different times.

Q: Where was your mother standing at the time this shot was fired?

A: Just inside the threshold of the bedroom door.

Q: Where were you standing at the time that your father was shot?

A: I stood in the same tracks I was when he was standing against the wall.

Q: On which side of the stove from your father?

A: On the further side of the stove from him.

Q: After your father's return, that afternoon, when did you first see the rifle with which he was killed?

A: Just at it was fired.

Q: Did you see your mother pick up the rifle before this time?

A: I did not.

Q: Where had the rifle been kept in the house previous to this occurrence?

A: Generally in the closet behind the bedroom door.

[What followed of this witness' testimony (as well as what preceded) substantially agrees with what he testified at the inquest.—Rep.)

Following is new evidence: Explaining the presence of a cartridge in the rifle, witness said that just as he was about to shoot crows, three weeks prior to the shooting, Elmer Buncell drove up with a team and cutter; witness immediately put away the gun, and the two went down town together. The room in which witness' father was shot is about 12 x14 feet. After the shooting witness got blood on his hands by lifting his father's head a little way from the floor, and laying it down again. The only language he heard his mother use after the shooting was pleading with him to stay at home with his father until she gets back.

The defense rests.

Adjourned until Thursday morning, at 10 o'clock.

J.L.G. SMITH'S WILL

The next day C. G. Smith, second son of J. L. G. Smith, deceased applied for letters of administration on the estate of his father.[34]

"J. L. G. Smith's Will[35]

It is Found Among the Papers in the Hands of John M. Cannady

It now turns out that J. L. G. Smith, made his last will and testament at Idaho City in 1880, in the presence of two witnesses. Shortly after the death of Mr. Smith, his son Charles called upon Judge Cannady to look at papers, which had been left in his charge for safekeeping. Among them were found a number of deeds, Government Patents, and a sealed envelope, on the outside of which was nothing to indicate its contents. Upon opening this envelope it was found to contain the will as above stated. The property is disposed of as follows.

To his eldest two sons, by his first wife, Pitt and Charles, he gave $100 cash. To his second wife and her four children, he gave the balance of his estate to be divided share and share alike. This will divide the majority of the estate into fifths, which we are informed will not be acceptable to Mrs. Smith, and there is strong probability of a protest."[36]

In the will situation [19 April 1888]: "In opposition to the petition of Charles Smith to be appointed administrator of the estate of his father, Mrs. Margaret Smith now comes into the Probate Court, and files her petition, accompanied by the will of her late husband, asking the appointment of Dr. W. W. McKay. Mrs. Smith, by the will left, was made executrix, which right she relinquishes in the petition asking for

Dr. McKay's appointment. A day will be set for the hearing of these petitions by the Court."[37]

[12 May 1888] " MRS. SMITH ASKS FOR AN ALLOWANCE FOR HER CHILDREN. Mrs. Margaret F. Smith has applied to the Probate Court for an allowance, out of the estate of her deceased husband, for the support of her family. She states that J. W. Smith is 17 years old, Mary is 15, Joseph L. G. is 12, and J. D. A. is 14 years old—the same being children of said deceased—and that they are wholly dependent upon said estate for their maintenance. She asks that $100 per month be allowed, from April 1, 1888, and payable the first of each month, until the further order of the Court."[38]

[25 May 1888] "No order in the Smith case today, the Probate Court having been occupied" with the will of Captain Settle.[39]

HELD WITHOUT BAIL

Dr. W.W. McKay was appointed executor of Smith's estate.[40] Back in court 3 days later Probate Judge Lemmon rendered this decision: "It appearing to me that the offense in the within depositions mentioned has been committed—that is, the crime of murder—and that there is sufficient cause to believe that the within named Mrs. Margaret Smith is guilty thereof, I order that she is hereby committed to the Sheriff of Alturas County.

N. M. Ruick, of counsel for the defense, moved that she be admitted to bail.

Judge Lemmon will decide upon this application Monday next, at 10 o'clock a.m."[41]

Judge Lemmon Decides the Motion Adversely in the Case of Mrs. Margaret F. Smith.

The motion to admit Mrs. Margaret F. Smith to bail, which was argued and submitted on Monday, was this morning decided adversely by Judge Lemmon, who holds the prisoner to await the action of the grand jury at the May term. The May term convenes on the 15th, and the grand jury will in all probability be impaneled that day.

This disposes of the Smith case until that time, unless the attorneys for the defendant bring it before the Chief Justice or one of the Associate Justices of the Supreme Court on a writ of habeas corpus. To do this, the writ must be granted by one of the Judges of the Supreme Court, and the body of the prisoner must be taken by the Sheriff before the Judge granting the writ, at the time and place specified therein.

As none of the judges are in the county at present, and not likely to be until the 15th of May, Mrs. Smith will, in all probability, remain in the custody of the sheriff until her case comes up for trial in the District Court."[42]

The next day [19 April 1888]: "J. H. Harris, of Bellevue, came up this morning and repaired at once to the office of the District Attorney. He comes to assume the duties of Deputy District Attorney and will assist General Roberts in the Margaret F. Smith and other important cases now pending. The General is to be congratulated on this appointment, as it brings to his aid the legal acumen of one of the ablest attorneys in Idaho."[43]

[23 May 1888] The attorneys of Mrs. J. L. G. Smith have filed certificates signed by Drs. Brown and Figgins, testifying to her serious illness, and given notice that they will move the Probate Court that she be admitted to bail."[44]

[24 May 1888] " In the Probate Court today the arguments upon the motion to admit Mrs. J. L. G. Smith to bail were heard. Judge Lemmon reserved his decision until tomorrow morning."[45]

[22 June 1888] "Close confinement is beginning to tell on Mrs. J. L. G. Smith, and she appears thin and careworn. She is allowed to take a walk in the jail yard every evening, after dark, in company with her daughter or one of her other children."[46]

Late in the summer [14 August 1888] the bail issue arose again. "In the case of Mrs. J. L. G. Smith, who applied to be admitted to bail, the court will render an opinion next Monday."[47]

[20 August 1888] "In the case of the Territory of Idaho vs. Mrs. J. L. G. Smith, the Court granted her application to be admitted to bail, and fixed the amount at $5000. The bond being promptly furnished, the defendant is at liberty. The bondsmen and the amounts in which they justified are as follows: T. E. Picotte, $2000; A. J. Rupert, $1000; P.A. Regan, $1500; Frank Garbutt, $500; D. Agnew, $500."[48]

[17 May 1889] "The People vs. Margaret F. Smith, arraigned on a charge of murder.—Demurrer overruled. Defendant excepts, and pleads "Not Guilty."[49]

[22 May 1889] "Territory of Idaho vs. Margaret F. Smith. Motion for change of venue granted."[50]

[30 October 1889] District Attorney Waters left today for Boise City, expecting to return …to attend the preliminary examination of the Chinaman accused of murder, after which he will go to Shoshone to prosecute the case against J. L. G. Smith."[51]

[6 Nov 1889] "The case against Mrs. J. L. G. Smith is set for trial at Shoshone Friday morning of this week. District Attorney Waters will therefore be compelled to leave for Shoshone tomorrow."[52]

When Waters returned from Shoshone he reported the jury returned the verdict in less than one hour after leaving the box.[53]

Boise newspapers reported on the trial in much briefer fashion. The couple was quarreling and he allegedly started toward her.[54] She feared another beating and grabbed a rifle and shot him through the head, killing him instantly. Smith was known to be a violent and quarrelsome drunk. The body was taken to Boise to be buried by the Masonic Lodge.[55] A preliminary hearing was held in the Probate Court and the crowd overflowed.[56] Mrs. Smith was held for murder but the Boise newspaper editorialized in her defense.[57]

In Rocky Bar the newspaper report said: Mrs. Smith was tried for the crime of murder and acquitted after a "long and tedious trial" at Hailey [erroneous].[58] "Mrs. Margaret Smith, of this city [Boise], was on trial last week before the court at Shoshone, Logan County, charged with the murder of her husband, J. L. Smith at Hailey more than a year ago. The jury were out less than an hour, and returned with a verdict of acquittal."[59]

The initial report in Hailey said: "MRS. SMITH ACQUITTED. The case of the Territory of Idaho vs. Mrs. J. L. G. Smith, for the shooting of her husband, which was on trail in Shoshone last week, came to an end Saturday night by the acquittal of Mrs. Smith. J. S. Waters and Vic. Bierbower appeared for the prosecution, while N. M. Ruick and Angel and Sullivan were counsel for the defense. The case has excited more or less interest from the beginning to the close, and attendance at the courtroom was large. Sunday, Attorney Angel received a telegram from his partner in Shoshone stating that the defendant had been acquitted."[60]

About a week after the trial, The Salt Lake *Herald* reported said Mrs. Smith and family and the Agnew family, her relatives, would make their future home in South America.[61] This never came to pass.

"Mrs. J. L. G. Smith has bought a farm within a half mile of Emmett, Payette Valley, and will occupy it. It contains eighty acres, part of which is set to clover. It also has a comfortable dwelling and a fine orchard. Herself and two younger sons will carry on the farm this season, while William, the older son, and his sister, Miss Mollie, will attend an eastern school."[62] She bought a farm at Emmett in the Payette Valley and moved there in 1890. The two younger sons lived with her while the older children, William and Mollie, attended an eastern school.[63]

On the 28th of May 1891 Mrs. Smith and a Mrs. Davis and the Davis' little daughter attempted to ford the Payette River in a buggy.[64] The treacherous current upset the buggy and swept Mrs. Smith to her death. Mrs. Davis held to the harness with one hand and her child with the other and managed to be miraculously pulled to shore by the horses.[65] The Smith children were complete orphans. J.L.G. Smith was another follower of Gambrinus who lived a violent frontier life.

THE HAILEY HOT SPRINGS

"SMITH'S SPRINGS. Notice To The People of Wood River.

The undersigned, having been this day put in charge of Smith's hot Springs, near Hailey, will endeavor to so manage them as to meet with public approval.

The hack will take passengers to and from the Springs at all hours

Hailey Hot Springs.

Grand Opening Festivities June 20, 1889---Low Railroad Rates.

Robert Strahorn & Co., proprietors of Hailey Hot Springs, announce the formal opening of that delightful re- resort on Thursday, June 20. In order to give residents of Idaho, Montana, Utah and Oregon an op- portunity of becoming acquainted with the resort and the attractions of the great Wood River Region, the Union Pacific company has ordered a rate of one fare for the round trip from all stations to Hailey and re- turn, good from June 17th to the 25th inclusive. This will give all visitors ample time to enjoy the opening fes- tivities, which will be more than us- ually varied and attractive. It will also enable the disciples of Izaak Walton to tempt the gamey trout, of which Wood River and tributary streams are said to be fairly alive this year. The glories of Wood River scenery, the bracing mountain atmos- phere, the unequaled natural drives and the allurements and hospitality of Hailey will also not be lost sight of.

Of course there will be music and dancing and feasting on June 20, and everybody who can should go. We are informed that no special invita- tions will be issued, but, as on all such occasions, the doors will be open wide. A general invitation is of course extended to all who care to encourage enterprises of this nature —enterprises of which Idaho has stood so much in need.

of the day or night. Fare for the round trip (including bath) 75 cents.

Orders left at the Alturas or Merchant's Hotels promptly attended to.

B. F. OLIVER, MANAGER

Hailey, I. T., May 18, 1888."[66]

[22 June 1888] "THE HAILEY HOT SPRINGS.

The rumors of a change of ownership of this property which have been in circulation for some time have this state of facts for a foundation: About a week ago, a gentleman looked the property over and offered to purchase it at a stipulated price, cash in hand, provided it could be got within 30 days. The offer was deemed to be a liberal one enough, under the circum- stances; and if the owners had been free to do so it would have been accepted. But, owing to the recent death of Mr. Smith and the consequent legal entangle- ment of the estate, no one can be accepted, unless some safe way can be found to convey the title—one that will satisfy all parties in interest."[67]

SMITH'S SPRINGS

Notice to the People of Wood River. The undersigned, having leased Smith's Hot Springs, near Hailey, will endeavor to so manage them as to meet with public approval.

The hack will take passengers to and from the Springs at all hours of the day or night. Fare for the round trip (including bath) 75 cents.

Orders left at the Alturas Hotel or Rupert's drug store promptly attended to, A. R. Sullivan, Lessee. Hailey, I. T., June 27, 1889.

THE HAILEY HOT SPRINGS

They are now the Property of Robert Strahorn & Co.

Today Robert Strahorn & Co. took up the deed conveying to them all the right, title and interest of the Smith estate in and to the Hailey Hot Springs, which has been in escrow for some time past, by paying the purchase price, which is $800. This, although a fair consideration under the circumstances, is a mere song when the present and prospective value of the property is taken into consideration; but it is better for the old owners, for the community, and for the world at large that the property should have changed hands.

The new owners have practically unlimited resources, and will work in harmony with the Union Pacific Railway officials. They will at once proceed to plow up a considerable portion of the grounds surrounding the springs, build an elegant dwelling for the residence of the manager, Robert E. Strahorn and his wife, also erect an hotel with a limited number of rooms for the exclusive use of invalids who may not be able to ride back and forth between the town and springs, set out ornamental shade and fruit trees and shrubs, and a large

WOOD RIVER TIMES

HAILEY, IDAHO.

SATURDAY.................................JUNE 8, 1889

variety of choice flowering plants, build a fence around the whole, and make other improvements as they suggest themselves. They will not only work for the present, as they will move after the view of attaining to the highest degree of development of which the business and property shall be capable.

In the execution of this plan care will be taken to extensively advertise the springs in the hundreds of thousands of copies of the various publications of the literary bureau of the Union Pacific Company, as well as in other publications; and by this time next year the Hailey Thermal Springs will be almost as widely known as Wood River country is today, and wealthy tourists will be coming to visit them in ever increasing numbers.

In order to be able to properly accommodate the expected flood of tourists Strahorn & Co. will doubtless soon find that one or two of our first class hotels are indispensable; and they will therefore either purchase the Merchants and Alturas, or build one that will be equal to these two in every respect."[68]

AT THE HOT SPRINGS

Ground Broken for a New Ladies Plunge—A Fine Stable to be erected.

Ground was broken, at the Hailey Hot Springs today, for a new ladies' plunge which will be 30 X 60 feet, and which will have at least six dressing rooms 6 X 10 feet each. This, like all the work of Strahorn & Co., will be located 100 feet west of the pavilion, which, in turn, is located 300 feet north of the Croy Gulch Road.

In a few days ground will be broken for the Hot Springs stable. This will be a two-story-and-cellar structure 24 X 60 feet. It will be located on the Croy gulch road, about 300 feet south of the pavilion.

By the end of this fall Robert Strahorn & Co. expect that their investments in Hailey and vicinity will reach somewhere between $50,000 and $60,000."[69]

HAILEY HOT SPRINGS

Grand Opening Festivities June 20, 1889—Low Railroad Rates.

"Robert Strahorn and Co. proprietors of Hailey Hot Springs, announce the formal opening of that delightful resort on Thursday, June 20. In order to give residents of Idaho, Montana, Utah and Oregon an opportunity of becoming acquainted with the resort and the attractions of the great Wood River Region, the Union Pacific has ordered a rate of one fare for the round trip from all stations to Hailey ad return, good from June 17th to the 25th inclusive. This will give all visitors ample time to enjoy the opening festivities, which will be more than usually varied and attractive. It will also enable the disciples of Izaak Walton to tempt the gamey trout, of which Wood River and tributary streams are said to be fairly alive this year. The glories of Wood River scenery, the bracing mountain atmosphere, the unequalled natural drives and the allurements and hospitality of Hailey will also not be lost sight of.

Of course there will be music and dancing and feasting on June 20, and everybody who can should go. We are informed that no special invitation will be issued, but, as on all such occasions, the doors will be open wide. A general invitation is of course extended to all who care to encourage enterprises of this nature—enterprises of which Idaho has stood much in need."[70]

AT THE SPRINGS

How Thanksgiving Day Was Observed There—Some of the Prize Winners. Thanksgiving was a red-letter day at the Hailey Hot Springs, the Hotel being crowded with visitors from 10 o'clock in the morning until late into the night.

The day's fun opened with turkey shooting, in which quite a number participated at 50 cents a shot ...."[71]

Smith's hot springs resort continued operating while the indispensable man continued his residency in the cemetery.

FAMILIES OF JOHN LAWSON GREEN SMITH

John Lawson Green "Shanghai" Smith (HUSBAND)

Birth:	30 Jun 1831
Place:	Maine
Death:	4 Apr 1888
Place:	Hailey, Idaho
Father:	John Smith
Mother:	Martha Ann Green
Mary Hamilton	(1st wife)

of Camptonville, California

Children:	Pitt, Charles

Pitt Smith

Birth:	1854
Place:	Wisconsin

Charles Smith

Birth:	1860
Place:	Washington Territory
Margaret Francis Agnew	(2nd wife) married 1869
Birth:	1841
Place:	Missouri
Death:	28 May 1891
Place:	Payette River, Idaho
Children:	William, Mary, Joseph, J.D.A.

William B.

Birth: 1871

Place:	Boise, ID

Mary

Birth:	ca 1873

Joseph Lawson Green

Birth:	ca 1876

J. D. A.

Birth:	ca 1874

END NOTES

1, 2 *Idaho Daily Statesman*, Boise, Idaho, 5 April 1888, p. 3, c. 2.

3   MyFamily.com. Gardiner, Kennebec County, Maine, Birth & Death records, 1800-1892. Internet site.

4   Elliot, Wallace W. *History of Idaho The Territory: Showing Its Resources and Advantages*. San Francisco: Wallace W. Elliot, 1884. pp. 27-28.

5   Federal Tax Records, 1865-66,University of Idaho Library, Microfilm # 58.

6   *Idaho World*, Idaho City, 19 August 1865, p. 1, c. 1.

7   *Idaho Tri-Weekly Statesman*, Boise, Idaho, 20 November 1866, p. 2, c. 3.

8   *Tri-Weekly Statesman*, Boise, 2 April 1867, p. 2, c. 3.

9   Ada County Deed Book, p. 578 and 580.

10 *The Capital Chronicle*, Boise, Idaho, 21 July 1870, p. 3, c. 1.

11 *The Boise Weekly News*, Boise, Idaho, 12 November 1870, p. 2, c. 4.

12 *Idaho Tri-Weekly Statesman*, 30 October 1873, p. 3, c. 1.

13 *The Semi-Weekly Idahoan*, Boise, Idaho, 28 September 1877, p. 3, c. 1.

14 *Idaho Tri-Weekly Statesman*, 13 December 1877, p. 3, c. 1

15 *Idaho Tri-Weekly Statesman*, 10 September 1878, p. 3, c. 1.

16 *Idaho Tri-Weekly Statesman*, 25 November 1879,p. 3, c. 5.

17 *Idaho Tri-Weekly Statesman*, 25 December 1879,p. 3, c. 1.

18 *Idaho Tri-Weekly Statesman*, 8 June 1880, p. 3, c. 1.

19 Boise County Records, ISHS, Reel 12, p. 112.

20 Blaine County Judicial Records, Idaho State Historical Society, microfilm reel 13, Alturas County Records.

21 *Idaho Tri-Weekly Statesman*, 16 July, 1881, p. 3, c. 3.

22 *Idaho Tri-Weekly Statesman*, 24 April 1883, p. 3, c. 1-3.

23 *Idaho Tri-Weekly Statesman*, 14 July 1883, p. 3, c. 2.

24 *Idaho Tri-Weekly Statesman*, 28 February 1885, p. 3, c. 1.

25 *Idaho Tri-Weekly Statesman*, 10 July 1886, p. 3, c. 3.

26 *Wood River Times*, Hailey, Idaho, 4 November 1885, p. 4, c. 4.

27 *Wood River Times*, 2 April 1888, p. 3, c. 3.

28 *Wood River Times*, 3 April 1888, p. 3, c. 1-4.

29 *Wood River Times*, 3 April 1888, p. 3, c. 1-4.

30 *Wood River Times*, 4 April 1888, p. 3, c. 3.

31 *Wood River Times*, 5 April 1888, p. 3, c. 1.

32 *Wood River Times*, 9 April 1888, p. 3, c. 1-4.

33 *Wood River Times*, 10 April 1888, p. 3, c. 1-4.

34 *Wood River Times*, 11 April 1888, p. 3, c. 2.

35 *Wood River Times*, 16 April 1888, p. 3, c. 3.

36 *Wood River Times*, 16 April 1888, p. 3, c. 3.

37 *Wood River Times*, 19 April 1888, p. 3, c. 3.

38 *Wood River Times*, 12 May 1888, p. 3, c. 3.

39 *Wood River Times*, 25 May 1888, p. 3, c. 1.

40 *Idaho Daily Statesman*, 16 May 1888, p. 1, c. 3.

41 *Wood River Times*, 14 April 1888, p. 3, c. 2.

42 *Wood River Times*, 18 April 1888, p. 3, c. 3.

43 *Wood River Times*, 19 April 1888, p. 3, c. 3.

44 *Wood River Times*, 23 May 1888, p. 3, c. 1.

45 *Wood River Times*, 24 May 1888, p. 3, c. 1.

46 *Wood River Times*, 22 June 1888, p. 3, c. 1.

47 *Wood River Times*, 18 August 1888, p. 3, c. 3.

48 *Wood River Times*, 20 August 1888, p. 3, c. 3.

49 *Wood River Times*, 17 May 1889, p. 2, c. 1.

50 *Wood River Times*, 22 May 1889, p. 3, c. 1.

51 *Wood River Times*, 30 October 1889, p. 4, c. 3.

52 *Wood River Times*, 6 November 1889, p. 4, c. 1.

53 *Wood River Times*, 6 November 1889, p. 3, c. 3.

54 *Idaho Daily Statesman*, 5 April 1888, p. 3, c. 3-4.

55 *Idaho Daily Statesman*, 6 April 1888, p. 3, c. 1.

56 *Idaho Daily Statesman*, 15 April 1888, p. 3, c. 2.

57 *Idaho Daily Statesman*, 18 April 1888, p. 3, c. 2.

58 *The Elmore Bulletin*, Rocky Bar, Idaho, 6 June 1891, p. 3, c. 6.

59 *The Elmore Bulletin*, 6 June 1891, p. 3, c. 6.

60 *Daily News Miner*, 5 November 1889, p. 3, c. 2. The information spread throughout Idaho. See *Idaho World,* Idaho City, Idaho, 12 November 1889, p. 1, c. 3.

61 *Daily News Miner*, 10 November 1889, p. 3, c. 2.

62 *Wood River Times*, 28 March 1890, p. 3, c. 1. They cite the *Boise Democrat*.

63 *Idaho Daily Statesman*, 14 November 1889, p. 3, c. 2.

64 *The Elmore Bulletin*, 29 March 1890, p. 3, c. 5.

65 *The Elmore Bulletin*, 6 June 1891, p. 3, c. 6.

66 *Wood River Times*, 18 May 1888, p. 3, c. 2.

67 *Wood River Times*, 21 June 1888, p. 3, c. 2.

68 *Wood River Times*, 27 August 1888, p. 3, c. 1.

69 *Wood River Times*, 5 September 1888, p. 3, c. 2.

70 *Wood River Times*, 8 June 1889, p. 2, c. 2.

71 *Wood River Times*, 4 December 1889, p. 3, c. 4.

22

W. F. SOMMERCAMP, SR.

Mining Accident Victim

William Franz Sommercamp was an early arrival in Silver City, Idaho, and remained in that area until his tragic death. Another of the renaissance men who used the frontier condition to rise to the top in numerous fields, he was notable as a brewer, saloonkeeper, farmer, stock raiser, and mine owner. Even before his Idaho days, he had experienced a generous slice of frontier excitement.

Sommercamp was born in Hanover in 1828 of parents native to that German locality.[1] In 1847, he immigrated to the United States and settled at Independence, Missouri, for five years. He moved to Albany, Oregon, in 1855, and then on to Yreka, California. He married Mary Slack, and the family moved to Shasta Valley, California.[2] There William F. Jr. was born, and William Sr. worked in mining. In July of 1856, W. F. Sommercamp was on the committee to solicit money from the citizens of Yreka, California, to buy equipment to outfit the new fire department, Siskiyou Hook and Ladder Company, No. 1.[3] On the fire department membership list of 23 December 1856, W. F. Sommercamp, Axe Man, was found. So many brewers seemed drawn to firefighting.

Sommercamp had an adventure while a resident of Yreka that entered the pages of written history.[4] California's most famous group of desperadoes, the Tom Bell Gang, pulled their biggest robbery, the Trinity Mountain pack train holdup, on 12 March 1856.[5] On 10 March 1856, Rhodes and Whitney's express left Yreka, California, for

Shasta, 110 miles to the south, with $17,000 in gold dust. Solomon D. Brastow, the messenger in charge, had $13,000 of that, and Ithamer Hickman, a Yreka merchant, had $4,000 in dust on his mule. Packer Larry Delass and Sommercamp were the others accompanying the shipment. On the third day, they reached the base of Trinity Mountain and then started up. The train labored a mile and a half up the trail when suddenly bandits jumped out on both sides of them. Delass spotted them first and yelled, "Don't shoot!"

Most of the outlaws had double barrel shotguns, while one held a rifle. They all wore their red flannel shirts with the tails out and had a brace of six-shooters and a Bowie knife in each belt. They covered their faces with black silk handkerchiefs with eyeholes cut out and attached to skullcaps made from red blankets. Brastow had two revolvers in pommel holsters, but his mule was spooked by the grotesque figures the outlaws presented and bucked and lunged, making it impossible for Brastow to grab the guns. One of the robbers said, "Stop that! We don't want to kill you, but we must have your money."

One packer later said the bore on the robber's shotgun looked "as big as a hog's head." The Bell gang marched the men 600 yards from the trail and lashed them to trees before taking their watches and money. One packer warned them that they would be tracked down and caught. "You might as well hunt for a coyote," a robber replied.

The highwaymen had barely left when Hickman whispered, "Boys, I'm loose. Hold on 'til they get off a little way and I will unfasten you." Soon they all were free and they ran back up the trail just in time to see the bandits, now without their masks, mounted on mules and driving Brastow's pack animal ahead of them. The victims started on foot, and soon news of the robbery reached Shasta and Yreka and a huge manhunt began.

A man in Chico identified them and four men-members of the Tom Bell gang-were arrested. William Carter, one robber, was taken out to show where the loot had been buried by Shasta Sheriff and future Idaho brewer William Nunnally. After several trips to the spot, $14,000 was dug up. The gang was finally all caught, but the remainder of the money was never recovered.

On the 1860 U. S. Census, recorded on 26 March, William was 32; Mary, who was born in Ohio, was 21; and William Jr. was 4 months. The father's profession was farming, and he had $2,000 in real estate and $5,863 in personal estate. Another clue to his lifestyle was that in August of 1861, Robert Lehmann advertised his Ice Cream Saloon in Yreka as "Summercamp's (sic) Old Stand."[6] A notice in the Yreka, California, newspaper in November 1862 said that Mrs. William F. Sommercamp had been delivered of a daughter.[7] Apparently, this little girl did not live long, and she was not with the family by the 1870 Census. Our subject next went to Humboldt County, Nevada, briefly and then, in company with future Idaho brewer John Brodbeck, went by ox-team to Idaho.[8] In 1864, he arrived in Silver City and brought his family the following year. A son, Charles E., was born in July 1865 but lived less than two years. Eventually, 10 children, four reaching adulthood, were born to the Sommercamp family.

BUSINESSMAN

Sommercamp was first mentioned in the *Owyhee Avalanche* in August of 1865 when he and a partner named Stevens advertised their Challenge Saloon, with billiard table.[9] Late one night, thieves broke into the saloon and found about $10 in gold dust and small change but neglected to swipe several half dollars.[10] Sommercamp had removed the large deposits before he went home that night.

In September, Sommercamp and Stevens dissolved their partnership, with Sommercamp taking over the Challenge Saloon and Stevens later opening his own place.[11] An anonymous letter to the editor of the *Owyhee Avalanche* held some strong opinions on the situation.[12]

"I had some notion of having them [Stevens and Sommercamp] arrested for getting money from me under false pretense. I went in there the other evening to look at things as any josh is apt to do, when Bill Stevens said he'd give me 99 points and discount me then. Although I never had played any, I thought here was a good chance to begin. Billiards is said to be a fashlenab's game, and dates back a long time. It is said to have originated with some small boys while shooting bulltoads in a green-scummed mud-hole, with rake handles. But I digress. We proceeded to chalk our cues; we procured the chalk at the bar, as suggested by Bill. To string the balls was a comparatively easy matter for me—in fact; I strung things around generally, Stevens got the lead and as far as billiards were concerned kept it. To be sure, he'd give me an occasional shot—in the neck. The only carom I made during the game was on a bottle of something behind the bar, and on the bald headed man who was watching the game; in the excitement I mistook his pate for a white billiard ball, and he came pretty near taking my pate with a chair. In trying to ward off the chair, my cue knocked the chimney off the lamp overhead, some of the droplets of hot glass getting down the back of my neck, – when a scene took place almost as interesting to behold as a fellow with bumble-bees in his trousers. In the meantime, Bill Stevens was keeping count of the game. I have concluded that billiards are a swindle, and am glad Stevens & Sommercamp have dissolved—the latter may be all right, but Stevens won't do."[13]

In October, Sommercamp was on the jury in the case of People vs. Hargrave.[14] In mid-December, the *Owyhee Avalanche* editor walked up to see how the town of Silver was doing and "found Sommercamp's about the best winter camp in camp."[15]

In February, a call went out for volunteers to meet at Sommercamp's saloon "for the purpose of devising means to raise a volunteer force to chastise the savages who brutally murdered Andrew Hall at his ranch yesterday, and who have so long been thieving and murdering generally."[16] The Snake Indian War lasted from 1864 to 1868 and has been termed "The Deadliest Indian War in the West."[17] On February 13, about 30 Indians attacked Hall's ranch at Jordan Valley, Oregon, on the Idaho border. Rounds of attack and revenge characterized the war.

Early the next spring—for spring comes very late in mountainous Silver City—Sommercamp and his new partner, Thomas W. Bray, were building, on the south bank of Long Gulch, a brewery and saloon.[18] The paper said they had machinery and ingredients and expected to be in operation inside of a month. A rival brewery owned by the Grete Brothers (John and Fred) was also under construction at that time.

Sommercamp and Bray dissolved their partnership in the brewing business on 3 September 1866.[19] Sommercamp was to deal with all outstanding debts, and lager would still be available at his Challenge Saloon and Star Brewery.[20]

During these early years, Sommercamp was also prominent in placer mining near Ruby City (two miles from Silver) and he constructed one of the big ditches on Florida Mountain with extensive flumes to carry water to his ground.[21] He was one of the men involved with the Potosi mine when it was discovered in 1867. Almost 40 years later, his son W. F. Jr., led a reopening of the mine.[22]

The new Sommercamp brewery of 1866 had a cellar and two upper rooms that were to be neatly furnished and rented. The first story and saloon were below street level and "fixed up invitingly."[23] As the newspaper said, "Sommercamp knows how to make good lager and sell it too."[24] In May 1866, the Federal Tax Records listed Sommercamp and Bray and then the entry was crossed out with no collection listed. On a later page, they were shown to have paid their brewers' license. On June of 1866, the next month, Sommercamp and Bray paid Federal tax on 20 barrels of beer from their Silver City Brewery.[25] In July, Sommercamp and Bray paid $10.33 tax on the beer they brewed.[26] In August, Summercamp (sic) and Brey (sic) paid for brewing 9 barrels

84. W. F. Sommercamp portrait.

of beer, and for his brewers license.[27] In September, Sommercamp alone paid his brewers assessment and on 10 barrels brewed.[28] In November of 1866, Sommercamp paid Federal Tax for fermented liquors.[29] The 1867 Pacific Coast business directory listed Sommercamp as the proprietor for the Challenge Saloon.[30]

Mrs. Sommercamp arrived in Silver on Beachy's Boise stage line on 5 November 1866, apparently after a visit to the capital.[31] On 24 February 1867, son Charles E., age 1 year and 7 months, died at Silver City.[32] On the 19th of July 1867, she gave birth to a daughter.[33] The family added a son on 10 June 1869.[34]

Just over a year from his last building project, Sommercamp was again in the building expansion game. The *Owyhee Avalanche* said his new building with brewery in the cellar and a "magnificent billiard saloon" at street level will be the largest "edifice in Owyhee."[35] Sommercamp announced, at the end of November, the grand opening of this new building fronting on Washington and Jordan Streets a few doors north of the former location.[36] Two months later, the local gymnastic club was meeting on the ground floor.[37] This may have been a Turnverein branch or a German gymnastics club such as was also in Boise—and wherever a few Germans gathered.

In spring of 1868, Sommercamp replaced his billiard tables with three new ones and his saloon was proclaimed the largest saloon in the Territory.[38] Sommercamp had the largest safe in town in his saloon by 1868.[39] He was also a trustee of the joint stock company set up to build a city water works. Sommercamp had a shaft down 38 feet on the Red Jacket Mine by late September of 1870.[40] He joined with a Miller and Hoffer in working on placer diggings on Florida Mountain, one of the major mines sites in view of Silver City.[41] By May of the next year, the sluices were running.[42]

Sommercamp owned a store for many years too. It was next to the barbershop and bathhouse, and bathers would buy fresh clothes before taking their rare baths.[43] Lea Farris, an African-American, operated the bathhouse and the laundry that picked up the dirty clothes was Chinese.

Sommercamp ran business ads in Boise newspapers during 1870. One of these read: "Star Brewery and Billiard Saloon! Wm. F. Sommercamp, Proprietor. Fronting on Washington and Jordan Streets, Silver City, I.T. /Largest and Best-fitted up saloon in the territory. Three No. 1 billiard tables with Phelan's Patent Combination cushions. Good Wines, Liquors and Cigars. Orders left at the Saloon for Lager Beer in Barrels, Kegs or Bottles, promptly filled at Moderate Charges, W. F. Sommercamp."[44]

Early in the 1870s, there was a downturn in the mining industry, which was the economic base of Silver City. The Bank of California failed and brought on a money crisis that paralyzed the backers of the mines and indirectly led many miners to move on. Sommercamp led the subscription list for the destitute.[45] Sommercamp did not seem to be too badly hurt financially by the recession. In 1871, he was reported as painting and fixing up his billiard room to resemble a new one.[46] Later that winter, Q. A. French, bartender for Sommercamp, left for a tour of the Atlantic states.[47] In 1872, the newspaper reported the repainting and reopening of Sommercamp's saloon.[48] Apparently, the saloon was closing each winter at this time.

Sommercamp's seemingly sudden interest in stock raising during this period may have been caused by the decline in income of his other enterprises. Along with his mining partners, Hoffer and Miller, Sommercamp brought in Durham cattle and Berkshire hogs from Kentucky and Illinois and brought them to the Camp Lyon area of Owyhee County.[49] Subsequently, his winter stock ranch was described as three miles up Squaw Creek and 15 miles below Snake River Ferry.[50] This area had little snow most years and the livestock thrived. At his death, he had large cattle and horse interests there.

He also expanded his beer line with ale and porter, which few Idaho brewers ever made, and added a fireproof storeroom and bottling department.[51] About this time, he also opened a saloon in nearby Fairview. It was often called a brewery, but apparently had beer hauled in from Silver City. In 1874, it was reported that it was being renovated.[52] The newspaper called the Star Brewery and Billiard Saloon at Fairview one of the "largest and finest in Idaho Territory."[53] It was called a branch of the Silver City establishment and offered lager beer, ale, and porter.[54] The two billiard tables had "Phelan's patent combination cushions." Unfortunately in 1875, most of Fairview burned and Sommercamp's saloon was lost.[55] That year, Sommercamp was listed as a brewer of ale and porter in the Silver City directory carried in newspapers around the territory.[56]

Postmaster Rufus King left Silver after embezzling quite a bit of money. After a failed suicide attempt, he was sentenced to the penitentiary, leaving his bonds men to make up the missing money. James Graham, J. M. Short, and W. F. Sommercamp settled with the government for $281.28.[57]

Sommercamp sold a claim to the Golden Chariot Mining Company in April of 1875 for $1.[58] He purchased the claim of William Townsend known as the Morning Star Lode in May of 1875 for $300 in gold coin.[59] The same month, he bought a claim from John Gebhard for $270.[60] In October, Sommercamp bought yet another mining claim from James Spray for $250.[61] Also in October, he gave George Hicks $240 for a mining claim.[62] In January the next year, Sommercamp sold "The Discovery of the Leviathan" to Fred Warnke for $200.[63] In December of 1876, Sommercamp bought the "Crown Point" mineral location from Gilmore Hayes for $240.[64] Obviously, Sommercamp had sufficient cash flow to support his mining investment during these two years.

POLITICS

In 1876, Sommercamp was elected a delegate to the state Democratic Territorial Committee from Owyhee County.[65] He continued his slight interest in politics in 1878, when he ran for county commissioner and received 222 votes.[66] Sommercamp was the patentee on four pieces of Owyhee County land in March of 1877.[67] In June, Sommercamp represented Owyhee County at the Democratic Central Committee meeting in Boise.[68] Sommercamp went to Boise in June of 1878 as an Owyhee County delegate to a meeting of the Democratic Territorial Central Committee.[69] That same year, he ran as an Independent for county commissioners and finished tied for second for one of the three seats.[70]

About 1877, Sommercamp had bought two quartz claims in the Carson District of Wagontown adjacent to the then famous Wilson Mine. One of his claims, the St. Clair, sat nearly parallel to the summit there and had yielded a rich crushing of ore. Sommercamp paid $850 for it.[71] The other was lower down the summit, but parallel to the St. Clair. Sommercamp started a new tunnel below his claim to cut into his property at a depth while also cutting into those owned by others in the area. Sommercamp bought up these other claims as they became available and he kept at least two men constantly busy working on his claim. By the time of this report, the tunnel was 1,000 feet long, had gone through six claims, and was about to reach the St. Clair. There were "drifts" or side tunnels run to most of the other claims. These claims had the colorful names of Crown Prince, Bismarck, Hope, Ophir, J. B. Dodd, Oro East, Oro West, and Pacific. Most of these milled out at 25 to 50 dollars per ton. The newspaper article predicted hundreds of thousands of dollars would be taken out.

Mary Sommercamp was one of the young ladies on the Liberty Car in the Fourth of July Procession in Boise in 1877.[72]

In October of 1877, Sommercamp sued John Catlow in Owyhee County. Two trials were held without a verdict and Catlow asked for a change of venue to Ada County. The Idaho State Supreme Court ruled against the move and also made Catlow pay the costs, which were great due to the 100 affidavits he filed in the case.[73] Catlow appealed in the case of John Catlow, appellant vs. W. F. Sommercamp, respondent in the Supreme Court, and the order changing the place of the trial was reversed.[74]

In 1878, his brewery produced only 33 barrels of beer but was up to 60 by 1879.[75] In 1878 Sommercamp sold to Fred Warnke for $500 the "First Extension North of the Rising Star Quartz Lode."[76] In 1881, Sommercamp acquired the Potosi mine, which had been located by

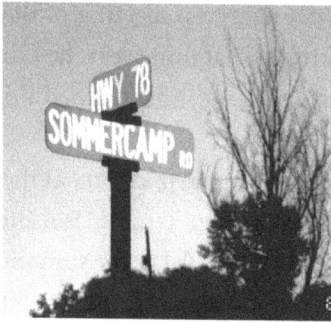

*85. Sommercamp road
& Hwy 78 sign.*

C.S. Peck in 1867.[77] A Boise reporter who spent several days in Silver City in 1881 said, "Father Sommercamp was as glad to see me as he always is to see an old Yreka man, and glad was I to see the old gentleman so prosperous."[78] Sommercamp filed a patent on a piece of Owyhee county property known as Perseverance on October 31, 1881.[79] Sommercamp was also the patentee on mineral property of 15.63 acres identified as "First N Ext Rising S" which was filed on November 17.[80] This was a mineral patent.

In 1881, apparently Sommercamp tried another unique financial venture. The Boise paper reported that on his Snake River ranch "are grown grapes of as fine flavor and perfect form as those of California's most favored vineyards."[81] In 1882, a gold brick valued at nearly $10,000 was displayed at Sommercamp's. It was the result of 14 days run of five stamps from the Empire State Mine.[82]

The R. G. Dun Mercantile Reference Agency of 1883 (p. 117) listed Sommercamp as Saloon and Brewery owner in Silver City, and also a Sommercamp and Coakley general store in Silver. In 1884, Sommercamp was named to the committee on permanent organization of the Idaho Cattle-Growers Association.[83] A famous gunfight between mining magnate William Dewey and Sommercamp employee Joseph Koenig took place at the brewery in 1884.[84] Koenig was shot dead.

In late summer of 1885 he shipped 224 head of cattle from Caldwell, Idaho, to Chicago.[85] About 1884, he ended his involvement in the brewing business.

During the late 1880s, mining seemed to be the focus of Sommercamp's business activities. Regrettably, not all of it was safe. In December of 1886, he had his leg broken in a cave-in while excavating on his ranch on Squaw Creek.[86] He made a couple of visits to Boise during 1888 as side trips from visiting his stock camp south of Snake River, and *The Statesman* reported that he was able to walk with a cane.[87] In 1889, the *The Statesman* repeated a report from the *Avalanche* that the Sommercamp group of mines at Wagontown was looking better than ever as work progresses, and they joined with his friends in congratulating him.[88] *The Statesman* gave a half page to telling the story of those mines later that year.[89]

FAMILY AND PERSONAL LIFE

The 1870 U.S. Census listed Sommercamp as 42 years old with real estate of $6,000 and personal estate of $8,000.[90] William F. Jr. was 10 years old and living at home with sister Mary 3, and Henry, 1, the younger two who were born in Idaho.

On 13 October 1871, Frederick C. Sommercamp, the 5-month-old son of William and Mary, died. This poem was printed about the infant:

> *"Whom the gods love die young" was said of yore,*
> *And many deaths do they escape by this:*
> *The death of friends, and that which slays e'en more,*
> *The death of friendship, love, youth, all that is,*
> *Except mere breath; and since the silent share*
> *Awaits at last even those who longest miss*
> *The old archer's shafts, perhaps the early grave*
> *Which we weep over may be meant to save.*[91]

On 5 October 1872, daughter Annie was born to the family.[92] Less than three years later, another tragedy struck the family with the death on 10 March 1874 of Annie, who was only 18 months old. Her poem was:

> *Only our neighbors' little girl*
> *On the opposite side of the street,*
> *With her gleesome call and laugh of joy,*
> *And winning ways so sweet.*

Only our neighbor's little girl
The darling of our hearts;
But her name begins ever that tender joy
Which the loved and lost imparts.
We glance with a sign at one neighbor's door
As children look out in their play-
There's a little face we shall see no more
At window or door over the way.
But a golden cord from a little hand
Seems reaching down to us here,
And our hearts are drawn to us here,
And our hearts are drawn to a better land,
As we feel that our treasurers are there.[93]

In 1871, son William F. Jr. arrived home from St. Augustine's College for summer vacation and then left again in August for Bernicia, California, for the new college term.[94]

A son was born to the Sommercamp family on 1 September 1875.[95]

In 1877, daughter Mary Sommercamp was on the Car of Liberty at the Boise Fourth of July parade representing one of the states.[96] On 15 October 1878, S. W. Babcox sold a claim to Sommercamp for $100.[97]

The 1880 U.S. Census found daughter Mary A., age 12, son Henry J., age 10, and son James A., age 4 at the Sommercamp home along with their border, the brewer Fred Shaffers.[98] In May 1881, Sommercamp was on the Grand Jury impaneled in the District Court in Silver City.[99]

"Silver City, Idaho. December 23. [1881]— Wm. F. Sommercamp, Jr. was married last evening at 8:30 o'clock, to Miss

86. Sommercamp house, 1899.

Alice Harley, both of Silver City, at the bride's home, by Judge Wickersham. The bride is one of the most accomplished and beautiful young ladies that our country boasts of. The young gentleman is one of our rising young merchants, of the firm of Sommercamp & Coakley. Only relatives and a few friends were invited. Miss Alice was attired in satin de Lyons, trimmed with plush and white Spanish lace; the groom was dressed in black. After the ceremony all repaired to the bounteous feast which was most elegantly gotten up. No cards having been issued the presents were not so numerous as might have been; but they were very handsome. The following is a list of a few: jewel case from Mrs. Miller, the bride's sister; album from James Coakley; silver cake basket from W. G. Kellogg; silver cake basket and set of silver tea and table spoons and butter knife from Mrs. Sommercamp. After merry making for an hour or more, the young couple were escorted to their new home, opposite the War Eagle Hotel, all wishing them joy."[100]

A son was born to Mr. and Mrs. William F. Sommercamp Jr. on 7 November 1882.[101] Another son was born on 11 June 1885.[102] A daughter was born on 18 August 1887.[103]

In 1884, Sommercamp, Sr. was on the committee to set up a permanent organization of Idaho cattle-growers.[104] One goal was registering stock brands for the whole region.

William. F. Sommercamp, Jr. was the treasurer of Owyhee County for the first time during 1885-86. He served again during the 1887-88 term, and 1889-90 term.[105] W. F. Jr. paid $165 for the lot in Silver formerly owned by A. F. Wells and used as a barbershop and shoe repair shop at various times before it burned.[106]

Henry Sommercamp Sr.'s son was mentioned in the Boise paper in 1885 when he passed a creditable examination in mathematics in college in Chicago, Illinois.[107] The family tradition of strong education was continuing.

The statewide Grand Lodge of the Rebekahs, the sister group to the Odd Fellows, elected Mary Sommercamp treasurer at their meeting.[108]

About 1887, while Sommercamp Sr. was spending much of his

time at his stock ranch at Succor Creek, he was severely injured. One of his thighbones was so badly broken that "nothing but his indomitable spirit and energy have kept him in active business."[109] In late October 1888, when Sommercamp visited Boise, the newspaper said he visited his stock ranch the other side of Snake River and would spend a few days in the Capital. They mentioned his broken leg of the year before and said he had recovered enough to be able to walk with a cane.[110]

On the Bradstreet Commercial Reports of September 1889, William F. Sommercamp, Jr. was listed as general store owner in Silver City and his father was not listed at all.[111]

In March of 1890, Sommercamp Jr.'s store nearly burned.[112] The residence of Mr. and Mrs. Dougal near the rear of the store burned during a strong wind. The iron roof on the building and the snow that was thrown on it saved the building. That same month, Sommercamp went to Wagontown for one day to look at his bonanza.[113] The mine was producing rich ore and the vein had widened out to 22 feet.

Just as great wealth in mining seemed within his reach, Mr. Sommercamp met an unfortunate accident.[114] While working with his son, Henry, on his mining property near the De Lamar mine in Owyhee County on 7 August 1890, he stumbled and fell headfirst into a 40 foot shaft with 15 feet of water in the bottom. He called to Henry to get a rope and some help, but the only nearby help was at the De Lamar mine. The men from there ran to the shaft but there was no answer to their calls. They dragged the pit and recovered the still warm and bleeding body, which had been injured in the fall. William Jr. in Silver City had been alerted by telephone, and, with Albert Cordell and Anthony Brooks, hurried to the scene, arriving just as his father's body was pulled from the water.

His remains were brought back to Silver City during the afternoon and were interred in the cemetery on Friday afternoon at 3 o'clock.[115] The funeral took place from the Masonic Hall with the Odd Fellows officiating. He was described as an "energetic, liberal and public spirited man."

In Boise, he was remembered as "one of the most respected and wealthiest miners and stockraisers in Idaho."[116] He left a widow, three sons and one daughter to mourn his loss.

The next day, it was reported that New York Life Insurance Company had insured him for $5,000.[117] The next year, W.F. Jr. reportedly returned to Weiser where he was engaged in the wholesale mercantile business as Sommercamp Bros. & Company after a two-week trip to Silver on family business.[118] Even before the tragedy to the father, W.F. Jr. owned, but leased out, a valuable silver mine in the Silver City vicinity.[119] Two months after his father's death, son Henry J. was listed as a wealthy mine owner when he visited Boise.[120]

THE SOMMERCAMP LEGACY

The work on the Sommercamp mines progressed until a shaft connected it to the De Lamar mine. Waste from the De Lamar "will be dumped on the west side and Sommercamp's ore will come out the east side."[121] In 1906, the old Potosi mine owned by the Sommercamp family was cleaned out, drained, and prepared for working again.[122]

Three months after her father's death, Miss Mary Sommercamp married Albert Cordell at Silver City with Reverend D.C. Pattee of Boise officiating.[123] The whole family eventually left the harsh winters and perhaps mixed sad and happy memories of Silver and joined W.F. Jr. in Weiser. Mrs. W. F. Jr. visited her mother, Mrs. Harley, in Bruneau valley.[124] When Anna G. Harley married Jefferson D. Whitson at Bruneau on October 21, 1896 the whole Sommercamp family turned out.[125] James Sommercamp was a groomsman.

In 1897, W. F. Jr. was still prominent enough to be mentioned as a visitor from Weiser when he went to Boise.[126] On the R. G. Dun Mercantile Agency list for January 1897, M. E. Sommercamp had a store in Weiser.[127] In February of 1901, M.E. Sommercamp and Co. were among the investors in a distillery that opened in Weiser.[128]

W.F. Jr. was a force in getting the Pacific and Idaho Northern Railway Company to Weiser. He spoke at a public meeting in its favor and then donated right-of-way through his land.[129] He was also a director of the Salubria and Weiser Telephone Company in 1893.[130]

That same year, the firm in Weiser was sold to Mrs. Sommercamp Sr., the mother, in a restructuring.[131] She controlled most of the business anyway as representative of the minor children. All debts were paid and it continued to run as before. It had been having financial difficulties as many businesses during that year of financial depression.

In 1894, the case of John McCullough vs. W. F. Sommercamp raised a stir.[132] McCullough gave Sommercamp $3,600 that was deposited in the Idaho Commercial Company's bank, which failed. McCullough died before he could appear in court. Future Senator Borah was one of Sommercamp's attorneys.

The September 1894, R. G. Dun Mercantile Agency Reference Book listed Mrs. Mary E. Sommercamp as general store owner in Weiser, Washington County. She had permanently left Silver after all those years.

Henry Sommercamp and Lou Johnson made a gold strike in the Warren area about one mile from the Iola mine in 1897.[133] In 1898, W. F. Sommercamp was a director in the newly formed creamery corporation in Weiser.[134]

"I" John, aged about 65, died on 13 February 1898 and was buried in the Chinese burial ground adjacent to the Pioneer Cemetery in Silver city. He had been the house servant of the Sommercamp family for years.[135]

Mrs. Sommercamp's home in Weiser was mentioned in a book on Idaho architecture. The home of Mary Elizabeth Sommercamp at 411 W. 3rd in Weiser was a Queen Anne-Colonial style designed by Tourtellotte and Hummel, Idaho architects.[136] In 1899, Mrs. Sommercamp was building what was described as a "palatial residence" in Weiser.[137] Mrs. Sommercamp, Jr. and her daughter visited in Mountain Home for 10 days that same month of June 1899.[138]

In December of 1899, son Henry J. Sommercamp married Miss Gertrude Shawan, another resident of Weiser.[139] Mr. and Mrs. William Sommercamp, Miss Ora, and Walter Sommercamp were all in attendance. On 19 March 1900, son James married Miss Ruby Peyton in Weiser at St. Luke's Church.[140]

William Sommercamp was the manager of the Weiser baseball team in June of 1900.[141] This was the team that at one time featured Walter Johnson, arguably the greatest pitcher in baseball history.

In June of 1900, Will Sommercamp, grandson of our subject, home from military academy in the East, went to Mountain Home to visit his grandmother and aunt, Mrs. Harley and Mrs. Whitson.[142]

In 1901, William was treasurer of the newly formed Weiser Distilling Company.[143] The family continued the business interests begun by the father. In August of 1901, Mr. and Mrs. W. F. Sommercamp and family returned to Weiser after a trip to Seven Devils and Payette Lake.[144] Mrs. St. Clair came to Weiser about this time to visit her daughter, Mrs. J. A. Sommercamp, who delivered an 8½-pound daughter on August 19.[145] Will Shawhan of Payette was in Weiser visiting his sister, Mrs. Henry Sommercamp, in November 1901.[146]

The M. E. Sommercamp & Co. firm of Weiser announced it was insolvent in January of 1904.[147] They had liabilities of $30,000 and considerable more assets, but had failed to collect on many debts from the construction days of the P. & I. N. railroad. They expected to get things in order and continue in business.

The R. G. Dun Idaho business list for 1904 (p. 9) had J. A. Sommercamp as a grocery store owner in Weiser, and Walker and Sommercamp as a drugstore partnership in Weiser. In September of 1904, a rich strike of gold and silver in the Crown Prince on Sommercamp ground at De Lamar was announced.[148]

In 1905, William Sommercamp, Jr. visited Silver City to look at the old Potosi mine and other properties.[149] Soon, he reported there were good prospects for opening the mine up again.[150] Silver City rejoiced that the "Home" and the "Potosi," both within the city limits at Silver, would be working again and hopefully producing $70 (per ton) ore.[151] In August of 1905, Mary Sommercamp of Weiser and Mrs. Mary Grete of Silver City and several other ladies were guests at Mr. and Mrs. Handy's house in Caldwell.[152] In December of 1905, Sommercamp traveled to Pittsburgh to deal with his investors.[153]

April, the following year of 1906, saw more movement in this area. Sommercamp went east and organized a company to develop the mine.[154] He announced he had ordered material for a shaft house and other buildings for the Potosi and the Home mines.[155] The claims were diagonal through Silver City and the editor there said they would be working about 400 yards from his office. In May, he went to Silver with a mining engineer to take measurements for the new machinery at the mine.[156] When he returned to Weiser, he was described as the general manager of the mine.[157] He left Mr. Masters, superintendent of the Potosi in Silver, in charge of a crew building a shaft house.[158]

Mrs. W. F. Sommercamp and daughter Oro, and Mrs. James Sommercamp and children went to Silver for an extended visit in the cool mountains.[159] While there, Mrs. Ed Masters gave a big party for Miss Oro.[160] In October 1906, Mr. Sommercamp, general manager of the Potosi mine, announced a rich strike.[161]

Early in 1907, Mrs. Henry Sommercamp, daughter of Captain and Mrs. J. H. Shawhan, left for Monterey, Mexico, to join Mr. Henry Sommercamp, who was there on mining business. She expected to be there for two years and spend considerable time in Mexico City.[162]

The Potosi Mining Company Ltd. bought the mine from the Sommercamp heirs in 1908.[163] William was both an heir and a stockholder in the new company.

In May of 1907, Mr. Sommercamp was one of the judges in a six-day horse race meet in Weiser.[164] Mrs. W. F. Sommercamp, Jr. was taken to Josephine hospital in Weiser in May to undergo serious surgery.[165] Sons Walter and Will were there, and her many friends were anxiously awaiting the results.

In September of 1907, Oro Sommercamp, granddaughter of our subject and daughter of Mr. and Mrs. W. F. Sommercamp, married Mr. J. H. Ricker at the Episcopal Church in Weiser.[166] In November, Sommercamp was checking on the Potosi again and the work on the new mill was progressing.[167]

A historical reminiscence in the *Evening Capital News* in January of 1908 by Silver City pioneer, African American barber Lewis W.

Walker, had a strange glitch about the history of the Sommercamp family and mines.[168] Walker said, "W. F. Sommercamp, now of Weiser, who is still interested in valuable mining property at Silver City, was proprietor of the Star Brewery and billiard saloon." He had skipped a generation.

A few days later, J. E. Masters, superintendent of the Potosi, reported that Silver City was the most prosperous it had been since the bank failures in California in 1873 had shut down many mines.[169] Over 800 people in the camp were working.

Walter Sommercamp, several years the assayer at the White Knob mine at Mackay, went to Silver to do the same job at the Potosi in late January of 1908.[170] A report by J. F. Nugent on the condition of Silver City in early April of 1908 said that the possibility of good times were better than they had been in a long time. In particular the Sommercamp group of mines had "thorough and systematic development work being prosecuted." "As the Sommercamp group is virgin ground it is highly probable that it will furnish a vast quantity of good milling ore."[171]

Three of the investors from Pittsburgh, H. E. Peterson, William Caldwell and R. L. Ream, went with Sommercamp to inspect the Silver City mines in late April of 1908.[172] Sommercamp said they were working 14 men at the mine and had three chutes going. "If Silver City was in Nevada," said Sommercamp, "it would be the greatest camp in the world today. Excellent properties are being opened up and the old mines that have been furnishing wealth to the world for years still continue to contribute the bullion in large quantities. For a practically new property, the Village Blacksmith is one of the best in the camp and is already taking out ore valued at $1,000 per ton, while all other properties in the camp are showing up well."

A month later, the good news continued. J. E. Marsters, foreman of the Potosi mine, brought news to Boise of an exceptionally rich strike made in the 300-foot level where an 8-inch vein of ore on a 16-inch ledge which averaged $2,000 per ton in gold.[173] He spoke in glowing terms of the many other strikes in the camp.

Mrs. James Sommercamp and her two daughters came to Silver in July to spend the rest of the summer with Mrs. Frank St. Clair.[174] In September of 1908, William, Jr. was again in Silver City and said the Potosi was showing better than ever expected.[175] In November, a rich strike there was announced and all the stockholders in Weiser were greatly pleased.[176] Mr. Sommercamp and his wife went to Portland on the train to see a specialist in regard to his health.[177] Early in December, Sommercamp returned from Portland and immediately went to Silver City.[178]

In March of 1909, Ernest Rammelmeyer, mining engineer and former Idaho brewery owner, was in Boise to consult with W. F. Sommercamp about the Potosi Mine in Silver City.[179] Sommercamp was remembered at that time as the son of early brewer William Sommercamp, who first owned the mine.

In May of 1909, Mrs. Mary E. Sommercamp, our subject's widow, died from "la grippe."[180] Son Henry was in Mexico, but the other two sons and her daughter were all with her in Weiser at the end. He death was "calm and peaceful, as the venerable lady called to her last rest had knowledge of a life well spent." She was remembered as a pioneer of the early 1860s.[181]

Mr. and Mrs. Henry Sommercamp came from their home in Mexico to visit his two brothers and sister in Weiser in October of 1909.[182] About this time, Frank Dunham and T. D. Fry filed liens against the Potosi Mining Co., Ltd. for wages they claimed they were due.[183] Dunham wanted $302.12, and Fry wanted $293.68. The legal papers named Mary E. Sommercamp, administrator of the estate of W. F. Sommercamp as the original owners of the mining claim worked on.

87. Tombstone Sommercamp children.

In 1910, Fry and Dunham filed a civil complaint in the District Court of the Seventh Judicial District in Owyhee County, Idaho. In the files of William Healy, Silver City attorney, there are several letters to and from the Sommercamps that are interesting and enlightening.[184] First, Connors & Brumbaugh of the Idaho Hotel could not collect from W. H. Sommercamp and asked William Healy to collect the debt of $19.55. Sommercamp responded on December 14 that his wife had had two operations in the last three weeks and his medium salary was all going to doctor bills. He would settle with the hotel people as soon as he was able. On February 22 of 1911, Sommercamp reiterated his problems, claimed a monthly salary of $75, and said he would settle as soon as possible. In March, Healy sent the bills to Ed Coulter of Weiser to see if he could get them paid. Before a Mr. A. Pettit came forward with a bill for $15 that Sommercamp owed him. There is no letter indicating the matters were ever resolved in the attorney Healy's papers, but the matter finally ended.

In September of 1911, Mrs. W. F. Sommercamp, Mrs. J. H. Ricker, and Mrs. J. A. Sommercamp were all in Mountain Home due to the illness of Mrs. William Harley.[185] The former is a daughter and the later granddaughters of Mrs. Harley. Mrs. Harley seemed to be improving at that time. The next month, Mrs. W. F. Sommercamp and Mrs. W. H. Sommercamp gave large luncheons in Weiser.[186]

In 1913, Joe Meingassner—formerly a brewer in Juliaetta, Idaho—sued the Potosi Mining Co., W. F. Sommercamp as Administrator of the estate of Mary E. Sommercamp, and a number of other businesses.[187] Mein-gassner received $375.82 plus $50.00 attorney's fees for the first action. Sommercamp had to pay $15,433.34 plus $1,500 attorney fees on the second action. The list went on and on, as nearly 30 actions were contained in the specifications. A sheriff's sale of the mine premises was ordered.

William Harley Sommercamp, born 6 November 1882, registered for the World War I draft at Washington County, Idaho, with a note attached that his wife lived in Portland, Oregon.[188]

W. F. Sommercamp Sr., our brewer, has a road named for him in Owyhee County. Also Sommercamp Basin is on Cow Creek in

Owyhee County; Sommercamp Mountain is 12 miles west of Silver City and this is where his fatal mining fall happened. There was, in addition, a small town in the French Hill area of Owyhee County named Sommercamp.[189]

Sleep well, Herr Sommercamp!!

END NOTES

1   U.S. Census 1880. The basic outline of Sommercamp's life is from *Historical Directory of Owyhee County*, 1898, p. 136. Two biographies of W. F. Sommercamp, Jr. say that senior first settled in New Orleans and worked in the confectioner trade. See "William F. Sommercamp," in H.T. French, *History of Idaho*, vol. II, Chicago, Lewis Publishing Company, 1914, p. 781; and "William F. Sommercamp," An *Illustrated History of North Idaho*, Chicago, Lewis Publishing Company, p. 480 .

2   The Grete brothers, John and Fred, also lived in Shasta before going to Silver City and becoming brewers and businessmen.

3   *History of Siskiyou County, California, Illustrated with Views of Residences, Business Buildings and Natural Scenery, and Containing Portraits and Biographies of Its Leading Citizens and Pioneers.* Oakland, CA: D. J. Stewart & Co., 1881. p. 188.

4   *History of Siskiyou County, California, Illustrated with Views of Residences, Business Buildings and Natural Scenery, and Containing Portraits and Biographies of Its Leading Citizens and Pioneers.* Oakland, CA: D. J. Stewart & Co., 1881. pp. 163-5.

5   John Boessnecker, *Gold Dust and Gunsmoke: Tales of Gold Rush Outlaws, Gunfighters, Lawmen, and Vigilantes.* New York: John Wiley & Sons, 1999, pp. 227-8.

6   *Semi-Weekly Journal*, Yreka, California, 2 August 1861, p. 3, c. 6.

7   *Semi-Weekly Journal*, Yreka, California, 19 November 1862, p. 3, c. 2.

8   *An Illustrated History of Idaho*, Chicago, 1899, "John Brodbeck," p. 179.

9   *Owyhee Avalanche*, Ruby City, Idaho, 26 August 1865, p. 4, c. 3.

10 *Owyhee Avalanche*, 16 September 1865, p. 3, c. 1.

11 *Owyhee Avalanche*, 23 September 1865, p. 3, c. 3. 7 October 1865, p. 3, c. 5.

12 *Owyhee Avalanche*, 30 September 1865, p. 3, c. 2.

13 *Owyhee Avalanche*, 30 September 1865, p. 3, c. 3.

14 *Owyhee Avalanche*, 14 October 1865, p. 3, c. 3.

15 *Owyhee Avalanche*, 16 December 1865, *The Weiser World*, 24 February 1905, p. 7, c. 3. 3, c. 1.

16 *Tri-Weekly Statesman*, Boise, Idaho, 17 February 1866, p. 2, c. 1.

17 Michno, Gregory. *The Deadliest Indian War in the West: The Snake Conflict, 1864-1868.* Caldwell, Idaho: Caxton Press, 2007.

18 *Owyhee Avalanche*, 10 March 1866, p. 3, c. 2. Over the years this building housed saloons, shops, a candy store and then burned in the great fire of 1907. It was rebuilt as a furniture store. Helen Nettleton, *Interesting Buildings in Silver City, Idaho*, Homedale, Idaho, Owyhee Publishing Co., Inc, revised edition, 1994, p. 41.

19 *Owyhee Avalanche*, Silver City, Idaho, 8 September 1866, p. 3, c. 4.

20 *Owyhee Avalanche*, Silver City, 8 September 1866, p. 2, c. 2.

21 *Historical Directory of Owyhee County*, Silver City, Idaho, *1898*.

22 *The Weiser World*, Weiser, Idaho, 24 February 1905, p. 7, c. 3.

23 *Owyhee Avalanche*, 26 May 1866, p. 3, c. 2.

24 *Owyhee Avalanche*, 26 May 1866, p. 3, c. 2.

25 Federal Tax Records, 1865-66,University of Idaho Library Microfilm # 558.

26 Federal Tax Records, 1865-66,University of Idaho Library Microfilm # 558.

27 Federal Tax Records, 1865-66,University of Idaho Library Microfilm # 558.

28 Federal Tax Records, 1865-66,University of Idaho Library Microfilm # 558.

29 Federal Tax Records, 1865-66,University of Idaho Library Microfilm # 558.

30 MyFamily.com. Internet site.

31 http://www.usroots.com-idmining/ar1866sc.html.

32 *Idaho World*, Idaho City, 9 March 1867, p. 3, c. 5.

33 *Semi-Weekly World*, Idaho City, 3 July 1867, p. 2, c. 4.

34 *Owyhee Avalanche*, 5 October 1867, p. 3, c. 3. Statham, Wilma Lewis. *Owyhee County Gleanings*. Boise, Idaho: The Idaho Genealogical Society and the Idaho Historical Society, 1964, 2nd printing, Copyright 1986. p. 11.

35 *Owyhee Avalanche*, 30 November 1867, p. 2, c. 3.

36 Statham. Wilma Lewis. *Owyhee County Gleanings*. Boise, Idaho: The Idaho Genealogical Society and the Idaho Historical Society, 1964, 2nd printing, Copyright 1986. p. 11.

37 *Owyhee Avalanche*, 25 January 1868, p. 3, c. 2.

38 *Owyhee Avalanche*, 2 March 1868, p. 3, c. 3.

39 *Owyhee Avalanche*, 19 September 1868, p. 2, c. 2.

40 *Boise Weekly News*, Boise, Idaho, 1 October 1870, p. 2. c. 2.

41 *Owyhee Avalanche*, 29 October 1870, p. 3, c. 2. *Boise City Weekly News*, 5 November 1870, p. 2, c. 3.

42 *Idaho World*, Idaho City, Idaho, 11 May 1871, p. 2, c. 3.

43 Helen Nettleton, *Interesting Buildings in Silver City, Idaho*, Homedale, Idaho, Owyhee Publishing Co., Inc, revised edition, 1994, p. 34-35.

44 *Semi-Weekly News*, Boise, 2 July 1870, p. 4, c. 4. *Boise City Weekly News*, 17 September 1870, p. 3, c. 4.

45 Ronnenberg, "Brewed in Silver: The Brewing Business in Idaho's Premier Gold Camp," *American Breweriana Journal*, May-June 1991, p. 5. Welch, *Gold Town to Ghost Town*, Moscow, Idaho, pp. 31-2.

46 *Owyhee Avalanche*, 1 July 1871, p. 3, c. 2.

47 *Owyhee Avalanche*, 2 December 1871, p. 3, c. 2.

48 *Owyhee Avalanche*, 22 June 1872, p. 3, c. 2.

49 *Idaho World*, 30 May 1872, p. 2, c. 3.

50 *Owyhee Avalanche*, 25 January 1873, p. 3, c. 1.

51 *Owyhee Avalanche* 19 October 1872, p. 3, c. 1. The first ad for the new products appeared in the same issue on p. 2, c. 4.

52 Owyhee Avalanche, 24 January 1874, p. 3, c. 1.

53 *Owyhee Avalanche*, 28 March 1874, p. 3, c. 1.

54 Galey, *Headlines Idaho Remembers*, p. 10. From the *Owyhee Daily Avalanche*, 17 October 1874, p. 2, c. 4.

55 *Idaho Tri-Weekly Statesman*, Boise, Idaho, 12 October 1875, p. 1, c. 2.

56 *Idaho World*, Idaho City, 31 March 1875, p. 2, c. 3.

57 Julie Hyslop, *Foundations of Silver City*, Vol. III, Nampa, Idaho, p. 31-33.

58 Owyhee County Judicial Records, Idaho State Historical Society, Microfilm reel 4, original pages 220-221.

59 Owyhee County Judicial Records, Idaho State Historical Society, Microfilm reel 4, original pages 259-260.

60 Owyhee County Judicial Records, Idaho State Historical Society, Microfilm reel 4, original pages 245-246

61 Owyhee County Judicial Records, Idaho State Historical Society, Microfilm reel 4, original pages 537.

62 Owyhee County Judicial Records, Idaho State Historical Society, Microfilm reel 4, original pages 535-536.

63 Owyhee County Judicial Records, Idaho State Historical Society, Microfilm reel 4, original pages 568-569.64Owyhee County Judicial Records, Idaho State Historical Society, Microfilm reel 4, original pages 776-777.

65 *Idaho Tri-Weekly Statesman*, 17 October 1876, p. 3, c. 2 & 3.

66 *Idaho Tri-Weekly Statesman* 21 November 1878, p. 3, c. 2 & 3.

67 Bureau of Land Management, Land Patent Records, on line. Accession/Serial #: IDIDAA 003201. Document # 251. These were Aliquot Parts SWNW, Section 3, Township 1-N, Range 4-W. Aliquot SENE, Section 4, Township 1-N, Range 4-W. Aliquot parts 3. Section 3, 1-N 4-W. Aliquot 4, Section 3, 1-N, 4-W. These were apparently all close together and may have been city blocks.

68 *The Semi-Weekly Idahoan*, Boise, 7 August 1878, p. 2, c. 5.

69 *Idaho Tri-Weekly Statesman*, 18 June 1878, p. 3, c. 3.

70 *Idaho Tri-Weekly Statesman*, 9 November 1878, p. 3, c. 3.

71 Owyhee County Judicial Records, Idaho State Historical Society, Microfilm reel 4, original pages 140-142.

72 *The Semi-Weekly Idahoan*, Boise, 20 June 1877, p. 3, c. 1.

73 *Idaho Reports*, January 1878, pp. 716-722.

74 *Idaho Tri-Weekly Statesman*, 7 February 1878, p. 3, c. 4.

75 Salem, *Beer, Its History*, 1880, Hartford, Connecticut, p. 200.

76 Owyhee County Judicial Records, Idaho State Historical Society, Microfilm reel 4, original pages 375-377.

77 *Idaho Daily Statesman*, 20 July 1908, p. 3, c. 1-4.

78 Owyhee in a Hurry: One Reporter's Rambles in and about Silver City," *Idaho Tri-Weekly Statesman* 5 November 1881, p. 3, c. 4.

79 Bureau of Land Management, Land Patent Records. Accession/Serial # IDIDAA 012455. Document #5057. It was sections 2 and 11 of Township 6-S, Range 4-W and contained 16.9 acres.

80 Bureau of Land Management, Land Patent Records. Accession/Serial # IDIDAA 012458. Document #5076, It was at Section 11 of Township 6-S, Range 4-W.

81 *Idaho Tri-Weekly Statesman*, 8 November 1881, p. 4, c. 1.

82 *Idaho Tri-Weekly Statesman*, 28 February 1882, p. 3, c. 1.

83 Idaho Tri-Weekly Statesman, 27 November 1884, p. 3, c. 3.

84 See the biography of Koenig in this volume.

85 *Idaho Tri-Weekly Statesman*, 1 September 1885, p. 1, c. 3.

86 *Idaho Tri-Weekly Statesman*, 7 December 1886, p. 3, c. 1. *Idaho Daily Statesman*, 12 December 1926, Section 2, p. 2, c. 7. Forty Years Ago Column.

87 *Idaho Tri-Weekly Statesman*, 19 September 1888, p. 3, c. 1. 19 October 1888, p. 3, c. 1.

88 *Idaho Tri-Weekly Statesman*, 19 June 1889, p. 2, c. 2.

89 The details on the mine that follow are all from this article. *Idaho Daily Statesman*, 15 December 1889, p. 2, c. 2 & 3.

90 *U.S. Census*, 1870, Silver City.

91 Jamison, *Cemeteries of the Idaho Ghost Towns of Fairview, Ruby City and Silver City. 1986,* Melba, Idaho, p. 71.

92 Statham. Wilma Lewis. *Owyhee County Gleanings.* Boise, Idaho: The Idaho Genealogical Society and the Idaho Historical Society, 1964, 2nd printing, Copyright 1986. p. 13.

93 Jamison, *Cemeteries of the Idaho Ghost Towns of Fairview, Ruby City, Silver City,* p. 70-71.

94 *Owyhee Avalanche*, 17 June 1871, p. 3, c. 2. 5 August 1871, p. 3, c. 2.

95 Statham. Wilma Lewis. *Owyhee County Gleanings.* Boise, Idaho: The Idaho Genealogical Society and the Idaho Historical Society, 1964, 2nd printing, Copyright 1986. p. 14.

96 *The Semi-Weekly Idahoan*, Boise, 20 June 1877, p. 3, c. 1.

97 Owyhee County Judicial Records, Idaho State Historical Society microfilm, reel 4. Original page 378. Owyhee County Judicial Records, Idaho State Historical Society microfilm, reel 4. Original page 378

98 1880 United States Census, Silver City, Idaho.

99 *Idaho Tri-Weekly Statesman*, 26 May 1881, p. 3, c. 3. John Grete was also on the jury.

100 *Tri-Weekly Statesman*, 24 December 1881, p. 3, c. 1.

101 Statham. Wilma Lewis. *Owyhee County Gleanings*. Boise, Idaho: The Idaho Genealogical Society and the Idaho Historical Society, 1964, 2nd printing, Copyright 1986. p. 4.

102 Statham. Wilma Lewis. *Owyhee County Gleanings*. Boise, Idaho: The Idaho Genealogical Society and the Idaho Historical Society, 1964, 2nd printing, Copyright 1986. p. 4. 16.

103 Statham. Wilma Lewis. *Owyhee County Gleanings*. Boise, Idaho: The Idaho Genealogical Society and the Idaho Historical Society, 1964, 2nd printing, Copyright 1986. p. 17. 18

104 *Idaho Tri-Weekly Statesman*, 27 November 1884, p. 3, c. 1.

105 *A Historical, Descriptive and Commercial Directory of Owyhee County*, Silver City, Idaho: Press of the Owyhee Avalanche, 1898, p. 18.

106   Hyslop, Julie, *Foundations of Silver City*, Vol. III, p. 34.

107 *Idaho Tri-Weekly Statesman*, 13 January 1885, p. 3, c. 3.

108 *The Elmore Bulletin*, Rocky Bar, Idaho, 19 October 1887, p. 3, c. 3.

109 *The Elmore Bulletin*, 16 August 1890, p. 2, c. 2.

110 *Idaho Statesman*, 20 October 1888, p. 3, c. 1.

111 "Bradstreet's Commercial Reports," vol. 87, September 1889, p. 4.

112 *The Idaho Democrat*, Boise, Idaho, 19 March 1890, p. 1, c. 1.

113 *The Idaho Democrat*, 19 March 1890, p. 1, c. 1.

114 *Idaho Daily Statesman*, 8 August 1890, p. 4, c. 1 & 2.

115 *The Elmore Bulletin*, 16 August 1890, p. 2, c. 2.

116 *The Idaho Democrat*, 10 August 1890, p. 1, c. 2.

117 *Idaho Daily Statesman*, 9 August 1890, p. 4, c. 1.

118 *Idaho Daily Statesman*, 16 August 1891, p. 4, c. 2

119 *Idaho Daily Statesman*, 18 March 1890, p. 3, c. 2.

120 *Idaho Daily Statesman*, 4 October 1890, p. 4, c. 1 & 2. Just after his father's death Henry went to Boise.

121 *Idaho Daily Statesman*, 5 May 1891, p. 5, c. 2. The impending connection between the mines was first reported in *The Daily Statesman* 22 October 1890 (p. 4, c. 2) but it took longer than expected

122 *Weiser Semi-Weekly Signal*, Weiser, Idaho, 25 August 1906, p. 1, c. 3.

123 *Idaho Daily Statesman*, 5 November 1890, p. 4, c. 2. 8 November 1890, P. 4, c. 2.

124 *The Elmore Bulletin*, Mountain Home, 9 October 1895, p. 3, c. 3.

125 *Elmore Bulletin*, 4 November 1896, p. 3, c. 2.

126 *Idaho Daily Statesman*, 13 March 1897, p. 6, c. 1.

127 R. G. Dun and Company, *Mercantile Agency Reference Book and Key*. January 1897, Idaho, p. 39.

128 Fern Coble Trull, *They Dared to Dream: Builders in the Purple Sage*, p. 16

129 Fern Coble Trull, *They Dared to Dream*, p. 43.

130 *Idaho Daily Statesman*, 23 April 1893, p. 2, c. 2.

131 *Idaho Daily Statesman*, 30 September 1893, p. 6, c. 4.

132 *Idaho Daily Statesman*, 11 October 1894, p. 1, c. 1.

133 *Idaho Daily Statesman*, 20 October 1897, p. 3, c. 1.

134 *Idaho Daily Statesman*, 27 October 1898, p. 8, c. 2.

135 *Idaho Daily Statesman*, 15 June 1899, p. 4, c. 1.

136 Wright and Reitzes, *Tourtellotte and Hummel*, 1987, Logan, Utah, p. 86.

137 Wilma Lewis Statham, *Owyhee County Gleanings*, Boise, Idaho: The Idaho Genealogical Society and the Idaho Historical Society, 1964, 2nd printing, Copyright 1986. 1986, p. 37.

138 *The Elmore Bulletin*, 29 June 1899, p. 3, c. 1.

139 *Idaho Daily Statesman*, 11 December 1899, p. 12, c. 2.

140 *Idaho Daily Statesman*, 17 March 1900, p. 6, c. 1. Statham. Wilma Lewis. *Owyhee County Gleanings*. P. 9.

141 *Idaho Daily Statesman*, 18 June 1900, p. 6, c. 1.

142 *The Elmore Bulletin*, Mountain Home, 21 June 1900, p. 3, c. 3.

143 *Idaho Capital News*, Boise, Idaho, 9 March 1901, p. 5, c. 4.

144 *Evening Capital News*, Boise, Idaho, 21 August 1901, p. 3, c. 2.

145 *Idaho Daily Statesman*, 24 November 1901, p. 2, c. 2

146 Statham. Wilma Lewis. *Owyhee County Gleanings*. Boise, Idaho: The Idaho Genealogical Society and the Idaho Historical Society, 1964, 2nd printing, Copyright 1986. p. 22.

147 *Evening Capital News*, 29 January 1904, p. 1, c. 5.

148 *Evening Capital News*, 26 September 1904, p. 1, c. 3.

149 *Idaho Capital News*, 22 June 1905, p. 5, c. 6.

150 *Idaho Daily Statesman*, 4 July 1905, p. 2, c. 5.

151 *Evening Capital News*, 26 September 1905, p. 8, c. 7.

152 *Idaho Daily Statesman*, 26 August 1905, p. 4, c. 4.

153 *Idaho Daily Statesman*, 1 December 1905, p. 6, c. 1.

154 *Evening Capital News*, 27 March 1906, p. 1, c. 6.

155 *Idaho Daily Statesman*, 4 April 1906, p. 2, c. 4.

156 *Evening Capital News*, 11 May 1906, p. 6, c. 2.

157 *Evening Capital News*, 18 June1906, p. 6, c. 1.

158 *Evening Capital News*, 20 June1906, p. 6, c. 2.

159 *Evening Capital News*, 16 July 1906, p. 4, c. 4.

160 *Evening Capital News*, 9 August 1906, p. 3, c. 2 & 3.

161 *Evening Capital News*, 10 October 1906, p. 3, c. 3

162 *Evening Capital News*, 28 January 1907, p. 5, c. 4.

163 *Idaho Daily Statesman*, 20 July 1908, p. 3, c. 1-4.

164 *Idaho Daily Statesman*, 14 May 1907, p. 2, c. 4.

165 *Evening Capital News*, 8 May 1907, p. 6, c. 3.

166 *Evening Capital News*, 14 September 1907, p. 3, c. 2.

167 *Evening Capital News*, 7 November 1907, p. 2, c. 2.

168 *Evening Capital News*, 30 January 1908, p. 5, c. 2.

169 *Evening Capital News*, 1 February 1908, p. 7, c. 3.

170 *Evening Capital News*, 25 January 1908, p. 2, c. 4.

171 *Evening Capital News*, 6 April 1908, p. 1, c. 6.

172 *Evening Capital News*, 30 April 1908, p. 10, c. 2.

173 *Evening Capital News*, 22 May 1908, p. 7, c. 4.

174 *Evening Capital News* 22 July 1908, p. 8, c. 3.

175 *Idaho Daily Statesman*, 14 September 1908, p. 4, c. 5.

176 *Idaho Daily Statesman*, 21 November 1908, p. 6, c. 3

177 *Evening Capital News* 19 November 1908, p. 3, c. 2.

178 *Evening Capital News* 9 December 1908, p. 3, c. 3

179 *Evening Capital News*, 24 March 1909, p. 2, c. 2.

180 *Idaho Daily Statesman*, 8 May 1909, p. 7, c. 1-2.

181 *Evening Capital News*, 7 May 1909, p. 1, c. 7.

182 *Evening Capital News*, 25 October 1909, p. 6, c. 1.

183 William Healy, Manuscript Collection, University of Idaho Library, Special Collections, file folder # 28.184William Healy, manuscript collection, University of Idaho Library, Special Collections, file folder #28

185 *Idaho Daily Statesman*, 7 September 1911, p. 4, c. 4.

186 *Idaho Daily Statesman*, 22 October 1911, p. 5, c. 1-2.

187 Ada County Judicial Records, Idaho State Historical Society, Microfilm reel 34, Judgment Book K, original pages 61-66.

188 WWI Civilian Draft Registrations, Internet site.

189 Mary Walsh Taylor, "Owyhee & Nez Perce County Place Names," English Thesis, University of Idaho, 1968, p. 104.

23

AUGUST THOMMON
Suicide

GUS THOMMON WAS A DISCIPLE of Gambrinus whose life during his years as a brewer was little noted in the press.[1] The U.S. Census of 1880 listed August as a resident of 244-246 Main Street of Boise, where he roomed with two other men. He was a native of Switzerland, and his parents were both Swiss.[2] He was 27, single, and a bartender. Thommon was born in Basil, Switzerland, 2 March 1852.[3] In 1871, he made a trip to the United States but only stayed a year. In 1877, he returned to stay and went to Boise to be near his uncle, brewery owner John Brodbeck.

To finally get mentioned in the local press, Thommon had to be a victim, a fate that befell him on the 4th of July 1879.

"A Wanton Case of Stabbing. —James Chapman, a painter, who has lived here for many years and has a family, occasionally goes on a drunk, generally by himself, and on such occasions manifests a vicious disposition, though a man of not very much muscular force. On election day he was on one of his periodical drunks, about 12 o'clock at night, shortly after the vote was counted, while he and several others were standing in front of John Brodbeck's saloon. And among the number was August Thommon, a young man and the nephew of Brodbeck's without the least provocation or warning he struck out with his right hand with a knife in it and gave Thommon a thrust in his bowels, cutting through

his pants in the upper portion of this left hand pocket. The
cut through the pants was over the seams and the flap of the
pocket as clean as could be cut with a razor. The gash on his
body was deep and nearly two inches long, allowing the
intestines to protrude, but Dr. Treadwell, the attending
physicians says the intestines were not cut due to the upward
direction given by Chapman to the knife. The doctor sewed
up the wound and stayed with his patient until morning. He
is doing as well as can be expected. Chapman never had a
word of trouble with Thommon, but made the thrust treach-
erously, as if he were under a ban or promise to commit a
felony on some person and did not care who it was, but he
knew enough to run, and did so as soon as he made the single
stab, and has not been found up to this date. This case of
stabbing was the most treacherous of any that we have heard
for a long time, and came within a hairs breadth of a murder.
No such person as Chapman is a safe man to live in a community. He would do no harm if he would keep sober. That
he will not do; and he should be arrested and dealt with
severely. There is no doubt but Chapman is secreted somewhere in the city, and the officers will do themselves some
credit in hunting him up."[4]

The search for Chapman went on.

"Not Found. George Chapman who stabbed August
Thommon on the night of the 8th instant has thus far
escaped the vigilance of the officers. We understand from
Sheriff Oldham and others that the most vigilant search has
been kept up, and every hiding place where there could be
any suspicion of his being found has been watched night and
day. Mr. Oldham informs us that he had not slept for three
nights after the warrant was placed in his hands. He has had
several men watching Chapman's house and other places,

and has run down every story and rumor in regard to his whereabouts, but no reliable trace of him can be had. Chapman was at Mr. Dunn's place Tuesday noon and said he would give himself up, but could not give bail and would have to lie in jail. Oldham heard of his being there soon after and went to Dunn's and searched the premises, but Chapman had gone. He kept guard around this place Tuesday night thinking he might return; and the rumor that he was heard running from there originated from a little confusion between the guards. One heard the other fall in crossing a ditch and in the dark took him for Chapman. The rumor that he got a horse of a soldier at the garrison has also been traced up and proven to be false. No soldier has a horse at the garrison. The last rumor is that he was seen on the hills between here and Dry Creek with a bridle in his hand, supposed to be looking for his own horses that are probably running in the Dry Creek hills. The rumor however wants confirmation. Sheriff Oldham and parties who have been on the hunt for him are inclined to think that he is not secreted anywhere in the city, although it is difficult to find a man these dark nights. There is scarcely a garden in town but what affords a good hiding place among the briers and trees, and you might pass within four feet of his hiding place and not discover him. The chances are that Chapman will be heard of in some of the mountain towns probably Yankee Fork or Challis before a great while. The town is not much loser if he is not found, though we believe the officers are doing their best to hunt him, and if he is caught he will find a steady boarding house for a while."[5]

Soon August recovered. "August Thommon, who was stabbed by George Chapman on the night of the 4th of July, is out of danger; the wound has healed nicely and Dr. Treadwell pulled the stitches out of it yesterday."[6]

Thommon was not content to be an employee all his life. In May of 1881, an announcement in the Boise newspaper said August Thommen had bought Frank Miller's soda factory and commenced making this delightful beverage. He gave the newspaper a dozen bottles to test, which they did, to their satisfaction.[7]

A notice in the *Statesman* in 1882 announced that Gus was starting his soda water works for the season to supply families with a superior summer drink at very low rates.[8] In May of the next year, the newspaper again thanked him for the box of soda he gave them that he had manufactured at Brodbeck's City Brewery.[9] His ad in the *Statesman* ran from 1881 to at least 1888, and said: "Having opened a soda factory at the City Brewery, next door below the *Statesman* office, we are prepared to furnish the citizens of this town and vicinity with soda water and syrups at most reasonable prices. Soda and Sarsaparilla delivered to any part of the city free of charge. Orders left at the City Brewery will receive prompt attention. August Thommon."[10]

The 1883 edition of the Dun Mercantile Agency list (p. 102) said August Thommen (sic) manufactured soda in Boise. On 25 April 1884, Thommon applied to be a United States citizen.[11] Soon he planned to marry. On July 24, 1894, August married Eva Katzenmeyer at Boise.[12] On 5 June 1895, Mr. and Mrs. Thommon had a son.[13]

In February 1896, Thommon was listed as a liquor seller when he became of member of the Idaho Mining Exchange.[14] In a biographical sketch of John Brodbeck in 1897, Thommon was credited with working for Brodbeck for 19 years.[15] In another biographical sketch of Brodbeck in 1899, August Thommon was listed as being in charge of the brewery when Brodbeck was away. He was also in charge of the saloon.[16] The second account said he had 21 years experience as a brewer.

Gus stayed in Boise a few more years, as indicated by his Rocky Mountain Bell Telephone Co. phone at his residence, number 14-B, listed during April of 1901.[17]

In 1902, according to the *Statesman*, John and Sara Brodbeck sold two city lots to Thommon for $1.17. Then, somehow, according to the newspaper, he bought the same lots from the Woodcocks—Brodbeck's daughter and son-in-law (Thommon's cousins), for the same price of $1. Perhaps the Woodcocks and Brodbecks jointly owned the lots or the land was being consolidated. At any rate, August and Eva Thommon immediately sold one of the lots to H. W. Clement for $800.

In 1902, Thommon moved to Emmett and opened a hotel in the Blackman building. A few years later, he opened the Russell Hotel. In 1904, his visits to Boise were duly noted in the newspaper.[18] Later that summer, his wife and children were visitors too.[19] The R. J. Dun listing of Idaho businesses for 1904 had A. Thommon as hotel and saloon owner in Emmett.

In 1905, March and June, the newspaper noted the visits to Boise of Thommon, proprietor of the Russell hotel.[20] Thommon still owned Boise property, for in 1905 he was assessed $32.40 for concrete curbs around lot 12, block 60 of the original town site, a total of 90 linear feet.[21] Thommon sold lot 12, block 60 in Boise's original town site to S. P. Jensen in early July of 1906 for $3,000.[22]

When Thommon visited Boise in September of 1905, his new position as landlord of the Russell Hotel in Emmett was proclaimed in the *Statesman*.[23] They said he had made the house "a popular head-quarters," and was helping to bring Emmett to "the front as one of the promising towns of the state."

By chance, Thommon was an important informant in the suspicious death of John Talty.[24] Talty was a contractor who was found dead one morning on the main road three miles from Emmett. He apparently fell off his horse and landed on his face. Five dollars in silver was in his pocket. The problem was that he had received $1,100 in a business deal and still had $200 at midnight, an hour before he left town. He drank a lot that night, and some thought he might have been drugged. The horse went back to his ranch after the rider fell. Thommon testified that Talty had paid several accounts, one for $400, and did not have nearly as much money on his person as people supposed.

In 1906, Thommon, still an Emmett hotel man, went to Boise to attend the funeral of former Governor Hunt.[25] He reported business was good in his hometown. He also visited Boise in June and July of 1906, once with his son.[26] In September, he was back in the capital again briefly.[27] In February of 1907, Thommon spent two days in Boise on business before returning to Emmett.[28] A casual observer would have thought Thommon was doing well.

In September 1908, Thommon went to the hotel about 10 a.m. and shortly said he felt badly and retired to his room to lie down. A half hour later, his wife came by to have some papers signed. The door was locked, so she knocked. Upon asking to be admitted, she heard the report of a gun. She got help to open the door. Thommon was lying unconscious on the bed with a gaping hole in his head. There was a 32-caliber revolver in his hand. He died about two hours later without regaining consciousness.

The local newspaper said it did not care to discuss what had prompted him to this action. It had no desire to expose family or business secrets nor to peddle current gossip. They did say he was carrying a load of trouble that was too much for him and it preyed upon his mind until "reason was unthroned."

The *Statesman* of Boise said he had been drinking heavily for several weeks and when his wife returned from Soldier, where she had been visiting relatives, she upbraided him for the condition he was in.

The funeral was held in the Russell hotel parlor.[29] Rev. S.A. Parker officiated and the Alfalfa quartet assisted. A large number of friends and relatives, including many from Boise, attended. Thomas Woodcock, John Brodbeck's son-in-law, went to Emmett to attend the funeral.[30]

The Emmett newspaper evaluated Thommon's character: "He was a man of strong likes and dislikes. To his enemies he was fiercely unrelenting; to his friends, strongly attached and lavishly generous. While he had his faults, he also had his virtues. He had a great big heart and a generous nature. As a citizen he was public spirited and optimistic, and never turned down an appeal for aid to help along any public enterprise."[31]

Mrs. Thommon reopened the Russell Hotel in a few days.[32] The next month, son Arnold won the prize at school for rapid improvement in penmanship.[33]

In October 1909, Mrs. Eva Thommon—along with many others—was voted a refund on her liquor license of $450 by the commissioners of Canyon County.[34] They wanted to prorate liquor licenses and then close the saloons under the recently passed local option law, but the Attorney General said they had to be allowed to keep them until they expired. She continued to operate the hotel personally.

In October of 1911, the Boise *Evening Capital News* published a special issue highlighting the progress of southern Idaho.[35] The report on the Russell Hotel of Emmett said that Mrs. Eva Thommen was the proprietress of the three-story brick structure. It had 31 guest rooms, a quality dining room, and was operated on the American plan from $2 per day and up.

Mrs. Eva Thommon remarried to Frank Knox on 5 September 1911 at Emmett.[36] There was an Eva A. Thommen who married H. M. Glover at Coeur d'Alene on 9 December 1911. If these were indeed both marriages of the widow of our subject, she was certainly going through husbands rapidly at this point in her life. Gus' daughter, Margaritha A. Thommen, married Thomas A. Wokersien on 5 July 1922 at Boise.[37]

END NOTES

1   Some sources spell the name Thommen

2   Thommon's genealogy is included with his uncle John Brodbeck's.

3   *The Emmett Index*, Emmett, Idaho, 24 September 1908, p. 1, c. 1.

4   *Idaho Tri-Weekly Statesman*, Boise, Idaho, 17 July 1879, p. 3, c. 2.

5   *Idaho Tri-Weekly Statesman*, 19 July 1879, p. 3, c. 3 & 4.

6   *Idaho Tri-Weekly Statesman*, 26 July 1879, p. 3, c. 1

7   *Idaho Tri-Weekly Statesman*, 21 May 1881, p. 3, c. 1.

8   *Idaho Tri-Weekly Statesman*, 20 May 1882, p. 3, c. 1-3.

9   *Idaho Tri-Weekly Statesman*, 8 May 1883, p. 3, c. 1.

10 *Idaho Tri-Weekly Statesman*, 14 June 1888, p. 3, c. 4.

11 Alturas County Records, ISHS, Reel 5, p. 8.

12 Idaho Marriage Index, 1850-1951.

13 *Idaho Daily Statesman*, 7 June 1895, p. 6, c. 4.

14 *Idaho Daily Statesman*, 23 February 1896, p. 2, c. 1 – 3.

15 *Boise Sentinel*, Boise, Idaho, 10 June 1897, p. 14, c. 3

16 *The Weekly Capital*, 23 December 1899, p. 11, c. 3.

17 *The Evening Capital News,* Boise, Idaho, 27 April 1901, p. 2, c. 2-4

18 *Idaho Daily Statesman*, 23 January 1902, p. 8, c. 2.

19 *Idaho Daily Statesman*, 21 June 1904, p. 5, c. 7. 28 July 1904, p. 5, c. 4.

20 *Idaho Daily Statesman*, 15 August 1904, p. 5, c. 3.

21 *Evening Capital News*, 7 March 1905, p. 8, c. 4. 8 March 1905, p. 5, c. 5. *Evening Capital News*, 27 June 1905, p. 5, c. 2. 30 June 1905, p. 6, c. 3.

22 *Idaho Daily Statesman*, 11 March 1906, p. 6, c. 1-2.

23 *Idaho Daily Statesman*, 20 May 1905, p. 5, c. 4.

24 *Idaho Daily Statesman*, 30 September 1905, p. 6, c. 4

25 *Evening Capital News*, 7 July 1906, p. 5, c. 2.

26 *Idaho Daily Statesman*, 1 December 1906, p. 3, c. 2.

27 *Idaho Daily Statesman*, 16 June 1906, p. 3, c. 3. 8 July 1906, p. 4, c. 1.

28 *Evening Capital news*, 21 September 1906, p. 8, c. 4.

29 *Evening Capital News*, 13 February 1907, p. 8, c. 5.

30 *The Emmett Index*, 24 September 1908, p. 1, c. 1.

31 *Idaho Daily Statesman*, 24 September 1908, p. 8, c. 1. There is a listing for August Thommon being married on 23 September 1908 to Cora N. Corrull at Caldwell in the Idaho marriage Index CD ROM. This was the day of his suicide. This may relate to the reason he killed himself. It is certainly a bizarre factoid.

32 *Evening Capital News*, 22 September 1908, p. 6, c. 4.

33 *Idaho Daily Statesman*, 25 September 1908, p. 8, c. 4.

34 *The Emmett Index*, 8 October 1908, p. 5, c. 3.

35 *Idaho Daily Statesman*, 28 October 1909, p. 2, c. 5.

36 *Evening Capital News*, 14 October 1911, p. 6, c. 4.

37 Idaho Marriage Index 1850-1951.

24

MIKE WEIMANN
Died at Insane Asylum

Weimann was the proprietor of the Eagle Rock Brewery in Idaho Falls for about six years.[1] Apparently he came to town in late 1888 and took over from Heath and Keefer, who had previously owned the brewery. His new ad in November of 1888 listed him as manager, with William N. Thomas as proprietor of the business.[2] The September issue of Bradstreet's Commercial Reports that year listed M. Weimann as brewer in Eagle Rock and Jacob H. Keefer as a saloon owner.[3] One of the few mentions in the press in the early years was when *the Idaho Register* of Idaho Falls reported in 1890 that the previous year, Weimann had 2,000 bushels of barley shipped in for him.[4] The paper said that would no longer be necessary; all he needed would be raised locally. This could make Weimann a father of barley growing in an area now world renown.

By July of 1890 ads for the Eagle Rock Brewery listed Weimann as the proprietor.[5] In 1891 a listing of the businesses of Idaho Falls said the brewery was now called the Idaho Falls Brewery and it had enough capacity to supply the surrounding towns as well as the local market.[6] Weimann's ad in July of that year still used the name Eagle Rock Brewery and offered lager in kegs or bottles.[7] Life must have been less than exciting, for there was no mention of the brewery again till the next year. *The Times* gave him a plug at that time, saying the beer was refreshing and not adulterated.[8]

In August of 1892, Casper Sauer took over the brewery as agent for Weimann.[9] Weimann was at least temporarily incapacitated.

91. Brewery and malt plant.

Weimann had a family. His wife was mentioned in the local paper when she made a quick trip to Omaha when her father was seemingly on his deathbed.[10] He recovered, and she came home. Early in 1893, Weimann was busy with that dreaded winter chore of every brewer—ice cutting. Mike built a slide and slid 400 tons from the Snake River directly into his icehouse.[11] Every team in town was hauling ice for somebody at that particular time.[12] The next month, a cryptic message in the paper said Weimann would be the next one "pulled" for stealing coal, as he had been hauling willows that he cut for fuel off the island below town.[13]

In 1893, newspaper ads for the brewery listed beer and lunch as the inducements.[14] Weimann was still the proprietor.

In May of 1894, the *Times* reported that Dr. Jones had performed skillful surgery on Mike to remove nose polyps and restore his nasal breathing.[15] A month later, Mike was reported acting strangely. Watchmen kept an eye on him, and Dr. Jones said there were strong symptoms of insanity. He was taken to Blackfoot, where the state

92. Bird's-eye view of Idaho Falls.

93. Skogg saloon with Eagle Rock beer.

asylum was located, and brought before a probate judge to determine if he should be committed.[16] He was committed. The next month, Mike must have come home for a visit or been released because the newspaper said just that he "came up from Blackfoot this morning."[17] The September 1894 R. G. Dun, Mercantile Agency Reference Book listed Mrs. M. Weimann as brewery owner in Idaho Falls. Mike was obviously not considered competent. Little was heard of Mike for the next year, but we did learn later that he suffered a stroke and was back in the asylum.

In May of 1895, John "Jack" R. Edwards purchased the brewery, which was apparently not in operation.[18] On the 14th of September 1895, Mike Weimann died at the asylum. The cause of death was attributed to a stroke he had suffered about a year before.[19] He was buried in Idaho Falls. No children were mentioned, but his wife was staying with Mr.

94. Closeup of Idaho Falls Brewery from Bird's-eye view drawing.

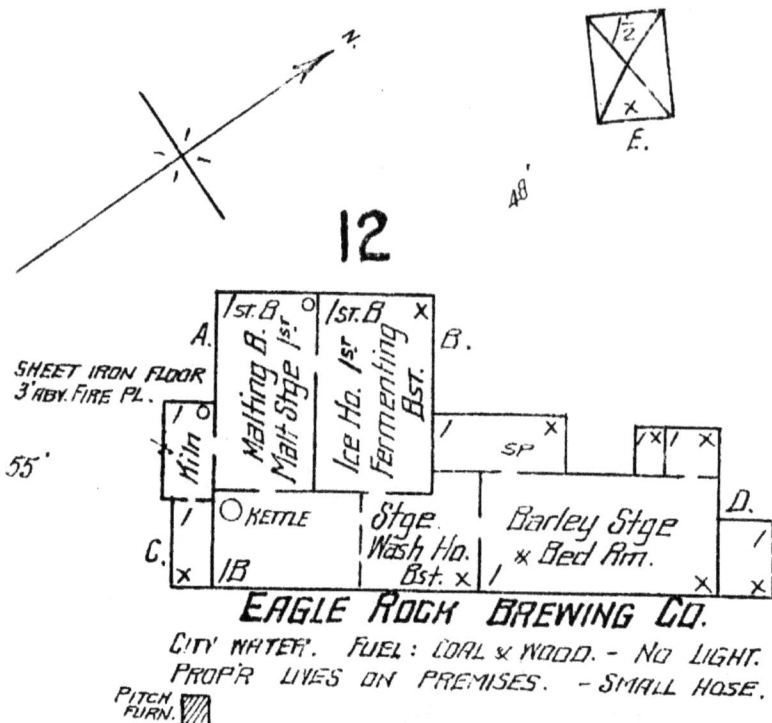

95. Eagle Rock Brewery 1903 fire map.

and Mrs. Joe Streibich at that time. Mike is another of those men of Gambrinus whose sad life story remains mostly obscure.

END NOTES

[1]There are at least three men with this name on the immigration lists for America but I cannot make a positive identification of him or a relative.

[2]*The Idaho Register*, Eagle Rock, 10 November 1888, p. 3, c. 4.

[3]"Bradstreet's Commercial Reports," vol. 87, September 1889, p. Idaho 2.

[4]*The Idaho Register*, Idaho Falls, 25 February 1890, p. 3, c. 1.

[5]*The Idaho Register*, 18 July 1890, p. 3, c. 8.

[6]*The Idaho Register*, 2 January 1891, p. 1, c. 3.

[7]*Idaho Falls Times*, Idaho Falls, Idaho, 9 July 1891, p. 4, c. 6.

[8]*Idaho Falls Times*, 28 July 1892, p. 5, c. 1.

[9]*Idaho Falls Times*, 11 August 1892, p. 5, c. 2.

[10]*Idaho Falls Times*, 22 December 1892, p. 7, c. 1.

[11]*Idaho Falls Times*, 19 January 1893, p. 5, c. 1

[12]*The Idaho Register*, 27 January 1893, p. 1, c. 4.

[13]*Idaho Falls Times*, 9 February 1893, p. 5, c. 1.

[14]*Idaho Falls Times*, 22 June 1893, p. 7, c. 5.

[15]*Idaho Falls Times*, 4 May 1894, p. 5, c. 2.

[16]*The Idaho Register*, 8 June 1894, p. 1, c. 3.

[17]*Idaho Falls Times*, 16 July 1894, p. 5, c. 1.

[18]Mr. J. R. Edwards had engaged George Bloom, who had once brewed in Chicago and also with the Fischer Brewing Company of Salt Lake, as the brewer. J. R.'s son, Hyrum, was in charge of the brewery. They intended to get their liquor licenses and have beer on the market by July first. They were indeed open on June 28, 1895, two days ahead of schedule.

[19]*Idaho Falls Times* 19 September 1895, p. 5, c. 4.

25

JOHN WILLIAMS

Stole From Retorts

IN JUNE OF 1866, WILLIAMS appeared on the Silver City scene as a brewer with John Grete as his partner.[1] At that time, Grete and Williams had their brewery "under full headway and can furnish any amount of the best lager at a moments notice."[2] The newspaper reporter, who prided himself on being a good judge of lager, tasted the new brew without complaint. The men were also erecting a 20 -by 40-foot building with a 12-foot second story and a basement fronting the brewery.[3] Grete and Williams paid federal tax for their brewer's license in May 1866, and on the 6 1/2 barrels of beer they brewed in June 1866, according to Federal records.[4] Their first newspaper advertisement read: "Miner's Brewery/Grete and Williams/Washington Street, Silver City/Manufacture the very best article of Lager!/Constantly on hand at wholesale and Retail/Will deliver in Ruby and Boonville/Fresh Yeast everyday/All orders receive prompt attention."[5]

Grete soon left the partnership, and William Slagle, a carpenter recently of California, became William's partner.[6] Slagle shot himself within a month or so. Ironically, the new newspaper ad that changed the ownership from Grete and Williams to Williams and Slagle never appeared until after Slagle's suicide.

On the Federal Tax assessment records, John Williams paid for brewing six barrels of beer in August of 1866.[7] He was definitely in the beer-making business.

Early in 1867, Williams bought out Slagle's share of the business, according to reports.[8] Maybe he made payment to some heirs.

Williams's newspaper advertisements in 1867 indicate he was operating the brewery on Washington Street alone.[9] Since Williams always
stayed with brewing as others came and went, this author assumes he
was the actual technician who cooked up the beer while the others
were business investors. Sometime in 1867, Williams sold out to T.
G. Rudelhuber and left no further tracks on the Idaho brewing scene.
Yet he continued to retail liquor and remained in the Owyhee area.

In early July of 1868, John Williams and J. C. Hepworth, former
employees in the mill of the Golden Chariot Mining Company, were
convicted of stealing several thousands of dollars worth of bullion
from the retorts of the company.[10] I cannot guarantee this was the
same John Williams. Hepworth was given a fine of $1, paid costs of
prosecution, and served eight years in prison. Williams was so low
from the effects of a pistol shot wound he received at the time of his
arrest that sentence was deferred in his case until the next term of the
court. I do not know how this was resolved.

Williams was back in Silver City 13 years later, in 1886, in the
saloon business as the following newspaper reports attested.

"Silver City, Idaho, May 14—Some men came near killing the
little son of Mr. Leslie, the photographer, here to-day. At Williams

96. Idaho Hotel, Silver City, C. E. 2008.

saloon, they kettled a dog and tied a rope on him and started him. From the saloon he ran around Jones corner toward the Idaho Hotel. The little Leslie boy was crossing the street from the printing office, the rope caught him and he was dragged from Jones' corner to the Idaho Hotel, where the men caught hold of the rope and checked the dog, and when they cut the rope the poor boy was insensible. He fell on his back when the rope caught him. He was carried into a saloon and washed, and was as limber as a rag. He came to after about two hours, and when his ma spoke to him he cried, and now when they speak to him he cries hard and don't say a word. He don't seem to know anything. Probable result is brain fever."[11] How the little fellow fared after this is unknown.

Williams had but a brief life as a follower of Gambrinus, and not one about which to brag.

END NOTES

1   *Owyhee Avalanche*, Silver City, Idaho, 9 June 1866, p. 3, c. 2. p. 2, c. 4

2   *Owyhee Avalanche,* 9 June 1866, p. 3, c. 2. The Pacific Coast Directory for 1867 listed Grete and Williams, general merchants in Silver City, Owyhee, Idaho Territory. Internet site.

3   *Owyhee Avalanche,* 9 June 1866, p. 3, c. 2.

4   Federal Tax Records, 1865-66, Microfilm # 58.

5   *Owyhee Avalanche* 9 June 1866, p. 2, c. 4.

6   See the biography of William Slagle in this volume.

7   Federal Tax Records, 1865-1866, University of Idaho Library, Moscow, Idaho, Microfilm #558.

8   *Owyhee Avalanche*, 12 January 1867, p. 2, c. 4.

9   *Owyhee Avalanche*, 10 January 1867, p. 1, c. 5.

10 *The Idaho Semi-Weekly World*, Idaho City, Idaho, 8 July 1868, p. 2, c. 1.

11 *Idaho Tri-Weekly Statesman*, Boise, Idaho, 17 May 1881, p. 1, c. 4.

TURN VEREIN

German Citizens and Culture in Idaho and Their Relation to the State's Brewing Industry

"Reviewing the brewing history of a city is like reading a novel of which one already knows the plot and ending: German brewers arrived in the 1840's to introduce lager beer, which quickly replaced the British-style ales. They produced an opulent culture of brewer's mansions, singing societies, gymnastic clubs, and in particular, intermarriage with each other's children. Prohibition was devastating; some brewers survived, but others did not. The larger survivors did well until the 1950s, and then the national brewers came on strongly and in the later decades, one by one knocked off the traditional local firms. Then, after 1980, local brewing revived with brewpubs and microbreweries." Professor George W. Hilton, Editor Emeritus of *The Breweriana Collector.*[1]

Idaho brewers do not perfectly fit this national pattern. Idaho brewers arrived later than the Eastern brewers—the earliest in the 1860s—and there were no established British or any other ethnic group of brewers to displace. All Idaho brewers were not Germans and certainly all Idaho Germans were not brewers, but there was a disproportional German influence in brewing in Idaho, as elsewhere. This can be traced to the high status of beer and brewing in areas of Europe that had Germanic culture, the saturation level of such businesses, and the common idea that going to America to brew was the road to a fortune. Looking at German-American culture in Idaho is instructive for understanding the lives of brewers.

Another question is, "What was going on in Europe to cause so many brewers and would-be brewers to come to America?" Between 1827 and 1856, at least 150 tracts written by Germans already in America were published in Germany. In particular, Gottfried Duden's *Report on a Journey to the Western States of North America*, published in 1829, and written in the form of believable letters to home, described the idyllic nature of Mid-western farming. He also said the one group that had particularly prospered during the mass movements (Volkerwanderung) were the men skilled in brewing. Another of Duden's books, *A Stay of Several Years along the Missouri*, said brewers could quickly get rich if they could find farmers to grow barley and hops. Germany was world-renown for its beer-making mastery, brewery schools, and model breweries, and for its 46 1/2 gallons per capita beer consumption. The right sort of men could transfer this tradition to America. Duden recommended moving to cities and bringing enough capital to build a brewery. Nicholas Hesse wrote a similar report in 1838, saying brewers must have the means to erect their breweries.[2] Brewers who found their way to Idaho were influenced by such propaganda and the success of those Germans in the East who preceded them.

The *Idaho World* newspaper in Idaho City had an ad in November 1869 that was headlined "Germans Attention" and went on to invite everyone interested in a German literary club to attend an organizational meeting at—where else?—the Idaho Brewery in Idaho City.[3] In the 1870 U. S. Census in the Boise Basin, Germans were the third most numerous foreign population, behind Chinese and Irish. For all of Idaho that year, there were 599 individuals born in the region the German Empire would soon encompass. That was only about 4 percent of the Idaho population of 14,999—a much smaller territorial population total than a few years before, when the mining rush was at its height. Classification was based on political rather than ethnic origins. "Germany" was still a geographic expression rather than a nation, a condition that persisted until the end of the Franco-Prussian War in 1871. Germanic culture was found in parts of Switzerland,

Italy, the Austrian Empire, the Volga and Black Sea areas of Russia.[4] Yet, within the various areas of "Germany" were islands of Poles, Slavs, French, Danes, etc. The German-speaking states represented in this 1870 Census of Idaho included Prussia with 232 representatives, Bavaria with 78, Hesse with 42, Hanover 32, and an ill-defined "Germany" with 100.[5] Many of these Germans were Jews who, both in Europe and America, constituted a separate ethnic group. Though separated by culture and religion, the German Jews were bound by language and seemed to intermix easily with gentile Germans in early Idaho. German Lutherans and Catholics still exhibited long-standing mistrust. When the immigrants of the 1880s arrived they failed to mix well with the earlier immigrants. Germans in America were as fractured a group as they had been in Germany.

In Idaho City, Dr. Herman Zipf, physician, was a graduate of the University of Heidelberg, and many merchants, butchers, and shoemakers were also Germans. The Idaho City Brass Band was composed, at least from time to time, of nothing but Germans, causing it to be labeled the German Band.[6] German-born Adolph Ballot, a watchmaker and jeweler, was a driving force in Idaho City music, and when he moved to Boise in the 1880s, helped start the Boise Philharmonic Orchestra.

There was also a strong German influence among the women of early Idaho. Every camp had a hurdy-gurdy—a place where men paid to dance with women. Fifty cents a dance plus a fifty-cent drink gave a man the opportunity to spend a few minutes with a female companion. When future governor McConnell arrived in Idaho, he found the hurdy-gurdys were populated with German girls.[7] These girls later became respectable wives in McConnell's recollection. Others took a different view. Editor James S. Reynolds of the *Idaho Tri-Weekly Statesman* of Boise urged the 1864 legislature to tax the hurdy-gurdy girls. He alleged that "they are Swiss, chubby, black, can't talk English, and live in the rear of the dance house on the cheapest kind of plunder." H. C. Street of the *Idaho World* of Idaho City jumped to the girls' defense. They were from Germany, he said, and "hundreds of our citizens, whose fathers and mothers are waiting for their wandering sons and daughters to return to the sunny banks of the Oder, Elbe, and the Rhine, do not feel very highly complimented by the *Statesman's* slurs on their complexion."[8] Early editors always invented something to feud about to try and keep their papers interesting. Whether either editor actually cared about German culture was questionable.

The 1870 Census located four young German girls working in a hurdy-gurdy house in Granite Creek in the Boise Basin.[9]

In Boise by that year, 35 German residents had banded together to form the Turn Verein and Harmonie Society—an organization long needed in Boise, according to the *Statesman*.[10] The new group held a big ball at Slocum's Hall in March of 1870—music and supper cost $7.[11] Social activities continued through this time of stress, including a grand ball at Slocum's Hall in September of 1870.[12] The singing society sang, the Turners did gymnastics, and everyone danced until dawn. The reporter of the *Boise Weekly News* went into more detail.[13] "...We say it was one of the most social and agreeable parties that has ever taken place in the city." Music was by Steitel, Pefferlee, Chapman, Harpham, and Moss. Sheffer & Company catered an elegant supper, and "Manager Goldbaum, with the rose star of authority pinned upon his breast, looked the very personification of the able commander, and, in appearance at least, would reflect no discredit upon the Staff of the Crown Prince of Prussia."

> *They danced with spirit and vigor*
> *Until the lark, the herald of the morn,*
> *Announced that jocund day stood tip toe*
> *Upon the misty mountain tops.*

The event was declared a success, "socially, numerically, and financially."[14]

The Turners mentioned here were members of the newly formed Boise Turn Verein. This organization, which is also known as the Turner Bund, began in America in 1848 in New York. Father Frederich

Ludwig Jahn originally formed the group in Germany in the early 19th Century.[15] His goal was to restore the German people to the level of physical vigor they enjoyed when their warriors first bounded from the forest to terrify the Roman legionnaires. In America, the organization soon adopted social and political goals and had activities for every member of the family. Anti-slavery, anti-prohibition, and anti-nativism were the principles of the movement in its American branch.[16] Turnen translates as gymnastics, and Verein means a union or club. TurnVerein—pronounced toorn-fair-ine—means "athletic club."

In Siskiyou County, California, many of the early settlers were Germans.[17] In October of 1855, in Yreka, California, the Lieder Tafel was formed, and in a few years became the Yreka TurnVerein. Many Yreka people later moved to Idaho during the gold rush. There was also a TurnVerein Society in Portland as early as 1862.[18] It was logical for the organization to be transported with the miners who came in droves to Idaho, and it spread quickly to the newly settled mining areas.

In March of 1870, the word was already put out in Boise to expect a great picnic from the "Turners, belonging to the German Society Hamonie" in May.[19] After only two weeks of practice, the boys' performance was the envy of all. The May Day picnic of 1870 was the largest gathering ever held in Boise to that point.[20] The school children were escorted

94. Grand Ball ad.

to Slocum's hall, where the procession formed. Preceded by the brass band, they marched to the picnic site for gymnastics, lunch, and games.

THE FRANCO-PRUSSIAN WAR

Political and regal machinations in Europe in 1870 would prove to have unpredictable repercussions in Idaho. First, Spain's Isabella II abdicated the crown. It was offered to Prince Leopold of Prussia, but Kaiser Wilhelm I, as head of the House of Hohenzollern, persuaded him to refuse it. The French were terrified that a Spanish-Prussian alliance would upset the balance of power. France's Napoleon III wired Wilhelm demanding a letter of apology and assurance that Leopold would not accept any future offer from Spain. Prussia's Count von Bismarck made the telegram public to show that Napoleon had tried to humiliate the Kaiser and that Wilhelm had refused the demands. On July 19, France declared war on Prussia and invaded the Saar basin while Prussia sent three armies to invade France.

Later that year, all Boise TurnVerein members were requested to assemble on July 4th to deal with the issues raised by the war in Europe.[21] Most experts thought France had the greatest army in the world, Emperor Napoleon III was the greatest threat to peace and stability, and the Prussians were in for a very difficult time. The war seemed to have given the Turners an issue with enough power to cement the new organization solidly together. In mid-August, there was another mass meeting of Germans. The Boise newspaper said, "it will be seen that the Germans of Idaho are not behind their fellow citizens of the eastern cities in sympathy for their kindred in the struggle through which they are now passing."[22]

At that time, Moses Moritz was teaching gymnastics to the newly formed Turners and their 30 members.[23] Those who worked hard were getting good at the ball and ring exercises. Soon, the Boise Turners bought a lot north of the Episcopal Church to build a hall, a symbol of "their permanency and prosperity."[24]

On the national level, Germans came in for criticism that received nationwide coverage during 1870.[25] The *Chicago Times*, the leading Democratic newspaper of the West, criticized the German participants in the Civil War, the German-American generals that led them, and their politics in general. "The Dutch of this country have proven a most stupendous fraud. The records of the War Department at Washington show of the 'Dutch generals' that during our late row, Chancellorsville was repeated on a smaller scale wherever Dutch battalions were placed in battle array. They vote just as they fought, on the side offering the most lager beer and the most money. It is useless for the Democracy to pander to the Dutch vote. It is a curse to any party." The old Know-Nothing ideas of the 1840s were still reverberating.

The elected leaders of the Boise Turners in January 1871 were John Lemp, (brewer) president; Moses Moritz (brewery owner), First Turner leader; and Chris Sans (brewer), steward.[26] Brewing was obviously a respected profession among the Germans. The Turners held another big ball later in January—the European war had not destroyed their social inclinations.[27]

In Idaho City, the widows and orphans fund for the war was headed up by S. G. Rosenbaum, Charles Bernstiel, and brewer Charles Lautenschlager.[28] Local brewer Alois Riid headed for Europe to enlist with the Germans, but died tragically a short distance into the trip.[29] The Society for the benefit of the German widows and orphans during the Franco-Prussian War accepted members who gave 25 cents or more per week.[30]

Charley Bernstiel was Idaho's most noted German advocate for the war.[31] He once decorated the horses on the Idaho City stage with little Prussian flags. He traveled between Boise City and Boise Basin haranguing his fellow Deutschers. When the Prussians captured Napoleon III at the Battle of Sedan in September of 1870, the Germans rejoiced. Bernstiel gave a case of champagne to George Anslie, the editor of the *Idaho World,* to celebrate the victory. Some French miners refused to accept the news and bet large sums that it was wrong.

When news arrived in Idaho City that Paris had surrendered to the

Prussians, the celebration among the Germans erupted with the force of a breached beer barrel. "The favorite beverage of old Gambrinus flowed in sufficient quantities to have run a ground sluice and heavy requisitions were made on Brodbeck' and Haug's brewery to supply the demand. At present, we believe all is well on Elk Creek."[32] In Boise, 50 or so Germans sat around a large table singing and drinking John Lemp's beer.[33]

In 1871, the *Tri-Weekly Statesman* had a whole political column written in the German language and signed "a Deutscher Democrat."[34] In April, the Turners gave a grand Easter ball.[35] The same year, the Turners had a May festival.[36] Boise was deserted and school closed for that big event.[37]

Robert Heuschkel and his future wife, Miss Bergold, arrived in Boise in 1871 and 1872, respectively.[38] Years later, they remembered that their fellow Germans were "very clannish and enjoyed many customs of the fatherland. "There was a dramatic society under the auspices of the TurnVerein, and Mrs. Nathan Falk and Mrs. Heuschkel took the principal female roles. Mrs. Epstein and Mrs. Wolters also were frequent participants, and Messrs. Wolters, Bayhouse, Richard Adelmann, and William Jauman took the male roles.

The dominant Anglo citizens of America found Germans funny. Their sometimes futile attempts to master the English tongue led to humorous stories of their fractured speech. Some of these stories were in good humor, and some may have not been. The following is an example of "Dutch" humor from 1872.[39]

"I pese clad to see you, like ash niver vas, Mister Cris; when did Zinzinnaty goome away from you?"

Such was the warm salutation of a Teutonic friend whom we met the other day in a distant city, where he had gone to reside. The reader might not guess in a long time what business our friend from Cincinnati was engaged in, so we can tell you he kept a lager beer saloon.

"How do you like your new location?" We inquired after his raptures at meeting a Cincinnatian had somewhat abated.

"Nice poys in this towns; nice poys. The first night vot I opens my saloon, they goomes in and calls for lager peer; doo, eight, scez, half a tozzen ove 'em; und ven I says 'Who makes pay for this too soon already?' by tam, dey says, 'you better as send out und puy a schlate.' Vel, I vants to aggommodate—there's no brincibal in dose things—so I bought a schlate. The peer kept calling for more poys, und I kept puttin der schlate unto dem. Pooty guick already I tells dem der schlate pese full on both sides, und uden they tells me if der schlate pese full I better as fill my tam Tuch head mid 'em! Well, dat is all right—there's no brincibal in dose things—dey are nish poys.

"Pooty bime by after leedle, they makes smash, mit mine bar, preaks mine pottles, unt knocks hail tamnation out of mine looking-class mit my head. Mine Cott! I vas mad. I radder you give me ten dollar so much as I vas mad. But dat pese all right, there's no brincipal in dose; dat makes nix tifference. Nice poys.

"Then they galls me a tam Tuch son 'f kun, unt I dells 'em they better as go to the tieful, their own tam American sconagun. Vash I right? Vell, that makes nottiage tifferent.

"They knocks the staircase down mine frow, unt throws the window out of the pany. That's all right—makes notting-tifference—there's no brincibal in dat—nice poys, but (growing very much excited and emphasizing each word on the bar with his fist) they put water into mine class peer—und Cott in himel, that ish not right—there's some brincibal in dose things—that makes somethings different!"

The Turner May picnic in 1876 was a high point in the history of the club.[40] The swollen Boise River dropped and did not fulfill its earlier threat to inundate the pavilion and grounds. The glee club sang:

Health to the fairest, we pledge;
Health to the fairest.
Quaff it at Beauty's shrine,
Pledge it in cups of golden wine;
In cups of golden wine.
Here's a health to all that's fair.

NEW TO-DAY.

MAY ✿ BALL

——o——

THE BOISE CITY

Turn Verein

WILL GIVE A BALL AT

SLOCUM'S HALL,

—ON—

MONDAY EVENING, MAY 2d.

— 0 —

COMMITTEE OF ARRANGEMENTS.
JULIUS OSTHEIM,   LOUIS HEYD,
W. BAYHOUSE.   M. P. FFERLE,
NATHAN FALK.

COMMITTEE OF RECEPTION.
A. ROSSI,   M MORITZ,
B. H. LEWIS,   WM. BRYON,
SAM. BECK.

FLOOR MANAGERS.
CHAS. GOLDBAUM,   JOHN LEMP,
GEORGE BAYHOUSE.

TICKETS,.....$3.00,.....COIN,
To be had from the Committee on the Picnic grounds,
A general invitation is extended.

95. May Ball ad.

Annie Bledsoe was crowned queen of May in a silent pantomime ceremony. Five young men then came out to demonstrate gymnastic and athletic training. Walt Coflin chinned himself with one hand, then the other; several performed feats on the parallel bars; then Coflin lifted one of his fellows with one hand. Finally, Ed Gaylord was selected Champion Turner. That afternoon, there was a two hour dance, and then at eight that evening, a grand ball. This plethora of events seems to cover all that Turn Verein sought to do.

In 1877, the May festival again involved music, gymnastics, food, and a grand ball in the evening.[41] Almost everyone in town was expected to visit the Turn Verein event sometime during the day.[42]

In far-off Russia in the early 1870s, a push for forced assimilation and forced military service drove the Volga Germans to look to America for a new home. Many took up farms in Kansas, Nebraska, or other Plains states. The conditions there were not favorable, and many soon looked to the Columbia Basin for farming opportunities. As a Germanic group, they became some of the earliest settlers in the Pacific Northwest.

In 1879, the Turner Hall in Boise was fitted up with a nice stage for a pinafore exhibition.[43]

The 1880 U.S. Census for the first time asked the national origin of each individual. This adds both light and confusion to the ethnicity of many people. 5,049 Idaho citizens were born in Germany. 637 Idaho citizens had a German-born father. 400 of these also had a German-born mother, and 237 had mothers of other national origins.

528 had a mother born in Germany. This included the 400 who also had German-born fathers.

When President Garfield died in 1881, Boise held a service in his honor.[44] The Turn Verein was among the lodges, such as the Masons and Odd Fellows that marched in the procession. The Germans of Boise rented the Good Templar Hall in February and watched a German play followed by a dance.[45] Only a few non-Germans were present, the newspaper editor noticed.

"Members of the Turn Verein are nearly all consumptives, and believe in the efficacy of extract of malt. Very pleasant evenings are those which they spend at the hall singing and other convivial content."[46] A Saenger (singing) Club was organized at George Kohlepp's brewery in Hailey in May of 1883. L. Schrepel was president, George Kohlepp vice-president, George Bayhouse Treasurer, George Schutze secretary.[47] Long-time resident and daughter of brewer August Exner, Barbara Exner Cobb, remembered quite a few Germans in Hailey when she was young.[48] In 1884, the Turn Verein Hall in Boise was fitted up for the accommodation of the Legislative Assembly, which was to meet there.[49] The December ball in 1885 was by invitation; "And it will prove an unapproachable affair, as all others that have been given by this society composed of our best citizens."[50] By 1889, Turner dances were still held, but they seemed to be smaller affairs with smaller mention in the newspaper.[51]

The Turner picnics seemed to retain their earlier vigor and popularity, however. In June of 1890, 60 members met at John Lemp's ranch at Lemp Gulch. They danced, sang, ate, and "enjoyed themselves as only Germans can."[52] They played football, had several boxing matches, and then concentrated on target shooting.

In September of 1891, the Boise Turn Verein held their annual picnic as always. The Committee that organized this was William Jauman (brewer Lemp's brother-in-law) brewer John Brodbeck, and saloonist Dick Adelmann.[53] The Germania club sang and they had lunch at Davis Grove on the banks of the Boise River.

The results of the 1890 U.S. Census were partially released in 1893.

It found 1,939 German-born Idahoans that year.[54] Other sources say 2,974.[55] This was out of a total state population of 161, 772.

When William Jauman died in 1895, his obituary mentioned his helping to form the Turn Verein.[56] The organization was still significant enough to deserve and require mention in such situations.

In the mid 1890s, a new German American organization was frequently mentioned in the Idaho press. They officially organized in November of 1894, but had an informal existence before that.[57] The German American Athletic Association was holding dances and other activities to raise money for a gymnasium in Boise in 1894.[58] Prominently mentioned was the fact that no intoxicants would be allowed in the new facility. So bold was the new group that they made an unsuccessful bid to host the Corbett-Fitzsimmons Heavyweight Championship fight.[59]

Some social events of the 1890s were referred to by a new slang term as "Germans," as in "Monday evening a bright and successful German was given at the Natorium in honor of Miss Arthur."[60] Whatever this involved, it took place after the dancing and supper of the evening.

During this period, Charles Sonnleitner in Hailey strived to conduct his brewery's retail facility as a German-style beer hall, not a frontier saloon.[61]

Boise had a visit by the Reverend C.A. Wentsch of La Grande, Oregon, in April 1900.[62] He wrote of his experiences in a letter to the *Am Stillen Meere*, a German paper in Rosalia, Washington, and it was translated in the Boise *Statesman*. He succeeded in finding a few Germans in Boise and was allowed to hold a religious service in the M. E. Church. He was pleased to see some "Americans" there who had come to feel at home in the German language through serious study. Wentsch also went to a German language class taught by Mrs. M. Heuschkel which was all in *Deutsch*, and where he heard the best German he had ever heard from Americans. Rosalia is near the Idaho border, and many Volga Germans settled in that area.

In 1900, *The Idaho Post*, a German-language newspaper, began publication in Boise.[63] It was started by Carl Wohlfarth, who at one time wanted to start a German newspaper in Lewiston, Idaho, but abandoned the idea to throw in with the Washington Post of Spokane. Wohlfarth left Boise without paying his debts and sold what was left of his paper to the Spokane publication. What is significant here is that someone, at least, thought Boise had enough people literate in German to make a foreign language paper feasible.

In August of 1901, in Butte, Montana, adjacent to Idaho, was the largest statewide gathering of the Sons of Hermann ever held in the state.[64] In Portland, the General German Aid Society and the German Ladies Relief Society were active for decades. German-America was seemingly making inroads in the Rocky Mountain West and Pacific Northwest.

The Turner Hall in Boise was leased to the Salt Lake Dramatical Company for two weeks of shows in August of 1901.[65]

In February of 1902, John Lemp (brewer), John Brodbeck (former brewer), Charles Leyerzapf, General John Green, Rupert Maxgut (brewery manager), John Nagel, Louis Koehler (former brewer), M. Klinge, Ben Kury, and August Mortiz sent out a call for all Germans of Boise to join them at the Grand Army of the Republic Hall for a social.[66] Dancing and speech-making in the German language were the order of the day.[67] Refreshments were served at intervals throughout the evening. Brewery owner John Lemp made a short address in which he spoke of the pleasure it gave him to see the German citizens all gathered together after so many years, and he hoped it would be the first of many to be held in the future. Rupert Maxgut then spoke, followed by a humerous recitation by Mrs. Heusckel and C. E. Kaufer.

Another meeting was held on 1 April.[68] Rupert Maxgut presided for the evening. There was an address by Mrs. Heuschkel, a song by Pearl Haines, a recitation by Charles Kaufer, and a comic dialogue by Mrs. Heusckel and Mr. Kaufer to entertain the 150 guests.[69]

In April of 1902, the Sons of Hermann, a branch of the German American Alliance, was organized in Boise with 54 charter members.[70] "Officers elected included C. Kauffen, C. Hummel, John Salfer, W. E.

Steineck, Henry Konrad, Louis Koehler, and Drs. Blitz and Boeck."[71]
A sister lodge was to be organized the next day. Nationwide, German
groups were forming at this time. That same month, 24 Germans
from Nebraska, previously experienced in sugar beet agriculture in
Germany, arrived in Boise to take up land and grow their crops.[72]
They claimed over a hundred of their countrymen waited in Nebraska
to see if this experiment was successful. This must have stimulated
German culture in the area.

At the end of June of 1902, a free German gathering was held at
Avenue Park at the end of the streetcar line.[73] Again in August of 1902,
a German picnic was held at Avenue Park in Boise under the auspices
of the Sons of Hermann.[74] There were athletics, refreshments, and
dancing day and night. There was a turn-of-the-century revival of
German culture in Boise.

The Sons of Hermann elected officers in September of 1902: Ex-
president Rupert Maxgut (brewer) was among the six electees.[75] At
the Christmas party on the night of December 25 that year, Maxgut
was the master of ceremonies.[76] The event featured a Christmas tree,
gifts for children, refreshments, and dancing until the wee hours.

In 1903, another big German picnic was held near the Natorium
with athletics contests and dancing.[77] A body of members of the Sons
of Hermann Lodge attended the funeral of Miss Freda Michel in
December of 1903.[78]

In a 1904 biographical sketch of John Lemp, he was identified as
one of the five surviving members of the old TurnVerein.[79] The sketch
also said that the organization had gotten new life and new members
that very year. Former brewer John Brodbeck was the secretary of the
organization in the spring of 1904.[80]

Back East in Indianapolis, 3,000 Turners and many times that
number of visitors held the national assembly of the North American
Gymnastic Union in June of 1905.[81] The national TurnVerein seemed
to be prospering.

In April of 1904, a large meeting of the Boise Turners was held
and committees were appointed to study the feasibility of building

a new hall for the group.[82] The first rough version of the building plans were published in the *Statesman* in June.[83] The plans drawn up by J. E. Tourtellotte & Co. were submitted to the committee and accepted with only slight changes.[84] The estimated cost at that time was $20,000. The tentative plans were released that September and called for a $30,000 building.[85] In January of 1905, the *Statesman* said the building was to be built soon.[86] In 1906, the renewed vigor of the TurnVerein led them to actually build the new building, designed by Tourtellotte and German-American Hummel, at the corner of 6th and Main.[87] This became a historic landmark. Before their new-found strength, the organization had owed $711.84 in delinquent property tax in Boise in 1897.[88] The new hall had a stage, a 400-seat auditorium, balcony, an exercise area, locker rooms, showers, gents parlor, kitchen and dining room.[89] A planned bowling alley never materialized. The building was 50 by 122 feet and two stories high with an entrance on Sixth Street.[90] It was expected to cost $15,000. At a meeting in September of 1905, the trustees of the TurnVerein submitted to the organization their plan to borrow enough to complete the new building.[91] The plan was adopted without dissent and $2,500 for seed money was raised in one day. The contract was let to Frank Rathmann & Co. for $16,200 in April of 1906.[92] In early February of 1906, the architectural plans of Tourtellotte & Co. were accepted.[93] Before the building was erected, there was a special street-paving levee assessed against the TurnVerein and many others. The Germans owed $608.03 for lot 7 of block 6 and $229.77 for lot 8, block 6.[94]

On the national level, the German American Alliance was lobbying Congress against passage of the Hepburn-Dolliver bill, which would give federal recognition to local prohibition laws. Ex-sheriff Edward J. Tamsen of New York led the delegation. He said, "The Germans are intensely interested in this subject. They see a disposition to push prohibition through federal channels. They are not only opposed to anything of this kind, believing prohibition to be the greatest farce ever inflicted upon a public, but they are far more strongly opposed to the features of the bill that take away individual liberty that the German-American citizen stands for."

"Any bill that prevents a man getting what he wants to drink or eat, in any part of the United States, is an infringement on the constitution of the country and a worse restriction of individual liberty and action. We feel that the constitution gives a man the right to order whatever he wants in one state and have it delivered to him without interference in another. Any law that prevents that will be bitterly fought by Germans, and we will carry it into the campaigns of the future. We are aroused on this subject, as we find that gradually the prohibition vagaries are encroaching on the liberty of the citizen. This whole thing is a matter of state legislation, and the government has nothing to do with it." Tamsen said that New York City alone had 200 lodges of the German-American Alliance.[95]

In Coeur d'Alene, there was a German club organized to celebrate the landing of the first Germans in America. After the turn of the century, they also had a chapter of the Sons of Hermann.

In a 1904 listing of the clubs and lodges of Boise the Sons of Hermann was said to have 40 members.[96] A German picnic was held at Wilson's park on Warm Springs Avenue in July of 1904.[97] It featured two different bands and "plenty of drinkables and eatables."[98] At the end of 1904, the Sons of Hermann held a New Year's dance with tickets selling for 50 cents.[99]

In November of 1904, the TurnVerein Association paid $262.50 in property tax in Boise.[100] A grand ball for New Year's Eve was given by the Sons of Herman at the G.A.R. Hall. Tickets 50 cents for gents and free for ladies, lunch included.[101]

In 1905, an Idaho Falls group of Germans, including brewer Gustave Fleigner, met to plan a remembrance for the death of Frederick Von Schiller, the German poet.[102] In Charleston, South Carolina, Germans and German-Americans met to celebrate the first German settlement in America. This distant event was important enough news to be printed in Boise.[103]

In 1905, the fortieth anniversary of the TurnVerein was celebrated in Boise.[104] The first week of January of 1906, the organization elected

W. G. Messersmith, August J. Moritz, and Henry Nieberding as new trustees.[105] In February, they had again decided to build using the third set of plans from architect Charles Hummell. Nearly $15,000 had been pledged, and the *Evening Capital News* said the building would be a sightly addition to the town, causing the removal of the old livery stable.[106]

In October, the Germans of South Carolina celebrated "German Day," the date of the first—supposedly—German settlement in America, which was near Charleston according to the local version of history.[107]

In June, a photo of the new Turner Hall as it neared completion was in the *Statesman*.[108] The details of its size and design were repeated again. In July, the TurnVerein elected Louis Koehler first speaker, C. F. Hummel second speaker, H. Nieberding secretary, and H. Konrad treasurer.[109]

The TurnVerein building was dedicated and the cornerstone laid on August first of 1906.[110] The band played *Die Wacht am Rhine* as well as *The Star Spangled Banner*. They followed with German cheers and then three cheers for President Teddy Roosevelt. There may have been a deep significance here about the problem of divided loyalties that the next decade would reveal. President L. Koehler delivered an address and T.C. Bouffler gave an address in the German language. They spoke of the first Turner location in 1870 and all they had contributed to build the area, and how much they stood for freedom and liberty. After Mayor J. H. Hawley spoke, real German cheers were given, followed by three cheers for President Roosevelt.[111]

By the 1910 Census, as pre-Prohibition brewing in Idaho was nearing its end, there were 5,049 citizens born in Germany. 7,036 were American born of two German-born parents, and another 5,138 were American born with just one parent German-born. These three groups together were only 5.2 percent of the population of Idaho. The state's population was 325,594.

After the dawn of the 20th Century, the German-American Alliance arose on the national level. It soon had 3,000,000 members

96. Turnverein name on their former building.

and seemed destined to become the first truly effective nationwide German-American organization.[112] The Sons of Hermann was an inner circle group of the Alliance. In 1906, the new officers of the Boise branch of the Sons were installed. President was C.F. Hummell, vice president was Frank Michel, treasurer was N. Steinfeld, and trustee was Chris Henkel.[113]

In November, the new Turner building was nearing completion with a final price tag approaching $17,000.[114] The organization was properly proud of having 100 members. A complete description of the hall was in the *Evening Capital News*:

"The elegant building put up by the Boise Turn Verein society was completed today and is now ready for occupancy. The building is one of the society structures in the city. It is finished in good style with native pine stained a dark green which blends with the light green wainscoting and red walls and ceiling. The entrance to the building is on Seventh Street. A wide door opens into a broad hallway off of which is the auditorium 38 x 58 feet, not including the stage. The auditorium contains a commodious balcony and will be well lighted as it contains over 200 electric lights. The society will rent this room for dances, parties and other social functions when they are not using it. The stage is a model of convenience and is almost as large as the Columbia.

The basement contains several small rooms besides the kitchen, and banquet hall. The latter is 25 x 68 feet in dimension. The kitchen and banquet hall are to be supplied with all the necessities for giving social functions. The lodge room on the second story is well furnished and is now being used by the society for holding its meetings.

Invitations are out for the dedication of the hall, which will take place Thursday evening, December 20, commencing at 8:30. A splendid vocal and instrumental program has been arranged for the occasion."[115]

In December, the dedication of the hall took place.[116] There were speeches and many musical selections. Gustave Kroeger spoke and emphasized that the organization was not just for Germans, it was an organization for physical and mental health.[117] He told how the territorial council had once met in the old Turner Hall. An address by Mr. Johnson emphasized the large number of Germans in some states, and the German origin of family names. In contrast to the Idaho situation, New York, with 320,000 Germans, was on its way to being the second largest German city in the world.[118]

On Christmas evening, 1906, the TurnVerein and the Sons of Hermann had a Christmas tree, dance, and supper for fifty cents.[119] When the *Statesman* celebrated the new architecture the year of 1906 had brought to Boise, the Turner Hall was prominently mentioned.[120] In January, the new Turner officers were Charles F. Hummel president, Gustave Kroeger, vice president; Antone Unternahrer, first secretary; Charles F. Bouffler, second secretary; Henry Konrad, treasurer; Chris Henkel, first turnward; Peter Groner, second turnward; William Messersmith and Anton Dolenz custodians; A. J. Moritz and Henry

97. Turnverein Building, Boise.

Nieberding, trustees; brewery manager William Stoehr was on the entertainment committee.[121]

Hartley and King, "builders of all kinds of stage effects and scenery," were busy in early January completing the scenic and stage effects for the TurnVerein.[122] Hartley had recently worked at the Basque in Portland and King had worked at the Lilliputian in New York. Their work in Boise was to be the equal of any on the coast.

The first ball at the new Turner Hall was held in February, and dancing lasted until after two in the morning.[123] The "best people of the city" attended and a "most tempting supper" was served at midnight.[124] The Mannerchor or male chorus, under the direction of Prof. C. O. Breach, was a highlight, as well as the orchestra, which did not use a piano. Very soon, all kinds of entertainments were presented in the hall, which seated close to 500.[125] Franklyn Fox was the manager, and the plan was to rent the theater out for dramatic play and light opera companies.[126] The introductory show was "Pilgrim Rest," which employed the local Union orchestra.[127]

The Sons of Hermann was continuing its lodge activities also.[128] In March, they elected a new slate of officers including, as trustee, former Moscow, Idaho and Spokane, Washington brewer Louis Koehler.[129]

The TurnVerein hired Professor Louis Rains of Denver, Colorado, to be their physical director, organize classes, and purchase equipment.[130] The society also made plans for the 35th anniversary celebration in April. Soon, the organization built a fence around the vacant lot adjoining their hall and prepared it for use by the physical culture classes.[131] They were going to attach swings, horizontal bars, and rings to the large trees, and build benches for spectators. A month later, the equipment was all installed and Professor Kauntz conducted several classes.[132]

In April of 1907, the Turners celebrated their 35th anniversary with a gala event; featured speaker was Gustave Kroeger.[133] Kroeger told how a meeting between William Bayhouse and Julius Ostheimer led to the founding of the Boise Wesangverein in 1870.[134] In a year or two, it became the Boise TurnVerein and among the charter members, still living were John Lemp and John Krall. Kroeger looked forward to a 70th or 80th anniversary of the organization.

That same April, the first gymnastic classes started and the organization reported rapid growth in membership.[135] The Turners continued to give their traditional socials with music and dance.[136] In July, the Turners purchased a piano and they were used by the Eilers Piano House for advertising.[137] July was also the month for their annual picnic, which drew almost 600 people to the Gess grove down the valley.[138]

A more ominous and frequent Turner activity was gathering the membership to attend the funerals of older members.[139] There were some new Germans moving to Idaho from the Mid-west to judge by letters of inquiry that state officials were receiving.[140] There were almost 5,000 German speakers in the state already.

For Christmas of 1907, the Turners held a large celebration at their new hall.[141]

In the New Year 1908 edition of the *Statesman* there was a list of the lodges of Boise.[142] Among these was Germania Lodge No. 1, founded in 1902, which seemed to have the same officers and members as the Turners and/or the Sons of Hermann. The 1909 article of the same type listed the TurnVerein and the Sons of Hermann as separate organizations.[143]

In February of 1908, the Columbia Club had a German conversation section, which met to speak German exclusively and enjoy German food.[144]

The 37th anniversary of the Turners in Boise was celebrated in April of 1908.[145] Gustave Kroeger was again the featured speaker. He alluded to the organization in Germany and how it had aided in the defeat of Napoleon.[146] There was music and food for the 100 or so guests.

In July of 1908, the international Turnfest in Frankfort-on-the-Main drew between 20,000 and 25,000 with the United States sending over 1,000 delegates.[147] The event eclipsed the Olympic games that were being held in London the same week.

For the 1908 Christmas celebration, 250 adults and 150 children turned out for a Christmas tree, musical programs, and a sumptuous supper.[148]

In February, they had a banquet and dance to celebrate the 100th anniversary of the birth of Abraham Lincoln, a German American hero.[149]

At the 38th anniversary celebration of the TurnVereins in Boise in April of 1909, Kroeger was again the featured speaker. He spoke against excessive alcohol consumption and likewise against the tyrannical laws of prohibition. He said of the drunkard: "...recognize his condition as more of a disease and less of a crime and you will have better results and we may count upon some degree of success."[150] Kroeger's thinking was very advanced for that era.

In July of 1909, the Billings, Montana, lodge of the Sons of Hermann lost a boatload of picnickers on the Yellowstone River in a tragic accident.[151] In Chicago in August was the Turnfest sponsored by the Bohemian Turnbund of North America.[152] Twenty thousand visitors were expected.

In October, a meeting of the National German Alliance in Cincinnati sought to oppose prohibitory laws.[153] This was the last great German American organization before World War I, and its membership probably included most Turners.

In January of 1910, a TurnVerein social in Boise still drew 50 members.[154] The annual meeting in April drew 500.[155] By this time, local option was in force in Idaho and many issues were of serious concern. After the usual music, local attorney Karl Paine gave the address. He had some extremely thoughtful comments on the philosophy of prohibition and other issues of the day. He said that if all must forgo alcoholic beverages because few imbibe, then consistency must extol that "because a few men are libertines, make the rest eunuchs, and wipe out mankind."

Paine went on to say how laws against boxing were still on the books but ignored because of the example of President Roosevelt sparing. Colored men had been disfranchised and universities that once spoke for freedom now taught that slavery was a boon to the black man. His point, in full prediction of the consequences of prohibition, was that unpopular laws are ignored. Personal liberty must be saved at all costs. He quoted the bishop of Durham: "Better England free than England sober."

In November 1910, the German language students of Boise High School started a Deutscher Verein club to get together to practice their language skills.[156] Little did they know how un-American this would seem in a few years.

In 1911, the influence of the great German immigration that started in 1848 on the increased beer consumption in America was noted. Many from wine-drinking countries switched to beer after a few years in America. The change to drinks of lower alcoholic level was considered a "cause for encouragement."[157]

A number of Turn Verein members attended the North Pacific Sangerbund in Seattle in August of 1911.[158] The chorus had over 500 in it, including Boise brewery manager William Stoehr and his wife.

In late October of 1911, the Idaho Supreme Court ruled that social clubs needed to have a liquor license if they intended to operate a bar for their members.[159] The *Statesman* opined "the saloon is the poor man's club," and that many club members belonged chiefly so they could drink liquor at the club. Therefore, requiring a liquor license was just common sense. The Boise Commercial Club was one of the first to announce it would abide by the decision.[160]

In early 1912, there was another sign of a vibrant Germanic culture in Boise. Reverend R. J. P. Kraus, the German Lutheran pastor of New Plymouth, preached in Boise with the idea of starting a congregation in the Idaho capital city.[161] This was to be a Missouri Synod branch of Lutheranism with the German language being the principal tongue.

The Turn Verein offered a program of folksong that was "the peer of any previous effort of the organization" in February of 1912.[162] Music director C. O. Breach had made great strides in the previous year. After the program, everyone danced for several hours.

In March of 1912, the male chorus entertained their families and friends at an "impromptu banquet and concert" at the Turner Hall.[163] August Mortiz was in the chair for the event. The second chorus concert of the Boise TurnVerein, under the direction of Professor C. O. Breach was given in May of 1912.[164] Their program ranged from "Tannhauser" by Wagner to Foster's "Old Kentucky Home."[165]

In August of 1912, Rudolph K. Stephen, who at 24 attested to the new young membership of the group, died of appendicitis and the Turners and Sons of Hermann were requested to attend.[166] The group was prospering, but it was the last flare up before the fire went out. On the horizon loomed statewide prohibition and thus the end of beer, the natural glue that bound the organization. Also, World War I would eventually cause all things Germanic to be despised with an irrational zeal.

Barbara Exner Cobb, brewer August Exner's daughter, remembered German children being persecuted in Hailey during World War I.[167] This is but one example of a nationwide hysteria that eradicated, almost overnight, German culture in America.

Vigilante groups rode out into the Idaho countryside to torment German farmers and force them to kiss the ground. The German language was no longer spoken openly, and families forbade their children to learn it. Architect Charles Hummel recalled that his grandmother Marie would speak German only when visiting with other "old-timers," some of who never learned English. It was obvious, he said, that she derived much pleasure from these opportunities to use the *Muttersprache*.[168]

In Boise, the German organizations dissolved in 1916. World War I made Germans an object of suspicion all over the country.[169] As historian Merle Wells said, "With a German population larger than any other group's at the time, Boise suffered a substantial cultural loss."[170] The TurnVerein Hall was only 10 years old, but was sold.[171] It first went to Amelia Sonna, and then to the South Idaho Conference of the Seventh Day Adventist Church that owned it until 1951. Overt public displays of Germanic heritage were not found in Idaho from World War I until well after World War II. The German backgrounds of the brewers were no longer of any greater significance than any other heritage would have been. It was not just a coincidence that statewide prohibition engulfed Idaho that year.

German-born Nampa brewer Jacob Lockman lost a son in World War I. Proving one's loyalty to America was suddenly an imperative to the extent of slaying relatives left across the Atlantic or being slain by them.

An article in the *Statesman* in 1988 lamented the demise of Jake's restaurant in the old TurnVerein building.[172] The building's karma had been to house restaurants for Boise.

To compare Idaho with other states, a study of the correlation between the number of breweries in Illinois and the German population (pages 296-299) found "a powerful locational factor in the U.S. brewing industry."[173] This was an attempt to show a quantitative correlation between Germans and breweries rather than a loose discussion of observations. The four factors that have been analyzed as determinates of the number and location of American breweries are cultural factors, such as those that effect consumption; economic factors, such as the raw materials and transportation costs; legal factors, including temperance legislation and taxes; and other factors, including historical inertia. In Idaho, all of these can be seen at work.

CHART I

GERMAN-BORN BREWERS OF IDAHO AND
THEIR GERMANIC AREA OF ORIGIN

If anything, this chart understates the Germanic influence. Only those born in Europe are listed, not those of Germanic parentage and culture born in America.

Brewer	Germanic Area	Places of Settlement
Albiez, Frederich	Baden	Challis
Bakle, George	Baden	Centerville
Becker-Jurgen, Leonard	Germany	Grangeville
Botzett, John	Prussia	Albion
Deesten, J. Henry	Prussia	Juliaetta
Exner, August	Selisia	Hailey
Fuchs, George	?	Challis
Gans, George Bar	?	Buena Vista
Gans, Jacob Bar	?	Buena Vista
Garrecht, Jacob	Bavaria	Idaho City
Geiger, Joseph	Baden	Genesee
Gindorff, Frank	Prussia	Jordan Creek, Custer, Bay Horse
Gooding, George	Bavaria	Granite Creek
Grete, John	Hanover	Silver City
Grete, Fred	Hanover	Silver City
Grunbaum, Leo P.	Austria	Boise
Haubrich, Leonard	Prussia	Pioneer City
Haug, Nicholas	Wartemburg	Idaho City
Hermann, John	Germany	McAuley
Kern, George	Wartemburg	Gibbonsville
Koehler, F.L.	Bavaria	Spokane, WA, Moscow
Koeninger, Robert	Furshanbach	Ketchum
Koeninger, Conrad	Furshanbach	Ketchum
Koeninger, Herman	Furshanbach	Clayton
Kohler, Christian	Baden	Idaho City

Kohny, Charles	Hanover	Placerville
Krall, John	Germany	Placerville,
Rocky Bar, Boise		
Kremer, Julius	Holstein, Kreis Pinnoberg	Idaho Falls
Lautenschlager, Charles	Hesse Darmstadt	Pioneer City,
Eureka, NV		
Lemp, Jacob	Hesse Darmstadt	SouthMountain,
Payette		
Lemp, John	Hesse Darmstadt	Boise, South
Mountain		
Lux, Conrad	Germany	Idaho Falls
Mackert, Charles	Rincheim, Germany	St. Anthony
Meniel, John	Bavaria	Coeur d'Alene
Mosler, John	?	Custer City
Muntzer, Henry	Alsace	Boise, Butte,
MT		
Natter, John B.	Baden	Centerville
Nutz, Xifer	?	Buena Vista
Bar, Leesburg		
Paul, Philip	?	Atlanta, Boise
Pelkes, John	?	Colfax, WA,
Palouse, WA, Wardner		
Reiniger, Henry	Wittenberg	Colville, WA,
Rathdrum		
Rambour, George	Munich area	Silver City,
Schuyler, NB		
Riid, Alois	?	Idaho City
Schleifer, Fritz	?	Silver City,
Fountain Springs, PA		
Sommercamp, W. F.	Hanover	Silver City
Spahn, Michael	Hesse Darmstadt	Idaho City,
Bonanza City,		
Salmon City		
Stadtmiller, Joseph	?	Pioneer City,
Vienna, Hailey,		
Gibbonsville, Salmon		
City, MT		
Utsch, John	Prussia	Hailey
Weisgerber, Christ	Duchy of Hesse	Lewiston
Weisgerber, Ernest	Duchy of Hesse	Lewiston
Weisgerber, John	Duchy of Hesse	Lewiston
Werneth, Sylvester	Baden	Franklin, Weiser
Zapp, Nick	Prussia	Silver City

CHART II

BREWERS OVERTLY ENGAGED IN
GERMAN CULTURAL ACTIVITIES

Only those with a direct reference to German culture are listed here.

Brewer	Germanic Activity
Brodbeck, John	TurnVerein leadership
Keefer, W.W.	German-style beer garden ownership
Kern, George	German band member
Kohlepp, George	Vice president of Sangerbund in Hailey
Lemp, John	TurnVerein leadership
Maxgut, Rupert	Sons of Herman officer
Misseldt, Joseph	Wrote German language letters to the newspaper
Moses Moritz	TurnVerein member and exercise leader
Riid, Alois	Went to join the Prussian army
Sans, Chris	TurnVerein member
Sonnleitner, Charles	German-style beer hall proprietor
Vorberg, Herman	Collected for German orphans while in Eureka, NV, 1871

CHART III

BREWERIES PER CAPITA, AND PERCENT
GERMAN-BORN IN EACH STATE IN 1880

State or Territory	Number of breweres per capita	Percent German-born
Nevada	1/1,886	3.6%
Montana	1/2,061	4.4%
Idaho	1/2,717	2.3%
Wyoming	1/3,464	3.9%
Arizona	1/3,464	3.7%
Washington	1/4,173	3.0%
California	1/4,574	5.0%
Oregon	1/5,461	2.9%
Wisconsin	1/6,4171	4.0%
Colorado	1/7,197	3.6%
Minnesota	1/7,570	8.5%
Utah	1/10,283	0.6%

State or Territory Number of breweries per capita percent German-born

State or Territory	Number of breweries per capita	percent German-born
Dakota	1/13,517	4.4%
Iowa	1/13,767	5.4%
Michigan	1/13,872	5.4%
Pennsylvania	1/14,181	4.0%
New York	1/15,218	7.0%
Maryland	1/16,402	4.9%
Nebraska	1/17,400	6.9%
District of Columbia	1/17,762	2.8%
Ohio	1/19,602	6.0%
New Jersey	1/23,084	5.7%
Illinois	1/27,728	7.7%
Indiana	1/29,526	4.1%
Connecticut	1/32,773	2.5%
Kansas	1/33,203	2.8%
Missouri	1/33,880	5.0%
Delaware	1/36,652	0.8%
New Mexico	1/39,855	0.6%
Kentucky	1/51,521	1.8%
Rhode Island	1/55,306	0.7%
Massachusetts	1/57,519	0.9%
West Virginia	1/68,717	1.1%
New Hampshire	1/69,398	0.2%
Texas	1/75,797	2.2%
Louisiana	1/104,438	1.8%
Vermont	1/332,286	0.1%
South Carolina	1/497,778	0.3%
Tennessee	1/514,119	0.3%
Virginia	1/756,282	0.2%
North Carolina	1/1,399,750	0.1%
Alabama	0	00.3%
Arkansas	0	00.5%
Florida	0	00.4%
Georgia	0	00.2%
Maine	0	00.1%
Mississippi	0	00.2%

Source: *One-Hundred Years of Brewing*, 1903, p. 610.

END NOTES

1 George W. Hilton, review of *The Breweries of Cleveland*, by Carl H. Miller, in *The Breweriana Collector*, vol. 102, summer, 1998, p. 5.

2 Internet:http://cgi.ebay.com/1922-Gottfried-Duden-German-Immigration-to-Missouri_0QQitemZ6587308QQcategoryZ29223QQrdZ1QQemdZviewItem., p. 2-3

3 *Idaho World*, Idaho City, 11 November 1869, p. 2, c. 5.

4 Carole Simon-Smolinski, "Idaho's West European Americans," in *Idaho's Ethnic Heritage*, Boise, Idaho, 1990, p. 45.

5 Other principalities represented were Saxony 14, Wurtemberg, 35, Austria 26, Baden 50, Bavaria 78, Hamburg 14, Hanover 32, Hessen 42, Mecklenburg 1, Nassau 1. See Simon Smolinski, p. 46

6 Hart, *Basin of Gold, Life in the Boise Basin, 1862-1890,* Idaho City, Idaho: Idaho City Historical Foundation, 1986, p. 56.

7 William J. McConnell, *Early History of Idaho*. Caldwell, Idaho: Caxton Printers, 1913. p. 186-7

8 Hart, *Basin of Gold*, p. 57.

9 Hart, *Basin of Gold*, p. 11.

10 Anderson, "Boise's German Heritage," *Idaho Statesman*, Boise, Idaho, 1981, p. 1.

11 *Idaho Tri-Weekly Statesman*, Boise, Idaho, 15 March 1870, p. 2, c. 1. *Idaho Daily Statesman*, 20 March 1910, Section II, p. 5, c. 3. Forty years ago column.

12 *Boise City Weekly News*, Boise, Idaho, 17 September 1870, p. 2, c. 7.

13 *The Boise Weekly News*, Boise, Idaho, 24 September 1870, p. 3, c. 1.

14 *Idaho Tri-Weekly Statesman*, 24 March 1870, p. 3, c. 1.

15 John Felix Vandracek, "The Rise of Fraternal Organizations in the U.S., 1868-1900," *Social Science*, Vol. 47, Winter, 1972, p. 26.

16 Herman Ronnenberg, The Politics of Assimilation, The Effect of Prohibition on the German Americans, New York: Carlton Press, 1973, p. 15.

17 *History of Siskiyou County, California, Illustrated with Views of Residences, Business Buildings and Natural Scenery, and Containing Portraits and Biographies of Its Leading Citizens and Pioneers.* Oakland, CA: D. J. Stewart & Co., 1881. pp. 183-4.

18 *Morning Oregonian*, Portland, Oregon, 4 March 1862, p. 3, c. 1.

19 *The Capital Chronicle*, Boise, Idaho, 26 March 1870, p. 3, c. 1.

20 *Idaho Daily Statesman*, 1 May 1910, Section II, p. 5, c. 3. Forty years ago column.

21 *Idaho Tri-Weekly Statesman*, 2 July 1870, p. 2, c. 3.

22 *Idaho Tri-Weekly Statesman*, 13 August 1870, p. 3, c. 1.

23 *Idaho Daily Statesman*, 14 August 1910, Section II, p. 2, c. 3. Forty Years Ago column.

24 *Idaho Tri-Weekly Statesman*, 15 October 1870, p. 3, c. 1.

25 *The Elko Chronicle*, Elko, Nevada, 9 October 1870, p. 2, c. 5.

26 *Idaho Tri-Weekly Statesman*, 12 January 1871, p. 3, c. 2. *Idaho Democrat*, Boise, 11 January 1871, p. 3, c. 1.

27 *Idaho Tri-Weekly Statesman*, 28 January 1871, p. 3, c. 1.

28 Hart, *Basin of Gold*, p. 56. See Lautenschlager's biography.

29 See Riid's biography for more details.

30 *Idaho Tri-Weekly Statesman*, 26 November 1870, p. 3, c. 2. *Idaho Daily Statesman*, 20 November 1910, Section II, p. 7, c. 3. Forty Years ago column.

31 Hart, *Basin of Gold*, p. 56.

32 *Idaho World*, Idaho City, 9 February 1871, p. 3, c. 1.

33 Hart, "Idaho Yesterdays: Lemp Helped Raise Funds," *The Idaho Statesman*, 8 January 1973, p. 11, c. 1-4. *Idaho Daily Statesman*, 5 February 1911, Section II, p. 8, c. 3. *Forty Years Ago* column.

34 *Idaho Tri-Weekly Statesman*, 24 May 1871, p. 2, c. 3.

35 *Idaho Daily Statesman*, 2 April 1911, Section II, p. 5, c. 1-3. Forty Years Ago column. *Idaho Democrat*, 5 April 1871, p. 2, c. 4.

36 *Idaho Daily Statesman*, 7 May 1911, section II, p. 5, c. 6. Forty Years Ago column. *Idaho Democrat*, 10 May 1871, p. 3, c. 3.

37 *Idaho Daily Statesman*, 14 May 1911, Section II, p. 5, c. 1-3. Forty Years Ago column.

38 *Idaho Daily Statesman*, 7 January 1912, Section II, p. 3, c. 1. This was a historical and biographical sketch of this couple

39 *Idaho Signal*, Lewiston, 24 August 1872, p. 4, c.4.

40 *Idaho Tri-Weekly Statesman*, 27 May 1876, p. 3, c. 2 & 3.

41 *The Semi-Weekly Idahoan*, Boise, 11 May 1877, p. 2, c. 4.

42 *The Semi-Weekly Idahoan*, 25 May 1877, p. 3, c. 1.

43 *Idaho Daily Statesman*, 10 October 1909, Section II, p. 3, c. 3.

44 *Idaho Tri-Weekly Statesman*, 27 September 1881, p. 3, c. 1.

45 *Idaho Daily Statesman*, 4 February 1912, Section II, p. 3, c. 1-3. Thirty Years Ago Column.

46 *Idaho Tri-Weekly Statesman*, 24 February 1883, p. 3 c. 1.

47 *Wood River Times*, (Weekly) Hailey, Idaho, 9 May 1883, p. 2, c. 5.

48 Barbara Exner Cobb, interview with Jean Arkell, 1985, p. 5. Oral history collection.

49 *Idaho Tri-Weekly Statesman*, 27 November 1884, p. 3, c. 1.

50 *Boise City Republican*, Boise, Idaho, 28 November 1885, p. 1, c. 1.

51 *Idaho Daily Statesman*, 18 January 1889, p. 3, c. 1.

52 *Idaho Daily Statesman*, 24 June 1890, p. 3, c. 2.

53 *Idaho Daily Statesman*, 2 September 1891, p. 8, c. 1.

54 *Idaho Daily Statesman*, 19 March 1893, p. 5, c. 1. Much of the 1890 U.S. Census data was destroyed by fire.

55 Ronnenberg, *Beer and Brewing in the Inland Northwest*, Moscow, Idaho, 1993, p. 24.

56 *Idaho Daily Statesman*, 8 October 1895, p. 3, c. 3.

57 *Idaho Daily Statesman*, 2 November 1894, p. 6, c. 4.

58 *Idaho Daily Statesman*, 6 December 1894, p. 6, c. 4. 11 December 1894, p. 3, c. 2.

59 *Idaho Daily Statesman*, 4 December 1894, p. 6, c. 4.

60 *Idaho Daily Statesman*, 18 November 1894, p. 3, c. 1.

61 *Wood River Times*, Hailey, 12 April 1893, p. 1, c. 3.

62 *Idaho Daily Statesman*, 24 April 1900, p. 4, c. 3-4

63 *Idaho Daily Statesman*, 27 January 1901, p. 8, c. 2.

64 *Evening Capital News*, Boise, Idaho, 23 August 1901, p. 4, c. 4.

65 *Idaho Daily Statesman*, 23 August 1901, p. 5, c. 3.

66 *Idaho Daily Statesman*, 10 February 1902, p. 5, c. 4. *Evening Capital News*, 10 February 1902, p. 6, c. 1.

67 *Idaho Daily Statesman*, 12 February 1902, p. 5, c. 2.

68 *Idaho Daily Statesman*, 28 March 1902, p. 6, c. 2. *Evening Capital News*, 27 March 1902, p. 8, c. 1.

69 *Evening Capital News*, 2 April 1902, p. 6, c. 4.

70 *Idaho Daily Statesman*, 18 April 1902, p. 6, c. 3. 19 April 1902, p. 5, c. 1. *Evening Capital News*, 3 April 1902, p. 5, c. 5.

71 Carol MacGregor, *Boise, Idaho, 1882-1910, Prosperity in Isolation,* Missoula: Montana Press Publishing Company, 2006, p. 37.

72 *Idaho Daily Statesman*, 25 April 1902, p. 8, c. 1.

73 *Idaho Daily Statesman*, 27 June 1902, p. 6, c. 2.

74 *Idaho Daily Statesman*, 25 August 1902, p. 3, c. 1.

75 *Idaho Daily Statesman*, 7 September 1902, p. 5, c. 1.

76 *Idaho Daily Statesman*, 26 December 1902, p. 5, c. 4.

77 *Idaho Daily Statesman*, 22 June 1903, p. 5, c. 1.

78 *Idaho Daily Statesman*, 21 December 1903, p. 5, c. 2.

79 Patricia Wright and Lisa B. Reitzes, *Tourtellotte and Hummel of Idaho: The Standard Practice of Architecture.* Logan: Utah State University Press, 1987.1904, p. 71.

80 *Idaho Daily Statesman*, 2 April 1904, p. 3, c. 4.

81 *Evening Capital News*, 21 June 1905, p. 1, c. 6.

82 *Idaho Daily Statesman*, 3 April 1904, p. 7, c. 4. 4 April p. 5, c. 4.

83 *Idaho Daily Statesman*, 7 June 1904, p. 3, c. 1-2.

84 *Evening Capital News,* 27 June 1904, p. 1, c. 4.

85 *Idaho Daily Statesman*, 12 September 1904, p. 4, c. 3.

86 *Idaho Daily Statesman*, 1 January 1905, p. 13, c. 3.

87 Wright and Reitzes, *Tourtellotte and Hummel*, p. 91.

88 *Idaho Daily Statesman*, 16 September 1897, p. 4, c. 4.

89 Simon-Smolinski, p. 71.

90 *Idaho Daily Statesman*, 9 August 1905, p. 5, c. 4. *Evening Capital News*, 8 August 1905, p. 8, c. 3.

91 *Idaho Daily Statesman*, 26 September 1905, p. 4, c. 3.

92 *Idaho Daily Statesman* 5 April 1906, p. 5, c. 1.

93 *Idaho Daily Statesman*, 8 February 1906, p. 3, c. 2.

94 *Idaho Daily Statesman*, 11 February 1904, p. 2, c. 4.

95 *Evening Capital News*, 13 March 1906, p. 3, c. 1-2.

96 *Idaho Daily Statesman*, 1 January 1904, p. 15, c. 6.

97 *Idaho Daily Statesman*, 10 July 1904, p. 7, c. 4.

98 *Evening Capital News*, 11 July 1904, p. 5, c. 4.

99 *Idaho Daily Statesman*, 31 December 1904, p. 8, c. 3.

100 *Evening Capital News*, 27 November 1904, p. 2, c. 2.

101 *Evening Capital News*, 30 December 1904, 30 December 1904, p. 2, c. 3.

102 *Idaho Falls Times*, 21 March 1905, p. 2, c. 4.

103 *Idaho Capital News*, 12 October 1905, p. 5, c. 2.

104 *Idaho Daily Statesman*, 13 April 1905, p. 5, c. 2. The next year was the 35th anniversary, which is a problem to explain.

105 *Idaho Daily Statesman*, 9 January 1906, p. 5, c. 1

106 *Evening Capital News*, 8 February 1906, p. 4, c. 2.

107 *Evening Capital News*, 5 October 1905, p. 1, c. 7.

108 *Idaho Daily Statesman*, 16 June 1906, p. 7, c. 2 & 3.

109 *Idaho Daily Statesman*, 4 July 1906, p. 5, c. 4. *Evening Capital News*, 4 July 1906, p. 1, c. 4.

110 Steve Anderson, "Boise's German Heritage: A Casualty of War," *Idaho Statesman*, 19 July 1981. *Idaho Daily Statesman*, 29 July 1906, p. 6, c. 4. 1 August 1906, p. 5, c. 3. Announcements were published that all members of the TurnVerein and the Sons of Hermann were expected to be present. *Evening Capital News*, 31 July 1906, p. 4, c. 5 & 6.

111 *Idaho Statesman*, 16 July 1993, p. C1, c. 1-7.

112 "Public Sentiment and Defense Measures," *Current History* VI (March, 1917), p. 980.

113 *Idaho Daily Statesman*, 7 April 1906, p. 5, c. 4.

114 *Idaho Daily Statesman*, 14 November 1906, p. 5, c. 1 & 2.

115 *Evening Capital News*, 8 December 1906, p. 3, c. 4.

116 *Idaho Daily Statesman*, 19 December 1906, p. 8, c. 2 & 3.

117 *Idaho Daily Statesman*, 21 December 1906, p. 5, c. 1-2.

118 *Evening Capital News*, 21 December 1906, p. 3, c. 3-4.

119 *Evening Capital News*, 24 December 1906, p. 5, c. 4.

120 *Idaho Daily Statesman*, 30 December 1906, Section IV, p. 4, c. 1-2.

121 *Idaho Daily Statesman*, 3 January 1907, p. 6, c. 3. *Evening Capital News*, 2 January 1907, p. 3, c. 3.

122 *Evening Capital News*, 8 January 1907, p. 3, c. 3.

123 *Idaho Daily Statesman*, 6 February 1907, p. 5, c. 2.

124 *Evening Capital News*, 6 February 1907, p. 5, c. 4.

125 *Idaho Daily Statesman*, 13 February 1907, p. 5, c. 4. 17 March 1907, p. 13, c. 3.

126 *Evening Capital News*, 13 February 1907, p. 8, c. 3.

127 *Evening Capital News*, 18 February 1907, p. 5, c. 6.

128 *Idaho Daily Statesman*, 22 March 1907, p. 5, c. 2.

129 *Evening Capital News*, 22 March 1907, p. 5, c. 4.

130 *Evening Capital News*, 26 March 1907, p. 2, c. 3.

131 *Evening Capital News*, 22 April 1907, p. 5, c. 3.

132 *Evening Capital News*, 20 May 1907, p. 6, c. 2.

133 *Idaho Daily Statesman*, 4 April 1907, p. 2, c. 4.

134 *Idaho Daily Statesman*, 7 April 1907, p. 10, c. 2 & 3.

135 *Idaho Daily Statesman*, 14 April 1907, p. 10, c. 4. 19 May 1907, p. 15, c. 1.

136 *Evening Capital News*, 31 May 1907, p. 2, c. 3.

137 *Idaho Daily Statesman*, 6 July 1907, p. 3, c. 1. *Evening Capital News*, 6 July 1907, p. 3, c. 3.

138 *Idaho Daily Statesman*, 22 July 1907, p. 4, c. 3. *Evening Capital News*, 14 June 1907, p. 3, c. 4.

139 *Idaho Daily Statesman*, 18 August 1907, p. 5, c. 2. 16 December 1907, p. 4, c. 2. Hubert Pitz and Fred Schimpf were the deceased in these two examples

140 *Idaho Daily Statesman*, 13 October 1907, p. 15, c. 2.

141 *Idaho Daily Statesman*, 26 December 1907, p. 4, c. 4.

142 *Idaho Daily Statesman*, 5 January 1908, p. 13, c. 3.

143 *Idaho Daily Statesman*, 3 January 1909, p. 6, c. 5.

144 *Evening Capital News*, 22 February 1908, p. 7, c. 4.

145 *Evening Capital News*, 3 April 1908, p. 5,c. 1.

146 *Evening Capital News*, 4 April 1908, p. 6, c. 3.

147 *Evening Capital News*, 18 July 1908, p. 5, c. 2

148 *Evening Capital News*, 28 December 1908, p. 2, c. 4.

149 *Evening Capital News*, 11 February 1909, p. 5, c. 5.

150 *Evening Capital News*, 15 April 1909, p. 6, c. 2. 16 April 1909, p. 3, c. 1-2.

151 *Idaho Daily Statesman*, 26 July 1909, p. 1, c. 6.

152 *Evening Capital News*, 26 August 1909, p. 1, c. 3.

153 *Evening Capital News*, 2 October 1909, p. 1, c. 2.

154 *Idaho Daily Statesman*, 10 January 1910, p. 5, c. 2.

155 *Idaho Daily Statesman*, 15 April 1910, p. 3, c. 1-2.

156 *Idaho Daily Statesman*, 27 November 1910, Section II, p. 6, c. 3.

157 *Idaho Daily Statesman*, 1 March 1911, p. 5, c. 2.

158 *Idaho Daily Statesman*, 25 August 1911, p. 5, c. 2

159 *Idaho Daily Statesman*, 3 November 1911, p. 4, c. 1.

160 *Idaho Daily Statesman*, 3 November 1911, p. 5, c. 1.

161 *Idaho Daily Statesman*, 17 February 1912, p. 7, c. 4.

162 *Idaho Daily Statesman*, 9 February 1912, p. 2, c. 3.

163 *Idaho Daily Statesman*, 3 March 1912, p. 5, c. 2.

164 *Idaho Daily Statesman*, 5 May 1912, p. 5, c. 3.

165 *Idaho Daily Statesman*, 15 May 1912, p. 4, c. 4.

166 *Idaho Daily Statesman*, 3 August 1912, p. 2, c. 3.

167 Barbara Exner Cobb, interview with Jean Arkell, 1985, tape side one, minute 26.

168 *Idaho Statesman*, 16 July 1993, p. C1, c. 1-7.

169 This is the reason for the sale of the Turn Verein H'all according to the essays on Idaho ethnicity in http://imnh.isu.edu/digitalatlas/geog/imem/text/main. htm.

170 Merle Wells, *Boise, An Illustrated History*, Woodland Hills, California, p. 86.

171 Simon-Smolinski, p. 76.

172 Tim Woodward, "Ghost of the TurnVerein," *Idaho Statesman*, 16 June 1988, Sec. C, p. 7, c. 2.

173 Mark L. Healy, "The Importance of German Immigration as a Locational Factor in the Illinois Brewing Industry: 1870-1920." Non-Thesis research paper, Northern Illinois University, May 2000. http://www.harpercollege.edu/ mhealy/geg108i/chapters/ch06/breweries/beerfinal.htm.

GAMBRINUS SERIES BIBLIOGRAPHY

1. Books, Periodicals, Interviews, Letters to the Author, Bylined newspaper articles, CD-ROMS, and historical files

"Ada County Death and Cemetery Records," Idaho State Historical Society, Boise, Idaho.

Ada County Judicial Records, Idaho State Historical Society, microfilm.

Adams, F. *Idaho Queen of the Gold Camps*. Idaho City: Idaho World Publishing, 1958.

Adams, Mildretta. *Historic Silver City, The Story of the Owyhees*. Homedale, Idaho: Owyhee Printing Co., 1981.

Adams, Mildretta. *Sagebrush Post Offices, A History of the Owyhee Country*. Pocatello: Idaho State University, 1986.

Alturas County Records, ISHS

Ambrose, Elaine. "Brewing Beer in Boise," *Boise Magazine*, Winter, 1999, pp. 58-111.

American Breweriana Journal. 1984.

American Brewers Review, 1909-1912.

Anderson, Eloise H. *Frontier Bankers: A History of Idaho First National Bank*. Boise: Idaho First National Bank, 1981.

Anderson, Steve. "Boise's German Heritage: A Casualty of War," *Idaho Statesman*, 19 July 1981.

Anthamatten, Brad. "Ranger Beer: Tulsa's 'Zest of the West'," *American Breweriana Journal*, March-April 1996, p. 29-32.

Anthony, Mildred F. Letter to author 27 December 1982. Letter to author, 13 October 1982. Letter to author 9 March 1983.

Armstrong, Steve. "Wallace Idaho's Sunset Brewing Company," *Foam on the Range*, May, 1998, pp. 6-11.

Arrington, Leonard J. *History of Idaho*. Moscow: University of Idaho Press, 1994.

Badsteiber, Erna Rambour. Two transcriptions of oral history tapes on Rambour family.

Bailey, Robert G. *River of No Return*. Lewiston, Idaho: R.G. Bailey Printing Comp., 1983. Baltimore Passenger and Immigration Lists, 1820-1872 Record.

Baird, Mallickan and Swagerty, *Nez Perce Nation Divided*. Moscow: University of Idaho Press, 2002.

Ballard, Kendall Lee. Letters to Author. 3 January 1996. 17 January 1996.

Bancroft, Hubert Howe. *The Works of Hubert Howe Bancroft, History of Washington, Idaho, Montana, 1845-1899, vol. 31*. San Francisco: The History Company, 1890.

Baron, Stanley Wade. *Brewed in America: A History of Beer and Ale in the United States*New York: Arno Press, 1972. C. 1962.

Battien, Pauline. *The Gold Seekers: A 200 Year History of Mining in Washington, Idaho, Montana & Lower British Columbia*. Colville, WA.: Eastern Washington University Libraries, 1989.

Beal, Merrill D., and Merle W. Wells. *History of Idaho*, 3 vols. New York: Lewis Historical Publishing Company, 1959.

Bear Facts, Pacific Coast Breweriana Association, 1982, 1983.

Belyk, Robert C. *Great Shipwrecks of the Pacific Coast*. New York: John Wiley & Sons, 2001.

Bennett, Robert A. *Walla Walla: A Nice Place to Raise a Family, 1920-1949*. Walla Walla, Washington: Pioneer Press Books, 1988.

Bennett, Robert A. *Walla Walla: Portrait of a Western Town, 1804-1899*. Walla Walla, Washington Pioneer Press Books, 1980.

Betts, William E. "Prohibition in Moscow, Idaho—1908," term paper, University of Idaho, 1968.

"Bills of Sale, v. 1, Idaho County," Idaho County Recorder's Office, Grangeville, Idaho.

Bird, Annie Laurie. *Boise, the Peace Valley*. Caldwell, Idaho: The Caxton Printers, 1934.

Bird, Annie Laurie. *My Home Town*. Caldwell, Idaho: Caxton Printers, 1968.

Boessenecker, John. *Gold Dust and Gunsmoke: Tales of Gold Rush Outlaws, Gunfighters, Lawman, and Vigilantes*. New York: John Wiley & Sons, 1999.

Boise County Deeds, 1871-1875, vol. 13.

Boise County Judicial Records, Idaho State Historical Society.

Boise Idaho, Forty-Five Years of Progress. Boise: The Illustrated Idaho Company, 1911.

"Bonanza! Ghost Towns And Other Sights to See Along the Yankee Fork," *Living Idaho*, July 1981, p. 11-12.

Boone, Lalia P., "Post Offices of Latah County," *Quarterly Bulletin*, Latah County Historical Society, Moscow, Idaho, vol. 7, no. 4, October, 1978, p. 3.

"Bradstreet's Commercial Reports," vol. 87, September 1889.

Brandenburg, Dick. "Dubuque Star Brewing Company," *American Breweriana*, number 69, July-August, 1994, p. 4-9.

Brewery Age, 1939.

Brown, Mark H. *The Flight of the Nez Perce*. New York: G.P. Putnam's Sons, 1967.

"Building Operations and Improvements, " *American Brewers Review*, 1907, p. 270. *Butte Commemorative*. ?1974

Butte-Silver Bow Public Archives, *The Montana Standard, World Museum of Mining.*

Remembering Butte, Montana's Richest City. n.p.: n.p., n.d.

Byhe, Farnda R. *Then and Now: A Picture Book of Caribou County Idaho.* Published by author, 1977.

Byrd, Joann Green. *Calamity: The Heppner Flood of 1903.* Seattle: University of Washington Press, 2009.

Cain, Larry, "Jacob Lockman Story, A Man and His Beer," *Rivers, Trails and Rails*, Canyon County [Idaho] Historical Society, Fall-Winter 2009, pp. 8-10.

Capitols' Who's Who for Idaho, 1950-51, Boise: Capitol Publishing Company, 1951.

Carlson, Randy. *The Breweries of Iowa.* Bemidji, Minnesota: Arrow Printing, 1985.

Carlson, Randy. "From the Archives," *American Breweriana Journal*, November December 1984, p. 13.

Carrey, Johnny. and Conley, Cort. *River of No Return*. Cambridge, Idaho: Backeddy Books, 1977.

Carrey, Johnny. and Conley, Cort. *Snake River in Hells Canyon,* Cambridge, Idaho: Backeddy Books, 2003.

Cascade Breweriana Association, "Brew News," March, 2005, vol. 6, issue 1. p. 8.

Cassia County, State of Idaho License Record Book. 1890s.

Cecil, Molly O'Leary, "City Works to Restore Old Brewery," *The Post-Register,* Idaho Falls, 30 July 1987. The Associated Press sent this story to area newspapers and it was reprinted under various headlines.

Cemetery Records, Ada County, Idaho. Idaho State Historical Society.

Chedsey, Zona and Frei, Carolyn, eds. *Idaho County Voices: A People's History from the Pioneers to the Present.* Grangeville: Idaho County Centennial Committee, 1990.

"Christ Weisgerber, Early Contributor to Lewiston," *Nez Perce County Historical Society Journal,* Fall/Winter, 1985, p. 3.

Clark, Linda Campbell. *Nampa Idaho, 1885-1985: A Journey of Discovery.* Nampa, Idaho:Nampa Centennial Committee, 1985.

Clough, J.P. "Michael Spahn: A Pioneer of Lemhi," *Idaho Recorder*, Salmon, Idaho, 15 April 1927, p. 1, c. 3.

Cobb, Barbara Exner. Interviewed by Jean Arkell, Hailey Idaho, January 1985. Part of the oral histories conducted by the library in Ketchum.

Conley, Cort. *Snake River in Hells Canyon.*

Converse, George L. *A Military History of the Columbia Valley, 1848-1865.* Walla Walla, WA: Pioneer Press Books, 1988.

"Copperkingmansion." http://www.copperkingmansion.com/History.html. Web site for the William Andrew Clark Mansion in Butte, Montana.

Cornett, Chris. Letter with photos, clippings, and genealogy charts on William von Berge. 19 July 1999.

Crawford, Mary M. *Nez Perce Since Spalding*. Berkeley: Professional Press, 1936.

Crutchfield, James A. *It Happened in Montana*. Nashville, TN: Falcon Press, 1992.d'Easum, Dick. *Fragments of Villainy*. Boise, Idaho: Statesman Printing Company, 1959.

David, Homer. *Moscow at the Turn of the Century*. Moscow, Idaho: Latah CountyHistorical Society, Paper no. 6, 1979.

"Deaths: Joseph Pickett, Sr.," *Brewers Digest*, February, 1991, p. 38.

DeBellis, Steve. "The Beer That Became a Movie," *BCCA News Report*, July/August 1981, p. 4+.

Defenbach, Byron. *Idaho the Place and its people, A History of the Gem State from Prehistoric to Present Days*. 3 vols. Chicago: American Historical Society,1933.

Denny, Jennie. Interview With Author. 7 May 1998. Pomeroy, WA.

Derig, Betty B. *Weiser: The Way It Was*. Weiser, Idaho: Rambler Press, 1987.

Deesten, Betty Ruth. "John Henry (von) Deesten," Typescript, undated, August, 1998.

Dickens, Charles. *Great Expectations*. London: Chapman and Hall, 1861.

Diffendaffer, Marguerite Moore. *Council Valley: Here They Labored*. Boise, Idaho: Worthwhile Club of Council, Idaho, 1977.

Dolph, Jerry and Randall, Arthur. *Wyatt Earp and Coeur d'Alene Gold!: Stampede to Idaho Territory*. Post Falls, Idaho: Eagle City Publications, 1999.

Doolittle, Lucinda. "'For Sale' Sign Goes up at Historic Home," *The Idaho Statesman*. 29 December 1999, p. 2B, C. 2-5.

Dun, R. G. List of Idaho Businesses, 1904.

Edwards, Jonathan. *An Illustrated History of Spokane County, State of Washington*. N. P.: W. H. Lever, Publisher, 1900.

1850-1951 Marriage Index, ID, CA, Ariz, NV. Family Tree Maker. CD-ROM. *1867 Pacific Coast Directory*.

El Hult, Ruby. *Northwest disasters, Avalanche and Fire*. Portland: Binford and Mort, 1960.

El Hult, Ruby. *Steamboats in the Timber*. Caldwell, Idaho, Caxton Printers, 1952.

Elliot, Wallace W. *History of Idaho, The Territory: Showing Its Resources and Advantages*. San Francisco: Wallace W. Elliot, 1884.

Elsensohn, Sister M. Alfreda. *Idaho County's Most Romantic Character: Polly Bemis*. Cottonwood, Idaho: Idaho Corporation of Benedictine Sisters, 1979, 1987.

Elsensohn, Sister M. Alfreda. *Idaho Chinese Lore*. Cottonwood, Idaho: Idaho Corporation of Benedictine Sisters, 1993. C. 1970.

Elsensohn, Sister M. Alfreda. *Pioneer Days in Idaho County*. 2 Vols. Caldwell, Idaho: Caxton Printers, 1947, 1951.

Emery, W. G., "History of Moscow, Idaho With Sketches of Some of Its Prominent Citizens, Firms and Corporations," Supplement to the *Moscow Mirror*, Moscow, Idaho, 1897.

Emmons, David E. *The Butte Irish: Class and Ethnicity*. Urbana, Illinois: University of Illinois, 1989.

Encyclopedia of Northwest Biography, American Historical Co., 1943.

Everett, George. *Champagne in a Tin Cup" Uptown Butte and the Stories Behind the Facades*. Butte, Montana: Outback Ventures, 1995.

Fastabend, Faith. *William Dewey's Darkest Days: The Murder Trials in Silver City*. Nampa, Idaho: n.p., Third Printing, 2006.

Fisher, Don C. "The Nez Perce War," M.A. Thesis, History Department, University of Idaho, Moscow, Idaho, 1925.

Fisher, Vardis. *Idaho Lore* (Prepared by the Federal Writer's Project of the Work Projects Administration). Caldwell, Idaho: Caxton Printers, 1939.

Fisk, Dale. *Landmarks: A General History of the Council, Idaho Area*. Littleton, Colorado: Profitable Publishing, n.d. (2002)

Flenner, J. D. *Syringa Blossoms*. 2 vols. Caldwell: Caxton, 1912.

Flynn, Gary. "Salem Brewery Assn.," *American Breweriana Journal*, No. 149, September-October, 2007, pp. 13-16.

"Fort Walla Walla Cemetery," Typescript, recorded by Violet Ries Wells, Fort Walla Walla Museum, Washington state. n.d.

Francl, Antonio. Letters to *Vojta Napreska*, 1852-1855. Naprstkovo Muzeum, Prague.

Francl, F. letter to *Pokrok Zapadu* (Progress of the West) 2 March 1900 from Spokane, WA. From archives of the Naprstkovo Muzeum, Prague.

Francl, Joseph. *The Overland Journey of Joseph Francl*. Intro by Richard Brautigan. San Francisco: William P. Wreden, 1968.

Frazier, Neta L. "Early Idahoan," *Spokesman-Review Magazine*, Spokane, Washington August 4, 1957, pp. 3-4.

Frederick, Manfred, and Bull, Donald. *Register of United States Breweries, 1876-1976*.

Trumbull, Conn.: Donald Bull, 1976.

Freeman, Harry C. *A Brief History of Butte, Montana: The World's Greatest Mining Camp*. Chicago: The Henry O. Shepard Company, 1900.

Freidrich, Manfred, Bull, Donald, and Gottschalk, Robert. *American Breweries*. Trumbull, Conn.: Bullworks, 1984.

French, Hiram T. *History of Idaho, A Narrative Account of Its Historical Progress, Its People and Its Principal Interests*. Chicago: The Lewis Publishing Company, 1914.

Fuller, George W. *The Inland Empire Who's Who*. Vol. IV, Spokane: H. G. Linderman, 1928.

Galey, Romaine, editor. *Headlines Idaho Remembers (And Some Idaho Might Like To Forget:): Local, State, National and International Events As We Read About Them inIdaho Newspapers of the Day*. N.P.: The Friends of the Bishop's House, Inc., 1977.

A General Directory And Business Guide of the Principal Towns East of the Cascade Mountains, for the Year 1865. San Francisco: A. Roman & Co., [1865?]

Gibbs, Rafe. *Beckoning the Bold, Story of the Dawning of Idaho.* Moscow: University of Idaho Press, 1976.

Gilbert, Frank T. *Historical Sketches of Walla Walla, Whitman, Columbia and Garfield Counties, Washington Territory.* Portland: A.G. Waling, 1882.

Gittins, H. Leigh. Letter to author, 27 June 1983. (Pocatello Historian)

Gordon, Elizabeth Putnam. *Women Torch Bearers: The Story of the Women's Christian Temperance Union.* Evanston, Ill.: National Women's Christian Temperance Union, 1924.

Green, Roberta, *They Followed the Glory Trail.* n.p.: n.p. 1987

Gulick, Bill. *Outlaws of the Pacific Northwest.* Caldwell, Idaho: Caxton Press, 2000.

Gurcke, Karl. *Brick and Brickmaking: A Handbook for Historical Archaeology.* Moscow,Idaho: University of Idaho Press, 1987.

Hailey, John. *The History of Idaho.* Boise: Syms-York Company, 1910.

Hale, Betty, ed. *History of Bannock County, 1893-1993*, Logan, Utah: Herff Jones, Inc., 1993.

Hampton, Bruce. *Children of Grace: The Nez Perce War of 1877.* New York: Avon Books, 1994.

Hankel, Evelyn G. "Early Astoria Breweries," *Clatsop County Historical Society Quarterly.* vol.. 9, no. 4, Fall 1989, pp. 17-24.

Hart, Arthur A. *Basin of Gold: Life in Boise Basin, 1862-1890.* Idaho City: Idaho City Historical Foundation, 1986

Hart, Arthur A. *Boiseans at Home.* Boise: Historic Boise, Inc., 1984.

Hart, Arthur A. "Germans Cornered Market on Brewery Trade in Idaho," *Idaho Statesman*, 9 July 1979, 10A, c. 1-3.

Hart, Arthur A. "Idaho Yesterdays: Lemp Helps Raise Funds," *Idaho Statesman*, 8 January 1973, p. 11, c. 1-4.

Hart, Arthur A. "Joe Misseld, German Brewer Knew How to Make the Papers," *Idaho Statesman*, 26 December 2006.

Hart, Patricia and Nelson, Ivar. *Mining Town: The Photographic Record of T.N. Bernard and Nellie Stockbridge From the Coeur d'Alenes.* Seattle: University of Washington Press, and the Idaho Historical Society, 1984.

Hawley, James H. *History of Idaho, The Gem of the Mountains.* 3 vols. Chicago: S.J. Clarke Publishing Co., 1920.

Hawley, James H. "Hawley Manuscript, M52 H31," Idaho State Historical Society manuscript collection.

Hayes, Anna Hansen. "Rock Creek Station," *Eighteenth Biennial Report of the Idaho State Historical Society, 1941-1942.* p. 68.

Healy, Mark L. "The Importance of German Immigration as a Locational Factor in the Illinois Brewing Industry: 1870-1920." Non-thesis research paper, Northern Illinois University, May 2000.

Helmers, Cheryl. *Warren Times, A Collection of News About Warren, Idaho.* Wolfe City, Texas: Henington Publishing Co., 1988.

Herbst, Henry. "The Brewers Journal," *BCCA News Report*, March/April, 1991, p. 7.

Hilton, George W. "Review of *Breweries of Cleveland* by Carl H. Miller," in *The Breweriana Collector*. Summer, 1998, p. 5.

"Historic Buildings of Soda Springs," brochure. original author Page Rich, revisions by Anna Beauregard. n.d. (2004)

A Historical, Descriptive and Commercial Directory of Owyhee County, Silver City, Idaho:Press of the Owyhee Avalanche, 1898.

History of Siskiyou County, California, Illustrated with Views of Residences, Business Buildings and Natural Scenery, and Containing Portraits and Biographies of Its Leading Citizens and Pioneers. Oakland, CA: D. J. Stewart & Co., 1881.

History of the City of Spokane and Spokane Country Washington From Its Earliest Settlement to the Present Time. Spokane: S. J. Clarke Publishing Company, 1912.

History of the Pacific Northwest: Oregon and Washington. 2 vols. Portland: North Pacific. Publishing Co., 1889.

"Hit The Trail!" Pamphlet for the Rock Creek Station and Stricker Homesite near Twin Falls, Idaho. Idaho State Historical Society.

Hobson, G.C. editor, *The Idaho Digest and Blue Book*. Caldwell, ID.: Caxton Printers, 1935.

Hobson, George C. *Gems of Thought and History of Shoshone County*. Kellogg, ID: Kellogg Evening Press, 1940.

Hogseth, Venetta Murichison. *The Golden Years: A History of the Idaho Federation of Women's Clubs, 1905-1955*. Caldwell: Caxton, 1955.

Holbrook, Stewart H. *The Rocky Mountain Revolution*. New York: Henry Holt and Company, 1956.

Holm, Debra Nelson. *Nampa's People: 1886-1986, Discovering Our Heritage*. Nampa, Idaho: Nampa Centennial Committee, 1986.

House, Janet G. "Snake River Anthology," *Idaho Heritage Magazine*, vol. vi, no. 3, Winter 1976, p. 33.

Howard, Helen Addison. "Did Chief Joseph Slay Mrs. Manuel?" *Frontier Times*, January 1972, p. 22-48.

Howard, O. O. *Nez Perce Joseph: An Account of his Ancestors, His Lands, His Confederates, His Enemies, His Murders, His War, His Pursuit and Capture*. Boston: Lee and Shepard Publishers, 1881.

Hussey, Larry. *Fort Walla Walla, Then and Now*. Walla Walla, WA: Privately published, 1994.

Hyslop, Julie. *Foundations of Silver City*, vol. I, *Transient Accommodations*. Nampa, Idaho: Julie J. Hyslop, n.d.

"The Idaho Brewing Company," *Western Progress*, no. 17, April 1902, p. 62. Idaho County Commissioners Minutes, vol. 7, 1904.

Idaho County Deed Book

Idaho Digest and Blue Book. 1935.

Idaho Magazine, March, 1904, p. 30.

Idaho Marriage Index, 1850-1951. C-D ROM

Idaho Reports, vol. 2, 1881-1890, "People v. Dewey," p. 83-90.

Idaho Reports, vol. 4, 1894-1896, "State v. Hendel," p. 88-98.

Idaho Reports, 1912.

Idaho State Gazetteer and Business Directory, 1903-04, 1906, 1908, 1910-11, 1912-13, 1914, 1916. Place Varies: R. L. Polk.

Idaho State Historical Society, *Sixteenth Biennial Report of the Board of Trustees of the Idaho Historical Society for the Years 1937-1938*. Boise, 1938.

Idaho State Historical Society Reference Series, number 197.

Idaho State Historical Society Biography file: John Manuel. John Lemp, Michael Spahn, Nelson Davis, John Henry Casey, Mrs. John Henry Casey.

Idaho State Historical Society Photo file. Jacob Lemp. John Lemp.

"Idaho Yesterday and Today, Souvenir Handbook, Fort Hall Centennial, 1834-1934." Pocatello: Graves and Patter, 1934.

Illustrated History of Idaho. Chicago: Lewis Publishing, 1899.

An Illustrated History of North Idaho. Chicago: Western Historical Publishing Company, 1903.

"Immigration and Emigration,"http://imnh.isu.edu/digitalatlas/geog/imem/text/main.htm.

Jagels, Ed. Letter to the author, 11 June 1991.

James, Don. *Butte's Memory Book*. Caldwell: Caxton Printers, 1975.

Jamison, Don. *By My Own Hand I Perish: Suicide in the Owyhee Mining* Camps. Melba: War Eagle Enterprises, 1986.

Jamison, Don. *Cemeteries of Idaho Ghost Towns of Fairview, Ruby City, Silver City*. Homedale: Owyhee Publishing Co., Inc., 1984.

"Joe Pickett's Last Brew," *Newsweek*, 6 June 1983, p. 80.

"John Lemp: Foundation Builder of Boise," *The Idaho Magazine*, March 1904.

"Joseph Pickett, Sr.," *Brewers Digest* , February 1991, p. 38.

"Joseph S. Pickett," *Modern Brewery Age*, April 1940.

Kearney, Pat. *Butte Voices. Mining, Neighborhoods, People*. Butte: Skyhigh Communications, 1998

Kendrick-Juliaetta Centennial Committee. *A Centennial History of the Kendrick-Juliaetta Area*. Kendrick, Idaho: Kendrick-Juliaetta Centennial Committee, 1990

Kincaid, Garret D. and Harris, A. H. *Palouse in the Making: Being a Series of Articles About the Early History of Palouse, Written by Judge Kincaid and Published in the Palouse Republic in 1934*. n. p: n.p., n.d.

Klockmann, Albert, "A. K." *The Klockmann Diary: The Quest for North Idaho's Legendary Continental Mine*. Sandpoint, Idaho: Keokee Co. Publishing, 1990.

Kootenai County Records, ISHS.

Langely, Henry G. *Idaho Territory Business Directory*. San Francisco: Langely Publisher, 1866.

Langford, Nathaniel Pitt. *Vigilante Days and Ways: The Pioneers of the Rockies; The Makers and Making of Montana, Idaho, Oregon, Washington and Wyoming.* Missoula, Montana: University Press, 1957. (reprint of 1890 book.)

Larrison, Earl J. *Owyhee: The Life of a Northern Desert.* Homedale: Owyhee Publishing Co., Inc. 1984.

Lockman, Adah. and Lockman, Winette. Interview with author, Nampa, Idaho, May, 1983.

Lozar, Steve. "1,000,000 glasses a Day," *Montana, The Magazine of Western History,* Vol. 56, no. 4, Winter 2006, pp. 46-55.

Lukas, J. Anthony. *Big Trouble.* New York: Simon and Schuster, 1997.

Lyman, W.D. *Lyman's History of Old Walla Walla County Embracing Walla Walla, Columbia, Garfield and Asotin Counties.* 2 vols. Chicago: S.J. Clarke Publishing Co., 1918.

Macgregor, Carol. *Boise 1882-1910: Prosperity in Isolation.* Missoula: Montana Press Publishing Company, 2006.

McConnell, Verna Priest. "History" (typescript life of Robert Koeninger), 7 April 1981.

McConnell, Verna Priest. Interview with Author, 30 April 1983.

McConnell, Verna Priest. "Robert and Elsie Koeninger Home in Ketchum, typescript, 3 January 1982.

McConnell, William J. *Early History of Idaho.* Caldwell: Caxton Printers, 1913.

McCunn, *Thousand Pieces of Gold.* (Novel) New York: Dell Publishing, 1981.

McDermott, John. *Forlorn Hope: The Battle of White Bird Canyon and the Beginning Of the Nez Perce War.* Boise: Idaho Historical Society, 1978.

McDonald, Duncan, "Goaded to the War-Path," *The New Northwest.* Deer Lodge, Montana, 21 June 1878, p. 2.

McLeod, George A. *History of Alturas and Blaine Counties, Idaho.* Hailey, Idaho: Hailey Times, 1938.

McTraland, John A. Museum of North Idaho, Letter to the author, 2 August 1982.

McWhorter, L.V. *Hear Me My Chiefs: Nez Perce History and Legend.* Caldwell, Idaho: Caxton Printers, 1986.

McWhorter, Lucullus Virgil. *Yellow Wolf: His Own Story.* Caldwell: Caxton Press, 2000.

Magnuson, Richard G. *Coeur D'Alene Diary: The First Ten Years of Hardrock Mining in North Idaho.* Portland: Metropolitan Press, 1968, p. 70.

Manderfeld, Sister M. Catherine. Letter to author, 25 September 1998.

Mangam, Wiliam D. *The Clarks: An American Phenomenon.* New York: Silver Bow Press, 1941.

May, Keith F., and May, Christina Rae. *A Field Guide to Historic Pendleton.* Pendleton: Drigh Sighed Publications, 1997.

"Mayor Weisgerbers Address," *Nez Perce County Historical Society Journal.* Fall/Winter, 1985, p. 6.

Meier, Gary and Meier, Gloria. *Brewed in the Pacific Northwest: A History of Beer Making in Oregon and Washington*. Western Writers Series no. 3. Seattle: Fjord Press, 1991.

Mercer, Lourie. Simon-Smoliski, Carol. Editors, *Idaho's Ethnic Heritage, Historical Overviews,* Vol I, Boise: Idaho Centennial Commission, Idaho State Historical Society, 1990.

Metcalf, Jerry. Letter to the author, June 1982.

Milbert, Frank M. *Mining and Treasure on Gold Creek, 1861-1973*. Pullman: University Printing, 1987.

Miller, Cathleen. *Gibbonsville, Idaho: The Lean Years*. Bend: Maverick Publications, 1985.

Miller, Donald C. *Ghost Towns of Idaho*. Boulder: Pruett Publishing, 1976.

Miller, Joaquin. *Illustrated History of the State of Montana*. Vol. I. Chicago: Lewis Publishing, 1894.

Minutes of the State Supreme Court, Microfilm # 128. University of Idaho Library.

Misseldt, Joe. Will and probate records. Probate court. Ada County, Idaho. *Modern Brewery*. 1935.

Moody, Charles S. "The Bravest Deed I Ever Knew," *Century Magazine*, March, 1911, p. 783.

Moody, Eric N. and Nylen, Robert A. *Brewed in Nevada: A History of the Silver State's Beers and Breweries*. Carson City: Nevada State Museum, 1986.

Morgan, Andrew. *The Scribbler: Adams County Pioneer Memoirs*. Fairfield, WA.: Ye Galleon Press, 1983.

Morris, Stephen. *The Great Beer Trek*, 2nd edition, New York: Stephen Greene Press/Pelham Books, 1990.

Murphy, Regina (Mrs. Edward), Letter to author, 28 January 1985.

Mutch, John D. "Trade Tokens of the Past: High Country Money," *High Country*, December 1979.

Neil, J.M. "The Impossible Dream," *Idaho Yesterdays*, 42: 4, Winter 1999, pp. 12-18.

Nettleton, Helen. *Interesting Buildings in Silver City Idaho*. n.p.: n.p. 1971. edition 2006.

"New Plants and Improvements," *The Western Brewer: and Journal of the Barley, Malt and Hop Trades*. June 1906, pp. 320-321.

Newspaper Editors of Montana. *A Newspaper Reference Work: Men of Affairs and Representative Institutions of the State of Montana, 1914*. Butte: Butte News Writers Association, 1914.

Nez Perce County Deed Record Book

"Nez Perce War Letters," Orlando Robbins to M. Brayman, July 7, 1877. Fifteenth Biennial Report of the Board of Trustees of the State Historical Society of Idaho, 1935-36, p.p. 109-111.

1910 Idaho Census Index. CD-ROM, Family Tree Maker.

"North Custer Historical Museum," *Souvenir Guide to the Salmon River High Country*, Summer, 1980, p. 5.

100 Years of Brewing, Supplement to the Western Brewer. Chicago: H.S. Rich, 1903. Reprint Arno Press, 1974.

Ostberg, Jacob. *Sketches of Old Butte:* Printed by author, 1972.

Owyhee County Judicial Records, Idaho State Historical Society

"Owyhee History, Historic Silver City," Owyhee County Historical Society fact sheet, no. 31, June 1983.

Pace, Zatelle. Curator Cassia County Historical Society, Letter to Author, 6 April 1982.

Painter, Bob. *White Bird: The Last Great Warrior Chief of the Nez Perces.* Farfield: Ye Galleon Press, 2002.

Peltier, Jerome. "The Brief Inglorious Life of Cherokee Bob," *The Spokesman Review,* 10 February 1957.

Peterson, Keith. Letter to author, 31 January 1983.

"Pickett's Charge," *Newsweek,* 4 September 1978, p. 63.

"Pioneer Cemetery: A Self-Guided Tour," Pamphlet. Boise, Idaho: Idaho State Historical Society, n.d.

Polk City Directories, Pocatello, Idaho, 1902, 1907, 1918-1919, 1927, 1929.

Postal Money Order Book, Gibbonsville, Idaho Post Office, 1897 to 1913.

Pratt, Orville Clyde. "The Story of Spokane." Unpublished typescript, 1948. At the Spokane Public Library.

Progressive Men of Southern Idaho. Chicago: A.W. Bowen, 1904.

Progressive Men of the State of Montana. Chicago: A.W. Bowen & Co., 190?.

"Public Sentiment and Defense Measures," *Current History* VI, March, 1917, p. 980.

Putman, Edison K. "Prohibition in Idaho." Ph. D. Dissertation, History Department, University of Idaho. 1979.

Rambour, Louis. Manuscript of untitled article on Columbus Brewery.

Rambour, Michael. Letter to the author, 14 December 2001.

Randolph, Julia. (Researcher and Compiler) *Gibbonsville, Idaho: The Golden Years.* Gibbonsville: Gibbonsville Improvement Association, 1982.

Rassmussen, Dean. Letter to the author, 28 July 1999.

Real Beer Page, Internet news service (<slists@lists.realbeer.com>) 6 February 1999.

Reinhart, Herman Francis. *The Golden Frontier: The Recollections of Herman Francis Reinhart, 1851-1869.* Austin: University of Texas Press, 1962.

The Resources of Idaho, Eagle Rock, monthly, 1885.

Roesch, Carol. "Roesch Brewery Spans Six Decades," *Pioneer Trails,* Umatilla County Historical Society, vol. 23, no. 3, Fall/Winter, 1999, pp. 3-6.

Ronnenberg, Herman. *Beer and Brewing in the Inland Northwest, 1850-1950.* Moscow: University of Idaho Press, 1993.

Ronnenberg, Herman Wiley, "Boy Oh Boise: The Bohemian Club Story, A Rousing Tale of Brewing on the Frontier," *Beer Cans and Brewery Collectibles.* October/November 2005, pp. 4-7.

Ronnenberg, Herman W. "Brewed in Silver: The Brewing Business in Idaho's Premier Gold Camp," *American Breweriana Journal*, May-June 1991.

Ronnenberg, Herman Wiley, "The Brewery of Palouse, Washington," *Bunchgrass Historian*, vol. 32, no. 1, 2006, pp. 4-11.

Ronnenberg, Herman W. "Carl Mallon, Brewer of Wallace, Idaho," *Bear Facts*, Vol. 1, Number 2, Fall, 1982. Unpaginated.

Ronnenberg, Herman Wiley, "Colfax, Washington, Brewery History," *American Breweriana Journal*, No. 149, September-October, 2007, pp. 7-12.

Ronnenberg, Herman W. "The Drying of Moscow," *Latah Legacy*, vol. 19, no. 2, Fall 1990, p. 25.

Ronnenberg, Herman Wiley, "Ernest, John and Christ Weisgerber: The Brewing Brothers of Lewiston, Idaho," *The Golden Age*, Journal of the Nez Perce County Historical Society, Spring and Summer 2006, Volume 26, number 1, pp. 9-14.

Ronnenberg, Herman Wiley, "Francis Clemens Sels and The Breweries of Canyon City, Oregon." *American Breweriana Journal*, No. 154, July August 2008.

Ronnenberg, Herman Wiley, "Franklin, Hayes & Fleigner And the First Brewery in Pocatello, ID," *The Breweriana Collector*, #142, Summer 2008, pp. 6-9.

Ronnenberg, Herman Wiley, "Gottfried Gamble," *The Golden Age*, Nez Perce CountyHistorical Society, Vol. 27, no. 1, Spring and Summer, 2007, pp. 21-24.

Ronnenberg, Herman W. "History of the Brewing Industry in Idaho, 1862-1960," Ph. Dissertation, History Department, University of Idaho, 1989.

Ronnenberg, Herman W. "Idaho on the Rocks: The Ice Business in the Gem State," *Idaho Yesterdays*, 33: 4, Winter 1990, pp. 2-8.

Ronnenberg, Herman Wiley, "Joseph Schober: Early Cottonwood Brewer," *Echoes of the Past*. vol. 2, no. 1, March 2007. pp. 5-13.

Ronnenberg, Herman W. "Juliaetta, Genesee, Moscow: The Breweries of Latah County," *Quarterly* of the Latah County Historical Society, vol. 8, Spring, 1979, p. 2.

Ronnenberg, Herman Wiley, "Lewiston: Midwife for Idaho's Brewing Tradition," *American Breweriana Journal*, #139, January-February 2006, pp. 9-19.

Ronnenberg, Herman W. "The Nampa Brewery," *All About Beer*, January 1985, pp. 61-63.

Ronnenberg, Herman W. *The Politics of Assimilation: The Effect of Prohibition on the German Americans.* New York: Carlton Press, 1973.

Ronnenberg, Herman Wiley, "Raymund Saux: Idaho's French Connection," *Echoes of the Past*, vol. 1, No. 8, March 2006, pp. 5-11.

Ronnenberg, Herman Wiley, ""Six Bo's to Go Joe" The Life Story of Boise's BohemianClub Brewery," *Suds and Spuds*. September 2005, pp. 3-8.

Ronnenberg, Herman W. "Researching Your Hometown Brewery: The Fire Insurance Connection," *The Breweriana Collector*, Vol. 69, Spring 1990, 22-24.

Ronnenberg, Herman W. "This 'Bud' Is Not For You," *American Breweriana Journal*, #73, March-April 1995, pp. 23-25.

Ronnenberg, Herman Wiley, "William von Berge: Grangeville, Idaho's Brewer, Barley Grower, and Inventor," *Echoes of the Past*, March, 2008, pp. 15-24. pp. 16-17.

Rulau, Russell. *Standard Catalog of United States Tokens, 1700-1900*. Iola: Krause Publications, 1997.

Russin, Don. Phone interview with author, 23 January 1999. St. Louis, Mo. to Troy, Idaho.

Sahlberg, A.T. Letter to author, 27 June 1983. (Daughter of Hayes of Pocatello)

Sahlbert, Tom. "Hayes Family," *History of Bannock County, 1893-1993*, vol. 2, Betty Hale, ed., Logan, Utah: Herff Jones, 1993.

Salem, Frederick William. *Beer: Its History and Its Economic Value as a National Beverage*. Hartford.: F.W. Salem, 1880, Reprint: Arno Press, 1972.

Sanborn-Perris Maps, Silver City, June, 1903. Moscow, 1904. Pocatello, 1900, 1907. 1915. Cottonwood, 1929. Shoshone 1888. Genesee 1893, Rathdrum 1892, 1896, 1908.

Schober, Thelma. Interview with author, Cottonwood, Idaho, 23 June 1983; 21 April 1986.

Schramm, Walt. "Rocky Bar on the Spook Circuit," *Incredible Idaho*, vol. 1, no. 1, July, 1969, pp. 8-10.

Secrest, William B. *California Desperadoes: Stories of Early California Outlaws in Their Own Words*. Clovis: Word Dancer Press, 2000.

Sherfey, Florence E. *Eastern Washington's Vanished Grist Mills and the Men Who Ran Them*. Fairfield: Ye Galleon Press, 1978.

Shoup, George Elmo. *History of Lemhi County*, Boise: Idaho Historical Society, 1969.

Silverberg, Robert. *Ghost Towns of the American West*. New York: Thomas Y. Crowell, 1968.

Simon-Smolinski, Carole. "Idaho's West European Americans," in *Idaho's Ethnic Heritage*, 1990.

Singletary, Robert. *Kootenai Chronicles: A History of Kootenai County*. Vol. I. Coeur d'Alene, Idaho: Museum of North Idaho, 1995.

Slade, David. "History of the Billings Brewing Company," University of Montana masters thesis, 1971.

Sneath, Allen Winn. *Brewed in Canada: The Untold Story of Canada's 350-Year-Old Brewing Industry*. Toronto: The Dundurn Group, 2001.

Snowden, Clinton A. *History of Washington: The Record of Progress of An American State*. vol. 4, New York: The Century History Co., 1909.

"Social Security Death Records," CD-ROM, Family Tree Maker.

Sonnleitner, Charles. "Brewing Industry Flourished Once in Old Alturas: Expert Beer Maker Gives Some of the Salient Facts of Earlier Days," *The Hailey Times* Hailey: 50th Anniversary Edition, 1931, p. 16.

"Souvenir Guide to the Salmon River High Country," Pamphlet. Summer, 1980.

Sparling, Wayne C. *Southern Idaho Ghost Towns*. Caldwell, Idaho: Caxton Printers, Ltd., 1981.

State Historical Society of Idaho. *Fifteenth Biennial Report of the Board of Trustees of the State Historical Society of Idaho For the Years 1935-1936.* Boise: 1936.

Statham. Wilma Lewis. *Owyhee County Gleanings.* Boise, Idaho: The Idaho Genealogical Society and the Idaho Historical Society, 1964, 2nd printing, Copyright 1986. P. 38.

"Step Into the Past …: A Self Guided Tour of Pendleton's Historic Downtown District." Pamphlet, Chamber of Commerce, Pendleton, Oregon, n.d.

Stepanek, Ed. "If You Can Remember Grangeville's Two Breweries, Consider Yourself An Old-Timer," *Idaho County Free Press,* 30 June 1976, p. 12A-15A.

Swanson, Charles R., Chamelin, Neil C., and Territe, Leonard. *Criminal Investigation* 4th edition, New York: Random House, 1988.

"Take This Job and Shove It," Movie, Avco Embassy Pictures, 1981.

Taylor, Edith C. (Weisgerber), Philip O. Weisgerber, and Marie E. White. *A Man, His Family and His City.* n.p., 1982.

Taylor, Mary Walsh. "Owyhee & Nez Perce County Place Names," A Thesis, English Department, University of Idaho, 1968.

"Those Were the Days: Growing Up in Style," *Idaho Yesterdays,* vol. 14, no. 3, Fall, 1970, pp. 28-9.

"Tour of Mathews Grain Reveals Remnants of Brothel," *Signal American,* Weiser, Idaho, 9 July 1987, p. 1, c. 3-6.

"Town of Juliaetta," *Latah Legacy,* Vol. 17, no. 1, Spring 1988.

Trull, Fern Coble. *They Dared to Dream: Builders in the Purple Sage.* Fern Coble Trull, 1986.

Turner, Faithe, "Col. W. H. Dewey and the Dewey Palace," *Twentieth Biennial Report of the State Historical Society,* 1945-1946, pp. 129-131.

Van Wieren, Dale P. *American Breweries II.* West Point, PA.: East Coast Breweriana Association, 1995.

Vandracek, John Felix, "The Rise of Fraternal Organizations in the U.S., 1868-1900," *Social Science,* Vol. 47, Winter, 1972, p. 26.

Walker, Francis A. and Seaton, Charles W. *Compendium of the 10th Census,* June 1, 1880.

Washington: Government Printing Office, 1883.

Walker, Francis A. *A Compendium of the 9th Census, June 1, 1870.* Washington: Government Printing Office, 1872.

Warner, Glen. "Overland Brewery Adds Touch of Germany," *Modern Brewery,* January 1935, pp. 45-46.

Washington: Northwest Frontier. Vol. IV, New York: Lewis Historical Publishing Company, 1957.

Washington, Oregon, Idaho Gazetteer and Business Directory, 1886-1887, 1892.

Weis, Viola Owen Geisler. *Uniontown: Its Beginning, Its Centennial.* Uniontown: Published by author, 1994.

Welch, Julia Conway. *Gold Town to Ghost Town: The Story of Silver City, Idaho.* Moscow: University of Idaho Press, 1982.

Wells, Merle. *Boise, An Illustrated History*. Woodland Hills: Windsor Publications, 1982.

Wells, Merle W. *Gold Camps & Silver Cities: Nineteenth Century Mining in Central and Southern Idaho*. Bulletin 22 of the Idaho Department of Lands, Bureau of Mines and Geology. Moscow, Idaho, 2nd edition, 1983.

Wells, Merle W. *Rush to Idaho*, Bulletin 19 of the Idaho Department of Lands, Bureau of Mines and Geology. Moscow, Idaho: 1958.

Western Brewer, 1899-1909.

Western Brewer and Journal of the Malt and Hop Trades, 1897-1906.

White, Ernie. "Empire's End," *Incredible Idaho*, Vol. 5, no. 3, Winter, 1973-74, p. 21.

Wilfong, Cheryl. *Following the Nez Perce Trail: A Guide to the Nee-Me-Poo National Historical Trail with Eyewitness Accounts*. Eugene: Oregon State University Press, 1990.

Wilson, R. G. and Gourvish, T. R. editors. *The Dynamics of the International Brewing Industry Since 1800*. London: Routledge, 1998.

Woodward, Tim. "Ghost of the Turnverein," *Idaho Statesman*, 16 June 1988, Sec. C.

Wright, Patricia and Reitzes, Lisa B. *Tourtellotte and Hummel of Idaho: The Standard Practice of Architecture*. Logan: State University Press, 1987.

"You Must Remember This: Science: How the Brain Forms False Memories," *Newsweek*, September 26, 1994, pp. 68-89.

Zanjani, Sally. *Glory Days in Goldfield, Nevada* Reno: University of Nevada Press, 2002.

Zhu, Liping. *A Chinaman's Chance: The Chinese on the Rocky Mountain Mining Frontier*. Niwot.: University of Colorado Press, 1997, p. 130.

2. Newspapers

The Atlanta News, Atlanta, Idaho, 16 May 1885.

Bellevue Press, Bellevue, Idaho, 1889.

Boise Capital News, Boise, Idaho, 1935.

Boise City Republican, Boise, Idaho, 1881-1887.

Boise City Weekly News, Boise, Idaho, 1870.

Boise News, Idaho City (then called Bannack, or Bannock), 1863, 1864.

Boise Sentinel, Boise, Idaho, 1897.

Caldwell Tribune, Caldwell, Idaho, 1894-1910.

Camas Prairie Chronicle, Cottonwood, Idaho, 1900-1910.

The Capital (aka, *Idaho Capital News, Idaho Evening Capital, The Weekly Capital*), Boise, Idaho, 1899-190?.

The Capital Chronicle, Boise, 1869-1870.

Caribou County Sun. Soda Springs, Idaho, 1986.

Cassia County Times, Albion, Idaho, 1892.

The Coeur d'Alene Barbarian, Warder and Wallace, Idaho, 1892-1896.

Coeur d'Alene City Times, Coeur d'Alene, Idaho, 1889.

Coeur d'Alene Evening Press, Coeur d'Alene, Idaho, 1909.

The Coeur D'Alene Miner, Wallace, Idaho, various dates. 1894.

Coeur d'Alene Morning Journal, Coeur d'Alene, Idaho, 1908.

Coeur d 'Alene Nugget, Eagle, Idaho, 1884.

Coeur d'Alene Press, Coeur d' Alene, Idaho, 1905-1907.

Coeur d'Alene Sun, Murray, Idaho, 1885, 1897.

The Commonwealth of Idaho, Boise, Idaho, 1892.

Cottonwood Record, Cottonwood, Idaho, 1901.

Cottonwood Report, Cottonwood, Idaho, 1898 – 1900.

The Council Journal, Council, Idaho, 1901.

The Daily Evening Citizen, Boise, Idaho, 1891.

The Daily Idaho Press, Wallace, Idaho, 1909.

The Daily Times, Wallace, Idaho, 1909.

The DeLamar Nugget, D*Double Standard*, Moscow, Idaho, 1896.

East Washingtonian, Pomeroy, Washington. 1931, 1949.

Elko Chronicle, Elko, Nevada, 1870.

Elko Independent, Elko, Nevada, 1869-1870.

Elmore Bulletin. Rocky Bar, Idaho, 1888-1892. Mountain Home, Idaho, 1892-1900.

The Emmett Index, Emmett, Idaho, 1908.

Enterprise Times, Givens Hot Springs, Idaho, 1988.

Eureka Daily Sentinel, Eureka, Nevada, 1887.

Eureka Republican, Eureka, Nevada, (aka *Eureka Daily Republican*), 1871-1878.

Eureka Tri-Weekly Standard, Eureka, Nevada, 1885.

Evening Capital Journal. Salem, Oregon, 1893.

Evening Capital News, Boise, idaho, 1901-1907

Evening Journal . Moscow, Idaho, (aka *Moscow Evening Journal*), 1905-1906.

Ferdinand Enterprise, Ferdinand, Idaho, 1916.

The Florence News, Florence, Idaho 1898.

Fremont Republican, St. Anthony, Idaho, 1898-1899.

Genesee Advertiser, Genesee, Idaho, 1888.

Genesee News, Genesee, Idaho, 1892-1909.

Gibbonsville Miner, Gibbonsville, Idaho, 1896.

The Golden Age, Lewiston, Idaho, 1863-1864.

Goldfield Daily Tribune, Goldfield, Nevada, 1912

The Grangeville Globe, Grangeville, Idaho, 1913.

Hailey Times, Hailey, Idaho, various dates.

The Helena Independent, Helena, Montana, 1935, 1931, 1936

Idaho County Free Press, Grangeville, Idaho. 1886-1931.

The Heppner Gazette, Oregon, Special Edition, January 1902

Idaho Falls Times, Idaho Falls, Idaho, 1892-1904.

Idaho Free Press, Nampa, Idaho, 1932.

Idaho Herald, Boise, Idaho, 1872.

The Idaho Pioneer, Boise, Idaho, 1935.

Idaho Post, Moscow, Idaho, 1908.

Idaho Press, (aka *Wallace Press*), Wallace, Idaho, 1904.

Idaho Register, Idaho Falls, Idaho, 1886-1904.

Idaho Review, Boise, Idaho, 1915.

Idaho Scimitar, Boise, Idaho, 1908.

Idaho State Journal. Pocatello, 1986.

Idaho Statesman (aka *Idaho Tri-Weekly Statesman, Idaho Sunday Statesman, Idaho Daily Statesman*), Boise, Idaho, 1863 to 1917.

The Idaho Sun, Murray, Idaho, 1884.

Idaho Times, Idaho City, Idaho, 1866.

Idaho World (aka *Semi-Weekly World*), Idaho City, Various dates.

Idahonian, Moscow, Idaho, 1980.

Idanha Chieftain, Soda Springs, Idaho, 1903.

Kendrick Gazette, Kendrick, Idaho, 1911.

Kendrick-Genesee Gazette-News, 1979.

Ketchum Bulletin, Ketchum, Idaho, 1886.

Ketchum Keystone, (aka *Daily Keystone*) Ketchum, Idaho, various dates.

Kootenai County Republican, Sandpoint, Idaho. 1903.

Lewiston Journal, Lewiston, Idaho, 1867.

Lewiston Morning Tribune, Lewiston, Idaho, 1987.

Lewiston Teller, Lewiston, Idaho, 1880.

Mackay Telegraph, Mackay, Idaho. 1903.

Morning Oregonian, Portland, Oregon, 1862-1865.

Moscow Evening Journal, Moscow, Idaho, various dates.

Moscow Mirror, Moscow, Idaho, 1885-1899.

Moscow Star-Mirror, Moscow, Idaho, 1909.

Mountain City Times, Mountain City, Nevada, 1898.

Nampa Leader-Herald, Nampa, Idaho, 1915-1919.

Nevada State Journal, Reno, Nevada 1912.

The Nez Perce News, Lewiston, Idaho, various dates.

North Idaho Radiator, Lewiston, Idaho, 1865.

North Idaho Star, Moscow, Idaho. 1891-1899.

Olympic Transcript, Olympia, Washington, 1875.

Owyhee Avalanche (aka *Owyhee Daily Avalanche*), Silver City, Idaho, 1865-1871, 1914.

Owyhee Bullion , Silver City, Idaho.

Owyhee Tidal Wave (aka *Semi-Weekly Tidal Wave*), Silver City, Idaho, 1869.

Palouse Republic, Palouse, Washington, 1904.

Payette Independent, Payette, Idaho, 1891.

Pend d'Oreille News, 1892

Pocatello Tribune, Pocatello, Idaho, 1902-1918.

Post Register, Idaho Falls, Idaho, 1935-36.

The Rathdrum Tribune, Rathdrum, Idaho, 1903-1927.

Recorder-Herald, Salmon, Idaho, 1932.

Resources of Idaho, Eagle Rock (Idaho Falls), 1885.

*Scimita*r Boise, Idaho, 1907.

Semi-Weekly Journal, Yreka, California, 1862.

Semi-Weekly Mining News, Salmon, Idaho, 1867.

Semi-Weekly News, Boise, Idaho, 1870.

Signal Annual Number, (*Weiser Semi-Weekly Signal*), Weiser, Idaho, 1909.

The Silver Blade, Rathdrum, Idaho, 1895, 1903.

Soda Springs Chieftain, Soda Springs, Idaho, 1904-1920.

Soda Springs Sun, Soda Springs, Idaho, 1915.

The Spokesman-Review, Spokane, Washington, 1893-1913.

Spokesman Review Magazine, Spokane, Washington, 4 August 1957.

The Standard, Grangeville, Idaho, 1905.

The Standard, Ogden, Utah, 1892.

Star-Mirror, Moscow, Idaho, 1909.

Sun, Wallowa, Oregon, 1930s.

Teller (aka *Lewiston Teller*), Lewiston, Idaho, 1880.

Teton Peak-Chronicle, St. Anthony, Fremont County, Idaho, 1899-1905

Tidal Wave, Silver City, Idaho, Various dates.

The Times. Wallace, Idaho.

Twin Falls News, 1905-1907.

Walla Walla Statesman (aka *Washington Statesman*), Walla Walla, Washington, 1861-1875.

Walla Walla Union, Walla Walla, Washington, 1872-1876.

Walla Walla Union-Bulletin, Walla Walla, Washington, 1944.

The Wallace Democrat, Wallace, Idaho, various dates.

Wallace Free Press, Wallace, Idaho, various dates.

Wallace Miner, Wallace, Idaho, 1907-1937.

The Wallace Press-Times, Wallace, Idaho, 1934-36.

The Wardner News, Wardner, Idaho, 1894-1899.

Washington Statesman, Walla Walla, Washington, 1863-1865.
Weiser Leader, Weiser, Idaho, 1886.
Weiser Semi-Weekly Signal, Weiser, Idaho, 1905-06.
Weiser World, Weiser, Idaho, 1905.
The Wenatchee Advance, Wenatchee, Washington, 1903.
The Wenatchee Daily World, Wenatchee, Washington, 1905.
Wood River News Miner, Hailey, Idaho, various dates.
Wood River Times, Hailey, Idaho, 1883-1906.
Yankee Fork Herald, Bonanza, Idaho, 1879-1881.

3. Manuscript Material

Ada County Deed Books, ISHS Microfilm.
Ada County, Judgment Records, microfilmed records, Idaho State Historical Society.
Ada County Judicial Records, ISHS.
Alturas County Records, ISHS, Reel 5.
Blaine County Idaho Judicial Records, ISHS.
BLM Bureau of Land Management land records.
Boise County Idaho Deed, 1871-1875, Book V.
Boise County Idaho Records, ISHS, Reel 12.
Blaine County Idaho Judicial Records, Idaho State Historical Society, Microfilm reel 31.
Boise County Idaho Criminal Records, ISHS, reel #40.
Boise County Idaho Judicial Records, Idaho State Historical Society, Microfilm reel # 35.
Challis Brewery Historic District, U.S. Department of the Interior, Register of Historic
Places Inventory, Nominating Form.
Chattel Mortgage Index, vol. I. Shoshone County Court House, Wallace, Idaho.
Cottonwood Idaho Brewery Records. In possession of private party.
Crescent Brewing Co. Letters to Becker Brewing & Malting Co., Ogden, Utah. 1909.
Custer County Records, ISHS, reel 1, 3, 8.
Federal Tax Records, 1865-1866, University of Idaho Library Microfilm # 558.
Franklin Hayes Brewery, Letters to Becker Brewing Company, 1901. Photocopy in possession of the author.
Galland Burke Brewing, Spokane, Washington, Records. Washington State University Library Special Collections.
Geographic Reference Library, American Geographical Gazetteer. Internet.
Henco Brewing Company, Spokane, Washington, Records, Washington State University Library Special Collections.

James Hawley, Manuscript, Idaho State Historical Society, MS2, H31.

Healy, William. Papers, 1908-1913, Manuscript Group 389, Special Collections, University of Idaho Library, Moscow, Idaho.

Idaho County Commissioners Minutes, volume 7, 1904.

Idaho County Deed Books.

Idaho Department of Corrections, Central Records in Boise.

John Manuel, Records and Memorabilia, In Possession of Private Party, Pomeroy, Washington.

Koeninger Brewery Records. In Possession of private party, Boise, Idaho.

Latah County Title Company, Moscow, Idaho, Property ownership records.

Minutes of the Annual Meeting of the Board of Directors of Sunset Mercantile Company, 1938. Hard Rock Mining Records, Box 1359, University of Idaho Library, Special Collections.

New York Brewing Company, Spokane, Washington, Records, Washington State University Library, Special Collections.

Olson, William A., Papers 1946-1978, Manuscript Group 393, Special Collections, University of Idaho, Moscow, Idaho.

Overland Beverage Co. Letters to Becker Brewing Co., 1909.

Owyhee County Judicial Records, Idaho State Historical Society, Microfilm reel 4.

Photo Collection, Latah County Historical Society, Moscow, Idaho.

Rammelmeyer, Ernest. Diary. Partial copy.

Records of the United States Court of Claims, Record Group 123, John J. Manuel, case 3496.

Records of the Idaho Department of Corrections, "John Hendel," State Penitentiary, Boise, Idaho.

Roder, Louis, Penitentiary Records, Idaho State Historical Society.

Shepp, Charles. Diaries, 1902-1971. Copies of the dairy are in the Special Collections, University of Idaho library, Moscow, Idaho. A transcription by Marian Sweeney, Kamiah Idaho for part of the early years are also there.

Spokane Brewing and Malting Company, Spokane, Washington, Records, Washington State University Library, Special Collections.

St. Anthony Brewing Company. St., Anthony, Idaho, Letters, 1901, 1902. In private collection.

United States Alcohol Tax Stamp, Idaho, In Possession of Private Party, Pocatello, Idaho.

The Wallace, Idaho, Fire Department Records, 1902.

Weisgerber Brewery Records, Manuscript Group 110, Papers 1863-1918. University of Idaho Library, Special Collections.

4. Internet Sites

Bureau of Land Management, Land Patent Records. http://www.archives.gov/genealogy/land/

Toennises, Mullins & McAllisters of Idaho—Descendants & Relatives. http://worldconnect.genealogy.rootsweb.ancestry.com/cgi-bin/igm.cgi%3Fop%3DSHOW%26db%3Ddacrea%26recno%3D3560

Dayton, Washington, Cemetery Records. http://www.interment.net/data/us/wa/columbia/dayton/dayton.htm

http://www.eastoregonian.com/

Historic Landmarks Advisory Commission in Salem, Oregon. http://www.open.org/-sedev/Agenda726.htm

"History of Joseph and Temperance Brown."http://cgi.ebay.com/1922-Gottfried-Duden-German-Immigration-to-Missouri_W0QQitemZ6587308QQcategoryZ29223QQrdZ1QQemdZviewItem

Idaho Museum of Natural History. http://imnh.isu.edu/digitalatlas/geog/imem/text/main.htm

Joseph Pickett & Sons. http://www.falstaffbrewing.com/jos__pickett_%26_sons.htm

List of Mayors of Juneau, Alaska. http://www.juneau.lib.ak.us/history/mayors.htm

"The Kemsleys of Sublett, Idaho." http://homepage.mac.com/icafe/KemsleyCafe/Stories/Kemsley/TheKemsleysOfSubletIdaho.html

Montana Cemetery Records: Rootsweb. com. http://www.rootsweb.ancestry.com/~mtmsgs/death_records.htm

Placerville, Idaho. Boise County. Cemetery Records. https://wiki.familysearch.org/en/Placerville,_Idaho

Platte County, Nebraska Probate Index. http://www.usgennet.org/usa/ne/county/platte/vitals.html

San Francisco Call newspaper vital records, 1869-1891. http://censuslinks.com/United-States/California/San-Francisco/San-Francisco-Call-Database-Vital-Records-1869-1875-1887-l569.html

Santa Fe Saloon and Motel, fifth Avenue, Goldfield, Nevada. http://www.freecasinos.ws/land_casinos/UnitedStates/Nevada/Santa_Fe_Saloon_Motel_and_Casino.html

Twin Falls Newspaper Index. http://twinfallspubliclibrary.org/newspaper/index.html

World War I Draft Registration. http://search.ancestry.com/search/db.aspx%3Fdbid%3D6482

Index

Note: Page numbers appearing in *italics* refer to photographs or illustrative material. Women are indexed under their last married name with a cross-reference from their maiden name.